D1355811

A PASSING FURY

ALSO BY A. T. WILLIAMS

A Very British Killing: The Death of Baha Mousa

A Passing Fury

Searching for Justice at the End of World War II

A. T. WILLIAMS

JONATHAN CAPE
LONDON

1 3 5 7 9 10 8 6 4 2

Jonathan Cape, an imprint of Vintage Publishing,
20 Vauxhall Bridge Road,
London SW1V 2SA

Jonathan Cape is part of the Penguin Random House group of companies
whose addresses can be found at global.penguinrandomhouse.com.

Copyright © A. T. Williams 2016

First published by Jonathan Cape in 2016

penguin.co.uk/vintage

A CIP catalogue record for this book is available from the British Library

ISBN 9780224099608

Printed and bound in Great Britain by Clays Ltd, St Ives PLC

Penguin Random House is committed to a sustainable future for our business, our readers and
our planet. This book is made from Forest Stewardship Council® certified paper.

For Kathy

Contents

Prologue ix

1: Neuengamme 1

2: Buchenwald 17

3: Lüneburg Heath 65

4: Neustadt 135

5: Lüneburg 203

6: Dachau 263

7: Hamburg 305

8: Hamburg Revisited 345

9: Nuremberg 405

Epilogue 429

Sources and Bibliography 433

Notes 439

Acknowledgements 473

Picture Credits 475

Index 477

Prologue

In 1945, the British took part in the most extensive scheme of war crimes trials in history. It was a unique endeavour. The criminal prosecution of men and women of another nation, Germany, who had abused, killed, tormented uncountable numbers of human beings and who had sought to eradicate whole races and categories of peoples from existence, was lauded as a victory for rational and civilised behaviour. By bringing unimaginably cruel crimes before courts of law where the accused were treated with formal respect, where the evidence of their guilt was presented, where they were allowed to defend themselves and justify their actions or given the chance to establish their blamelessness, there was hope that a civilised humanity would reassert itself. It was the conquest of a system based on evil by a system founded on law. The fury unleashed by the discovery of atrocity after atrocity, of individual and collective brutality, of a concentration camp network whose purpose was the enslavement of the enemies of Nazi Germany and the deliberate extermination of peoples, was to be corralled by a legal process. Law was the cultured response and 'Nuremberg' the name that came to symbolise its form. And so a myth was born.

I

Neuengamme

1.

The bus pulled up. Quietly. On time. As German buses are supposed to do. I stepped onto the pavement. Few people were around: a couple of Sunday cyclists pedalling along the straight country road from the nearby village; some walkers amidst distant trees; a farmer on a tractor in the field behind me.

As the bus moved away, I stood and looked at the site stretching into the distance to left and right. Immediately in front of me a little steel bridge spanned the perimeter ditch, leading to the gatehouse. There was no grand entrance, no barbed wire fences, just a couple of modern glass and steel buildings separated by an iron gate. It could have been a local community project, an art exhibition, nothing imposing or remarkable. But there was a sign. It said this was once a *Konzentrationslager* (KZ), a concentration camp.

I'd never heard of Neuengamme before that day. I stumbled across it by chance, looking for somewhere to visit that would take me outside Hamburg during a long weekend I spent there several years ago. I thought I should make the effort when I saw a local guidebook mentioning the camp. It seemed appropriate given that I was in the middle of writing about allegations of brutality and torture and unlawful killing by British troops during their occupation of Iraq after 2003. I thought it might give me some perspective on the institution-alisation of cruelty.

Walking through the gate, I had an unobstructed view across an empty white paved square. It was large, like a redundant car park. My eyes squinted at the morning sun reflecting off the concrete. On a signpost with a tilted display board, I read that this was the *Appellplatz*, the parade ground. It was a tranquil place, open, bleak but inoffensive. Innocent even, though I knew this was an illusion of time not space.

To my left, standing about one hundred metres apart, and them-selves a hundred metres in length, twenty in width, were two long double-storey red-brick buildings. They looked like an architect's model: perfect in their symmetry, pristine and composed. Each had precisely forty-four sets of windows facing into the square: twenty-four on the first floor, twenty on the ground floor with four white glass doors positioned in the middle. No embellishments. The buildings were functional.

Between these blockhouses, and also to my right on the other side of the parade ground, were several identical unsettling structures. As long and wide as the brick buildings and laid in a row, maybe seven or eight of them, it was hard to count, they were flat plinths of grey rubble each surrounded by thick knee-high walls made of reddish stones encased in steel mesh. The ground about and between them was black. Hard black ballast, painful to walk on. The stones bit into the soles of my shoes, twisting my feet in awkward directions. It was impossible to stroll. I had to tread with circumspection, in discomfort, akin to a physical experience of memory. The signs said these structures marked the sites of the original wooden prisoners' barracks long since pulled down.

Beyond those shadow-buildings, at the head of the parade ground furthest from the entrance, was another strange structure: a steel frame and pitched roof, about the size of a double garage, covered a square pit, and above the pit was a large two-metre-square photograph superimposed on a board. From a distance it looked like the side of a cattle truck. This was the *Arrestbunker*, the *Lagergefängnis*, the camp's punishment cells, where the hangings and executions were conducted, and where one night in April 1945, a board said, seventy-one prisoners brought from Fuhlsbüttel prison in Hamburg were shot in waves, and grenades thrown into their cells when the prisoners rose up in a final and futile act of resistance.

Turning away, I walked along the side of the furthest brick block-house. A doorway in the middle gave access to the exhibitions. Inside, the history of the camp and its people was laid out in rooms full of glass cases, displaying the detritus of the prison: the camp's books where the names and fate of the captives, the *Häftlinge*, were recorded with meticulous care by the SS administration, books that had been hidden, buried by prisoners at the end of the war when records were being destroyed and the camp evacuated, and dug up after the British had finally come, revealing pages of names, proof of the scale of casualties; the reconstructed bunk cots of cheap wood, pressed together in an affront to the very notion of privacy; the striped rags of inmates barely capable of covering skin and wholly inadequate to keep out cold. Everything in those cabinets was an offence against life. There were no exhibits from which one could extract hope, a prospect of release or a return to a dignified condition. Even the accounts of liberation were simply stories of suffering heaped upon suffering. It felt like it was my duty to ingest all the names and incidents and information, as though it was feasible to comprehend a vast system and era of dehumanisation through individual human histories.

Two hours later I came out into the sunshine again. It took that long to see everything, all the diagrams and photographs. I couldn't walk past any of them quickly and feel comfortable doing so. I couldn't stop and feel comfortable either. That would have been tantamount to saying, 'I don't care enough.' The obligation to scrutinise every exhibit, to give it due attention, was intense.

But there was more. I walked on to the far end of the blockhouse. Beyond, looking east, was an innocuous scene: a path, a ditch, a little pedestrian bridge and across an overgrown field, behind a chest-high hedge, a white single-storey house. Solitary, incongruous, reminiscent of a farmer's cottage or a village schoolteacher's home.

By the time I reached the little white house, the camp with its parade ground and spectral barracks was almost forgotten. A brick wall with the number '61' on a blue marker beside the gate interrupted the surrounding hedge to the house. It was as if this were an ordinary house in an ordinary avenue in a quiet ordinary suburb. Except there were no other homes anywhere nearby. It sat entirely on its own in the middle of a grass lawn behind the hedge.

A grey metal gate opened onto a short drive. In the centre of the gate was a moulded circle within which was cast the shape of another building, one reminiscent of those pictures that appear on books about the Holocaust, of camp gateways to Auschwitz and other extermination centres.

I pushed through the gate and walked towards the house, no more than a bungalow with a single garage at its side, set on a brick base with a few steps leading to the porch and the front door. It was locked. I looked through the windows, trying to see a relic from the past, but there was nothing. Plain empty rooms, all small and homely.

The lawns, now rough and inhospitable, gave only the slightest suggestion of a family once playing around the house. It *was* a family home nonetheless. The board outside the hedge said that Max Pauly, the camp commandant, and his wife and five children had lived there from 1944 until 1945. And after they had been taken away, others moved in, including a British Army officer when the camp was adopted as an internment centre for suspected Nazi war criminals.

Retreating to the gate, I could see more buildings a little way off in the distance. These were thick and industrial, hulking constructions, joined to the main site by a long path through a mown field that had a broad clayey pit at its head.

The massive building was odd. It didn't look like a normal factory, if that was what it was. I could see it had the plan layout of a letter E, like the head of a fork. The three tines were the size of aircraft hangars, each pointed towards me. The middle one had two ramps leading from the second storey onto the ground in front. It was grotesque, though I learned later it was only a brick factory.

To the right was a canal basin. Next to that, a section of more modern concrete wall had been left in place and displayed a sequence of photographs and text. This was the site of the civilian prison built in the grounds of the concentration camp after the war and after the British had gone home. Neuengamme hadn't ceased to operate as a penitentiary even then. Only in 2003 had the detention facility finally closed down and the whole area been designated by the Hamburg Senate as a place of commemoration. It had taken nearly sixty years to alter the camp's function from incarceration to remembrance.

I walked between the building and the canal and on towards a small copse. A few prefabricated buildings were scattered amongst the trees. One was a café. I kept on going until I reached a modern walled enclosure. Monuments flourished here: a twenty-metre-high, thick slab-finger of concrete; a twisted sculpture of what looked like a person, though it might have been a dog or a writhing animal; a plaque on the wall with the words 'KZ *Gedenkstätte Neuengamme*'. And sitting amidst a little plantation of conifers was a square, black, apparently windowless box of a building. This was the House of Commemoration: as though all that I'd seen and walked amongst was insufficient to preserve the memory of what had taken place here.

I imagined there would be darkness within the building, but the hall was lit by a skylight that spanned the roof. It was bright, as bright as the parade ground I'd walked across earlier. A short flight of stairs led to another floor. Along the red walls, white scrolls hung from the ceiling to the floor. Each one had three columns. Names of the camp prisoners who'd died here were clustered beneath specific days. The record began in 1938. It ended in May 1945. Some dates, the earliest, had only one or two names. Dates in later years had more than I could count by sight. And one day, 3 May 1945, at the very end of the war, had thousands written below it. Name after name after name without explanation. I wondered what had happened *then*, on *that* day, to cause such loss of life.

Wearied by the weight of the lists of the dead, I left the building and wandered back to the main centre of the camp, more aware now of the scale of suffering endured over years and by thousands upon thousands of prisoners. I knew by then that this wasn't even an extermination centre, like Auschwitz or Treblinka or Belzec. It was a labour camp. Thousands of Jews had passed through here but many, many prisoners had been common criminals, political detainees, Soviet soldiers, French Resistance fighters, members of the Dutch underground, people from across Europe. Here they'd suffered together and died together.

On my way back to the camp's entrance, I passed a single-storey building, the SS garages where the camp automobiles were serviced, cared for, I realised, with greater affection than the inmates were afforded. Signs indicated an exhibition that purported to examine the 'relationship between individual deeds and individual responsibility'. This was the very question troubling me then, thinking of the Iraqi hotel worker Baha Mousa, whose killing in a British Army base in Basra 2003 I was writing about at the time.

Immediately inside the exhibition was a display of black-and-white photographs. They were very different from all the other pictures in glass cabinets or on walls about the camp. There was something courteous, something proper about the scene they depicted. On the left of one photograph was a fresh-faced, dark-haired young man in British uniform, sitting behind a desk, his hands clasped just beneath his chin, a textbook and notepad on the table before him. He was looking askance at something or someone out of shot. To his left, also behind the table, was another soldier, who sported a few more medals and braiding and an air of seniority. He had his head down, looking intently at a sheaf of papers. A sign was attached to their table: 'All present will stand when the president enters or leaves the court.'

The caption beneath the photograph said that the man on the right was Major Stephen Malcolm Stewart. He was senior prosecutor at the main trial of the camp's SS personnel, begun in March 1946 in a makeshift courtroom within an old building in the centre of Hamburg. The trial had been a British affair, with British lawyers, British judges, British guards. The exhibition notes said the trial had been held at the same time as the iconic Nuremberg tribunal, where leading Nazis like Goering and Hess and Speer were prosecuted over ten months in 1945 and 1946, but had been quite independent of those proceedings. I knew about Nuremberg. I had never heard of the Neuengamme trial.

I put on the headphones that were hanging from the table in front of the photographs and sat down to listen. In measured tones, the voice of the prosecutor talked about the crimes committed. His telling of the events and incidents in the Neuengamme camp avoided the histrionic. He described them as evidence of a criminal enterprise, and the SS members who'd served there as criminals. The speech was decorous, polite. Everyone was dressed respectably: prosecutor, defender, witness, accused, judge. They were all able to converse and think and ask and answer. All brought together as equal human beings, even the accused with their numbered cards around their necks, to confront the grossest of cruelties, the worst of human behaviour.

The recording and the photographs made me wonder whether this was the moment when those responsible for Neuengamme had been brought to account for the killings and beatings and tortures. Had this been the reckoning for a whole system that rendered people into tools if fit enough, deliberately murdered them if not, that from the moment of entry scraped away any vestige of human sociability, destroying the trappings that define us as humans, the clothes, the books, the tenderness, the enjoyment of food: everything civil replaced with indignity? Was this how justice was done?

A little later, before leaving the camp to return to Hamburg, I entered the visitor centre at the gatehouse. I bought a pamphlet on the history of the camp, wanting to know more about the British trial and about the mystery of the many thousands of deaths recorded on that final day in May 1945. Flicking through the pages I found nothing about the court case, but there was a section on the last moments of the camp. It was brief. With the British Army approaching, it said, orders were sent to evacuate the prisoners. The Nazi party chief in Hamburg commanded the inmates to be taken to ships moored near Lübeck, some fifty miles away. 'More than 9,000 prisoners were taken aboard these ships,' the booklet said. 'Crammed into the ships' holds, many of them died of starvation, thirst and disease. On 3 May 1945, the ships *Cap Arcona* [a great ocean liner that had regularly carried

passengers across the Atlantic to South America before the war] and
Thielbek, lying just off Neustadt in Lübeck Bay, were accidentally
bombed during a British air raid intended to stop German troops
from escaping across the Baltic. Almost 7,000 prisoners were either
killed in the flames, drowned or were shot trying to save their lives.
Only 450 people survived.'[1]

So that was it. A coda to the story of Neuengamme. After surviving
the horrors of the concentration camp, thousands had died in an
'accident' at the hands of the RAF. I thought the Ancient Greeks had
it about right: people's lives are but playthings of the gods.

2.

At first, there was no hint of obsession. But my feeling of ignorance
after leaving Neuengamme was a provocation. Gradually, the time I
spent searching for information about the camp, the Lübeck Bay
disaster or the British trial in Hamburg grew out of all proportion to
the initial curiosity. The archives at the Public Records Office in Kew
and the Imperial War Museum were a terrible attraction, encouraging
days then weeks of sifting through files and documents. Like some
possessed detective, I burrowed into library shelves too, listened to
recorded memoirs on old cassette tapes, unearthed long-forgotten
manuscripts. The more I looked, the more I wanted to find. I'd entered
a labyrinth.

It wasn't long before I became besieged, all sorts of information
accumulating around me like slag heaps of books and boxes of notes
and dust-coated piles of printed statements and courtroom documents,
files not just on Neuengamme but on hundreds of investigations,
transcripts from trials held by the British, and sometimes the
Americans, after 1945, intelligence reports on atrocities committed
and suspects sought for war crimes. Some records were mundane,
others came alive in the reading. Word-for-word records of the hearings were like screenplays, capable of revealing character and tension
and high emotion.

But the documents weren't enough. I returned to Europe, mostly Germany, visiting the sites where atrocities had occurred or retribution been meted out. Over a span of years I travelled to many places. To Neustadt, vainly and unreasonably seeking clues about the disaster now seventy years old. I stayed in Hamburg again, walked around the Curiohaus, where the Neuengamme and other trials were held in 1946. I visited Lüneburg, the location of the first and most extraordinary British trial of concentration camp personnel, the ill-named Belsen trial. I stayed in Dresden during a balmy weekend one March, captivated by the still-scorched walls and cobbled streets left by the inferno caused by British and American bombers in 1945. I drove into Poland, conscious of how the smooth autobahns of Germany suddenly gave way to potholed roads once across the border, and motored to Żagań and the half-preserved prison, Stalag Luft III, the *Great Escape* camp, where you can still see the entrance to the tunnels amidst the pine trees that threaten to smother what's left of the compound. I went to Colditz, one of the first 'protective custody' centres set up by the Nazi regime in 1933 long before it housed British and other Allied prisoners of war. I flew to Berlin and saw the prison at Plötzensee where nearly 3,000 people had been executed, most for acts of resistance against the Nazis, and tried to make sense of the concrete-block field that was the Holocaust memorial in the centre of the city.

Most of all I sought out the concentration camps in Germany, aware now that hundreds were dotted across the country. They encapsulated the multiple dimensions of Nazi atrocity, from genocide of the Jews and Gypsies and Slavs and disabled and gays and Jehovah's Witnesses to the complete suppression of political opposition, the transformation of human beings into tools for labour, the punishment of anyone who fell from official favour, the housing and ill-treatment of enemy prisoners of war, the torture of those thought to have information valuable to the German state. The camps, or rather what's left of them, still pimple the map of modern Germany, like little islands in the urban and rural landscape that are sometimes proclaimed, sometimes obscured, sometimes buried, sometimes erased, depending on the whim of the local authorities: Bergen-Belsen, in the sparse woodland of Lüneburg Heath; Dachau, a suburb of Munich that's become a tourist destination; Flossenbürg, barely noticeable in the Bavarian forest, close to the Czech border; Buchenwald, on the Ettersberg hill visible from the streets of Weimar below; Mittelbau-Dora, several miles outside Nordhausen and concealed in tunnels in the hills where the inmates built V2 rockets safe from Allied bombing but in the most terrible subterranean conditions; and lesser camps, no less horrific: Farge, where there still stands the hulking U-boat factory, the construction of which cost the lives of several thousand slave workers; Fuhlsbüttel, the Gestapo's prison close to Hamburg airport; Bullenhuser Damm, where twenty Jewish children were hanged for fear that they might tell of the experiments conducted upon them. Each was a shrine of sorts, recording the magnitude and nature of crimes committed and the need for justice in response. Each aggravated an intense emotion: anger at the atrocities; resentment when it seemed that insufficient respect had been shown to the victims. In every one, hundreds, thousands, hundreds of thousands had suffered, and hundreds, thousands had been responsible for that suffering.

Deliberately, I ended up at Nuremberg, the supposed apex of the reckoning for Nazi Germany. I sat on the benches of the courtroom, which is still used today, looking up at the judges' executive chairs, a large Christian cross on the wall behind lit up by the beams of an afternoon sun like some divine sign of affirmation. By then, after the travels through the archives and across Germany, I realised that for all its enduring significance, Nuremberg – the word, the idea, the trial – important as this was and continues to be, could not and did not capture anything but a fragment of the story of the justice exacted by the British and the Allies after the war's end. Often merely faint ghosts in the history books that extol the Nuremberg Tribunal, hundreds of other proceedings had fashioned the character and reality of the fury let loose, all part of a gargantuan effort to bring to justice those responsible for the wickedness of the Nazi regime.

And a fury I by then believed it to be, one I thought I understood, perhaps even shared, as I journeyed from camp to camp, a deep-seated anger that the natural order of the world had been violated, not just by bringing about such a catastrophic war, but by debasing every human value. As early as 1943, the Allies had agreed that there would be retribution. They'd declared that they would pursue those responsible for war and atrocity 'to the uttermost ends of the earth and will deliver them to their accusers in order that justice may be done'.[2] The fury was to be contained, though, passion replaced by rational, civilised process. Some had called for immediate execution of the most senior Nazis in government and military, but this was eventually dismissed in favour of a judicial process, purportedly founded on right and fairness, not vengeance. All those responsible for waging unlimited war against the whole of Europe and crimes ranging from the mass killing programmes in death camps to the most minor incidence of ill-treatment of Allied nationals were to be brought before a court, a charge laid against them and evidence produced proving their guilt. It was to be a procedure in accordance with standards of the most ordinary and parochial criminal courts. A distinction would be made between the 'Major War Criminals', the German leaders brought to Nuremberg, and all other perpetrators, 'Minor War Criminals', to be tried by the Allies independently, in courtrooms across the Continent. But everyone was supposed to be held accountable.

Faced with the thousands of camps spread across Europe, where millions of people had been murdered or abused over a decade or more, the scale of the task was overwhelming. And the crimes hadn't been confined to those compounds. There had been massacres on the battlefields, in villages and towns, in the woods. Individual Allied soldiers or airmen had been shot or tortured even though taken as prisoners of war. The potential pool of perpetrators deserving prosecution grew to colossal proportions. If the fury was to be fulfilled entirely, maintained until all had been punished, the process would have required a massive commitment of resources, time and political will.

Looking up at the judges' bench in the Nuremberg courtroom I was reminded again of the Ancient Greeks. I thought of the Furies, the Erinyes, implacable creatures of vengeance, pursuing Orestes for the killing of his mother in Aeschylus' *The Eumenides*. And I thought how Athene had resolved to place the question of Orestes' responsibility before a human jury rather than allow the goddesses of the underworld to decide his fate. Ted Hughes's version of the play has Athene say:

> This case is too deep for a man
> Nor should I let the law, like an axe,
> Fall mechanically on a murderer.
> … Let me select a jury of the wisest
> Among the citizens of this city.
> Let them be the first of a permanent court
> Passing judgement on murder.
> They shall be sworn in
> To integrity and truth.[3]

It seemed to me the fury of the Allies was to be similarly contained.

3.

In the autumn of 1946, Clement Attlee, then Prime Minister, introduced the British lawyer Geoffrey Lawrence, who sat as the President of the recently completed Nuremberg Tribunal, to an audience at Chatham House. With unselfconscious hubris, Attlee said, 'At the Nuremberg trial it fell to Lord Justice Lawrence to show the whole world what British Justice means.'[4]

When I first read this, I laughed. Even with the most solemn of international cooperative judgements just delivered, the British had to claim moral ownership. This book is, if only in part, a search for the truth behind Attlee's assertion. It's about the justice seen at Nuremberg. But it's also about the broader justice delivered beyond that court by the British. It's a story of a time when people looked upon humanity's capacity for systematised cruelty and tried to respond, a story of retribution that ultimately descended into indifference. But more, it's a personal story, part travelogue, part investigation into the past, part reflection. All that I searched for, all that I discovered, remains relevant and personal. Too many parallels exist with the present, with our probable future, with our own natures, for it to be consigned to History alone. As I write this, I only have to think that Britain has recently been at war for almost twelve years, in Afghanistan and Iraq, to know the landscape of conflict and crime is pressingly close.

I haven't attempted to be comprehensive, though. I understood soon enough that I couldn't write about all the thousands of investigations and prosecutions run by Britain, let alone other countries, particularly the Soviet Union, France, Poland, the US and Germany itself. I didn't want to write *the* history of post-war justice in any case. Instead, this is an idiosyncratic account, driven by fascination. I've written about how the Allied scheme was constructed, so that I could understand the context. I've written about the crimes uncovered in the camps which provoked so much immediate demand for justice. I've written about some of the investigations carried out by the British immediately after the war's end. I've written about the story of the disaster off the coast of Neustadt, driven by my ignorance revealed that afternoon in the camp outside Hamburg. I've written about a few of the people involved, whether as detective, lawyer, judge or perpetrator, in an attempt to appreciate who they were and why they acted as they did. I've written about the trials that I found the most compelling, particularly Bergen-Belsen and those associated with Neuengamme concentration camp.

And I've written about Nuremberg, its story coursing through and weaving amongst the early British proceedings, making sense of them as they make sense of that supposed great icon of international justice. They were then and remain intertwined and inseparable.

2

Buchenwald

1.

The town of Ohrdruf is easy enough to find. Take a right at Gotha off the A4 from Frankfurt to Weimar and drive for about seven miles. The memorial site is not so accessible, though. It lies behind fenced land to the east of the town and is still used as a training ground for the German Army, just as it was in 1945. You can only see what was left of the camp if you write to the Bundeswehr and ask permission for someone to show you around. I hadn't realised this when I arrived there one bleak November afternoon. It was cold and drizzling with hardly a breeze.

Ohrdruf was the first camp to be liberated by US forces, or so it was announced at the time. Quickly followed by others – Buchenwald, Dachau, Nordhausen, Mauthausen, Flossenbürg – the encounters provoked an intense reaction. Each revealed atrocities too sickening for even the hardiest soldier. Places that should have been innocuous, insignificant militarily, forced American troops to halt as they advanced through Thuringia and southern Germany during April 1945. Within the space of a few weeks they came upon camp after camp, mostly anonymous to start with but soon to become infamous. The photographs and film taken by the accompanying journalists provoked a desire for vengeance, not only for the unjust waging of total war, but for all that the Nazis had done and believed.

A satellite of Buchenwald, Ohrdruf wasn't like the huge camps. It had been constructed at the end of November 1944 to house labourers building a communications centre outside the town. The prisoners came from across the KZ network. They had to undertake brutally policed excavation work. Already weakened from years in other camps, the prisoners fell sick and many were carted back to Buchenwald, unable to work any longer. When news came through that the Allies were approaching, the inmates, nearly 10,000 in number,

were evacuated en masse. Of those too ill to travel many were
executed by the SS, their bodies dumped in sheds or scattered about
the camp. Others, too decrepit to move, were left to die.

Not long after the evacuation, units of the US 4th Armoured
Division and 89th Infantry Division chanced upon scenes that
would soon become all too familiar: barbed wire enclosures;
regimented barracks; watchtowers; bodies strewn over the ground;
stinking piles of emaciated corpses dusted with lime. It was beyond
their understanding, provoking disgust and anger. Colonel Hayden
Sears, the commander of the tank force that had entered Ohrdruf
on 4 April, spoke with a few survivors, learning about the savage
conditions in the camp and the recent removal of most of the
inmates. They told him that the SS had shot those unable to walk,
but hadn't finished off everyone. Some had survived. Incensed,
Sears had his men round up nearly thirty civilians from the town,
including a few dignitaries. They were shown the pits of rotting
and burned bodies. *The Times* reported that the Burgomeister and
his wife had committed suicide after they'd been forced to view
the camp and its victims.[1]

Unable to gain entry to the memorial, or see what had been
preserved of the site, I left Ohrdruf and, following the route taken
by the US Army in 1945, carried on driving the forty kilometres to

Weimar, to the north of the city, to the overlooking hills where I knew the Buchenwald site to be. Plenty of the brown road signs with white lettering that mark all German KZ memorials pointed the way.

Unlike its satellite Ohrdruf, now hidden from any chance visitor, Buchenwald was impossible to miss. The monument erected by the East Germans in the 1950s could be seen for miles sitting atop the Ettersberg hill. At first I thought it was some huge control tower, a giant concrete block, but something about the shadow it cast across the valley towards the city betrayed its nature. Perhaps that was the point. A permanent reminder. No other concentration camp I've visited has such an obvious and widely visible cenotaph. I suppose if I had been living in Weimar I might have become indifferent to the sight of it, but it looked too imposing to put out of one's mind completely.

The Buchenwald camp complex was enormous. Following the crest of the hill, on the five-kilometre route labelled the *Blutstraße*, the 'Blood Road', I began to feel very uneasy. Not because of the lurid notice, but because the imprint of the camp, spread across the contours of the woodlands and hillsides, became increasingly oppressive. Derelict concrete huts or broken markers or disused railway tracks appeared by the side of the road, dozens of indicators of the past drawing you in to an accursed place long before you enter the main camp.

I parked in front of the old SS quarters and then followed the footpath as directed down the hill. The harshness of the place was accentuated rather than alleviated by the peaceful wood within which the camp stood. It came as a shock when, emerging from the trees, I saw the guard towers, then the main entrance building of the prisoners' compound looking like some cricket pavilion with a pathetic, small, cream-painted iron gate set in its middle, the only way in for the thousands of inmates. The gate was stiff and swung heavily when I pushed through it. Inside, I could see the blockhouses, the dark crematorium, the remnants of the rectangular prisoners' barracks fanning out over the grounds, mocking the quiet rural location.

I thought I would be prepared for Buchenwald after seeing Neuengamme, but I wasn't. The prisoners' enclosure housed exhibitions that were cruel in their honesty: the cell next to the crematorium, just visible through a locked greasy glass door, was full of hundreds of small urns neatly stacked on the floor, ready to be filled, a terrifying symbol of certainty. People were expected to die here, I realised. They were expected to be killed by one method or another. The disposal of their remains was integral to the design and operation of the camp. But the urns also seemed incompatible with their surroundings. Why use them when the living bodies were deemed worthy of no regard at all? It wasn't the only incongruity.

After a couple of hours inside the main prisoners' compound, I walked quickly away from the last building I'd entered, the crematorium with its meathooks and industrial ovens served by metal carts. I was glad to be escaping, fed up with the reminders of death and torture. Then I saw that the little gate, the only way out of the compound, which was ringed by wire, was closed. It was late afternoon, 4 o'clock, and the exhibition halls were already shut. No one was about. I experienced a sudden rush of fear that the gate had been locked, trapping me inside as though I too were one of those thousands imprisoned here all those years ago. It was a fleeting, irrational panic and of course the gate opened easily when I pushed it.

Outside, relieved but unnerved, I followed the track running parallel to the compound fence. It passed before an odd concrete structure, a mound with ramps and walls and small dens that reminded me of one of those ersatz ruined castles built as follies in the grounds of British country mansions in the nineteenth century. A stone wall with curved metal spikes encircled it. I couldn't understand what it might be, situated so close to the inmates' camp. It was unclassifiable. I looked at the explanatory panel that was attached to the wall of the enclosure. This was the camp zoo, it said, built for the wild animals kept by the SS. A black-and-white photograph from before the war showed two bear cubs play-fighting behind the walls.

Maybe it was my aggravated imagination, but this fragment of Buchenwald, visible to all the prisoners just beyond the perimeter fence, shocked me more than all those bunkers and barracks behind the barbed wire. I thought it to be the most inhuman of structures in that vast site, an affront, mocking the human beings inside the camp, the animals by contrast receiving careful attention and proper feeding from the guards. Later I found out that the SS had also built a falconry alongside the zoo on Heinrich Himmler's orders. Inmates had to tend to the birds of prey and were responsible for their welfare, but were given no protection from their talons; yet another cruelty to add to the daily brutality of the camp's regime.[2]

I doubted the Americans who liberated Buchenwald would have thought much about the zoo. When later I examined the camp's history, I found that the obvious and multiple outrages uncovered there and at Ohrdruf were enough for General Eisenhower, Supreme Commander of Allied Forces in Europe, to be called to see the horrors. He arrived on 12 April 1945, with Generals Patton and Bradley, the most senior commanders of the US Army. They were taken to Ohrdruf first, where survivors were brought to tell them about the conditions in the camp. The generals and their entourage were photographed looking grim-faced, standing in line over the camp debris. Patton walked away and vomited, unable to stomach the smell of decomposing bodies despite his reputation for toughness. Eisenhower wrote that the things he saw 'beggar description'. He cabled his staff at headquarters insisting that all units should come and see what the Nazis had done. He wrote to the British to invite members of parliament to fly to Germany and visit the newly found camps to see the 'evidence of Nazi infamy'. He wanted the world to know what they'd been fighting against, what they had been fighting for.

When the British Parliamentarians visited Buchenwald a week later, Lord Stanhope 'marvelled at the cold-blooded, thorough organisation behind it all'.[3] The Nazis were shown to be 'worse than brutes', the evidence convincing the visitors of the 'utter depravity of all tainted with Nazism'. Language simply wasn't sufficient to communicate the scale and depth of cruelty they saw. The 'inmates were pitiful wrecks through lack of food, hard work, and the ever-present fear of beatings or violent death', The Times reported, estimating that 60,000–75,000 had died there, figures extrapolated from the SS records, which item- ised the deaths of 6,477 in January 1945 alone.

But words and statistics couldn't fully convey the enormity of what was being uncovered. Photographers and film-makers were summoned to the camps to record the scenes. People *had* to be shown the evidence if they were to be convinced that the incredible stories were true. The British Ministry of Information even announced that they would provide an extra allowance of film stock (like all things, subject to rationing) so that 'full scenes of the conditions in the concentration camps' could be captured. The Times wrote: 'the printed word can glance off an inattentive mind, but the moving picture bites deep into the imagination'.[4]

Those photographs and films, thrust at the public in the spring of 1945 as more camps were discovered, were both horrific and accusa- tory. Lord Justice Lawrence, the British lawyer who six months later would sit as President of the Nuremberg Tribunal, would say that the images of the liberated camps were so 'appalling that the civilized world stood aghast'. And that was how it appeared: as a profound shock. The pictures from Ohrdruf and Buchenwald and then many other camps made the nature and scale of Nazi atrocity real and tangible and incited an instant disgust and mood for vengeance. For the first time, the public were forced (and allowed) to look at the emaciated bodies, piles of dead, the detritus of nameless, faceless victims of the Nazi regime.

I walked away from the prisoners' camp at Buchenwald thinking of Susan Sontag's instruction, 'Let the atrocious images haunt us', and drove back to Weimar, that clean and neatly laid-out city which now enraged rather than charmed me.[5] In the antagonistic comfort of a café close to the Goethe Museum, I could understand, even at this distance of time, why the shock of the encounter with the concentration camps might have stimulated a cry for justice. It made sense.

Then, as the smiling, moustachioed waiter took my order, as I looked at the other customers sitting at tables and laughing and chatting earnestly, inoffensively, I began to sober up, to think more dispassionately. Had the horrors of the camp been such a revelation? I wondered. They'd certainly provided the symbol *and* image of Nazi guilt once the war was won, galvanising the Allies and their citizens to demand retribution, hurrying them to undertake war crimes trials and punish those responsible. But was the official and public shock genuine? Should the British and Americans have been so surprised? The question was important. I already suspected from what I'd read that a lack of preparation had plagued the British efforts at retribution. If the discoveries could have been predicted, if the Allies had known of these systems of atrocity, then that would have a great bearing on gauging the quality of justice planned and eventually delivered.

2.

Overheard in a café: a young Nazi is sitting with his girl; they are discussing the future of the Party. The Nazi is drunk.

'Oh, I know we shall win, all right,' he exclaims impatiently, 'but that's not enough!' He thumps the table with his fist: 'Blood must flow!'

The girl strokes his arm reassuringly. She is trying to get him to come home. 'But, of course, it's going to flow, darling,' she coos soothingly, 'the Leader's promised that in our programme.'

Christopher Isherwood, 'Berlin Diary', Winter 1932/3[6]

Isherwood wasn't the only person to witness something amiss in Germany after the coming to power of Hitler and the Nazis. Even a cursory examination of writings in the British press and official records in the National Archives at Kew reveals that a great deal of information was known about the nature of Nazi rule from early on in Hitler's regime. Little of the ruthlessness of the usurpers was hidden from view. And given that travel to Germany in the 1930s was available to those wealthier individuals wishing to embrace the beauty of the country and the culture it offered, events there were never secret.

Patrick Leigh Fermor walked across the country in 1933 and later wrote about his travels. His first experience when entering Westphalia from the Netherlands was of National Socialist flags and an outfitter's shop which displayed a host of 'swastika arm bands, daggers for the Hitler Youth, blouses for Hitler Maidens and brown shirts for grown-up SA men'.[7] Hagiographic photographs of Josef Goebbels and Hermann Goering and, of course, Hitler too, the recognisable leaders of the new Germany, adorned the shop. Even in those early days when the Nazis first attained power, the violence induced by anger and hate directed particularly against Jews and communists was very clear.

In fact, ever since 1923 and the Munich putsch, when the young Adolf Hitler with his fascist supporters failed in their bid to overthrow the nascent democratic German government based in Weimar, the British press had reported on this faction forged in passion. Numerous accounts in the 1920s told of 'a political movement which exercises an unholy fascination on untold numbers of youths in Germany', of murder plots in Berlin, of battles on the streets of Stettin when National Socialists squirted syringes of hydrochloric acid at communists, of 'terrorist bomb plots' in Hamburg, all in the context of a Germany in perpetual political and economic crisis after the end of the First World War.[8]

By early 1930 references to the National Socialists, Hitler's political party, were commonplace. They were gaining ground in state and national elections, and stories of their ferocity, particularly in clashes with the far left, received due newspaper coverage. Initially, the general tenor of reporting was dismissive. The Nazis' political beliefs were described as 'peculiar', specifically their assumption that 'all ills come from Jews, Jesuits, Freemasons, foreigners, Socialists, and Communists'.[9] Their intention to preserve German culture from influences such as jazz was ridiculed. Wilhelm Frick's appointment as the Nazi party's first government minister in Thuringia in 1930 (Frick would be one of the Nuremberg defendants fifteen years later), and his election to a seat in the Reichstag, prompted The Times to express a half-hearted concern. Frick introduced a motion to the central parliament which was a warning, the paper said, of the 'outlook of a party which may take an increasing part in German politics for a year or two'. Frick proposed a law to imprison 'for racial treason those who injure or impede the natural fertility of the German race or who by inter-breeding with members of the Jewish or coloured races contribute to the racial deterioration and disintegration of the German people'.

The Nazis were now a political force and recognised as such in Britain. The brown-shirted storm troopers (the SA) and black-shirted party police (the *Schutzstaffel* or SS) were achieving notoriety, as were the Party's ideas: a strong Germany, a pure race, the disavowal of treaties forced upon the country after its defeat in World War I. 'No one knows', *The Times* said, 'whether this is a menace or whether it may develop into a constructive force.' But the paper's correspondent was willing to give it the benefit of the doubt: 'If Herr Hitler is correctly reported [in his desire to obtain power by legal and consti-tutional means] the prospect clears considerably. It is precisely the spirit of his party which has won it so much support, and his words suggest that he is going to guide this spirit into useful channels.'[10]

Total press condemnation was thus kept at bay, comfort found in Hitler's assertion that law would govern his party's acquisition of power. He was, besides, openly admired by many in Britain who liked his strong and uncompromising approach. Only in 1933, when the Nazi party finally gained control of the German government after national elections, did the dangerously dictatorial nature of the new regime and its violent spirit become a more persistent worry in the serious news-papers. The establishment of 'concentration camps' was pivotal in that shift of perspective. They quickly came to epitomise Nazi tyranny.

3.

The concentration camp as a place of abuse had already embedded itself in the British consciousness during the Boer War of 1901. Reports of 'enclosures' for Boer women and children and men who were not engaged in fighting the war against the British in South Africa shocked many when made public by a concerned Englishwoman, Emily Hobhouse. She had inspected the camps and led the initial cries of outrage. Officially, the claims of multiple deaths of the inmates through neglect or suspected ill-treatment were denied, but voices denouncing the practice of interning civilians would not be suppressed. David Lloyd-George alerted Parliament to the 'alarming rate of mortality among the women and children'[11] and the press erupted in indignation that Britain could operate such an inhumane policy.[12] The criticism was enough to warrant months of debate, public inquiry and the enduring association of the term 'concentration camp' with brutality, tyranny and suffering.

Two decades later, the term reappeared.[13] When reporting on the oppressive measures that Hitler had introduced immediately after becoming Chancellor of Germany in 1933, the *Manchester Guardian*'s 'own correspondent' in Berlin wrote about the opening of the first concentration camp in Germany at Dachau outside Munich. Five thousand men: communists, those who supposedly endangered the state, Marxists and socialists, had been rounded up and placed in custody in a newly constructed compound on the orders of the President of the Munich Police, Heinrich Himmler. 'This is the first clear statement hitherto made regarding concentration camps,' the paper reported. 'The extent of the terror may be measured from the size of this Bavarian camp – which, one may gather, will be only one of many.'[14]

Despite these fears, a slight touch of levity intervened when describing how the first 140 inmates had arrived at the former munitions factory, now surrounded by barbed wire, preparing the ground for a much greater influx. The reporter wrote of the prisoners: 'One cannot help asking oneself if the Communists will refuse to speak to the Socialists, and the Socialists to the Communists, and what the Pacifists will make of their new military surroundings.' I suppose it was meant as a joke.

By the summer of 1933, however, the British press were mentioning Dachau and other camps with increasing regularity and greater seriousness. On 4 May the *Manchester Guardian* reported on the creation of labour camps and the 'twenty thousand Jews' who would 'shortly be drafted into several depots throughout Germany'. Various stories were told: the paralysing of trade unions (as a move towards 'the absolute extermination of Marxism'); a draft law by the Prussian Ministry of the Interior ('which will permit sterilisation of mentally deficient degenerates and certain classes of criminals, provided their consent to the necessary operation is forthcoming'); the arrest of George Weideinger, a carpenter who had distributed a pamphlet 'describing as murder the shooting of Communist prisoners by Nazi guards at a concentration camp at Dachau a few days before Easter'. The official German story was that three inmates had been shot dead and another wounded whilst 'attempting to escape', a soon-to-be ubiquitous cliché.

In a series of later articles on 'Germany Under the Swastika', the paper was clear about the nature of the new regime. 'Terror remains a basic Nazi method of government,' it said. '[T]he number of persons incarcerated in concentration camps is estimated at tens of thousands.'[15] The report, by an 'American Visitor' (journalists remained largely faceless and anonymous in those days), filed from Berlin, went on to name Dachau as already renowned for its brutality. '[I]t is credibly reported that prisoners are frequently beaten and that ropes are left in their cells as a convenience for those who wish to commit suicide: and certainly the number of "suicides" reported from concentration camps is suspiciously high.' The regime's 'fanatical anti-Semitism' featured prominently in this 'terror'.

The British Parliament was alive to the issue too. Persecution of the Jews was observed soon after Hitler took power. 'There are still constant reports of individuals being spirited away to internment camps and their relatives being left without knowledge as to their whereabouts,' Barnett Janner remarked in a debate on Foreign Affairs.[16] The plight of the Jews was stressed time and again. No one demurred.

'[N]ight after night Nazi spokesmen proclaim on the wireless that Jewry will be destroyed,' Janner said to the House in April 1933.[17] Sir Austen Chamberlain and many others queued up to condemn the violence directed against Jews and political opponents across Germany.

The camp system became a recurrent theme denoting the character of the new German state. The *Manchester Guardian* in particular would not let the matter rest. The paper reflected on the secrecy which surrounded the newly formed installations. But enough information was available, it said, 'to leave no doubt at all as to the inhuman treatment of the interned prisoners'. The Brown Shirts (the SA) were in charge of the camps, not the usual prison authorities, and, according to the paper, inmates often arrived having already been tortured in one of the many 'Brown Houses' across the country. 'The camps are, so to speak, the continuation and amplification of the Terror in the streets.'[18]

And it wasn't just the *Manchester Guardian*. *The Times* reported in August 1933 on a 'Nazi camp for unbelievers'. The correspondent had been allowed to view the anonymous camp and had heard that flogging was sometimes used, and meals were uniformly bread and potatoes. He'd seen the cells for solitary confinement and he'd left 'with a feeling of repulsion,' he wrote, 'guilty of something approaching indecency, not only in having pried into the lives of human beings in dire misfortune, but in having been permitted to witness such inhuman treatment imposed by ruthless men on their own flesh and blood'.[19]

Later, a *Times* editorial reflected on the Nazis' Nuremberg Rally with disdain. It noted the 'vehement attack on the Jews and a caustic condemnation of the democratic system ... The unhappy Jews of Germany, with the exception of the smaller traders, are herded in concentration camps, or deprived of their means of livelihood, often forbidden or unable to leave the country, reduced to penury, and cruelly confronted with starvation.'[20]

The *Manchester Guardian*'s 1934 New Year's Day edition described in further detail the conditions experienced by the estimated 2,200–2,400 inmates of Dachau. The punishment cells (*Arrestzellen*) were damp, concrete, with chains attached to the walls, wooden planks for a bed, nothing to eat for a day then only bread and water with a hot meal once every four days. Corporal punishment was mentioned: flogging with an 'ox-hide thong that has a strip of steel, three to four millimetres wide, running along its whole length', twenty-five to seventy-five lashes depending on the offence, dispensed by an SS man. New inmates were beaten on arrival with wet towels in the reception showers and rubber hoses and fists. Many had died, perhaps fifty within nine months of its opening.[21]

Apart from the formal reportage, the newspapers also published correspondence on the subject from their readers. Rennie Smith recounted his visit to Dachau in 1934 on behalf of a Christian group when he was allowed access to the camp to speak to the commandant and inmates. He confirmed the brutal conditions that the *Manchester Guardian* had revealed. And he was scathing about the rationale that the authorities gave for them: they were all part of a 'cure', a 'healing' of 'poisoned minds', he said. With a lament, Smith ended his letter:

> When I was leaving the camp I turned round to see what seemed like the whole 2,000 assembled, as in a silent mass meeting, before the barracks. The mute anguish and appeal of this multitude rose in streams to the blue sky of the sunny afternoon. What I found most terrible, in its human degradation, was not the detailed incidents of cruelty but the wicked fact that a group of Germans should have the audacity to arrogate to themselves the right to 'heal' in ways like these, another group of Germans.[22]

Within the month, the Terror in Germany was depicted as an 'organic part of the Hitlerite regime: it has grown systematic as the regime itself has grown systematic'. The SS and Gestapo were referred to regularly (along with the SA Brown Shirts) as orchestrators of the cruelty. Executions, terroristic trials, terrible conditions in prisons: anyone minded to read the serious press, at least, couldn't be in any doubt about the political atmosphere in the new Germany.[23] Oppression in its many forms was set out in detail: the anti-Semitic laws, individual acts of violence, acute public humiliation. Though systematically collected evidence was lacking, this could not hide the scale of 'the beatings, the murders, the torture, the robbing, the blackmailing, the arrests and imprisonments, not to speak of the humiliations (both public and private) that have been perpetrated by the Nazis on the Jews'. The experience across Germany wasn't uniform, it was reported, but it was widespread and organised, and from top to bottom incited by Nazi party newspapers and journals.[24]

4.

As I trawled though the newspaper archives, I could see that the stories of concentration camps rarely varied in this early period of Nazi rule. A hiatus set in as the new regime eradicated all effective opposition. But the British reading public were still informed consistently of the existence of the camp system, individual camps were named, and what happened within them reported. The SS and Gestapo had become synonymous with remorselessness and brutality too. 'In the Sachsenburg camp the prisoners are constantly being beaten by their Blackshirt guards with rifle-butts ... [who] habitually refer to the prisoners as "those swine" who ought to be slaughtered.'[25]

Stories of abuse meted out to Jews, Christians, communists, socialists, political opponents, the mentally and physically disabled, homosexuals and everyday criminals were there for anyone to see if they cared to look. It wasn't simply a case of ill-treatment, either. On 16 April 1935 Leonard Montefiore of the Jewish Board of Deputies presented a report to the effect that the fate of Jews in Germany was 'starvation or exile'. The closure of businesses, dismissal from employment, the cumulative effect of small, petty humiliations accompanied by frequent and deadly physical violence were all part of the treatment. As the *Manchester Guardian* reported in mid-1935, the purpose was to 'destroy the German Jewry altogether in the course of time'.[26] Lists of the executed were published to demonstrate the intent of the regime.[27]

By November that year, *The Times* recorded that persecution was at 'a new pitch'. Described as a 'cold pogrom', the effects of the policy of ghettoisation established by the Nuremberg decrees were unpicked in detail. 'The laws are being interpreted as meaning that a Jew, as a second-grade citizen, is not fit to exercise any occupation within the German national community.' The article spoke of 'savage fanaticism' directed at 'the total destruction of the whole Jewish community in Germany'. It quoted the catchphrase *'Juda verrecke'* ('May Jewry perish!'), and itemised the way in which the livelihoods of all Jews were being squeezed to a level of unsustainability. But even with this bleak assessment the writer assumed either Hitler was 'unaware of all that is being done' or 'that fanatics are beyond control'.[28]

In Britain, political protest followed the revelations. The Durham Miners' Association passed a resolution in November 1935 expressing 'horror and indignation at the brutal and inhuman treatment meted out by the Nazi Government to the Jews'.[29] Lord Mount Temple resigned as chairman of the Anglo-German Fellowship on the same grounds. Public protests by representatives of the university, the churches and the city council were held in Glasgow; and the whole of Bedford College for Women of the University of London (principal, staff and students) signed a resolution condemning the persecution and calling on the British government to allow Jewish refugees into the country and its colonies in greater numbers than had so far been allowed.[30]

Much more information was available for those who wanted to see. Hans Beimler was one of the early inmates of Dachau. A prominent communist in Munich, he endured a month in the camp before escaping. He wasn't the type to accept his imprisonment placidly. Strangling his SA guard, dressing in the man's uniform, walking out of the camp and eventually finding his way to Spain, Beimler wrote a book about his experience. *Four Weeks in the Hands of Hitler's Hell-Hounds* may have been a lurid title, but it turned out to be an accurate portrayal, the first detailed insider account. Translated into English and published in the UK in late 1933, albeit with limited distribution, it provided raw material for the press reports.[31]

But did all this reportage and memoir and Parliamentary comment create a fixed view of Nazi malevolence? Ambivalence rather than uniform condemnation of Germany under the Nazis would be a more accurate interpretation. By 1935 letters to newspapers had multiplied on whether the reports of Germany's descent into bestiality and terror were true. Eleanor Rathbone, suffragette, independent MP for the Combined English Universities (a constituency disbanded after the Second World War), and persistent advocate for women's rights, wrote to the *Manchester Guardian* in July of that year warning of the impact of the Nazi regime.[32] 'Visiting Germany: A bad mistake, morally and politically' was her acerbic missive directed not only at the Nazis, but also those who viewed them with favour. 'Sir,' she wrote, 'Your organ and a few others continue to publish side by side evidences of the German government's continuing disgusting crimes against humanity and letters – usually anonymous – expatiating on the pleasures of visiting Germany. No wonder your correspondents find a warm welcome there. Every sign that British people are willing to condone their crimes by accepting the protection and authority (as visitors must do) of those responsible for them must be gratifying to the Nazis.'

A small flurry of supportive and contradictory responses followed. One travel agent from Conway wanted a tourist boycott, remembering banners in the streets of pretty Rhineland towns saying 'The Jews are the enemies of the State' or 'Who buys from a Jew is a traitor'. Others disagreed. Everywhere was cordiality and hospitality, according to them. 'My friends who have accompanied me to Germany with doubts and fears, have all come back with the feeling that these people are our own kith and kin and that war against them is unthinkable.'[33]

The issue became inflamed when the British Legion organised a visit of ex-servicemen to Germany in June 1935 to 'stretch forth the hand of friendship' strained by the Great War. Major Francis Fetherston-Godley and Colonel Crosfield led a deputation that was heartily welcomed and supported by the Prince of Wales. The latter's liking for Germany, and Adolf Hitler in particular, prompted a warm regard for the initiative by the intended hosts. Both Goering and Rudolf Hess were reported as welcoming the visit. Anglo-German cooperation, burying any animosity left from the trenches, was a peaceable act, it seemed.[34]

In its itinerary the Legion included not only meetings with German veterans, but also, rather strangely, a visit to a labour camp. It was exploited by the German media. Hitler and Goering played host. On his return, Major Fetherston-Godley spoke of his impressions. He'd been taken to Dachau and said 'all the prisoners seemed extraordinarily fit, and it appeared to be an excellent idea for prisoners to be kept in such a way rather than incarcerated in a prison'. There were 'trees and flowers and sports grounds where the prisoners can play games', the Major added. The delegation hadn't seen any sign of Jewish persecution.

Wilful blindness? Or simply clever propaganda by the Nazis? Whichever, the visit, and Fetherston-Godley's account, attracted withering criticism. 'Innocents abroad' was the charge. 'Does Major

Fetherston-Godley really believe that a visit of a delegation (did any of this delegation know German?), filled up with banquets and other ceremonies, can give a clearer impression of the real state of affairs than the daily experience of responsible journalists?' one letter-writer remarked.[35]

5.

By the late 1930s the many accounts of inhuman treatment, killings and oppression were accepted as fact in British media and political circles. As relations between the two countries deteriorated and it became apparent that Hitler's Germany was intent on expanding its control into Austria and Czechoslovakia, British politicians became worried. Geoffrey Mander spoke in the Commons at length in April 1938 about the 'hated Gestapo' and the 'concentration camps'. James de Rothschild mentioned Dachau in June of that year, saying, 'I need not describe the conditions which reign there; everybody in this House knows of them.'[36] The problem of Jewish refugees from Germany, and whether they should be allowed to enter Palestine, haunted some of the conversations. 'It is better for a Jew to starve in Palestine, in his home, than to be killed at Sachsenhausen, or Dachau, or some of those foul torture places to which they are being sent at the present time. The only way out is Palestine,' Colonel Josiah Wedgwood said in a Parliamentary debate in late November 1938.[37]

Whether or not prompted by the need to reinforce images of German bestiality as a propaganda tool, accounts of atrocities and systemic brutality and killing became pervasive once Germany invaded Poland and war was declared with Britain. In October 1939, the British Foreign Office published a White Paper (on sale for 3d) that reported on the treatment of German nationals in Germany during the previous two years. Conditions were reminiscent of 'the darkest ages in the history of man'. The Paper said evidence gathered had been withheld from the public previously so as not to endanger the prospects for peaceful settlement of the developing dispute with Germany.

The Times commented that '[e]ven after the outbreak of war the British Government felt reluctant to take action which might have the effect of inspiring hatred',[38] but anti-British propaganda spread by the Germans (which included reference to the concentration camps operated by the British in the Boer War) forced the government to reveal what it knew. The White Paper listed first-hand accounts of the 'plight of the Jews', 'sadistic cruelty', and the 'City of Sorrow' that was Buchenwald, where the SS used the most vicious punishments.

Similar reports appeared regularly after this, with the Polish government in London speaking of atrocities in its country.[39] Terrorism through mass executions and deportation to concentration camps was a recurrent theme throughout 1940 and the subject of a joint statement by the Polish and Czech governments in exile on 12 November that year.[40] The Gestapo's oppressive actions merited particular attention, as did the treatment of the Jews. A 'grim story of Nazi oppression' was related in numerous leaders and articles. The murder and evacuation of men and women in occupied Poland ('it is reckoned that more than 5,000 persons have been executed either individually or in mass'[41]) as fulfilment of *Lebensraum*, the Nazi policy of removal of Poles and Jews from lands so that Aryan Germans could occupy them, was revealed.

Even before the USA became fully embroiled in the conflict, Prime Minister Churchill and President Roosevelt conspired in October 1941 to produce parallel statements denouncing 'German savagery' and promising a 'fearful retribution'.[42] In January of the following year, after the attack by Japan on Pearl Harbor on 7 December 1941 had led to war being declared by Germany on the USA, representatives of nine nations under German occupation gathered in London to condemn Nazi atrocities and propose how those responsible should be punished when the war was over. There would be 'vengeance'. The declaration made at the conference introduced the idea that justice would be done. International law was cited to indicate why the Germans' actions were criminal. Punishment was demanded but only through 'the channel of organised justice'.[43]

Over the next couple of years, debates in Parliament, international declarations, newspaper reports of massacres and extermination and torture and any number of other crimes identified Nazi figures as war criminals who would be punished once the war was won. In October 1942, Lord Maugham, the former Lord Chancellor, suggested that 'it would be a condition of the Armistice that named criminals wanted for war crimes should be caught and handed over'.[44] President Roosevelt had announced the day before that a United Nations Commission for the investigation of war crimes was to be established. It would record testimony and name suspects and assemble the 'evidence against those responsible for atrocities'. Sumner Welles, Under-Secretary of State, was asked at a Washington press conference on 7 October 1942 if the list would include Hitler. He replied caustically that he would leave the answer to 'the questioner's excellent judgement'.[45]

The idea of a UN War Crimes Commission (UNWCC) was supported by the British government. The Lord Chancellor, Viscount Simon, said the Commission's aim was not to 'promote the execution of enemy nationals wholesale, but to secure the punishment of individuals guilty as ringleaders or perpetrators'. Sumner Welles also made it clear that mass reprisals weren't envisaged. Roosevelt's statement at the White House on 7 October had emphasised that the 'number of persons eventually found guilty will undoubtedly be extremely small'. Both the US and British administrations were anxious to avoid German reprisals and the killing of more captured Allied troops. If the Nazis believed they might face mass execution, then what would they have to lose by committing yet more horrendous crimes? *Wenn schon, denn schon*, the Germans might think.

It was a reasonable fear. The Allies had already accumulated considerable information about atrocities against civilian populations and against Allied troops on and off the battlefield. Communiqués intercepted by the British code-breakers revealed a wealth of detail about atrocities. The information traffic contained repeated reports. In July 1941, a summary of this traffic included reference to a 'laconic' message reporting to Himmler that 'in the cleaning up operations in SLONIM by Pol. Reg. Mitte of 17.7.1941 1153 Jewish plunderers were shot'. Further messages reported that an SS cavalry brigade had liquidated 3,274 partisans and Jewish Bolsheviks without incurring a single casualty. In August 1941, they intercepted a message that referred to 30,000 executions during the Russian campaign then underway. The names of officers and their actions were all laid out in detail. There was frequent mention of 'Jew-operations' and the listing of numbers executed (700 Jews incapable of work shot in July 1942) – the level of detailed knowledge was extraordinary.[46] There was no doubt the government understood the capacity of the Nazi regime to be ruthless. Lord Maugham, again, told the House of Lords in a debate on war crimes on 7 October 1942 that evidence of German outrages had been received from every country the Germans had attacked. What value was there in being coy when the world was learning of the extermination of the Jewish people in Europe?

Only a couple of months after Viscount Simon's and President Roosevelt's announcements, a formal declaration was issued in London, Moscow and Washington accepting as truthful the reports of the institutionalised massacre of Jews at the hands of the Nazi forces. Released to the press by the US Department of State on 17 December 1942, the statement conveyed remarkable awareness of the enormity of what was happening on the Continent. The German authorities, it said,

> are now carrying into effect Hitler's oft-repeated intention to exterminate the Jewish people in Europe. From all the occupied countries Jews [no mention was made of German Jews] are being transported in conditions of appalling horror and brutality to Eastern Europe. In Poland, which has been made the principal Nazi slaughterhouse, the ghettos established by the German invader are being systematically emptied of all Jews except a few highly skilled workers required for war industries. None of these taken away are ever heard of again. The able-bodied are slowly worked to death in labor camps. The infirm are left to die of exposure and starvation or are deliberately massacred in mass executions. The number of victims of these bloody cruelties is reckoned in many hundreds of thousands of entirely innocent men, women, and children.[47]

As a sketch of the Holocaust, this came close to reflecting the policy of extermination undertaken by the Nazis. Whether people believed it, thought much about it, considered that anything could be done in response other than promise retribution, I can't tell. But the principle of retribution for such atrocity was established here. Some might think it was bravado, given that the Battle of Stalingrad had not yet been won by the Soviet Army, the USA was still engaged in a bitter conflict with the Japanese in the Pacific, Britain had only recently achieved a land victory against the Germans in North Africa at the Battle of El Alamein, and the prospect of liberating any part of mainland Europe was many months away. Then again, the thinking of the Allied leadership was starting to be shaped by the sense that the war would eventually be won by the USA and the Soviet Union, who were now able to mount two equally strong fronts against the German forces. Optimism that the Nazis would be defeated eventually allowed expressions of retribution to have political weight. It was good for morale.

In such confident spirit, the registering of suspected war criminals began. On 16 October 1942, the Soviet authorities named Hitler, Goering, Hess, Goebbels, Himmler, von Ribbentrop and Rosenberg at the head of the list, and agreed with President Roosevelt that these and other most senior Nazis should eventually be put on trial and punished. They would cooperate fully to this end, declaring that 'the clique of Nazi leaders and their cruel accomplices must be judged in accordance with penal laws'.[48]

Despite the political rhetoric on both sides of the Atlantic proclaiming that the Nazis would suffer punishment for their crimes through some legal procedure, significant resistance to the whole idea of a war crimes tribunal existed within British government circles. The failure of a similar enterprise at the end of the First World War was very much in the minds of many officials. If a repeat of that debacle (as many saw it) were to take place, then justice would not be done. Worse: it would be a waste of money.

6.

What had happened after the armistice in 1918, at the Leipzig Trials, as they became known, was a cause of concern for some.[49] Just as the Allies now looked for a form of procedural retribution, so too had France and Britain after the First World War. Even the language was the same. In October 1918, the French government issued a notice stating that 'acts so contrary to International Law, and to the very principles of human civilisation, should not go unpunished'. Calls for 'war criminals' to be brought to justice were made. A provision was inserted in the Treaty of Versailles signed with Germany in June 1919. And the German government (which exercised sovereign control of its territory at the end of World War I, unlike in 1945) acknowledged that the Allied powers would be entitled to bring the accused before military tribunals.

The plan was to conduct trials of those accused of violating the laws of war, trials that would mirror normal domestic criminal proceedings where laws of evidence and 'fair trial' standards would be respected. A very long list of individual suspects was drawn up by both the French and British and submitted to the new German government. But the German authorities stalled and raised objections. Conditions in the country were chaotic. The Germans argued that pursuing all the people on the list would be impossible and might even bring the government down. After considerable delay, their pleas were heard and a reduced list of forty-five was presented. It was also agreed that the trials would be conducted before the Supreme Court of Leipzig according to local procedural rules, though the evidence was to be provided by the Allies. Even then, it took until the middle of 1921 before any case was heard and that was only concerned with the conditions and treatment in some of the prisoner-of-war camps in Germany.

I came across a lovely little book written in 1921 by a lawyer, Claud Mullins, which told the story of the Leipzig Trials.[50] I say 'lovely' because its innocence is a beautiful thing. His faith in the legal process as a civilising and necessary expression of complete justice on this earth has a childlike quality to it. Mullins may have found fault with the way the trials were conducted, disapproving of the lenient sentences that were handed down, but throughout he seemed to have an unshakeable belief that the law properly followed would resolve any moral questions on how war should be conducted. Given the terrible slaughter experienced on all fronts, where millions perished through methods of war that were never the subject of legal condemnation, I thought Mullins's views quaint.

Of more practical concern from the vantage point of World War II, however, was that the few trials which did take place and the limited punishments imposed were little more than symbolic. Only junior officers were prosecuted. None of the German leadership was held to account for war crimes. Though Kaiser Wilhelm II had abdicated after the end of the First World War, he was given asylum in the Netherlands, which, being neutral throughout the conflict, wouldn't contemplate extradition. Any demand to hold the head of the German state responsible for the whole conflagration was thus lost amidst the practical operation of international law. The Kaiser escaped justice, so the Allies believed, eventually dying in 1941, when the Germans occupied most of Europe.

As far as many in the British establishment were concerned, the Leipzig Trials set a poor precedent. If applied to the Nazis, they feared the law would hinder retribution, not channel it.

7.

Whatever doubts the British may have had, the Allies agreed that some form of trial-based procedure should be adopted as a means of obtaining retribution. In October 1943, the three Allied leaders, Roosevelt, Churchill and Stalin, met in Moscow and issued a defining statement.[51]

> The United Kingdom, the United States and the Soviet Union have received from many quarters evidence of atrocities, massacres and cold-blooded mass executions which are being perpetrated by Hitlerite forces in many of the countries they have overrun and from which they are now being steadily expelled.

Speaking for the United Nations, as the alliance against Germany was now called, the three leaders gave a warning in ferocious language:

> At the time of granting of any armistice to any government which may be set up in Germany, those German officers and men and

members of the Nazi party who have been responsible for or have taken a consenting part in the above atrocities, massacres and executions will be sent back to the countries in which their abominable deeds were done in order that they may be judged and punished according to the laws of these liberated countries and of free governments which will be erected therein. Lists will be compiled in all possible detail from all these countries having regard especially to invaded parts of the Soviet Union, to Poland and Czechoslovakia, to Yugoslavia and Greece including Crete and other islands, to Norway, Denmark, Netherlands, Belgium, Luxembourg, France and Italy.

Thus, Germans who take part in wholesale shooting of Polish officers or in the execution of French, Dutch, Belgian or Norwegian hostages, of Cretan peasants, or who have shared in slaughters inflicted on the people of Poland or in territories of the Soviet Union which are now being swept clear of the enemy, will know they will be brought back to the scene of their crimes and judged on the spot by the peoples whom they have outraged.

Let those who have hitherto not imbrued their hands with innocent blood beware lest they join the ranks of the guilty, for most assuredly the three Allied powers will pursue them to the uttermost ends of the earth and will deliver them to their accusors in order that justice may be done.

The above declaration is without prejudice to the case of German criminals whose offenses have no particular geographical localization and who will be punished by joint decision of the government of the Allies.

Here, then, was the plan for justice. Individuals were to be held responsible for the atrocities they had committed. Reparations by the German state would not be enough. Perpetrators would be identified and returned to the country where their crimes had been committed. Those of the leadership of the Nazi regime, who'd designed and operated pan-European atrocities (extermination, deportations, oppression, slave labour), would be dealt with separately.

On 20 October 1943, the UNWCC was finally instituted, having been approved in principle and promised by Roosevelt a year

previously. It was to be based in London. But the new organisation was slow to do anything of practical use. Much of its work
until 1945 was taken up with legal debate. In late 1944, when it
was proposed that a Central Investigating Agency be set up, it
was decided that the Commission had insufficient staff to do so.
Instead, a period of extended legalistic discussion followed its
creation. Simply defining the extent of 'war crimes' was a major
enterprise. Despite a reasonably rich history of international laws
of war, the known atrocities of the Germans far surpassed the
ambit of existing Conventions of The Hague and Geneva. These
hadn't been drafted with the wholesale oppression of populations
or the undertaking of systematised extermination in mind. Some
lawyers declared that strictly speaking a war crime could not be
committed by a German if the victim were a national of Germany
or one of its allies.

The British representatives on the Commission were the leading
voices supportive of this narrow interpretation. It was foolishly
pedantic in the circumstances. With German and Austrian Jews and
communists and opponents to the Nazis the first amongst the
persecuted and killed, how ridiculous it would be if their suffering
were ignored because of their nationality. A different language had
to be adopted if these strict legal objections were to be overcome.
Developing the term 'crimes against humanity' was the Commission's
proffered solution, accompanied by the novel notion of 'crimes
against peace' to reflect the world's outrage at the waging of aggressive war on such a grand scale by the Germans.

The idea of 'crimes against humanity' was promoted as early as
March 1944 by the US representative on the Commission, Herbert
Pell. He said the atrocities known to have been committed against
German Jews and Catholics, all part of a religious or racial persecution, demanded a response based on a 'law of humanity'. He met
with fierce resistance from the US State Department, who maintained
the line that the suffering of German nationals, whoever they were,
was not the legal concern of the Allies.[52] Only after a bitter battle
between lawyers was the new term accepted. Subcommittees were
then formed to draft the appropriate resolutions. They settled on a

definition of crimes against humanity as 'crimes committed against any person without regard to nationality, stateless persons included, because of race, nationality, religious or political belief, irrespective of where they have been committed'.[53] Clumsy and unassimilable for many, the provision was only finally accepted late in 1945, more than a year after it was first mooted by Pell.

It seems odd that in the middle of the bloodiest of conflicts a group of lawyers should have been sitting in London deliberating on terminology and definition and spending the best part of a couple of years doing so. Did they think they were engaged on a necessary project, I wondered, when I read the minutes and reports from the Commission. Lawyers have an extraordinary belief in the efficacy and essential character of their work regardless of what's happening around them. Perhaps that's a good thing, a reminder of the civilising nature of law when governed by a sense of right and fairness. But fear that the law can stultify justice often intrudes. Should so much angst have been felt about the definition of war crimes? Should its application to nationals of the enemy state have caused so much debate? Legal opinion will attest to the necessity of certainty and clarity in the law. And if the law is clear and excludes a situation from its application, then to bend it or distort it to make sure it can apply will weaken its power. No doubt that was what they were trying to avoid. It smacks now of bull-headed pedantry even so.

8.

The problem of how to deal with the Nazis after the war wasn't simply a legal matter. It was a political one too. Though Britain, the USA and the Soviet Union might have agreed some form of retribution was necessary, little consensus existed about the best way to undertake it. The Americans were particularly concerned by the question, though progress towards a solution was slow whilst the war was going on. There were good reasons for this.

In July 1943, the Allies invaded Sicily. After the German forces retreated across the Strait of Messina, the invasion of mainland Italy followed in September. It was the first time that Allied troops had occupied Axis home territory. It brought them into direct contact with the Germans' treatment of prisoners of war and civilian detainees. In August 1943, units operating under General Eisenhower's command discovered an internment camp on the island of Ustica off the northern coast of Sicily. Yugoslav partisans held there had been tortured and starved to death. Eisenhower asked for confirmation that he could put the prison officials on trial immediately in an Allied military court. The request was denied after the matter had been considered at the highest level. The Combined Chiefs of Staff decided on 1 January 1944 that 'immediate trial by civil or military court would result in reprisals by the enemy against arbitrarily selected allied prisoners of war'.[54] The German suspects should be held prisoner and not segregated so as to avoid alerting the enemy. Evidence should be collected confidentially and no publicity should be given to the 'capture and trial of war criminals'. It was 'believed that any temporary propaganda advantage that might be gained ... could be completely overbalanced by the danger of reprisals against Allied prisoners of war in enemy hands'. After some deliberation it was preferred that the UNWCC should take on the task of preparing for prosecutions once the war ended, receiving information and storing it for that purpose.

The policy was altered slightly after the D-Day landings in June 1944. The British and US command began examining many cases where their troops had been murdered during the fighting in France. The Canadians had suffered particularly at the hands of the 12th SS Panzer Division 'Hitler Youth', which had a reputation for barbarism. Massacres of captured Canadian soldiers had been uncovered. Outraged, General Eisenhower, now Supreme Commander of the Allied Expeditionary Force in France, ordered a court of inquiry into one of the incidents. It found that up to twenty-six men had been executed at the Château d'Audrieu on 8 June 1944. No prosecutions followed, however, as none of the suspected German perpetrators had yet been captured.[55]

The process nevertheless set a precedent. Similar procedures were instituted as more atrocities came to light. A Special Inquiries Branch was established with representatives from the US, British and Canadian armies. They operated much like any normal military criminal investigation. Witnesses were found and brought before a hearing and subjected to cross-examination with the aim of identifying whether a crime had been committed, whether an accused could be named and whether a good case could be made against him. It was scrupulously fair.

I found records of a number of these inquiries in the old Foreign Office files held at the National Archives. Relatively few were conducted and none related to mass atrocities of the kind the press and senior Allied politicians had been reporting for several years. They were generally concerned with localised incidents (usually the shooting of Allied prisoners of war) and attracted little attention beyond that of the investigating troops. A typical case was the shooting of two American airmen after they'd parachuted from their plane shot down over Longueil, France on 24 June 1944.[56] French civilian witnesses were brought to the inquiry. After lengthy cross-examination the military court concluded that one of the killings was murder, but insufficient evidence had been collected for the other death to be declared a 'killing as a fact provable at law'. A secondary allegation of stealing property was also dismissed.

The case was very detailed, very specific and very fair. No scream for retribution was heard. Any allegation had to be proven to the satisfaction of a legal standard. Even faced by the 'consistent pattern of brutality and ruthlessness' perpetrated by the 12th SS Panzer Division, which committed numerous atrocities in the Normandy campaign and again when re-formed in the Ardennes in late 1944, the process was scrupulous.[57]

Inquiries continued and expanded as the Allied forces pushed into France, Belgium and the Netherlands. More atrocities came to light and some were thoroughly investigated.[58] But a reticence to publish the details uncovered remained typical. Even when the camp at Breendonk Fort in Belgium, a Gestapo prison that retained the evidence of systematic torture, was overrun by the British 21st Army Group, caution was exercised. British Army investigators drafted a full report, but only a few details were released to the correspondents accompanying the military advance. Officials from the Ministry of

Information and the Foreign Office debated between them whether to release the whole story to the media in January and February 1945. 'I am not convinced', said one handwritten comment on the memo passing back and forth, 'that the British public is sufficiently aware of German abominations [or] that it is any use counting on being able to revive atrocity stories when the war is beginning to fade from people's minds.'[59] Sir Cyril Radcliffe at the Ministry of Information wrote to Lord Cadogan at the FO, 'We have always taken an austere view of the use of atrocity material in this war, considering that the Government should be scrupulous about lending the weight of its authority to such stories.'[60] The Foreign Office's position remained equally reserved:

> We agree with you in taking 'an austere view' of the use of atrocity material, not only because of being sure of its authenticity, but also because it seems to us that the public may be in danger of being sated with this as with other forms of war propaganda. Our material could often be more effectively put to use later on when memories of German conduct are beginning to fade and when it should be possible to combine information about war crimes with information about the punishment meted out to those guilty of them. Moreover, there is the danger that publication of the details of atrocity stories now may make it easier for those concerned to avoid justice and may also provoke the enemy to some form of reprisal.[61]

It was an approach that encouraged circumspection even when the first major concentration camp was overrun. In November 1944, a party of French troops operating with the US 7th Army moved into Alsace and the Vosges mountains behind the retreating German forces and found Natzweiler-Struthof KZ. Established in 1940, it had received thousands of prisoners from France and across Europe over the four years of its operation. Most had slaved in the nearby quarry. As with every other labour camp, the harsh conditions had led to thousands of deaths. From the central camp were run forty or so sub-camps, outposts for housing prisoners used as forced labour. Natzweiler had been evacuated a month before the Allied soldiers arrived, but a handful of former inmates remained in the district.

A team of intelligence officers, whose role it was to gather information that might be useful for propaganda purposes, was sent to the camp from their base in the south of France. Captain Yurka Galitzine, a British officer seconded to the unit, found not only the detritus of the camp (Galitzine said later the smell of death reminded him of a 'knacker's yard'), but also rumours indicating that British prisoners had been held there. Galitzine returned to Natzweiler in December to conduct a more thorough examination. His subsequent report described a spectrum of atrocity. He wrote about an operational gas chamber where, after days of various medical examinations, dozens of Jewish men and women had been killed and their bodies then sent to Strasbourg for detailed post-mortems. He wrote about SS *Hauptsturmführer* Josef Kramer, the camp commandant responsible. He wrote about 'experiments' undertaken on inmates by medical professors and doctors. He wrote about the large-scale torture of Russian and Polish prisoners of war; about the starvation rations. He wrote about the Frenchmen and -women brought into the camp to be worked to death. He wrote about mass executions and punishments.[62] It was a comprehensive account months before the revelations from Buchenwald and Ohrdruf.

Galitzine apparently presented the report to his superiors thinking it would serve as important information to expose the nature of Nazi rule. But nothing was done. No one was appointed to investigate further. No plans to prosecute were laid. The Supreme Headquarters Allied Expeditionary Force (SHAEF) court of inquiry wasn't involved.[63]

9.

None of this made much sense to me. During the war, the British and Americans had rarely tired of pronouncing their disgust at the Nazis' means of oppression. They'd known from before the war that these were centred on the concentration camp system. And they'd committed themselves to exacting retribution. So why were they so reluctant, so negligent, in their pursuit of atrocities when they were first uncovered? Perhaps the authorities hadn't truly believed their own propaganda. But I came to realise that that would have meant doubting the stream of information emanating from their intelligence services too.

During one of my trips to the National Archives, I asked to see a file labelled 'Papers recovered from Lt Col A.P. Scotland: German concentration camps; POW interrogation reports'.[64] The title intrigued me, particularly as I'd heard of Scotland and knew him to have been a controversial character in charge of the interrogation of German prisoners of war. It appeared that the War Office had had to demand confidential papers back from Scotland after he'd retired from the forces in the late 1940s. Whilst flicking through the bundle of documents, I found copies of numerous reports of interrogations of German troops who'd been captured towards the latter half of 1944. Some had been inmates in concentration camps, released and drafted into the German Army before being taken prisoner by Allied forces in France. A steady stream of cooperative soldiers had been sent to interrogation centres in Kempton Park and Lingfield for questioning.

Scotland's papers had been separated into various manila files. Each one had the name of a major concentration camp on its front cover: Dachau, Mauthausen, Natzweiler, Buchenwald, Sachsenhausen, Auschwitz. I was amazed at the level of detail that had been accumulated long before the Allied troops had invaded Germany. There were exact maps of the camps, setting out the layout of the huts and guardhouses and installations, and details of their operations. And there were lengthy statements taken from the German POWs. Each one must have made the interrogators shudder.

Václav Krejči told them he'd been in Dachau. He was able to give a complete description of the camp and the crimes committed there: terrible punishments amounting to torture; prisoners selected for experiments; submersion in tanks of ice-cold water after which resuscitation was attempted by women prisoners forced to 'revive the victim with the warmth of their bodies'; fatal pressure chamber experiments on Russian prisoners; malaria tests.

Wilhelm Kick told them about a gas wagon, loaded with prisoners, that travelled to and fro between Mauthausen and Gusen, driven by the commandant, *SS-Obersturmbannführer* Franz Ziereis, who would take the van to his home so that his wife could look through the peep-hole and see the 'death agony of the unfortunates inside'. Names of SS troops were provided. Details of their crimes noted.

Henryk Rygiol told them he and his wife had been interned in Auschwitz and had seen terrible things. He said there'd been a dog-training school where the animals had been taught to have an appetite for prisoners' flesh; hundreds of thousands of Jews had been gassed, the twenty-one ovens burning night and day to cope with the bodies. He gave the names of the SS men working at the camp.

Władysław Bulowski told them that his family had lived in the village destroyed to make way for the Auschwitz complex. They'd all known about the massed transports of Jews, he said. 'Old people were kept apart' when they'd arrived, 'likewise the ill and infirm. The latter ... were driven into gas chambers, poisoned and subsequently burned.' All of the information given would turn out to be brutally accurate.

None of this could have been a complete surprise. Though everything in Scotland's files was marked 'Top Secret', the Russians had by then overrun Majdanek concentration camp near Lublin during their 1944 summer push to Berlin, and had denounced the terrible conditions they'd found. On 11 August 1944, the *Times'* Moscow correspondent reported that the 'camp was not intended to provide permanent accommodation for the inmates. The barracks were cleared just as fast as the prisoners could be killed, though always there were some 20,000 kept alive to work on extensions to the camp. The favourite method of killing them was by gas. There were both mobile and permanent gas chambers, and the Russians captured many containers of the gas used.'[65] Majdanek, it said, suggested 'medieval conceptions of hell'. By October 1944, the paper was saying that Majdanek had seen the slaughter of as many as 1,500,000 people, mostly Jews. The British Foreign Office was also picking up Soviet reports of atrocities, 'monstrous crimes' in Lithuania, special camps built for executions, the 'fort of death' at Kaunas where 70,000 people had been murdered. There was more of the same from Lvov and East Prussia.[66]

And months before that, in March 1944, President Roosevelt had accepted and publicly confirmed reports that 'the wholesale systematic murder of the Jews of Europe goes on unabated every hour'. He'd said that mass transports of Jews from Hungary and the Balkans, 'innocent people', would 'perish on the very eve of triumph over the barbarism which their prosecution symbolises'.[67] Churchill too had acknowledged privately to his Foreign Secretary, Anthony Eden, that this was 'probably the greatest and most horrible crime ever committed in the whole history of the world'.[68]

Whether these stories were fully believed or not, and perhaps they weren't truly understood even if they were believed, the Allied leaders prepared for retribution nonetheless. They might have been driven by the desire to punish the aggressors, but that moral imperative was given greater heft by the atrocity stories. They suited a purpose.

10.

Martin Gilbert, the historian, spent years uncovering and dissecting the information the Allies had accumulated about the extermination of the Jews and of the atrocities in the camps, despite the Germans' attempt to keep the killing centres at Auschwitz and Belzec and Treblinka and elsewhere secret. He found that by 1944 a steady flow of data on the subject had been collected from many sources. But other than the general statements issued from time to time by the Allied leaders, little had been done to hinder or prevent the genocide. There were even official fears expressed in London and Washington that the Germans might alter their policy of 'extermination' and embarrass the Allies by 'flooding them with alien immigrants', as one government official recorded. Perhaps only the expression of an ignorant and faceless bureaucrat, but perhaps also a hint of indifference to the slaughter at a time when all attention was focused on winning the war.[69] Overall, though, Gilbert described the failures of the British and Americans throughout the course of the war as 'those of imagination, of response, of Intelligence, of piecing together and evaluating what was known, of co-ordination, of initiative, and even at times of sympathy'.[70]

If true, and Gilbert's thesis is strong, it's perhaps unsurprising that the practical measures for a reckoning, taken before the war's end and the sudden exposure to the stench of the camps, were half-hearted. Who would have had the imagination to convert all the available information into a full appreciation of the level and scope of atrocity? When Elie Wiesel reflected on his determination to write about his life in Auschwitz and Buchenwald, he knew 'deep down' his testimony would not be received easily given that it 'sprang from the darkest zone of man'. He wondered whether those who hadn't experienced the camps would 'at least understand' on reading his account. 'Would they be able to comprehend how, within that cursed universe, the masters tortured the weak and massacred the children, the sick, and the old?'[71]

I doubted it. I doubted that before the camps were revealed all those reports and words and statements could have conveyed the truth.

Even so, enough was known for President Roosevelt to be alerted in January 1945 of the difficulties that would likely ensue once German unconditional surrender had been achieved and the Moscow Declaration of 1943 could be put into effect.[72] A memo had been written by Henry Stimson (US Secretary of War), Edward Stettinius (US Secretary of State) and Francis Biddle (Attorney General), the leading figures in the US administration's development of war crimes policy, representing one stream of thought as to how to treat the Nazi leadership after victory had been achieved. But it wasn't the reports of the camps that drove them to formulate their proposed policy. The need for a coherent plan had been made imperative by a growing number of revelations about the murder of American servicemen by German forces.[73]

However publicly inflammatory these accounts of massacre, Stimson's memo recognised that the criminality of Hitler and his cohort of senior Nazis was 'the result of a systematic and planned reign of terror within Germany, in the satellite Axis countries, and in the occupied countries of Europe', starting in 1933 when Hitler had first been appointed Chancellor of the Reich. From the beginning, his reign had been 'marked by mass murders, imprisonments, expulsions and deportations of populations; the starvation, torture and inhuman treatment of civilians'. Total war had been pursued 'with utter and ruthless disregard for the laws and customs of war'.

The names of the chief German leaders are well known, and the proof of their guilt will not offer great difficulties. However, the crimes to be punished have been committed upon such a large scale that the problem of identification, trial and punishment of their perpetrators presents a situation without parallel in the administration of criminal justice.

A list of hindrances followed: 'The gathering of proof will be laborious and costly, and the mechanical problems involved in uncovering and preparing proof of particular offenses one of appalling dimensions.' Only a 'negligible minority of the offenders will be reached by attempting to try them on the basis of separate prosecutions'.

The recommended solution, the 'judicial method', one which would hold good for the whole of the retributive process, ultimately skated over the difficulties and insisted it was preferable to any other response. Summary executions of Hitler, Himmler and selected others would, it said, 'encourage the Germans to turn these criminals into martyrs'. Far better to condemn through trial. The public would be supportive and the method would 'receive the respect of history'. It would also 'make available for all mankind to study in future years an authentic record of Nazi crimes and criminality'. They would try both the German leadership *and* the organisations used to carry out their atrocious designs: the SA, the SS and the Gestapo in particular. A case would be made before an international tribunal that a deliberate plan had been crafted by the Nazi leaders to commit atrocities through these groups as an elaborate but clear conspiracy. A court would decide whether a criminal plot had been hatched, who of these leaders had been involved in bringing it to life, and which organisations were implicated. Individuals found guilty by the tribunal would be sentenced and that would conclude its work.

After that, all those accused of specific atrocities would be hunted down and put on trial. Using the findings of the first tribunal, defendants would be prosecuted as members of the condemned organisations. Guilt by association, in other words. Proof of the 'nature and extent of the individual's participation' in the concerned organisation was all that would be needed. 'Individual defendants', it concluded, 'who can be connected with specific atrocities will be tried and punished in the national courts of the countries concerned.'

It sounded very simple. But it didn't resolve how the barriers to pursuing so many perpetrators could be overcome. Spreading the load of prosecution across the nations wouldn't alleviate the complications of identification of the accused, accumulation of evidence or anything else. Still, a plan for dealing with the main leaders of the German Reich had been sketched out and with it a sense of what steps to take. Evidentially, they would need proof of the crimes committed, proof that a plan to commit these crimes existed and proof that the individuals selected for prosecution were intimately connected with the design of that plan.

There's no doubting the general thrust of this relatively early proposal: focus on the easily identifiable head of the monster, gather the documents establishing their guilt, try them as a select gang of individuals, convict and sentence, and then worry about the rest later. It became the preoccupation at the highest level: how to condemn the main leaders through legal process. Investigations into the specific atrocities committed by lesser figures would be viewed through that strategic prism, providing as they would the incontrovertible evidence of overall criminality.

The memo also recommended that the UN War Crimes Commission be wound up. It had done its job, although reading between the lines I wonder whether the authors of the memo valued its contribution at all. The UNWCC may have provided an institutional location for lamenting Nazi crimes, reports of which were being passed to it by various sources, but it hadn't been particularly well organised or focused. Instead, the memo suggested that representatives from the four powers, the United States, Britain, France and the Soviet Union, would lead a staff of attorneys and researchers to gather the information, analyse it and 'prepare the charges to conform to the proof'. The evidence would then be presented to the International Military Tribunal, as it would be known.

Here was the blueprint. It would undergo considerable shaping over the next few months, but the basic structure had been sketched out *before* the public were exposed to the pictures of mounds of rotting corpses, seething graves, skeletal armies of camp survivors; before the imagination was given form.

11.

A couple of hundred miles south-south-east of Buchenwald, on the German–Czech border, is the small town of Flossenbürg. It had snowed before I arrived, but the roads were clear. I was looking for the next major concentration camp that the Americans had discovered in April 1945. Driving slowly through the town, I missed the sign to the camp memorial and only realised my mistake when the signposts for the Czech border appeared. Returning to the town I saw the tiny KZ sign that pointed down a lane past a modern housing development.

As I pulled into the rough parking area, I wondered why the site was so hard to find, quite unlike the heralded presence of Buchenwald outside Weimar. It was, after all, of equal magnitude and brutality. I knew Flossenbürg KZ had been an important centre of military production, using slave labour brought from across Europe, and that some 90,000 people had passed through during its operation from 1938 onwards. Twenty-one thousand of these were recorded as having died, though that number didn't include those brought specifically for execution. The camp had a strong British connection, which was one of the reasons I'd travelled there. Several members of the Special Operations Executive, agents who had parachuted behind enemy lines to encourage resistance and conduct sabotage of their own, had been arrested in 1944 by the Gestapo and sent to Flossenbürg. At the very end of the war, as news of the Allied forces advancing across Germany had reached the camp, the agents had been taken from their tiny cells and hanged.

Once inside the camp, I read the inscriptions on the gatehouse walls. They said that the memorial and museum had been opened in 2007. Both had been a long time coming, over sixty years, and there

was a sheepish quality to the description of the memorial's history.
After the war, the site had become subsumed within the small town,
a few houses, a cemetery, some light industrial buildings appearing
within the grounds and walls of the once huge labour camp. A
commemorative stone had been erected in the late 1940s, but after
that the site had been allowed to blend into the slope of the hill
descending away from the small housing estates that pushed up to its
side boundaries. It was only when survivors from the camp gathered
in the town for the fiftieth anniversary of liberation and condemned
the state of the memorial (located down the hillside in the 'Valley
of Death' as it was known) that government plans were formed to
resurrect the KZ from its submersion.

Stamping my feet in the cold, surprised by the late spring weather,
I was puzzled as to why it should have taken so long for a conscience
to emerge. Perhaps a collective aversion had set in. I couldn't testify to
any general civic embarrassment across generations, though I knew
that when the camp had been found by the US troops at the end of
April 1945 (there was snow on the ground then too), local people had
denied limply any knowledge about the conditions inside. With much
slave labour working the quarries in the nearby hillside, with the
over-worked crematorium pumping human ash into the air around
them, with bodies littering the roadsides throughout the town after
the evacuation by the SS in fear of the approaching Americans, their
protestations of ignorance hadn't been believed. The camp simply
dwarfed the town.

Photographs I saw showed the camp's hulking presence. The entrance building alone, a red-tiled, stone-walled, three-storey-high grange, behind which stretched dozens of long barracks, proclaimed its purpose. No one could have been that blind.

The liberating Americans found a grave containing 800 bodies, disinterred them, forced the local population to look and then to rebury the remains. Later, evidence was uncovered of a close working relationship between some of the townsfolk and the camp since it had begun to operate in 1938: letters requesting labour to help with harvests or manual jobs in local businesses were unearthed. Even if the camp conditions hadn't been fully appreciated, it was certain the slave potential of its inmates had been understood.

It wasn't only the lack of acknowledgement by the local population that shocked and, in truth, angered me. Within the museum, in one of the renovated block barracks, immediately after walking through its entrance, I was confronted by a large map behind a glass screen on one of the exhibition walls. It depicted Europe and was peppered with square coloured markers, hundreds of them. Most were located in modern-day Germany, the Czech Republic, Austria, Poland.

The little coloured symbols clustered around several names in bold print with the letters KZ by their side: Dachau, Mauthausen, Theresienstadt, Niederhagen, Arbeitsdorf, Sachsenhausen, Ravensbrück,

Bergen-Belsen, Groß-Rosen, Flossenbürg and other names that had become familiar to me: Neuengamme, Stutthof, Natzweiler, Mittelbau-Dora.

There were several more markers, little motifs of a black factory, a solitary chimney jutting out: Auschwitz, Chełmno, Sobibór, Treblinka. They were the death camps, the extermination centres for the destruction of the Jews in Europe, though they killed others too: Roma, Sinti, the disabled, homosexuals, Jehovah's Witnesses, Russians, Poles. The desire to eradicate whole swathes of humanity was reflected in these little symbols.

Staring at the map, reading the explanation, I realised that all these little coloured squares represented the destruction of men, women and children through murder, work, neglect and viciousness. Each marker, both large and small, indicated the location of a camp. There were about 1,000 in all. They ranged from minor factories that had kept a couple of hundred inmates for production purposes to the massive encampments normally associated with our idea of a concentration camp. And for the first time I realised that to understand the magnitude of the Allies' task in prosecuting *all* abuses occurring since the Nazis had come to power in 1933, meant understanding the scale and breadth of the camp system, its history as well as its final discovery. The exhibition in Flossenbürg provided a brief account, an introduction, but it was enough.[74]

I already knew the first camps had been established in early 1933. Their initial purpose was to detain opponents of the new Nazi regime that took full control in March of that year, as the British press had reported. Even before the general election, Hitler and his supporters had constructed a plan to remove the political opposition, particularly of the Left. He was in a position to do so because he had been appointed German Chancellor by President Paul von Hindenburg on 30 January 1933. In February, one of Hitler's new appointments, Wilhelm Frick, Reich Interior Minister, issued a decree for 'the Protection of the German People'. This authorised the police to take into custody anyone they wished, as well as banning assemblies and enabling censorship to be practised against any publication. It was followed on 28 February, prompted by the Reichstag fire the night before, by a presidential emergency decree that introduced the notion of 'protective custody' or *Schutzhaft*.

The Nazi authorities used the new law to arrest opponents. Thousands were detained by the SA and SS as well as the police. Written orders to justify arrest merely read: 'You are taken into protective custody in the interest of public order. Reason: Suspicion of activities inimical toward the State.'

Political opponents weren't the only ones destined for the camps. Common criminals who appeared unwilling to give up their felonious habits were sent there too, detained under another regulation called 'police preventive custody' or *Vorbeugungshaft*.

About a hundred camps were established within a few months of these decrees coming into operation, many improvised to meet local Party and police 'needs'. Most didn't last long. As was reported in many debates in the British press about the nature of Hitler's rule at the time, the immediate suppression of opposition was supposed to be temporary. Once 'order was established' the camps would close, which many did, though not all.

With Himmler's appointment as Munich Police President on 9 March 1933, the former munitions factory at Dachau was identified as a permanent detention centre. It was quickly converted to house up to a couple of thousand inmates, who were to undergo 're-education'. *Arbeit macht frei*, 'freedom through work', was the slogan that became associated with the KZ institution.

The nature of the Dachau regime, and by extension other KZs already in existence or to be formed later, was established early on too. The first commandant, Hilmar Wäckerle, may not have lasted long (he was removed following complaints about executions that he'd ordered soon after the first prisoners had arrived), but public outrage only had a temporary effect. Wäckerle's replacement, Theodor Eicke, was as ruthless as his predecessor. He introduced the 'Disciplinary and Punishment Order' where severe penalties were decreed for the most petty offences: the use of corporal punishment by bullwhip or cane, solitary confinement and execution were all condoned and authorised.[75]

Into the camp came a hotch-potch of different people of whom political opponents were the most numerous in 1933. They were joined by many Jehovah's Witnesses, who were seen as non-cooperative with the Nazi regime particularly after their refusal to be conscripted into the armed forces after 1935. Thousands of vagrants and beggars who were specific targets of Propaganda Minister Josef Goebbels were also detained. Jews were arrested too, mostly for their political opposition at first rather than purely by reason of their race. Once in the camps, though, the anti-Semitism that defined much of the ideology of the Nazis played out in uncontrolled cruelty. By common account, the Jews were the ones to suffer most amongst the inmates.

With the SS under Himmler already assuming control of internal security and developing a policy of permanent state oppression, the camps that survived acquired a new purpose. Prisons were dotted across the cities of Germany, such as Spandau and Plötzensee in Berlin, Fuhlsbüttel in Hamburg and Colditz south-east of Leipzig. But at the heart of the new despotic system lay the *Konzentrationslager*, vast complexes designed to hold thousands of inmates under brutal conditions. Dachau became the early model for their governance, a prototype for many of the larger camps to follow.

Although the number of camps and inmates held within them decreased significantly in 1934, internal struggles in the Nazi party gave rise to an enhanced and different detention system, albeit one established in line with the Dachau model. Through a ruthless eradication of the SA – the Brown Shirts, whom Hitler and Himmler identified as a threat to the new order, but whose own brutality had ironically served to bring the Nazis to power – during the Night of the Long Knives, Himmler and his deputy, Reinhard Heydrich, were able to centralise the developing police state in the hands of the SS.

Part of this rationalisation saw Theodore Eicke (erstwhile Dachau commandant) appointed as head of a new administrative formation, the Inspectorate of Concentration Camps, or *Inspektion der Konzentrationslager* (IKL). A guard force within the SS was also formed: the SS Death's Head Battalions (*Totenkopfwachsturmbanne*). By 1936, Himmler had consolidated power over the camps and the policing of the state to such an extent that the camp system now lay outside any state control. He and the SS had complete authority over its operation.

Between then and 1939 the system expanded exponentially. It served a purpose as preparation for war by controlling dissent and using forced prison labour to undertake the extraction of raw materials or the production of military equipment. SS companies were created to benefit from these activities within an economic structure that saw many camps, such as Flossenbürg, built next to quarries or other industrial or mining complexes. But the system also enabled the realisation of the racial and social control philosophy that underpinned Nazi ideology. The persecution of the Jews, which since 1933 had assumed increasing importance in the life of the state, reached rabid proportions after Kristallnacht in November 1938, when 30,000 Jews were arrested and thousands of Jewish shops, businesses and properties looted and destroyed in a coordinated 'public' demonstration of hate incited by Goebbels and the whole Nazi structure. Camps modelled on Dachau at Sachsenhausen, Buchenwald, Flossenbürg, Mauthausen and Ravensbrück took the new detainees. After them any elements deemed 'antisocial' or a threat to the purity of the German people were also sent to these places.

The outbreak of war in 1939 reinforced the economic and racist dimensions of the KZ system. The SS under Himmler assumed greater control for internal security, and the camp population increased again. The newly conquered territories posed a threat in so far as their peoples were bound to be antagonistic towards German rule. And the Jews who lived in these places were deemed the most threatening. Mass killings began early on, but control needed to be exercised over those who weren't massacred. Not only Jews had to be contained. All those from the occupied territories who failed to conform or who looked likely to resist were rounded up. More camps were built: huge complexes in Germany and now in occupied Poland, at Auschwitz, Groß-Rosen and Neuengamme. After the invasion of France in 1940, Natzweiler, near Strasbourg, was built. The Jews of Europe were also herded into ghettos as a means of enclosing them, separating them from normal society, in Lublin, Warsaw and many cities and towns in Eastern Europe. The scale of repression was extraordinary. Hundreds of thousands were incarcerated. Hundreds of thousands were killed.

During 1941, the KZ system extended even further, to be used as the fulcrum for the eradication of peoples, as a vast resource of labour for war production, and as a means of repressing opposition. The invasion of Russia (on 22 June 1941) spurred on the systematic and institutionalised extermination of Jews, of Soviet prisoners of war, of Gypsies, of the disabled. Methods of killing were devised to match. Two new KZ complexes were constructed in October 1941: Auschwitz II-Birkenau and Majdanek near Lublin. Soviet POWs were handed over to the SS and incarcerated in these camps. Thousands were shot, but the vast majority of deaths occurred through starvation and disease.

Before long it was realised that the main purposes of the camps were contradictory. For how could reliable sources of labour for industry be maintained if the workforce was subjected to killing and ill-treatment that made them incapable of working efficiently or at all? It was a tension never to be resolved. At the Wannsee Conference outside Berlin in January 1942, a meeting of senior Nazi figures chaired by Reinhard Heydrich (head of the Reich Main Security Office, the RSHA), it was decided that the Jews of occupied Europe would be collected together, transported to Poland and exterminated in specially constructed killing centres. The Wannsee Protocol drafted at the conference was supposed to present the 'Final Solution' to the Jewish 'question'. The camps that were built to satisfy this policy produced another form of institution – the death camp. Birkenau was at the heart of this killing complex in Poland, with Belzec north of Lvov, Sobibór, Treblinka, Chełmno and Majdanek forming a star of relatively short-lived massacre centres. The numbers killed in these places are difficult to comprehend as people rather than soulless figures: they're estimates only: 400,000 to 500,000 in Belzec; perhaps 200,000 at Sobibór; over a million in Auschwitz.

The failure of German forces to overcome Russian resistance intensified the demands for labour. In March 1942, Himmler reorganised the system by establishing the SS-Business Administration Main Office (WVHA), incorporating within it the IKL under the command of *SS-Obergruppenführer* Oswald Pohl. By September 1942, agreement had been reached between Hitler, Himmler and Albert Speer (acting then as Production Minister) that KZ inmates could be 'leased' to armaments producers and housed in sub-camps of the main concentration camps.

Many of those dots I saw on the map at Flossenbürg represented these new, industrial-based sub-camps. Into the system came large influxes of forced labour. Polish and Soviet nationals were driven into the camps to work. But none of this war production role significantly lessened the deadly conditions. Though the death rate may have declined for a time in 1943, the killing never stopped. In late 1944, whilst maintaining its 'selections' (when new arrivals would be chosen as fit for work or to be sent to the gas chambers), 300,000–400,000 Hungarian Jews were transported to Auschwitz for extermination, the event that triggered Churchill and Roosevelt to issue public condemnation of the Nazi atrocities. The killing only stopped as the Soviet forces pushed ever closer into Poland. Then the SS began to evacuate all the camps that were threatened with being overrun by Allied troops.

And so the last stage of the KZ system began. Though maintaining its industrial and production role, the camps that remained in German hands were increasingly populated by the sick or those unable to work and left to die, useless objects to be discarded or ignored, merely herded behind the wire fences. Bergen-Belsen was identified as one camp where Jews could be 'deposited' for possible exchange, but few benefited from the plan. Instead, as the numbers transferred expanded month by month, it became a place where sick inmates from the other camps could be sent, a place that could not cope, a place of destination because the now-evacuated camps had nowhere else to send them.

At the end of 1944 and the beginning of 1945, the marches and transports from the closing KZ system represented the final killing orgy. No one would be allowed to dawdle as the emaciated prisoners were forced to walk in the bitter cold or were packed into cattle trucks without provisions. By April the evacuations were constant and deadly.

Then the liberating forces came.

* * *

Even from such a brief account I came away from Flossenbürg conscious of the magnitude of the KZ system and its hydra-like history. I knew it was impossible to calculate the total number of people who'd entered these places. Insufficient records existed, though there was enough information to appreciate that millions had lived and millions had died in the system. There had been immense order here that had as its purpose immense abuse. And it had spread throughout Germany and its occupied territories. The camps and their inmates had been everywhere. To suggest ignorance of their presence and purpose seemed ludicrous to me, just as it had been obviously ludicrous to the Americans when they'd arrived in the town of Flossenbürg to confront its citizens.

Nonetheless, to think the Americans could have been prepared for this encounter, one repeated across the landscape of southern Germany, when they'd already committed themselves to prosecute *all* war criminals, is perhaps equally ludicrous. Could those who planned to bring to trial and to punish everyone responsible, from the highest to the lowest, have foreseen the magnitude of the task? Each dot on that map was a multiple crime scene with multiple victims and multiple perpetrators. Maybe they should have been ready, given the information they'd accumulated about the camps over the preceding years. But then again, maybe the scale of atrocity had never been truly appreciated.

It was nonetheless a reality the British discovered for themselves when their troops walked into Bergen-Belsen in the middle of April 1945. That was *their* moment of awakening.

3

Lüneburg Heath

1.

The heathland around Horsell in Surrey where I grew up always terrified and excited me in equal measure. H.G. Wells set his *War of the Worlds* there on the outskirts of Woking and I could never put that out of my mind as a child. I thought the expanse of sandy ground, which encouraged little but heather and bracken and conifers to grow, was an obvious location for Martians to land and inflict defeat and suffering on the world. It made for a surprising and occasionally frightening playground, hundreds of acres of rough scrub and dense wood to explore, full of strange, incongruous spaces.

Once, when my brother and I had roamed a little further than usual, we'd come across a dilapidated walled enclosure deep within a grove of pine trees. It was as if we'd discovered the remnants of an ancient city. The oriental domed entrance gate and brick walls exuded a ghostly presence. We'd skirted its borders but hadn't dared enter. Only later did I find out it was the burial ground for a handful of Muslim Indian troops who'd died of their wounds from fighting in France during World War I (with a few other casualties of the Second World War added in the 1940s). Their bodies had been shipped from an army hospital in Brighton. Over the years, disrespect had replaced honour and locals had vandalised the site, causing the bodies to be moved to a different cemetery. The place had become derelict.

I imagined Lüneburg Heath would have the same disquieting quality. But none of that dark and lonely aspect manifested itself as I drove across it. It was a pleasant, cool, bland region of inoffensive farmland and woods and low hills of heather. Stretching from Hamburg in the north of Lower Saxony to Hannover in the south, the landscape was mostly flat and innocuous.

On the route from Hamburg to Bergen-Belsen, the first concentration camp liberated by the British, I stopped at the Commonwealth

War Cemetery at Becklingen. It felt an appropriate thing to do. The graveyard was tight against the roadside of the B3, an isolated place, unheralded and unanticipated when it suddenly appeared on my right with its lines of white headstones covering a slightly inclined plot surrounded by a thick hedge.

The perfectly maintained cemetery housed the graves of over 2,000 British casualties. The inscriptions were, as in every British cemetery of the Second World War, pitiable. Many were generic, I assume chosen from a list supplied by the stonemasons, but occasionally with a glimpse of something more personal. Those are the ones that make you weep.

As I walked the lines of graves I noticed how many had died in the last months of the war. I tried to imagine the pain of the families. Would it have been more acute when news of the surrender of German forces came through? They must have been ripped apart by the thought that their son, father, brother, husband had been within a few days of surviving the conflict. Gunner Alcock, for instance, who'd died on 1 May 1945. Or Lance Bombadier Booker, killed on 4 May. Or my namesake, Private Williams of the King's Shropshire Light Infantry, aged nineteen, on 25 April. So close to making it through. And so young too.

The weight of numbers killed in those few weeks remains testimony to the bloody fighting that had to be done right up until the end of the war. Though the British moved swiftly across this country, they still encountered occasional fierce resistance. They expected it. Swathes of troops may have been capitulating across the front, but many instances of brutal struggle occurred.[1] They induced intense caution and fear that the German forces would mount some kind of counter-attack or stand to the last man even though all was palpably lost. That was the presumption given the rabid pronouncements coming from the Nazi leadership even after the death of Adolf Hitler was relayed from Berlin on 1 May.

If confirmation was needed that the British were fighting an implacable foe, they found it several miles along the road from Becklingen Cemetery, across the heath towards Hannover, at Bergen-Belsen. They arrived in the town in April 1945 to encounter a huge concentration camp that would unman even the most battle-hardened of soldiers.

★ ★ ★

A bank of pine trees obscured the entrance to the camp on a bend of the L298 road a mile south of the British Army base still used as a tank firing range, but I caught sight of the discreet sign in time. I felt a tremor of discomfort when I pulled into the coach park full of school outings from across Europe. 'It's a theme park,' I thought to myself. 'A bitter and sickening theme park, but a theme park nonetheless.'

I knew this was irrational, if not wrong: wrong for me to think like that and wrong in fact. If the place had been erased and given no memorial I would have been angry at the suppression of history, the failure of the German nation to acknowledge its past. At least by making the camp accessible, free to enter and a destination for commemoration, due remembrance was and may remain possible.

But the frisson of distaste wouldn't go away. Maybe it was the cafeteria in the basement of the modern white concrete building that exuded architectural merit and housed the exhibition and documentation centre. Though no doubt artfully designed, tasteful, the sight of the café somehow made me bad-tempered. I thought: how could you eat here, beneath those pictures and artefacts and recordings in the exhibition floors above? How could you sit down and have a peaceful cup of coffee, a cake, a snack to alleviate a slight feeling of mid-morning hunger knowing those who'd been incarcerated here had suffered such deprivation of food and drink that they'd been driven mad, mad enough to claw the soil for any scrap of edible matter, mad enough to cut the flesh from a corpse and shove it into their mouths to chew raw? Then there were all the things you could buy in the bookshop: DVDs as well as publications and leaflets. If this were anywhere else, signs advertising 'gifts' and 'souvenirs', key rings, postcards and inscribed trinkets would hang on the walls and counters. I wondered how long it would be before that happened, the transformation of shrine into tourist attraction.

Mine was a ridiculous response. Of course it was. I reminded myself that even those who came to mourn had to eat. And buying books recounting the history of the camp and some of those who'd survived, which I'd done on many occasions, was important: keeping the past relevant and known and knowable. How easily it could slip into obscurity otherwise.

The logic didn't dispel the unease. It made me ask yet again: why visit these places? Was it macabre? Morbid and slightly odd? At the time I travelled to Lüneburg Heath and Bergen-Belsen, I was in the midst of examining more allegations against British forces during their occupation of Iraq after 2003. Hundreds were emerging. Invariably these mentioned military camps, places where detainees were held en masse for the purpose of interrogation. I'd read many victims' statements about their treatment in the army bases, camps like Abu Naji and Bucca and Shaibah, where techniques were used to break men down and reduce them to nothing, to numbers, sometimes to playthings. That was what the statements conveyed, though I couldn't vouch for the truth or falsity of any of them. And, of course, this was all in the shadow of the new 'camp' imagery from Guantanamo Bay and those 'black sites' condemned as destinations for victims of 'extraordinary rendition'. Wasn't that the reincarnation of the KZ idea, at least as regards its purpose in isolating, corralling, dehumanising and slowly shredding a body of its living qualities? Orange jumpsuits instead of striped pyjamas? Waterboarding instead of whatever torture one can imagine the Nazis practised? The comparison was trite, perhaps, but founded on a truth: the institutionalised breaking of a person's mind and body through a regimen of psychologically and physically inflicted pain was central to both. What touches in these places is not the deaths but the lives; stripped to the bone, to bare life. What possible reason could there be to do that? None. But some excuse is always found: you pose a threat to security; you're contagious; you're different. It never seems to take long before a reason justifies anything.

I was sick of it all, of reading about ill-treatment and torture, but I couldn't turn away and forget. Maybe the journeys to the past and to Germany were a substitute for those inaccessible sites in Iraq, a safer way of trying to gain some insight as to how a place, a 'camp', can induce the degradation of humanity in guard and inmate alike. But I also thought of another reason: if I didn't go, all my knowledge and understanding would be limited to literature or text. I was convinced that to touch the ground and smell the air, to walk amongst the buildings was necessary to gain a better sense of the atrocity that Nazi Germany had perpetrated. The experience might not communicate the raw suffering and boredom and moments of hope and ordinariness, the life and lives of the camp despite the prevalence of death (for whatever their nature, lives were led here, people did survive though in a state of decomposition of spirit and personality and body), but it might reveal something intangibly vital nonetheless. The chance of achieving *some* awareness was worth the danger of morbid fascination. I convinced myself it didn't matter who else was walking about the ruins, what their motivations were, how they felt. Every visitor had their own reasons for making the effort. That was their affair.

It helped that Bergen-Belsen has been preserved in good order as a memorial, a *Gedenkstätte*, without ostentation. Once through its gates, past the motley group of buildings both modern (to house the exhibitions) and original, you enter a great expanse of scrub and grass, surrounded by tall birches and conifers, and dissected by roughly bordered pathways curling around landmarks. Plinths and signboards indicate where barracks and crematoria and the hospital and other buildings used to sit (most were burned down by the British to stop disease spreading). Others are simple memorials: a small headstone for sisters Anne and Margot Frank, who died of typhus here; a tall concrete obelisk backed by a wall with inscriptions in various languages remembering the dead from numerous countries; a thick pedestal erected by the Central Jewish Committee in 1946 recording the deaths of thirty thousand Jews 'exterminated at the hands of the murderous

Nazis' screaming its anger with capital letters and an exclamation mark: 'EARTH CONCEAL NOT THE BLOOD SHED ON THEE!'

The mass graves were marked too. The bodies, pushed and thrown into vast pits, had to be covered quickly to stop the typhus spreading. Large stone plaques now rested on the side of compacted, rectangular mounds of earth. They recorded the number of people buried beneath, 1,000 and 2,500, like grim denomination bills. That was the scale of death in the camp at the end of, and just after, the war. They simply recorded the figures and said nothing about those who'd died.

It was tempting to be drawn in by the numbers. If said with authority their effect can be disconcerting. Five thousand, twenty thousand, a hundred thousand, six million: they quickly become symbols of something other than the individuals they're supposed to represent. They say more about the perpetrator than the victims, who dissolve collectively into unknowable fractions. Then it isn't long before the numbers are set as indicators against which other atrocities are measured. A ghoulish competition can erupt, the greater the quantity the more dreadful the deed, perhaps.

A little while ago I gave a reading at a book festival of *A Very British Killing*, the book I'd written about one case of ill-treatment of several Iraqi detainees. I spoke about the details of Baha Mousa's death, the man killed by British troops in an army base in Basra in September 2003. At the end of my talk someone said he'd read the book and was a little disappointed. He thought there would have been more revelations about torture and brutality. Quickly worried that the rest of the audience would misunderstand him (or it seemed to me), he said he didn't mean he wanted to *see* more cruelty. It was just that what happened didn't feel that ... that terrible. Bad, yes. Of course. But not horrific like the Nazis, if I knew what he meant. In the vacuum of my silence he carried on: we hear of so many deaths and atrocities these days, don't we? One death seems ... well, a little insignificant.

I asked the man, how many does it take before we get angry and do something? He shrugged. He couldn't say. In fairness to him, it was a hackneyed question of mine. I worried, though, that the man's comments echoed many people's views. Not that anyone else would voice them easily. They might be misinterpreted: how callous to support the idea that one death should count for little, should be incapable of provoking shock or concern?

Walking along those meandering paths of the Bergen-Belsen site I thought that the numbers carved into the stone laid on the mounds were callous too, albeit unintentionally so. I didn't believe that they contained 1,000 or 2,500 people exactly. I didn't believe that those who had to bury them counted and stopped at the exact figure and then filled in the grave. I thought they must have guessed, made a rough estimate, rounded up or rounded down, that it didn't matter whether it was 999 or 1,001 or some other figure around the thousand or whatever figure they ended up carving into the stone. The number was vast, signified by the multiple noughts. That was enough.

Do the mathematics of war crimes matter? Politically, legally, it would seem so. Arguments about the number of Jews killed in the Holocaust have never ceased since the initial investigations immediately after the war. In February 2006, as if oblivious to the moral ambiguity that equates quantity to seriousness, Luis Moreno Ocampo, then Chief Prosecutor of the International Criminal Court, responded to hundreds of written submissions he'd received (one of them related in part to Baha Mousa) about allegations of unlawful killings and war crimes committed during the British invasion and occupation of Iraq.[2] He wrote that 'while, in a general sense, any crime within the jurisdiction of the Court is "grave" ', no case would be investigated by his office unless it passed 'an additional threshold of gravity'. The criteria couldn't be expressed scientifically, but a 'key consideration', he said, was 'the number of victims of particularly serious crimes, such as wilful killing or rape'. For Iraq this 'was of a different order than the number of victims found in other situations under investigation' by him. He mentioned the Congo and Darfur, that featured, he said, 'hundreds or thousands of such crimes'. Four or five or twelve killings were insufficient for his office to do anything. He wouldn't sanction any further action until such time as evidence of more allegations came to light, if they ever did.

There were no such difficulties when British troops entered Bergen-Belsen in April 1945 and encountered the mounds of bodies, the scattered corpses, the thousands upon thousands of dying or barely living. Some of the soldiers may have been conscious of the concentration camps from all those news reports before and during the war. But could any of them have believed they were *this* terrible? From the accounts of the liberation, I didn't think so. I didn't think they were prepared, any more than the politicians and government officials were prepared when they were calling for retribution from the comfort of Whitehall.

2.

The news filtered through slowly. On 14 April 1945, amidst the general communiqué of battle success across Germany, *The Times* reported: 'British troops will soon be facing the problem of dealing with a big German concentration camp in their line of advance at a village called Belsen 10 miles north-west of Celle. Their information is that there are about 60,000 persons in the camp, some of them political offenders, some criminals, and among them are about 1,500 with typhus and 900 with typhoid fever, as well as about 9,000 sick with other complaints.'[3]

That was all, for the moment: a vaguely expressed fear that recent scenes from Ohrdruf and Buchenwald would be replicated. Even then it was strange language that was used, as though the paper thought it was important that some of the inmates were 'offenders' or 'criminals', information that could only have come from the Germans.

Unlike most of the camps to be liberated by the Allies, Bergen-Belsen was handed over in a relatively orderly fashion. Its situation was different as it had become the destination of last resort for prisoners transferred from many other camps to the east or south. Already a sinkhole for prisoners from the middle of 1944 onwards, Bergen-Belsen was a place where the sick had been sent, those too ill to work. Some camp prisoners had been told they were being transferred there to 'recuperate'. It was nothing more than a euphemism for gradual death as there were few if any medical facilities there to aid recovery. A tent camp had had to be constructed in late summer 1944 to cope with the increased numbers. It held 8,000 women transferred from Auschwitz until, in November 1944, a storm destroyed the tents. All the occupants had then to be shifted into the barracks. As Germany collapsed on all fronts, an even greater influx of prisoners arrived during the early spring of 1945, making the already overcrowded conditions in the camp untenable. From 15,000 inmates at the end of 1944, the camp housed over 42,000 by March 1945. No heating, limited food, next to no medical supplies, little shelter and the decay of those barely living caused disease to fester and spread throughout the camp. It was impossible to contain the lice. Dysentery and TB were predictably rife. But it was the onset of typhus that became an immediate and unstoppable killer. In March, 18,000 people died in the camp. Those who remained were surrounded by decomposing corpses. They were given little if any food. Water was scarce.

By the beginning of April, with typhus rampant and British forces moving more quickly than the Germans expected, the German command became terrified by the prospects of having to follow the general order recently emanating from Himmler to prevent concentration camp prisoners falling into the hands of the enemy. Himmler was persuaded to relax his position and the Allies were contacted with a proposal to surrender the camp to their care on 12 April. Some members of the SS administration were to remain with a detachment of Hungarian troops who were already guarding the camp for the Germans. The agreement with the British was that they would stay to continue their duties, although under British control.

Sometime on 15 April the first British soldiers entered the camp. From the moment they stepped through the gates they realised the hellish nature of the place. It may have been called a liberation, but the inmates were not free. Captain Derrick Sington of the Intelligence Corps commanding No. 14 Amplifying Unit (a small fleet of trucks with loudspeakers, used to relay information and commands to the public) was told to drive about the compounds telling everyone that the British had arrived and that no one was allowed to leave.

The amplifying truck used by Derrick Sington is pictured on the right: IWM

Many years later, Gerard Mansell, one of the first intelligence officers there, wrote about the environment the British troops had entered. He said that he and his colleagues 'were utterly unprepared for the scenes which greeted us – the shabby rows of flimsy wooden huts packed with hundreds of the dead and dying, lying heaped on the tiered bunks; the pathetic little knots of listless, skeletal figures with shaven heads, their grimy, striped prison garments hanging loosely from their protruding bones; the deep pits half-full of emaciated, naked corpses; the bodies lying everywhere in hundreds, the living often indistinguishable from the dead; the forlorn heaps of shoes, spectacles and other effects, all that remained of the thousands whose ashes now covered the ground with a fine powder'.[4]

On 18 April, the senior medical officer of the British unit which had taken control of the camp talked to the press about the conditions he'd found. It was 'the most horrible, frightful place', he said.[5] And indeed the picture he painted was terrifying. He said 'there was a pile, between 60 to 80 yards long, 30 yards wide, and four feet high, of the unclothed bodies of women all within sight of several hundred children. Gutters were filled with rotting dead, and men had come to the gutters to die, using the kerbstones as back rests.' He said that cannibalism had been reported by his men. He said there was no water, turnip soup was all that the Germans had been feeding the inmates, typhus was rampant, but starvation was the main killer. He said he was shown all this and around the enormous compound by the SS commandant, Josef Kramer, who had stayed to surrender the camp to the British. Kramer was described as 'a typical German brute – a sadistical, heavy-featured Nazi', who was 'quite unashamed'.[6] There were 'enormous covered death pits', but one was exposed: it 'contained a great pile of blackened and naked bodies'.[7] No one had been prepared for these scenes of concentrated carnage.

As part of the relief effort, a medical team was summoned. Some of the doctors were later compelled to write about their observations, to publish professional musings as though they had been suddenly thrust into a horrible experiment. Their articles may have been drafted for a specialist audience, but to me they shone light not only on the treatment that was needed, but also on the lives those in the camps had had to endure.

The *British Medical Journal* printed a shortened version of Captain Mollison's report for the British 21st Army Group that then occupied north-west Germany.[8] He described the state of a typical survivor whom his team had treated. It was a clinical assessment stripped of emotional rhetoric. Such is the nature of academic medical reference and perhaps more revealing for all that, though the language made me flinch.

The patient lay flat in bed with acute distress, yet with a miserable expression. He showed no interest in anything except his own needs, and appeared completely indifferent to the deaths that occurred so frequently. Moreover, death was a very public affair, since there were no screens and beds were crowded together. He talked with a whining voice and complained continually, usually of his severe diarrhoea. 'Scheiszerei' was the commonest word. Second only to this complaint was unfavourable comment on the diet, the soup being blamed for the diarrhoea. Black bread was next in unpopularity. Patients who were a little less ill asked continually for white bread and complained that they were being starved. The truth was that there was enough food in terms of calories, but much of it was unpalatable. Although starving, they were extremely particular about their diet and very difficult to please. Most of them did not fancy sweet things, and almost all wanted solid food rather than soup. When they wanted a drink, lemonade or something sour was most often asked for. They were all sure that soup and cold food made the diarrhoea worse. Although milk was available as an alternative to the full diet, many of the patients didn't want it, and, if given it, complained that they were not getting enough to support life. Because of their poor appetite, many of them left their food untouched, and as there were insufficient nurses to feed them their state rapidly became worse. The orderly simply put the food beside the bed and left it. Later the untouched food would be collected if the patient had not secreted it in his bedding for future use. Fear of being without food was so great that even dying patients would put bread-and-butter and meat under their pillows.

Mollison's account cast doubt on the nature of any liberation. For the prisoners, removal of the SS guards didn't mean escape from their torment. And if food was a problem, more so was bodily function. The minutiae of medical observation, rarely revealed in the sweeping press and courtroom accounts I'd read, exposed the predicament for both victim and medic. Mollison wrote,

All the seriously ill were incontinent of faeces, and their beds were continually soiled as there were not enough orderlies to change them, and, in any case, many of them had no sheets but simply lay on covered palliasses. Almost every patient when first seen had diarrhoea – varying from two to three loose stools a day to an almost continuous production of watery stools. In the latter cases a movement of the bowels invariably followed immediately after taking anything by mouth, so that the patient was afraid to eat or drink. The stools did not as a rule contain blood or pus. They were often light brown in colour, smelt offensive, and consisted of fluid and lumps of undigested food. On examination the patient had an appallingly thin face. The eyes were sunken and the cheek-bones jutted out. These extreme changes made all the patients look alike, so that it became difficult to distinguish one from another. This difficulty was accentuated by the fact that all patients had had the bulk of their hair shaved off. The skin of their arms, legs, and anterior abdominal wall was often rough, dry, and scaly. There were large bed-sores on the buttocks and the lower part of the back. The ribs stuck out, and it was difficult to use a diaphragm type of stethoscope because it simply bridged across two ribs and made no contact with the skin dipping down in between. The anterior abdominal wall was concave, falling away from the ribs above and from the anterior superior iliac spine below. The greatest muscle-wasting was around the pelvis. The ischial tuberosities stood out prominently and the posterior surface of the ilium was almost devoid of muscle. There was a depression below the anterior superior iliac spine, and the skin hung down to the thigh in a fold. The legs were fuller owing to oedema; but this was often confined to the ankles and feet, so that a common appearance was of a leg as thin as a stick with a fat swollen foot on the end of it. The face and hands were pale.

This wasn't the condition of just a few. Thousands of patients had been similarly affected, their massed misery hard to comprehend. In November 1945, fresh from his experience as part of the Royal Army Medical Corps at the camp, Dr Joseph Lewis delivered a lecture about it. 'In my Division,' he said, 'which had the care of approximately 4,500 cases, we were able to discharge as fit just under 2,000 patients after about two months' treatment. Sweden very generously agreed to accept our more chronic invalids who were fit to undertake the journey by rail and sea, and all our orphans. We disposed of about 1,500 in this way. At this stage we handed over to a small military unit and moved from Belsen, not without regret, for we realised that we had been privileged to see a clinical sight not easily forgotten.'[9]

'Privileged' wasn't the most apt word, I thought, but doctors were faced with unique circumstances. What language *could* do justice to the sights they observed? W. Collis and P. MacClancy reported on three paediatric cases of 'interest', as they called them, attempting to communicate the impact on inmates of the conditions in the camp.[10] But they betrayed some compassion nonetheless. Apart from detailing the consequences of starvation and disease, they told the story of a young boy they named Z., aged five.

He was admitted to the children's hospital, Belsen, from the general hospital on the death of his mother. His mother, an Austrian Catholic, died at Belsen of typhus. The father, a Slovak Jew, last heard of in Sachsenhausen, was probably dead. A sister, aged 6, was alive and well in camp. Two other children died in Ravensbrück *Lager*. Nothing was known of the patient's past history. On admission he was very emaciated. He lay rolled up in a ball under the bedclothes, moaning, and wouldn't eat or speak. Examination revealed pleurisy with an effusion on the right side, and some infiltration in the right and the upper zone of the left lung. The temperature was irregular, rising to 101°. Sedimentation rate, 101 mm. first hour (Westergren). Pirquet plus. 10 c.cm. of serous fluid was aspirated to exclude empyema. The child was hand-fed with specially appetizing meals while being talked to in his own language. He was given a high-protein diet with an addition of vitamins and calcium, and at first was kept in a warm room; later he was placed in the open air. After one week he began to talk; after two weeks his appetite returned; and after eight weeks the sedimentation rate was 50 mm. He was then evacuated to Sweden. The latest report states that he has put on 7 lb. (3.2 kg.) and is now almost well.

The doctors commented, 'The above case illustrates the final problem of the Belsen children. It is a social one of the most profound complexity. Here we have a little boy of 5, together with his sister of 6, whose parents have been cruelly murdered and whose family and home have been destroyed. What is to become of him? Is he to be brought up Jew or Catholic? Is he to be left in an orphanage? He has found a temporary refuge in Sweden, but what of the future?' They offered no answers.

The psychological impact of the camps was studied by another army medic, Captain M. Niremberski. He published an article in 1946 concluding:

Psychiatric study of the most affected of the 60,000 inmates of the Belsen concentration camp showed a concentration camp mentality: a dulling of social adaptation with depreciation of family ties and sense of values, low standard of bodily habits, and aggressive and masochistic tendencies. Terror and fear symptoms were common; memory for remote events was impaired. Passive types showed a marked reduction in activity, even up to complete immobility in some cases. Greatly exaggerated sexual appetites were noted. Young children, up to 8 years of age, showed no marked disorders, but older children showed fear reactions.[11]

3.

When the British entered Bergen-Belsen they placed under arrest SS camp commandant Josef Kramer, SS Dr Fritz Klein and the rest of the SS detachment who'd been left behind. There was confusion about what should be done with them. Brigadier Glyn Hughes, Deputy Director of Medical Services for the British 2nd Army, said he and Lt Col Taylor, the commanding officer of the British unit which had assumed control of the camp administration, were with Josef Kramer when they heard shots coming from the western end of the men's section. They all headed to the crematorium, where they found a stack of straw covered with potato plants. Hughes said, 'A number of male internees were foraging in the stack for food. Surrounding them were three or four individual members of the SS guards of the camp armed with automatic weapons ... As I approached the spot I saw and heard them firing single shots at the aforesaid internees and they made no attempt to cease firing when I came up to them, Josef Kramer made no attempt to prevent them or to interfere.' That the SS guards were still armed was surprising enough. That they should have been allowed to continue to act as ruthless guards even after this incident was incredible. Hughes said, 'We gave immediate orders to Kramer that all shooting at internees was to cease immediately and that any further case reported to us would result in one SS guard being shot for every internee killed.'[12]

Whether or not Hughes's threat was carried out is unclear: he admitted that more shootings by the SS occurred that day and some spontaneous retribution was inflicted. Gerard Mansell would recount much later that Kramer 'was severely beaten up as he was being taken away'. He said some 'guards were shot out of hand on one pretext or another. The rest were made to bury the dead and clean up the camp.'

The *Daily Mail's* correspondent Edwin Tetlow, accompanying the British Army liberators, wrote that '[w]e decided to give the awful task of burial to some of the SS guards and women SS'.[13] It was becoming a standard form of ad hoc punishment by the British and Americans. Leslie Hardman, a Jewish chaplain stationed in nearby Celle, was sent to the camp and later described the scene. I found his memoir by chance in my university library. He'd written: 'I went up to the officer in charge of the burial operations. Two SS men were working under his instructions. As the corpses were pushed to the edge of the pit, they took what bodies they could grasp – bodies interlocked, coagulated, disintegrated – and threw them into the huge open wound which was to be the common grave.'[14]

The immediate reckoning hadn't ended there. Tetlow reported, 'When our troops went into the cells in which these ghouls are being kept they found that one SS man had hanged himself. Two others have now committed suicide by trying to run away.'[15] It was an odd turn of phrase. Tetlow explained, 'They knew they would be shot by our men if they did this, and they were. They ran deliberately because they could face no more of the work they have been doing in the last four days.' Kramer, now nicknamed alliteratively in lurid press fashion 'the Beast of Belsen', was 'caged like a wild animal' in the camp to save him from being lynched. He was beaten like the other SS men, 'his pasty face' showing the lumps of the attacks by prisoners. Few felt any sympathy. With the state of the camp evident to everyone, who would intervene or condemn?

Alan Moorehead, another journalist, was also shown round the camp during those first days.[16] After walking amidst the crowds of prisoners ('there were many forms lying on the earth partly covered in rags, but it was not possible to say whether they were alive or dead or simply in the process of dying') his army guide asked him whether he wanted to see the SS men and women.

A British sergeant threw open the cell door and some twenty women wearing dirty grey skirts and tunics were sitting and lying on the floor.

'Get up,' the sergeant roared in English.

They got up and stood to attention in a semi-circle round the room, and we looked at them. Thin ones, fat ones, scraggy ones and muscular ones; all of them ugly, and one or two of them distinctly cretinous.

The last adjective, or similar, seemed to be one that would become ubiquitous over the coming years. In interrogations and courtroom cross-examination, many SS accused would be labelled as subnormal, moronic, cretinous. At times it was an easy way of explaining their brutalities. Their lack of intelligence supposedly made their actions understandable.

Moorehead was then taken to see the male SS prisoners.

As we approached the cells of the SS guards the sergeant's language became ferocious.

'We have had an interrogation this morning,' the captain said. 'I'm afraid they're not a pretty sight.'

'Who does the interrogation?'

'A Frenchman. I believe he was sent up here specially from the French underground to do the job.'

The sergeant unbolted the first door, and flung it back with a crack like thunder. He strode into the cell, jabbing a metal spike in front of him.

'Get up,' he shouted. 'Get up. Get up, you dirty bastards.' There were half a dozen men lying or half lying on the floor. One or two were able to pull themselves erect at once. The man nearest me, his shirt and face spattered with blood, made two attempts before he got on to his knees and then gradually on to his feet. He stood with his arms half stretched out in front of him, trembling violently.

'Get up,' shouted the sergeant. They were all on their feet now, but supporting themselves against the wall.

'Get away from that wall.'

They pushed themselves out into space and stood there swaying. Unlike the women they looked not at us, but vacantly in front, staring at nothing.

Same thing in the next cell and the next where the men who were bleeding and were dirty were moaning something in German.

'You had better see the doctor,' the Captain said. 'He's a nice specimen. He invented some of the tortures here. He had one trick of injecting creosote and petrol into the prisoner's veins.'

The Nazi doctor was Fritz Klein. He'd been at Auschwitz, Neuengamme and then Bergen-Belsen for the last few months before the end of the war. The technique of injecting petrol or phenol into the veins of prisoners hadn't been his invention. I found various references to the technique being used in other camps. The science of killing and torture is frequently one to share, distribute, even inculcate within a corrupted system. Not that this would have mattered much to his British guards. Moorehead was told Klein had just finished being 'interrogated'.

'Come on. Get up,' the sergeant shouted. The man was lying in his blood on the floor, a massive figure with a heavy head and bedraggled beard. He placed his two arms on to the seat of a wooden chair, gave himself a heave and got half upright. One more heave and he was on his feet. He flung wide his arms towards us.

'Why don't you kill me?' he whispered. 'Why don't you kill me? I can't stand any more.'

The same phrases dribbled out of his lips over and over again.

'He's been saying that all morning, the dirty bastard,' the sergeant said. We went into the sunshine. A number of other British soldiers were standing about, all with the same hard, rigid expressions on their faces, just ordinary English soldiers, but changed by this expression of genuine and permanent anger.

4.

Not long after I read Alan Moorehead's article and while I was looking specifically into the British investigation at Bergen-Belsen, a friend of mine lent me a book. It was a 'bestseller' called *Hanns and*

Rudolf about the parallel lives of a British Army war crimes investigator and a concentration camp commandant.[17]

As soon as I started reading, obliged now by the loan, I was astonished at the coincidence. It'd been written by a journalist, Thomas Harding, whose great-uncle was Hanns Alexander, a member of the investigation team sent to Bergen-Belsen in late May 1945. I recognised the name from the War Crimes Investigation personnel I'd seen listed in various War Office files. Like many in the unit, he was a German national who'd escaped to Britain before the beginning of the war, had served in the British Army and then found himself indispensable when the need for reliable interpreters arose at the conflict's end. With a Captain Alfred Fox (another member of the investigation team), he'd been sent to interview Dr Klein in a military hospital on 18 May 1945, about a month after Bergen-Belsen had been liberated and a couple of weeks after Moorehead had seen Klein lying in his own blood in the cells.

Harding told the story of Alexander's encounter with Klein as if he were there:

> Klein did not look well. Since his arrest he had been working without
> pause to clear the camp, carrying corpses into the mass graves. Hanns
> and Captain Fox took a seat next to his bed and the interrogation
> began.[18]

I knew Klein had been drafted in to help with shifting the piles of corpses, part of the liberating soldiers' rough retribution. Numerous photographs had been taken of him standing in the middle of a mass of dead prisoners, picking up the naked and emaciated, partially decomposed bodies and loading them onto trucks, or taking the arms or legs of a cadaver with another SS man to carry to a pit. One picture appeared on the front page of the *Daily Mirror*. It made a visceral connection between perpetrator and the multitude of dead victims: Klein surrounded by, up to his ankles in, breathing in the smell of, rotting corpses. For all the rhetoric about legal justice that the politicians and lawyers were emitting in London and Washington, the soldiers confronted by the reality of the camps couldn't contain themselves. It was an immediate reckoning.

The treatment of Klein, justified or not (and who then or now would have protested or said it wasn't warranted or shouldn't have been done?), would have been enough to unhinge most people. The photographs were dated between 18 and 25 April and Klein appeared, in the first of the series, reasonably close-shaven. Only as the days went by did he grow stubble and then a beard. And that was when Moorehead must have seen him, whilst Klein was undertaking his labours amidst the dead of Belsen.

Maybe Lt Alexander's interpretation of Klein's condition, as told by Harding, was the result of the corpse-carrying. But given Moorhead's account, the forced labour amongst the dead may not have been the only reason he'd been hospitalised. If Moorehead was right and the man was begging for mercy, he must have been in a bad way. Even with the lapse of a couple of weeks, the effects were unlikely to have worn off. Then again, the records suggested Klein had contracted typhus, a hazard of being immersed in graves of those who'd already died of the disease. So perhaps his condition when interviewed was the product of a confluence of factors.

Whatever the cause, nothing was made of this summary treatment. Though the 'laws and customs of war', upon which the British relied in order to condemn the Nazi accused, required prisoners of war to be 'humanely treated' and officers to be spared any labour, no one seemed to worry about the harm done to Klein or the gruesome work he was required to perform, or any ill-treatment by his guards. He wasn't the only one to be dealt with in this way. By 28 June reports confirmed the deaths of twenty SS guards under arrest in Bergen-Belsen.[19] They had all purportedly died of typhus. It was commonly believed that they'd contracted the disease from being forced to bury the bodies of the prisoners. Dr Klein, the man pictured astride that carpet of cadavers, also suffered. But he survived to face trial.

5.

As public demands increased for punishment of those responsible for the conditions at the camps, rather amateurish investigations into what had happened and who was responsible began at Bergen-Belsen. The scenes witnessed were enough to convince that something criminal had happened. But members of the liberating forces gathered evidence with little guidance or skill. Conversations were written down, rough notes taken, but records were sketchy and imprecise and of variable quality. Many surviving inmates, potential witnesses, were allowed to leave the camp and go home. Few left details of their destinations, anxious as they were to escape that still-hellish place.

In London, the War Office assimilated the reports arriving from across newly occupied Germany and decided that the Judge Advocate General (or JAG, head of the army's legal corps) would be in overall charge of pursuing war criminals. Plans were drawn up for a practical response. 'Owing to the numbers of war criminals now being uncovered,' the War Establishment Committee (WEC), responsible for allocating resources for any army operation, wrote towards the end of April, 'it is necessary to form as rapidly as possible War Crimes Investigation Teams for the purpose of eliciting and recording evidence required by JAG branch in preparation of the cases for trial of such criminals.'[20]

By 28 April, it was decided that a war crimes investigative team should comprise a lieutenant colonel (legally trained) in command, a major, four captains or lieutenants, a couple of clerks, and three drivers/batmen. They would need a four-seater saloon car and a 15cwt 4x4 truck. The officers and any photographer were to carry pistols and the other ranks Sten guns. Those holding the rank of lieutenant colonel would act as special investigators, as detectives in other words, and the majors would operate 'as a cross examiner on behalf of the presumptive accused'.[21] Even confronted by the terrible sights of the camps, fairness was to characterise the process. No one was to be officially condemned without careful examination of the facts.

Three days later, an order to the British Army of the Rhine (BAOR) HQ was sent commanding the creation of two of these investigative teams. Everything was supposed to be in place by 15 May.[22] The bureaucrats decided on the kind of equipment each team would need. The WEC set out a long appendix to the order. It listed five pages of items from braces and water bottles to chisels and screwdrivers to axes and shovels to brushes and lamps to goggles and gloves to cars and trucks to chairs and tables to set squares and T-squares to jugs, paddles, paper (blotting and printing), photographic film, tape, tents for a darkroom, tripods, kettles, pails, stoves, aprons, caps, masks and trousers: everything that could be imagined would be needed to dig up remains, photograph the scenes of crimes, carry out a criminal investigation in the field.

This was the level of planning. Some of the equipment arrived, but the personnel needed to use it didn't. The gap between administrative design and action on the ground was immense, as those already at Bergen-Belsen realised. Conditions were dreadful. Over forty thousand prisoners were still being kept in the camp for fear the typhus might spread beyond the perimeter. Troops who'd been there since 12 April were struggling to treat the survivors, who were dying at the rate of five hundred a day. They had to dispose of the mounds of corpses too, a task that still wasn't finished when the main investigating team arrived nearly a month later. If a proper investigation was to be conducted, if the accused were to be interrogated, witnesses of their criminality identified, and evidence mustered, it would take a massive effort. But no one in government seemed intent on taking the task seriously.

This may have had something to do with the official position held by the British on war criminals generally. The government was never that keen on the American plan to try both the major and minor war criminals in some splendid scheme of prosecution. Though they were happy to pursue and try individual Germans for specific crimes committed against *British* soldiers (crimes such as the killing of the fifty escapees from Stalag Luft III or the massacres remembered from the days immediately before Dunkirk in 1940, when British troops who'd surrendered to SS units were machine-gunned mercilessly at Wormhoudt and Le Paradis),[23] the preference was for instant measures. It was Winston Churchill who allegedly first suggested mass executions once the war was won. As early as July 1944 he wrote to the Foreign Secretary, Anthony Eden, in response to learning about the deportation and annihilation of the Jews from Hungary, making no distinction between major and minor culprits:

> It is quite clear that all concerned in this crime who may fall in to our hands, including the people who only obeyed orders by carrying out the butcheries, should be put to death after their association with the murders has been proved ... Declarations should be made in public, so that everyone connected with it will be hunted down and put to death.[24]

Nothing had changed with the end of the war. Bergen-Belsen merely confirmed the scale and spread of 'horrible' crimes. Nonetheless, with Hitler and Himmler and all the others still at large, political minds were focused on the broader issue of how to deal with the leaders of the Nazi regime.

6.

As the Bergen-Belsen investigators were clumsily uncovering the local stories of atrocity, operating with few resources and, left to get on with their work as best they could, struggling to cope with the enormity of their task, Sir Alexander Cadogan (Permanent Under-Secretary at the Foreign Office, a civil servant rather than politician, and one who had consistently expressed opposition to an overarching trial) handed an aide-memoire to Samuel Rosenman, US President Franklin D. Roosevelt's assistant.[25] The note of 23 April 1945 from His Majesty's Government expressed the absolute certainty that Hitler and 'a number of arch-criminals' (they must have been avid readers of Sherlock Holmes) should, when or if they were captured by the Allies, 'suffer the penalty of death for their conduct leading up to the war and for the wickedness which they have either themselves perpetrated or have authorised in the conduct of the war'. The reasoning for this definitive position was that otherwise it would be 'impossible to punish war criminals of a lower grade by a capital sentence pronounced by a Military Court unless the ring-leaders are dealt with with equal severity'.

The British government's favoured strategy was therefore clear: 'execution without trial is the preferable course.' Despite all the American arguments that a public and fair hearing should be held, the British wanted summary justice. The aide-memoire warned, at least as far as Hitler and his closest associates were concerned, that a trial, with its demands for proof, would be 'exceedingly long and elaborate'. Then there were those onerous rights that would have to be accorded to the defendants. 'There is nothing upon which British opinion is more sensitive in the realm of criminal procedure', the note went on, 'than the suspicion that an accused person – whatever the depths of his crime – has been denied his full defence.' His Majesty's Government would fight shy of an attempt to interfere with the normal arrangements of a criminal trial, even though fulfilling them might provide the Nazis with an opportunity to grandstand and subvert the whole process. Best then to avoid one altogether.

The sensibilities of the British weren't taken that seriously. They became less relevant when Hitler's suicide was announced on 1 May 1945. The Führer myth (as well as reality), inside Germany as well as out, was so strong that his absence from any trial would inevitably lessen the impact of the propaganda value that might be gained by Nazi leaders dragging out proceedings or complaining about procedural technicalities. Besides, the determination of the Americans to obtain justice through a recognisable criminal process had already been decided. President Roosevelt may have died on 12 April 1945, but newly sworn-in President Harry Truman wasn't about to change the American position. Plans were well advanced in Washington. Crucially, the Soviets agreed that some form of trial should take place. The British were isolated. Realising they were swimming against a tide of international and perhaps public opinion, the British government withdrew its long-held objection to a grand show trial and embraced the idea instead, albeit reluctantly.

On 2 May, President Truman formally engaged Robert Jackson as the Chief of Counsel for the proposed international tribunal. He had won the race to fashion the formal retribution process. He was a familiar figure in US legal circles, having served as Attorney General under President Roosevelt and then as Supreme Court Justice. A man of the establishment, as one would expect. Jackson's appointment represented a desire for a principled approach.[26]

By this time the Americans were distributing a draft protocol outlining how the proposed trial of Nazi leaders should proceed.[27] In San Francisco at the end of April 1945, whilst the Allies gathered at the United Nations Conference on International Organisation (the inauguration of the UN), the draft was handed to Anthony Eden, British Foreign Secretary, and his counterparts, Vyacheslav Molotov of the Soviet Union and Georges Bidault of France. This was the first attempt to put the idea of judicial retribution into some legalistic form. Only the basic principles were accepted by the four powers at this point (the detail would remain under negotiation for some months), though this was significant enough. By finally affirming that a military-style trial (and a 'fair trial' at that, as the draft declared) of 'Major War Criminals' would take place (rather than a scheme of summary execution), with evidence and charges prepared by a committee of representatives from each of the four Allied powers acting in cooperation, and by confirming that individual 'officers and men' directly responsible for atrocities and crimes would either be returned to the countries where those crimes were committed or tried by the Allies in some other procedure, the method of retribution was prescribed.

After that, it was all about the detail. What crimes were to be prosecuted? What were to be the charges? Who were to be the 'Major

War Criminals' brought to trial; who would be tried in separate local courts? Much of the legal logistics were made a little easier by the adoption of the military tribunal model. Some impossible fusion of legal systems and procedures in order to find a hybrid to satisfy every nation affected wasn't needed. Instead, agreement that a court martial, where there would be a prosecution, a defence and a bench of judges to decide the outcome, was an approach each of the powers could understand and embrace.

7.

Whilst these high political manoeuvres were going on in the Allied capitals, matters were improving slightly in Bergen-Belsen. Perhaps recognising the demands of criminal trial, perhaps finally convinced of the importance of gathering proper evidence, Majors Smallwood and Bell, both from the Judge Advocate General's Office, and Captain Fox of the Special Investigation Branch of the Military Police were sent to the camp. Even then it was a pitifully under-resourced response. German interpreters only arrived more than two weeks later, on 14 May, and these were, as would be noted in formal reports, 'of no value in dealing with a considerable number of possible witnesses who only spoke Czech, Polish, Russian etc'.[28] The officers were also without NCOs to act as 'searchers', to identify suitable witnesses and suspects. Three arrived with the interpreters, but it was late and hardly adequate given that there were 'some 55,000 potential witnesses sick or healthy, distributed over an area of several square miles'.

I imagined those thrown into the hellish conditions did what they could. Major Smallwood gave evidence at the Belsen trial (as it would later become known) and was explicit about how he'd coped.[29]

When we got there, there was no fixed plan.
There had been some investigations already made by members of the Military Government, but they had not taken any very definite statements. Statements had been taken, but no sworn affidavits or

anything like that. So the first thing was to get interpreters. None of us spoke any Czech or Polish, and very little German and perhaps a little French. With the aid of the Military Government we got hold of some interpreters and two girls who were extremely good. They were both ex-internees, Czech Jewesses aged about 25 or 26 respectively. One had been interned for four years and the other for five years in different camps which included Auschwitz and Belsen. They had only just come to Belsen ten days before the liberation and they escaped the full horrors and were therefore in pretty good health. With their aid we started to take statements. Of course, there were thousands of people there and it was difficult to know where to begin. To start with we got them to bring in their friends who were in a fit state to give evidence, and gradually the circle grew. With the aid of the Military Government we got various members of different nationalities to send people along if they could give statements that might be helpful. The procedure at first was that the witness was brought in and we explained to the interpreters, who understood the position very quickly, that what we wanted was evidence of definite acts committed by definite people on, as far as possible, definite dates. We did not want a whole series of people coming along to say that SS guards were brutal and cruel, because one knew that already. We gave these instructions to the inter-preters and we got a whole lot of statements from various witnesses. The procedure, speaking for myself, was that I took rough notes as we went along and the witness went away and I put those notes into ordinary affidavit form. The witness then came back and the affidavit was read out to her and translated in my presence by the interpreter. Sometimes small alterations were made then the witness was sworn and signed it.

It wasn't very sophisticated. Some statements taken by Smallwood were of dubious value. On 8 May he interviewed Hela Frank. All her statement said was: 'I am 24 years of age. I am of Polish nationality and was first arrested in May 1943. I have been in concentration camps ever since and came to Belsen on 1 November 1944. I knew in Belsen an SS woman called Frau Amper. She worked in the kitchen and often beat people both men and women with a whip who came there. She once beat me with her hands but not very badly.'[30]

That was it. Slightly more fulsome and useful statements would be taken (none were as detailed as the prosecution officers could have thought ideal), but this was hardly a definitive proof to convince any court to convict this SS woman or anyone else. Not if the standards of normal British justice were to apply. Other statements were better, but looking at the general quality, they were too short, too imprecise to be valuable. They gave no sense of the multitude and prevalence of abuse suffered. But then, how could they? Perhaps only a poet would have been able to do justice to these stories.

In the circumstances, it was all Smallwood and his fellow officers could reasonably manage, or so they claimed. A British War Crimes headquarters had been hastily established at Bad Oeynhausen, a small town west of Hannover, though it was an office dogged by frustration and lack of support from government back in London from the start. Only on 20 May 1945, more than a month after Bergen-Belsen had been liberated, was some kind of team, as originally envisaged by the War Office, finally assembled in the camp. What was now known as No. 1 War Crimes Investigation Team took shape and began work. A Lieutenant Colonel Leo Genn was appointed to command the operation.

At first, I didn't dwell much on the identity of those sent to investigate the atrocities at Belsen. They were just faceless names on a page. But then I came across the unpublished memoirs of Fred Warner almost hidden amongst the papers of another investigator, Anton Walter Freud, in the Imperial War Museum. Warner, it seemed, was one of the numerous German nationals who'd escaped Germany in 1939 and sought refuge in Britain. He was considered reliable enough to serve with the Royal Pioneer Corps in Britain before being recruited to the Special Operations Executive and parachuted into Italy behind enemy lines in early 1945. A few months later, he was invited by Major Gerald Draper at JAG to join the War Crimes Team as an interpreter and investigator.[31]

Warner, born Manfred Werner in Hamburg, had been posted to Bergen-Belsen as soon as he was recruited by Major Draper. The officer to whom he'd reported at the camp was 'quite a celebrity', he wrote. He mentioned the name Genn, which triggered a vague memory of one of those English actors who'd appeared regularly in numerous films during the 1950s and '60s. He was in *The Longest Day*, the iconic 1960s film about D-Day, and *The Wooden Horse*, another war movie about a notorious escape from a German POW camp. When I looked up his photograph, I remembered the polished English persona, exuding calmness whilst everyone else about him panicked – the quintessential Englishman of Empire. How, I wondered, had he come to command this vital first investigation?

Some details weren't difficult to find. Leo Genn was a lawyer. He'd studied law at Cambridge in the 1920s and even practised as a barrister in London for a short time. But acting was his true passion.

After a couple of years at the Bar from 1928 to 1930, he met the wonderfully named stage actor and producer Leon Lion. Lion encouraged Genn's theatre acting whilst having him help out as legal counsel. Genn's acting career flourished and by the mid-1930s he'd already appeared in films and had been taken on as a member of the Old Vic Company. His smooth voice and equally smooth features made him ideal for the movies and the stage. He appeared in a succession of plays both in London and New York as well as the odd film now and then. The war changed that. By 1940 he'd signed up with the Royal Artillery. His thespian skills weren't forgotten, though, and he was drafted in to narrate official war films. (You can listen to recordings of his voice-overs in the Imperial War Museum's archive.) In 1944 he was given leave to act in Laurence Olivier's *Henry V*. It must have been strange for him to leave his unit, fighting across France, to go home and pretend to be fighting the fifteenth-century French.

At first I had no idea how he'd been chosen as commanding officer of the Belsen investigation. He didn't seem to have the obvious profile for a war crimes investigator. But then I came across a comment made by Major Smallwood at the Belsen trial that was to take place later in 1945 that suggested Genn had served in the SHAEF Court of Inquiry, which I now knew had examined various massacres of Allied troops taken prisoner during the Battle of Normandy and in the campaign across northern France and into the Low Countries.

Whether this was true I couldn't say at first, though it would have explained his appointment. Few others would have had similar experience; the Court of Inquiry had only investigated a few dozen cases during its short life. Then again, it occurred to me ungenerously that perhaps his glamour and charm and growing celebrity, coupled with his rank of lieutenant colonel and the Croix de Guerre on his chest, might have made him an irresistible choice for the War Office. With a whole department of long-serving lawyers in the Judge Advocate General's Office back in Whitehall, why else would they have selected a man who clearly had only a cursory interest in the law, had little if any investigative experience in civilian life, and had never practised criminal law to any great degree? I thought legal counsel to theatreland during the 1930s hardly qualified him to take on the largest and most complex criminal investigation Britain had ever undertaken, perhaps would ever undertake. It reinforced the impression of amateurism, of a British military and governmental arrogance that an officer with limited experience in a specialist field would be able to cope.

I was wrong. Up to a point. Searching further amongst the Foreign Office records, I found that Genn had indeed been appointed as a member of the Court of Inquiry at the beginning of 1945 to serve alongside the Canadian, Col Bruce Macdonald, and the American, Col John Voorhees.[32] Travelling around France and the Netherlands they scrutinised the suspected murder of many Allied servicemen. At Tilburg they investigated the shooting by the Gestapo in July 1944 of three Allied airmen, an Australian, a Canadian and a Briton.[33] The men had been hiding at a Dutch underground address in the town when the house had been raided by the Germans. Witnesses were found who could testify to having seen the Gestapo members executing the airmen in the back yard. The Inquiry gathered them together and over the course of a day asked them questions about what they'd seen and then produced a reasoned set of findings. It was detailed work. Genn and his colleagues had surveyed the house, producing plans of the scene and marking the location of the shootings; they'd found photographs taken by the local Dutch police of two of the dead men (pictures of the tops of their heads wrapped in cloth like some 1940s charladies, their shirts soaked in blood, their mouths open); had taken their own photographs of the back yard from nearby windows where witnesses had watched the executions; and had identified the perpetrators. The report was composed and exacting in its attention to the 'facts'. But what could it offer? Simply, a recommendation that should the named Gestapo members fall into Allied hands they should be brought to trial and charged with murder.

Genn also visited the village of Le Paradis, where the infamous massacre had been perpetrated upon members of the Royal Norfolk Regiment and other units during the retreat to Dunkirk in May 1940. Ninety-seven men had been captured, gathered together in a farmyard and machine-gunned by an SS unit. But Genn and his fellow investigators couldn't identify the German troops involved with any certainty. They could only plead for the Allies to search for more information.[34]

There were several cases like this. Each produced a carefully typed report deposited with SHAEF headquarters. No doubt the details were passed on to London, but I couldn't quite understand why such work had been undertaken at a time when the war had yet to be won, when there was so much death and devastation to contend with. What had it achieved? A reaffirmation of decency formulated by legal process? Maybe that was enough.

Nonetheless, Genn's experience made him the natural choice for taking on the case of Bergen-Belsen. Few others had had to dig up remains of their comrades to determine a victim's cause of brutal death, had cross-examined witnesses, had sought the necessary information to identify German perpetrators, had acquired the skills to pursue an investigation in the best traditions of British justice.

The appointment of Genn was, I thought, a logical one after all. He was a lawyer, he was in the field, he was ready to move to Germany. But then I found out later, after finally tracking down his private papers, that ambivalence, perhaps even resentment, had accompanied Genn's acceptance of his new mission.[35] In his seemingly aborted memoirs (deposited with the IWM and amounting to only half a dozen pages, tailing off before he'd finished telling the story of his time at Belsen, perhaps having lost faith in his ability to write something worthy, the style laboured, doing little justice to the terrors he'd been recalling) he complained, first, about the way in which the SHAEF Court of Inquiry had been precipitously wound up, a decision he reckoned must have been made by 'a member of the Combined Staffs in Washington, under the influence, one can only imagine, of a good lunch on a Spring day'. It was a 'destructive order', he said, disbanding a functioning unit in the middle of vital war crimes investigation work, as he saw it. And as for his new commission, Genn wrote, it seemed to me acidly, 'the dictates of publicity were paramount and concentration camps must have priority over offences against our own serving personnel. This might perhaps be the place', he continued, 'to note that in the hearts of all of us who had any operational experience whatever, this particular fact remained one for exasperation and lasting regret.'

8.

Whatever his reservations, when Lt Col Genn took up his post at Bergen-Belsen he brought with him Major Savile Champion, a solicitor in the Royal Artillery, Lieutenant Robichaud (a Canadian army translator who'd served with Genn on the SHAEF Court of Inquiry), Lieutenant Alexander (the Hanns in *Hanns and Rudolf*, although he then called himself 'Howard' to assimilate into the British forces more easily), two other interpreters and about ten other ranks. It represented a significantly better investigative presence than before.

Surrounded by the Stygian scenes of the dead and barely living, these men had to undertake an unprecedented task, with experiences that were impossible to imagine for those who weren't there, breathing in the stench, witnessing the corpse-strewn grounds. Simply burying the dead was a daily terror for the British troops. If General Patton had thrown up in Ohrdruf and the stomachs of the army medics had turned, what chance did these lawyers have?

Even without the psychological impact of the conditions they had to bear, Genn and Champion recognised that simply bringing order to the camp would take a 'herculean' effort.[36] They grumbled that despite the expanded investigative team, they suffered from a 'desperate lack of personnel'. They believed there were only enough of them to conduct an 'ordinary investigation of a particular' war crime, not of a whole history and system of atrocity. The more they delved, the more the scale and spread of crimes committed were revealed. Genn and Champion later reported, 'Twenty such [investigation] units could well have been employed without being entirely adequate to cover the field.'

It didn't help that men assigned to their investigative team were being poached soon after arriving. Such was the apparent dearth of available lawyers of quality throughout the British zone of occupied Germany that Major Bell had been sent to the 1st Canadian Army on secondment and Major Smallwood was required to sit as Judge Advocate in other military cases. After some struggle with Legal Division, Genn managed to secure Smallwood part-time, hardly satisfactory given the huge demands of the investigation.

Carrying out a full inquiry in these circumstances was difficult enough, but they also felt they were operating in a legal void. They weren't clear about the limits of their jurisdiction or the charges that could be levelled against the SS men and women in custody: was it 'neglect', 'mass murder', 'gross cruelty', some other offence? The crimes they were hearing about were far outside their experience, anyone's experience, and the overwhelming suffering they could see in the prisoners who'd survived and the stories that were accumulating through their interviews made them wonder. A 'single instance of murder or brutality appears in the nature of a drop in the ocean in the light of the many thousands of deaths caused over a period of time by the joint deeds of all concerned', they wrote, as though they were seeing the evidence transcend the words and notions they had of 'crimes'. They needed new terms, a completely fresh language to express the enormity of all that they were hearing.

No one had briefed them on the discussions in the UN War Crimes Commission committees, which were toying with the idea of 'crimes against humanity' as a new internationally recognised offence. No one made reference to a category of crime being promoted by an unknown visionary called Raphael Lemkin, a Polish refugee who since the early 1930s had seen the rise of Hitler and the atrocities committed against the Jews under the Nazis. Lemkin coined the term 'genocide' to describe the planned killing of a race or people with the intent to annihilate such a group.[37] He itemised aspects of destruction from the economic and political to the religious and the moral and the physical too. Even in 1944, he was able to chart how the 'Jews for the most part are liquidated within the ghettos, or in special trains in which they are transported to a so-called "unknown" destination'.[38]

Though Lemkin didn't have the details of these final destinations, Lt Col Genn and his team did. As questioning of witnesses continued, they discovered that a large number of the inmates and SS members had been transferred to Bergen-Belsen from Auschwitz when that camp had been shut down at the end of 1944. The stories they were hearing about the latter camp were of gas chambers, industrial-scale killing, years of slaughter of the Jews and many others in installations built for that purpose. This was the reality of 'genocide', even if the word was yet to be commonly adopted. Initially focused on collecting evidence for prosecuting those responsible for the terrible scenes at Bergen-Belsen, they now had another priority: investigating the 'mass extermination in gas chambers at Auschwitz'.

The extension of their remit after their discovery wasn't reflected in any increase in resources. Lt Col Genn still had too few officers and men in his team and those he had were inexperienced. Matters were complicated, rather than helped, when investigators from other Allied armies came. The officer in charge of the camp, Brigadier Keith, complained at the end of May that two Czech investigating officers had turned up unannounced and a whole team of French officers had 'arrived with two broken down cars on temporary loan only'. 'They must come with proper cars,' he wrote to SHAEF headquarters. 'They have no typewriters or stationery either. Will you drum it into them that they must come properly equipped.'[39]

Meanwhile, Genn tried to ameliorate the pressure by jettisoning the plan thought up back in London that he should act as principal investigator and his second in command, Major Champion, should sit by his side making sure those accused were treated fairly and witness testimony was challenged before being passed to the prosecutors at JAG. Genn's report towards the end of June 1945 said, 'It has been found impracticable to use both the CO and 2 i/c on single deponents since it would have cut down the amount of work done in the available time by approximately half.' But the report affirmed that 'all officers of the unit taking depositions have, however, borne strongly in mind the fact that the interests of the accused should be watched. Witnesses have been questioned with this object in view and the testimony of those considered unreliable rejected.'[40]

The splitting of Genn and Champion to conduct interviews was a feeble measure. Tens of thousands of potential eyewitnesses amongst those left in the camp would have had something to say. All of them could testify to the conditions and the cruelties. But they couldn't all be examined and prepared to give evidence. Many were sick with typhus. Many were dying. And those who were well enough to be released had been let go before the investigating team had arrived. The investigators needed *good* witnesses, reliable figures, people who could say something specific against individual SS members. Genn estimated around 400–500 SS men and women had served at Bergen-Belsen, of whom they had 50 or so in custody. That was a lot of potential defendants who had to be tracked down and against whom some evidence would be needed.

Some of the investigative desperation was apparent from the way in which witnesses were sought. A public address announcement, broadcast about the camp by loudhailer, pleaded: 'Any person who can give evidence of brutal conduct or murder by any SS men or women at Belsen and has not already given evidence should call at War Crimes Investigation Office Camp 3 Block GB2 First Floor, Room 52 between 10 and 12 in the morning or 2 and 4 in the afternoon. Evidence as to any of the SS men or women having taken part in selection parades for gas chambers at Auschwitz or elsewhere is also required.'[41]

9.

Whatever was happening with investigations underway at Bergen-Belsen and other camps was incidental to the pursuit of those most senior Nazi figures wanted for the planned Major War Criminals trial. With Hitler's death confirmed by the Russians on 1 May, as was the suicide of Josef Goebbels, the infamous Propaganda Minister and another of those 'gangsters' identified throughout the war as central to the Nazi regime, the Allies began to round up anyone they could find. Franz von Papen, a key politician in Hitler's rise to power, but latterly a peripheral figure as German Ambassador to Turkey during most of the war, was taken early by the Americans in Stocklausen, Austria. Alfred Rosenberg, the Nazis' so called 'philosopher' who'd been prominent in defining their racial theory, was arrested in Flensburg near the Danish border on 18 April.

Then on 8 May the biggest catch so far was announced. *Reichsmarschall* Hermann Goering, Commander in Chief of the German Air Force, had been picked up by US General Patch and his 7th Army as they hunted for Nazis through the Austrian Alps. Goering was reported as having surrendered along with his wife, child and members of his staff near Salzburg. He was allowed an extraordinary degree of respect, in spite of the many stories naming him as one of those who would be tried as a war criminal. The Americans presented him rather naively at a press conference after his capture.

Goering expounded on any subject the reporters asked.

Why had he ordered the bombing of Canterbury?

'In revenge for the British bombing of a German university town, the name of which I cannot remember.'

Was Hitler dead?

He believed so.

And what about the concentration camps being unveiled across Europe?

The Times reported Goering as saying they 'were solely Hitler's concern and were run under his direct orders. He never discussed them with anybody but those actually in command of them.'[42]

Goering's defence was already in preparation. He denounced the idea that he was a wanted war criminal. He railed against the preposterousness of such a claim. He said he acted only in the best interests of Germany as a high-ranking minister of state of a sovereign country. There could be no question of him committing a 'crime' in this context, he said. That would undermine the whole concept of state sovereignty. He would take responsibility for his actions, but he was not a war criminal. The distinction was vital for his sense of honour.

Over the next few weeks other notorious Nazis were arrested. Many had gathered in Flensburg on the Danish–German border. Officials had made for the town with the imminent fall of Berlin and in the hope of maintaining some order away from the advancing Russians. The British found them there, but allowed them to pretend that they were still running the country whilst it was decided what to do with them. Only after a few days were the leaders placed under arrest. On 23 May, Admiral Doenitz, nominal President of Germany in the wake of Hitler's death; senior military commanders General Jodl and Field Marshal Keitel; Minister of Armaments Albert Speer; and numerous other lesser figures were finally taken into custody. It was the end of a ridiculous interval. Despite their outlaw status and despite the collapse of a functioning chain of command, senior Nazi figures had been left to act as though they still held some legitimate position as the government of Germany.

With the conclusion to this absurd situation came the naming of those who were to be considered 'criminal'. Many national administrations still in exile wanted to have a say. The Polish government in London issued a list of war criminals to be 'indicted' on 24 May. It included names such as Goering and Keitel and various other ministers such as Wilhelm Frick, Reich Minister of the Interior and Protector of Bohemia and Moravia for a time, and Walther Funk, President of the *Reichsbank*, as well as chiefs of German administration imposed across Poland during the Nazi occupation: Greiser, Forster, Koch. They also listed 15,000 others who'd been involved in the oppression of the Polish people, in the bloody suppression of the Warsaw rising and, most poignantly, the operation of the camps at Belzec, Majdanek, Auschwitz and Treblinka, where the horrors exceeded even those found at Bergen-Belsen and Buchenwald.[43]

One name soared above all the others on the Polish list now that Hitler was dead. He was the man who provided the most direct link between high Nazi policy and the brutal reality of the camps and the organisations that brought them and the terror across Europe into being. His photograph was released around the world the next day, 25 May.

10.

The picture was of a man lying dead on a hard wood block floor. It showed a 'paltry, obese figure' (at least according to one of the journalists, Selkirk Panton, who, by his own account was allowed to examine the body). The corpse was half covered by a coarse blanket. Shoes without laces, a white enamel basin, an overturned cup were scattered about the body. The eyes were closed and hands rested across the abdomen.

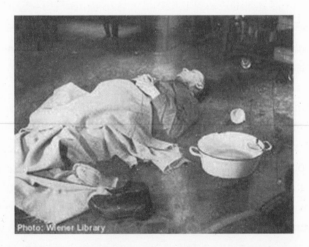

Photo: Wiener Library

The photograph had the feeling of a tableau, an artistic composition reminiscent of Henry Wallis's *The Death of Chatterton*. There was a touch of high Renaissance art in the way in which the man was surrounded by artefacts, each weighty with religious symbolism: the cup suggesting the loss of power, perhaps; the simple bowl an attempt to cleanse the soul; the discarded boots, the removal of hope. And the blanket? What could that signify, thrown half over the body after a frenetic death? What did it conceal?

All those details assumed importance because the dead man was Heinrich Himmler. The man responsible for the concentration camps, for the genocide against the Jews, for the operation of a police state in Germany, for systematised mass executions, for the whole regime of destruction and extermination of all those peoples across Europe. Next to Hitler, he was the person most intimately associated with all the atrocities committed by the Nazis and their allies. Leader of the SS, the Gestapo, the Secret Service, his character appeared on every page of the story of the descent into atrocity of a whole nation. If anyone, *he* was the person you would want to see on trial for all these crimes.

The story of Heinrich Himmler was tightly entwined with Nuremberg and every trial for Nazi crimes that took place after the end of the war. His personal orders directed to camp commandants and SS commanders were referred to again and again in court transcripts and witness statements. His instructions provided the intent, the *mens rea*, the mental element of the crimes that caused millions to die through deliberate killing and deliberate neglect, crimes made visible to the world as the camps were liberated by Allied forces. Though Hitler's overarching murderous directives provided the environment for atrocity, it was Himmler's crafted instructions that were proof of a plan to dehumanise and exterminate.

Announcing his death, *The Times* described Himmler as 'the most sinister figure in Germany',[44] the *Manchester Guardian* called him 'the most feared man in Europe'. He was 'second to none as an organiser of mass persecution and terrorism'.[45] The reign of terror in Europe was his doing, they said. His obituaries may have been sketchy, but enough was known to warrant these descriptions. Born in Munich in 1900, Himmler joined the National Socialists soon after the First World War. He worked initially for Gregor Strasser, one of the original figures behind the Nazi movement who was later executed in 1934 on Hitler's orders during the 'Night of the Long Knives'. By then, Himmler had already established himself as one of Hitler's closest associates and the leading member of the SS. In 1936 he was appointed Chief of the Police for the whole of Germany and as *Reichsführer-SS*, organising the security services so that he was responsible for both public order and state security. He developed the *Waffen-SS* as a military wing, thus bringing to the battlefield the same vicious ideology, brutality and ethos of total obedience as was applied to his system of oppression both in Germany and in occupied Europe. The vast empire he constructed was responsible for the Gestapo, the concentration camps, the persecution and extermination of the Jews and others deemed unworthy of existence in Nazi Germany, everything that was the essence of Nazi malevolence.

But there he was, dead on a hard wooden floor. Dead from biting down on a prussic acid capsule fixed in his teeth, on the floor of a house in Lüneburg occupied by British Intelligence. The man who would have given greater meaning to the proposed trials of the most senior Nazis was dead. The British had let him escape. Though he'd been captured and identified, he'd been allowed to commit suicide whilst in the hands, quite literally, of British soldiers who were supposed to have kept him alive.

Himmler's end was a bizarre one, odd enough to provide fodder for conspiracy theorists who wish to see some dirty dealing in the strangeness of the story. Sometimes it's far easier to believe that sinister forces have been at work rather than accept a ridiculous sequence of unintended events that the evidence otherwise suggests.[46] The story I tried to piece together from reports of the various British soldiers who were involved (though accounts differ in many little details) smacks of incompetence and occasional buffoonish decisions, but not conspiracy.[47]

The grotesque comedy of Himmler's final days began soon after Hitler committed suicide. As the Allies stormed across Germany, arresting the high-ranking Nazis and announcing their intention to put these leaders on trial, it was clear that an honourable surrender was impossible. With all lost and crumbling about him, Himmler decided not to stay with the Flensburg group of ministers and instead took two of his faithful adjutants, Major Heinz Macher and SS Colonel Werner Grothmann, and headed towards Bavaria, Himmler's old power base. Himmler shaved off his trademark moustache and placed a black eyepatch over his left eye. His papers identified him as Sergeant Hitzinger. He and his little entourage removed all SS badges and insignia. They reached Meinstedt, 70 kilometres south-west of Hamburg, on 21 May 1945, two weeks after the war in Europe had been officially concluded with unconditional surrender at Lüneburg Heath. At an Allied checkpoint they were stopped and questioned. Troops were on the lookout for anyone in the SS or in the Nazi hierarchy. The group looked suspicious. Particularly the little man with a pirate-like eyepatch. One of the soldiers lifted the patch and couldn't see any damage. The men were all taken into custody.

Himmler and his companions were then ferried from camp to camp. They were questioned a number of times. Eventually, they ended up at an internment facility outside the village of Westertimke, until recently a German-run prisoner-of-war camp. It was now 'Civil Internment Camp 9' and housed suspect characters, war criminals, Nazi party officials, captured SS men. Captain Thomas Selvester (later to become a detective inspector with the Salford police) was the commander.[48]

Soon after arrival on 23 May, Himmler revealed his identity. There are conflicting accounts of how this came about. Captain Selvester said Himmler asked to see him and at that meeting told the captain who he was. The sergeant interrogating Himmler recalled his detainee shouting in exasperation, 'Don't you know who I am?' before announcing that he was Reichsführer Heinrich Himmler. The sergeant tried to picture the person before him with a moustache, started to believe he might be telling the truth and called in the commandant. Whatever the exact sequence, Captain Selvester then telephoned headquarters of the British 2nd Army stationed at Lüneburg.

At about 7 to 8 p.m. that same evening, a Major Rice arrived. He confirmed Himmler's identity by asking the suspect to provide his signature. It matched a copy of one the Major brought with him.

A full body search was ordered, which Captain Selvester would later say he carried out personally. He found a glass phial inside a small brass case, which Himmler told him contained medicine for stomach cramps. Selvester wasn't fooled. It was common knowledge that SS men had been given poison capsules to insert in their teeth. They could snap them in a second, releasing the cyanide into their system, killing them within minutes and escaping the indignity of interrogation if they chose. Then Selvester found another brass case, but without any phial inside. He suspected it was hidden somewhere and he carefully examined Himmler's clothes and brushed his hair. But he didn't look inside his mouth. He was worried, he said later, that such a move would precipitate some drastic action on Himmler's part. Instead, he ordered thick bread sandwiches and a cup of tea for his prisoner, watching carefully to see how Himmler managed to eat. Selvester was satisfied and took no further precautions.

Arrangements were then made to transport Himmler to a villa on Uelznerstraße on the outskirts of Lüneburg. The house had been commandeered by the British as a temporary interrogation centre. Colonel Michael Murphy from Field Marshal Montgomery's intelligence office was there to welcome him. He saw to it that Himmler was stripped once again, searched and given British battle dress to put on. Himmler refused. He wouldn't wear British Army uniform. He was given a blanket to tie around his midriff instead, the one that ended up covering the lower half of his body in the photograph.

Captain Wells, an army doctor, was with Colonel Murphy and he asked to examine Himmler. The doctor, mindful of the danger, asked Himmler to open his mouth so that it could be inspected again. Inside, he saw a black capsule hidden in a gap in Himmler's teeth. But before he could thrust his hand in to prevent him, Himmler bit down hard on the capsule.

There was frenzy. Murphy, Wells and Sergeant Major Edwin Austin grabbed hold of Himmler and upended him, trying to dislodge the capsule. It was too late. They pushed an emetic down his throat and applied a stomach pump. For fifteen minutes Himmler was writhing in pain, but all they succeeded in doing was delaying his death. It was 11.14 p.m. The cyanide had killed him and they'd lost the chief culprit of those scenes at Buchenwald and Bergen-Belsen that had assaulted the world since the middle of April.

I found it difficult to equate the accumulated accounts of Himmler's convulsive death with the scene in the photograph in front of me and others I managed to dredge up from the Imperial War Museum and newsreel archives. It seemed too ordered as a depiction of the aftermath of such a dramatic happening. The chaos that followed Himmler's sudden crushing of the phial didn't manifest itself in the photograph. All the stories indicated desperate attempts to stop the poison working. Himmler's head was thrust in and out of a bucket of water, it was said. How had he ended up lying sedately on the floor with only an overturned cup and a polite basin of water next to him?

It's likely the truth was more prosaic. The photograph must have been taken the morning after the poison took effect. Himmler died close to midnight, but the room in the picture was lit by natural light, with the sun's rays shining through a window and slanting across the body. A motion picture film was recorded of the scene at the same time. It was shown on British Pathé news in the cinemas.[49] A different impression is conveyed if you watch the clip. When the camera pans back, although in exactly the same position and still surrounded by the objects visible in the photograph, Himmler now lies in what looks like an ordinary suburban living room. A light hangs above him decorated with a frilly lampshade. There are flowered print curtains. It's as though someone has come round for tea and had a nasty turn. A ghostly hand holds up a phial shaped like the head and casing of a bullet for the camera. A sentry stands guard, shifting uncomfortably, looking down at the body. And through the open windows can be seen a host of figures milling about in the garden. If the details of the suicide were correct and it occurred late in the evening, then everyone must have left the body and gone to bed.

Presumably during the night and before the photographs and film were taken, decisions had been made as to what to do next. These added another element of peculiarity to the story. Morticians moved in. Plaster casts were moulded of Himmler's teeth and feet and hands. Then a death mask was made, an almost quaint touch evocative of another age when photography wasn't available to prove a person had passed away. It reminded me of the wax mask of Oliver Cromwell on display in the British Museum. Himmler's mask was presumably to convince the world that he was dead. It appeared on Time magazine's front cover a few days later.

One further act was deemed necessary. Supposedly to avoid his grave becoming a focal point for Nazi worship, it was decided to bury Himmler's body somewhere out on the expanse of Lüneburg Heath. Early in the morning after the death and once the photographs and

filming had finished, a party of British soldiers, including Sergeant
Major Austin, loaded the body onto a truck and drove out to a forested
part of the heath. The corpse had no coffin. It was wrapped in blankets. They motored for some time then stopped in the middle of
scrub. A deep grave was dug and the body shoved into the hole. No
markers were left and no coordinates noted of the grave's location.
The soldiers returned to Lüneburg town.

Unsurprisingly, the circumstances of Himmler's death and burial
remain mysterious. Not only did various conflicting accounts from
the participants in the operation emerge, but the British government's
files were closed to the public under a 100-year embargo. That was
not necessarily suspicious in itself. It was common practice to stamp
files with such a long secure rating. But it indicated a sensitivity that
seems strange now. If the files exposed incompetence or stupidity by
lower or even senior ranks, then revealing it to the public soon after
the war would, no doubt, have been considered embarrassing. But
keeping the matter quiet encouraged conspiracy theories to flourish,
the most popular being that the British had deliberately killed
Himmler.

In retrospect, it mattered little whether Himmler was murdered
or committed suicide or whether the British were inept or not. The
manner of his death and the way in which it was represented afterwards fed neatly into the Allies' plan for Germany and its people.
Undoubtedly, those preparing to prosecute the Major War Criminals
would have seen Himmler's absence as a substantial setback. But
with the hated figures of Hitler and Goebbels also dead, Himmler's
pathetic end, the very insignificance of the man evident in the banal
details of his capture and death, could still serve a purpose: to dispel
the myth of the leading Nazis as godlike figures. That was vitally
important for the proposal to bring the German command hierarchy
to account personally for what had been done in their name and by
their design if not their direct order. Challenging the Nazi cult,
induced through propaganda and ruthless authoritarianism, was a
vital part of the Allied policy of denazification of Germany. It was
also central to achieving legitimacy for the prosecutions that were to
follow. Having the German public exposed to the very human falli-
bility of their once supreme rulers, and to the sordid little details of

their existence after capture, was a necessary act. Himmler's death mask and ignominious passing served that purpose at least.

11.

With Himmler's suicide, the list of potential defendants at an over-arching trial of Major War Criminals was 'all but complete' according to the *Manchester Guardian*.[50] That wasn't quite true. The Americans were still searching for a number of leading Nazis including Joachim von Ribbentrop (Foreign Minister) and Martin Bormann (Hitler's long-standing deputy), although they'd been told by Robert Ley, the Nazi Labour Minister, captured in the middle of May by the US 7th Army while attempting to pass through their lines to get to his family in Cologne, that Bormann was dead, killed in Berlin.

On the same day that Himmler died, US forces arrested Julius Streicher and Franz Ritter von Epp. Von Epp's photograph stereotypes him as *the* ardent fighting German. He was one of the original Nazi supporters. Over a twenty-year period he rose to *Reichskommissar* of Bavaria, though apparently with limited power or influence. When arrested in 1945 he was already in poor health. He would die in detention at the end of 1946. Streicher was popularly known in the Allied media as the 'Jew-baiter'. He'd led the persecution of the Jews in the German media throughout the Nazi era, being responsible for the magazine *Der Stürmer*, which barely included anything but anti-Semitic propaganda. Both were arrested together in Austria on a farm forty miles from Berchtesgaden, the mountain resort where Hitler had built his 'Eagle's Nest' retreat. With these men in custody the Americans, under Robert Jackson's direction, were gathering an impressive range of defendants for a major trial, sufficient anyway to justify a single dramatic hearing that would portray the full extent of Nazi crimes. The most senior suspects in American hands were trans-ferred to a hotel in a small town in Luxembourg.

The Palace Hotel at Mondorf was to become known as 'Ashcan'. Even the code names used by the British and Americans signified their disgust at the enemy. Over the next few months Ashcan was prison for forty-odd leading Nazis. Colonel B.C. Andrus was its US Army commandant, a man who had little time for any of his charges. He reportedly called Goering 'Old Fat Stuff' and insisted the inmates watched a film recently taken at Buchenwald. He introduced the movie in brutal fashion, or so an article written for *Collier's* magazine claimed. 'You are about to see a certain motion picture showing specific instances of maltreatment of prisoners by Germans,' he was reported as saying to his Nazi captives. 'You know about these things and I have no doubt many of you participated actively in them.'[51] Apparently, Hans Frank, von Ribbentrop, Kesselring and Streicher were horrified.

By the summer, forty-six Nazis had been collected at Ashcan. I found a list of the inmates in a British government file, and although I recognised some, the majority were unknown to me.[52] It took some time to discover their histories. Most were prosecuted for one crime or another, but many were released without charge after a year or two. They represented a cross-section of army and government personnel. Not all were notorious. Some were functionaries who had no influence within Hitler's inner circle, but hung about power like faithful pets. Men such as Erwin Kraus, head of the National Socialist Motor Corps, established in 1931, a little like a Nazi Automobile Association. Krauss had taken a team of motorcyclists to compete in the Isle of Man TT race in 1939, racing on BMW machines. They'd won the senior race, landing a propaganda victory for the swastika-emblazoned team. And there was Philipp, Prince of Hesse, who seems to have acted as liaison between the Nazi state and the fascists in Italy. Related by marriage to Prince Philip, husband-to-be of Queen Elizabeth II, he would be quietly released later. Jakob Nagel was State Secretary in the *Reichspost* Ministry. The American interrogator Major Giannini was mystified at how he'd obtained such a position. Nagel came across as a 'minor executive' at best. Despite his lowly status he would still be questioned as to the exact structure and operation of the German postal services, but evidence of any involvement in awful crimes wasn't forthcoming.

Several men, military staff officers and government bureaucrats, who couldn't be held responsible for the persecution of the Jews or the concentration camp system or any other atrocities, were held in detention for a number of years and a few were prosecuted. Most had secured their release by the early 1950s.

Various other such senior, but not top, Nazis were held in Ashcan and it was almost luck as to whether they stayed for years, were prosecuted in some trial or other, or were released to get on with their lives. Most of the military men avoided severe punishment: Ernst John von Freyend didn't stay in captivity very long. He was Field Marshal Keitel's adjutant and considered inconsequential. Friedrich von Boetticher was military attaché to Washington DC until 1941, then Chief of the Armed Forces Central Division. He wouldn't be prosecuted at all and died a free man in 1967. Leopold Bürkner, Vice-Admiral of the German navy, wasn't put on trial, but spent a couple of years in Ashcan before being released to eventually become a director of the airline KLM. He died in 1975.

Then there were people like Richard Darré. Originally from Argentina, his parents sent him to be schooled in Germany. He stayed, becoming attracted to the Nazi cause and to their supposed theories connecting race and land. As a member of the Party, he rose to be Minister of Food and Agriculture, helping to develop the *Lebensraum* idea used to justify the acquisition of territory by invasion and the exclusion of those who lived there. He was prosecuted as a member of the government in one of the later Nuremberg proceedings, and sentenced to seven years in prison, though he too would be released early, in 1950. And Wilhelm Stuckart, lawyer, chair of the Reich Committee for the Protection of German Blood and a leading theorist for the Nazis' racial laws, had been involved in discussions on the 'Final Solution', taking part in the infamous Wannsee Conference where he'd proposed the forced sterilisation of persons with Jewish grandparents so that although allowed to continue to live in Germany, they would die out naturally. He was also prosecuted in the 1948–9 so-called Ministries trial at Nuremberg, but released at its conclusion. He died in a traffic accident in 1953.

All of these men had their counterparts in every nation. They were mostly ordinary, dull bureaucrats. That didn't make them any less culpable or complicit in enabling the war to be fought and the Nazi regime to function. But it made them unattractive as figures to be presented to the world as the epitome of Nazi criminality. That was a central purpose of the Allies' plan for retribution: to demonstrate publicly and for posterity the criminal, corrupt men who directed the German state. For this they needed figureheads. It was for the Allies to pick them as if from a complex menu: Julius Streicher (anti-Semite propagandist) and Alfred Rosenberg (so-called Nazi philosopher) to represent the ideology of hate; Hermann Goering, Rudolf Hess (Hitler's deputy until 1941 when he made a bizarre flight to Scotland purportedly to bring an end to the war), Wilhem Frick (Minister of the Interior who constructed the anti-Jewish and generally suppressive laws of Nazi Germany) and Ernst Kaltenbrunner (second in command to Himmler and SS chief of the organisation that operated the Gestapo and secret police) to represent those who put Nazi ideas into practice; Doenitz, Keitel, Jodl, Erich Raeder (commander of the German navy) representing the military acquiescence to Hitler; Arthur Seyss-Inquart (Austrian Nazi Chancellor and later Commissioner for the Netherlands) and Hans Frank (Governor-General of occupied Poland, known as the 'butcher of Cracow') to represent those who imposed oppression on other lands; and several senior government men to make up the numbers: Joachim von Ribbentrop (Foreign Minister), Fritz Sauckel (chief of slave labour) and Walther Funk (Minister of Economics) to represent those ministers who made the oppressive system function so effectively.

12.

The Nazis held at Ashcan (and other main prisons) were subjected to interrogation just as the SS officers and guards were at Bergen-Belsen, but with significantly more rigour and certainly more resources. The American gaolers were seeking evidence about all aspects of the war, the operation of the German state and, with a prosecution in mind, their captives' connection to any atrocity. In a preliminary trawl for information, each inmate was given a 'General Prosecution Questionnaire' to answer. One of the questions pointedly asked: what was your knowledge of conditions in concentration camps?

The prisoners' squirming attempts to avoid any responsibility began immediately. That much was apparent from the thousands of pages of reports recorded of the questioning at Ashcan. Von Ribbentrop portrayed himself as a powerless onlooker once the war had begun. Hitler and Himmler acted without his knowledge on all matters. He said he tried to resign on several occasions, but eventually gave his 'word of honour' to Hitler that 'he would cause him no further trouble'.[53] *Generaloberst* Blaskowitz admitted he knew Jews had been spirited away by the SS, he thought sent to the Warsaw Ghetto, but he denied that he or the army in general had been involved. General Reinecke was incensed by the suggestion that the army had anything to do with atrocities. He said he went to see Hitler in 1939, telling him 'that there was so much talk in the Armed Forces circles about concentration camps that something must be done about it'. He asked to inspect one and was taken to Dachau along with over a hundred other officers to meet Hitler in person. They were allowed to go anywhere in the camp and were entirely satisfied that the inmates were well treated, he said. His impression made him doubt the reports in the foreign press from Bergen-Belsen and the other camps.

Robert Ley was more interested in helping the Allies rebuild Germany. Whilst sitting in his cell he wrote a full report on how this might be done, drawing on his experiences in building the West Wall defences in France in dramatically quick time. His recommendations were extraordinarily precise, down to naming the standardised building materials that would be needed for major reconstruction works. The report is an extraordinary insight into the man's character: even after all the destruction and death of war, after all the revelations about the Nazi regime, he hadn't lost his sense of self-importance as a minister of state.

Many interrogations were speculative and minute in the detail pursued. General Reinecke, again, was asked about the sexual hygiene in the army: he said he knew little about the subject. More relevantly, Reinecke admitted that 'Nazism was a catastrophe for the German people' but that was the extent of his confession.

The inquisitions at Ashcan were directly connected to the political machinations in Allied government circles. Senior politicians and high-ranking lawyers were battling for supremacy in the strategic game of designing the exact form of retribution to come. Now that they'd determined that criminal trials would be held, not only did they require identified defendants, but also credible evidence about their crimes. The interrogations produced some material (though few confessions), but it wasn't enough. In mid-May 1945, Justice Jackson was informed by his army legal colleagues that little in the way of hard evidence to charge *any* Nazi leader, let alone those now in custody, had been gathered. The *Daily Mail* may have thought that 'proving' self-evident crimes would be a mockery of a process, but once the fiction had been adopted of an independent tribunal, serving to judge the behaviour and acts of the Nazis objectively, then so too had the demands such a procedure implied. Even if the tribunal couldn't stand up to intense scrutiny as a wholly impartial process, it had to look like one. And that could only happen if the evidence was clear, comprehensive and overwhelming. It was a factor that would plague *every* trial conducted by the British and Americans in Germany (though the Soviets had fewer qualms about fair process).

Jackson travelled to Europe at the end of May to see how this vital element of his task could be fulfilled. His tour was heralded by the press. On 29 May, he held a press conference in Paris. 'We hope that the trials may begin within a few weeks,' he was reported as saying. 'We have had wars before, with victors and losers, but this is the first time that anyone has tried to fix the guilt and try those responsible for offences against humanity. This is our chance to do something now, and we must get on with all possible speed.'[54] He mentioned that national authorities would begin their own trials soon, drawing the distinction with his mission to stage one great hearing.

In London, Lord Wright, head of the UN War Crimes Commission, spoke at a conference of representatives from its sixteen member nations about a 'complex interlocking system'. The Commission, national authorities across Europe, and military trials run by the Allied occupying powers were all to operate simultaneously. They were to overlap when localised offences committed by individual accused were part of a 'general scheme'. Where acts were seen as elements of 'mass criminality' emanating from 'a master criminal and his entourage, and carried out according to plan by elaborate organized agencies and instrumentalities', 'special methods' to deal with them were needed. Lord Wright gave an example: 'membership in a body like the Gestapo or a particular section of it might in proper cases raise a *prima facie* presumption of implication in atrocities committed by the Gestapo'.[55]

On his return to the USA, Jackson drafted a report on his trip for President Truman. It was long, but impressive.[56] Whatever Jackson's failings (and an undeniably self-congratulatory tone permeates his writing), the report pieced together a coherent narrative for the kind of justice he had in mind.

'In brief,' he wrote, never failing to identify himself with each achievement,

> I have selected staffs from the several services, departments and agencies concerned; worked out a plan for preparation, briefing, and trial of the cases; allocated the work among the several agencies; instructed those engaged in collecting or processing evidence; visited the European theater to expedite the examination of captured documents, and the interrogation of witnesses and prisoners; coordinated our preparation of the main case with preparation by Judge Advocates of many cases not included in my responsibilities; and arranged cooperation and mutual assistance with the United Nations War Crimes Commission and with Counsel appointed to represent the United Kingdom in the joint prosecution.

Jackson succeeded in both distinguishing *and* joining inextricably the prosecution of the Major War Criminals and the rest of the culprits. He knew that the American public and the military and political constituencies wanted justice not only generally against the Nazis for the war that they'd been forced to fight, but also for specific killings of American personnel. He knew similar feelings existed across Europe. But he knew too that the pictures of the concentration camps, recently and widely disseminated, demanded a response. He told the President that immediate proceedings for war crimes committed against US troops was necessary for 'morale'. But he was adamant that they shouldn't interfere with the prosecution of the major figures he was preparing. He said trials under US military law were already underway and that some 'concentration camp cases are also soon to go on trial'. The British were doing the same, he said, with their primary focus on Bergen-Belsen. Though final agreement had yet to be achieved on the document defining the International Military Tribunal (to try the Major War Criminals), his vision was the right one to pursue 'preferably in association with others, but alone if necessary'.

More generally, Jackson justified once again this choice of judicial retribution. He asked, rhetorically, what they should do with the men the Allies had in custody. And he answered,

> We could, of course, set them at large without a hearing. But it has cost unmeasured thousands of American lives to beat and bind these men. To free them without a trial would mock the dead and make cynics of the living. On the other hand, we could execute or otherwise punish them without a hearing. But undiscriminating executions or punishments without definite findings of guilt, fairly arrived at, would violate pledges repeatedly given, and would not set easily on the American conscience or be remembered by our children with pride. The only other course is to determine the innocence or guilt of the accused after a hearing as dispassionate as the times and horrors we deal with will permit, and upon a record that will leave our reasons and motives clear.

Justice Jackson concluded his report with a flourish, demonstrating his ability to define the mood of the public, whilst containing, perhaps constraining, the craving for instant retribution.

When I read the whole document, there were certain passages I thought revealed something crucial about Jackson, about how one might express anger and yet maintain composure. Outrage bled through his words. For a lawyer used to dampening emotion through written judgment, this must have been a moment of release.

He said the people of the USA 'came to view the Nazis as a band of brigands, set on subverting within Germany every vestige of a rule of law which would entitle an aggregation of people to be looked upon collectively as a member of the family of nations'.

He said, 'Our people were outraged by the oppressions, the cruelest forms of torture, the large-scale murder, and the wholesale confiscation of property which initiated the Nazi regime within Germany. They witnessed persecution of the greatest enormity on religious, political and racial grounds, the breakdown of trade unions, and the liquidation of all religious and moral influences.'

He said, 'This was not the legitimate activity of a state within its own boundaries, but was preparatory to the launching of an international course of aggression and was with the evil intention, openly expressed by the Nazis, of capturing the form of the German state as an instrumentality for spreading their rule to other countries.'

He said, 'Once these international brigands, the top leaders of the Nazi party, the SS and the Gestapo, had firmly established themselves within Germany by terrorism and crime, they immediately set out on a course of international pillage.'

He said, 'The Nazis swooped down upon the nations they had deceived and ruthlessly conquered them. They flagrantly violated the obligations which states, including their own, have undertaken by convention or tradition as a part of the rules of land warfare, and of the law of the sea. They wantonly destroyed cities like Rotterdam for no military purpose. They wiped out whole populations, as at Lidice, where no military purposes were to be served ... They transported in labor battalions great sectors of the civilian populations of the conquered countries. They refused the ordinary protections of law to the populations which they enslaved. The feeling of outrage grew in this country, and it became more and more felt that these were crimes committed against us and against the whole society of civilized nations by a band of brigands who had seized the instrumentality of a state.'

He said, 'We propose to punish acts which have been regarded as criminal since the time of Cain and have been so written in every civilized code.'

He said, 'In arranging these trials we must also bear in mind the aspirations with which our people have faced the sacrifices of war.'

He said, 'As we expended our men and our wealth to stamp out these wrongs, it was the universal feeling of our people that out of this war should come unmistakable rules and workable machinery from which any who might contemplate another era of brigandage would know that they would be held personally responsible and would be personally punished.'

Shifting from grandiloquence to pragmatics, he said, 'I know that the public has a deep sense of urgency about these trials. Because I, too, feel a sense of urgency, I have proceeded with the preparations of the American case before completion of the diplomatic exchanges concerning the tribunal to hear it and the agreement under which we are to work.'

He said, 'We must now sift and compress within a workable scope voluminous evidence relating to a multitude of crimes committed in several countries and participated in by thousands of actors over a decade of time ... The evidence is scattered among various agencies and in the hands of several armies. The captured documentary evidence – literally tons of orders, records, and reports – is largely in foreign languages. Every document and the trial itself must be rendered into several languages.'

He said, 'An immense amount of work is necessary to bring this evidence together physically, to select what is useful, to integrate it into a case, to overlook no relevant detail, and at the same time and at all costs to avoid becoming lost in a wilderness of single instances. Some sacrifice of perfection to speed can wisely be made and, of course, urgency overrides every personal convenience and comfort for all of us who are engaged in this work.'

Jackson had established the rationale for the trials to come. But despite his powerful rendition of wrong and necessity for justice, I could find no explicit mention of the Jews or any other specific group persecuted by the Nazi regime. I didn't think that was a product of ignorance.

13.

Whilst in London during his short European tour, Justice Jackson met the man who would be his British counterpart throughout his mission and the Nuremberg process: Sir David Maxwell Fyfe. Brought up in Aberdeen, Maxwell Fyfe was an avuncular and ambitious lawyer and Conservative politician, polite, determined and a man who had risen through political and legal ranks more through ability than family contacts. He'd been Attorney General for a brief period during the last months of Winston Churchill's government, and would prove to be a better advocate than Jackson at the Nuremberg Tribunal. Privately, Maxwell Fyfe would often be critical of his American colleague's performance and though Jackson would collect many plaudits for the achievements of Nuremberg, Maxwell Fyfe would present the steadier and more comforting image of an objective lawyer pursuing the accused with professional skill, cross-examining in a manner that turned the attention to their crimes and responsibility rather than giving them space to perform to the crowd (as Jackson famously and negligently did with Goering).

Maxwell Fyfe had been asked to establish the team that would coordinate the British contribution to the Nazi trials. It was to be called the British War Crimes Executive (BWCE), a fusion of offices from various government departments which had some connection with registering war crimes during the war.[57] It would take until September 1945 before all its senior members were appointed, but the Solicitor General, Sir Walter Monckton, the Treasury Solicitor, Sir Thomas Barnes, and a handful of lawyers and representatives from the War Office and other departments would initially support Maxwell Fyfe. Their work began immediately from their allocated base at Church House in Westminster, much to the irritation of the Church of England whose property it was and who'd expected the building to be handed back to them once the war was over. The UN War Crimes Commission shared the third floor of the building with the newly developing United Nations Organisation. The BWCE occupied the second floor; its mission was to help the codification of procedure for the International Military Tribunal, gather and collate information to assist the prosecution and oversee the British effort at the trial. A European Section was posted to operate in Germany at BAOR Headquarters at Bad Oeynhausen, close to the dirty investigative work that was already underway at Bergen-Belsen and other parts of north-west Europe.

A directive was soon issued to the BAOR by the War Office to clarify areas of responsibility. Though the BWCE would deal with the Major War Criminals in cooperation with the Americans, it was for the British Army to catch, try and punish the so-called 'minor' war criminals in those zones of Europe it occupied and controlled. Special Army Order 81/45 gave it the power to set up military courts to try suspects. Legal advice and direction would be provided by the Judge Advocate General. Only those accused of crimes involving victims who were Allied nationals could be brought before these courts. Cases involving criminal acts against German nationals by the Nazis were specifically excluded.

The Army's duties didn't end there. The BWCE wanted information, documents, orders, statements by informers which could be used to prove the guilt of the major Nazis they had in custody as well as 'the criminality of Nazi State Organisations', meaning particularly the SS and Gestapo. They needed evidence of unlawful orders, atrocities in the field or on the high seas, torture as policy, the taking and execution of hostages, officially condoned reprisals, organised extermination in concentration camps. And they wanted help with the compilation of CROWCASS, the Central Registry of War Criminals and Security Suspects, designed to identify all those who might have committed war crimes. Detention reports were to be sent to Paris where CROWCASS was based at 53 rue des Mathurins. Fingerprints and photographs of suspects (taken in 'two positions: front face and side face' and without hat) were needed for each suspect captured.

It was a monumental task. At one of its early meetings, on 11 June 1945, representatives of the army, navy and air force, as well as government lawyers, gathered to consider how they could fulfil it. The meeting began with Major General the Viscount Bridgeman making a clear distinction between the pursuit of 'minor' war criminals (to be tried now by military courts under a soon-to-be-issued royal warrant) and prosecuting 'major' war criminals (such as Goering and those held at Ashcan). Though the Viscount recognised that these latter figures wouldn't be connected easily to specific violations of the laws of war, they would be vulnerable to charges holding them accountable for plans or policies that encouraged such crimes to be committed. Their mission now was to decide how they could help in bringing the *major* criminals to book.

As Justice Jackson had already appreciated, it was a question of evidence. They needed policies, orders, documents showing direct intent to commit atrocities. Fortunately, Allied forces had already acquired a vast array of Nazi archives. The Admiralty had the German naval records going back to 1900. 'Voluminous' was how the material was described. It would take time to sift through and they weren't quite sure whether they would find anything useful for a prosecution anyway. They decided to concentrate on a few barbarities: the sinking of passenger liners, for instance, or the deliberate shooting of the survivors from ships sunk by German U-boats. Whether this would demonstrate a plan to carry out such acts they couldn't then predict.[58]

The men from the War Office were even more speculative. They said the interrogation of SS and Gestapo personnel now in custody should reveal damning material about those organisations. The records of the OKW, the *Oberkommando der Wehrmacht* (the supreme command of the German armed forces), were intact in Germany, but these too would take months to analyse. At least they had information from British prisoners of war about the way they'd been treated. That had been card-indexed, with the POWs debriefed on return from Germany and providing details of their experiences. But the War Office officials were sceptical that this information revealed any major plan except for a few isolated issues like the treatment of captured commandos and parachutists (everyone knew Hitler had publicly ordered that these soldiers were to be shot if taken alive) and the specific execution of the fifty escapees from Stalag Luft III, the most celebrated atrocity against British officers and still very much in the public mind.[59] Other than these, there was little which would satisfy a proper court of law.

And then, finally, they mentioned the statements already being gathered from people (mostly 'foreigners', it was rather dismissively noted) who had been victims of the concentration camps. They had stories to tell, though how that would help with prosecuting the likes of Hermann Goering, they couldn't yet say.

14.

If the gathering of the BWCE members had been at Bergen-Belsen rather than in London, they might not have been so blasé about the stream of testimony coming from the witnesses at the concentration camp. They might have paid more heed to its significance and pressed for more resources to support its discovery. But they were far removed from the stench and squalor and as they were content to leave matters to the tiny investigation team under Leo Genn, they were unable to appreciate the strategic value of the information emerging from the camp. Not only were the inmates providing a picture of the ghastly last days of Bergen-Belsen, they were also constructing, collectively, an account of the whole system of mass extermination of the Jews and the history of the concentration camp organisation. Hundreds of competent witnesses were testifying about the worst of other detention centres, many having been evacuated from Auschwitz and Mittelbau-Dora and Ravensbrück, and taken to Bergen-Belsen as a last resort at the end of the war. And, unlike other investigations getting underway in north-west Germany, the investigators had leading perpetrators in their custody who were prepared to talk.

On 22 May 1945, Captain Stephen Malcolm Stewart, a member of the War Crimes Section of the Judge Advocate General's Branch at the BAOR HQ, travelled to the prison at Diest in Belgium with a typed statement taken from Josef Kramer. The 'Beast of Belsen', the SS commandant, had been moved to the citadel, a low-lying old fortress that served as one of the growing number of holding gaols for suspected war criminals. Stewart and his colleague, Major Pollard of the Special Investigation Branch, had already interrogated him and were now bringing back a typed statement for him to sign. Stewart read it out to Kramer in German, though it was transcribed in English.[60]

The statement was an extraordinary admission of complicity in the whole industry of oppression and killing constructed around the camps as its organisational skeleton. Kramer, who was thirty-nine years old, confessed that he'd volunteered for the SS in 1932 when he was only twenty-six. He had been assigned to the concentration camp service, something he said he hadn't asked for and hadn't wanted. It was a story told by many accused SS officers who'd served in the concentration camps – they would profess their disappointment at being kept from the fighting, even the Russian front, where the pitiful suffering endured by the German army was common knowledge. Kramer, though, said he'd been given his orders and whether palatable or not he had to follow them. He'd moved to Dachau in 1936, where there were political prisoners, criminals, beggars, 'gypsies and people who do not want to work', as he described them. He said no death sentences had been carried out whilst he was there, only prisoners shot whilst trying to escape, that by then overfamiliar euphemism.

From Dachau he'd been moved to Sachsenhausen. He'd been promoted, but only to be in charge of the mail department. He had no idea what was going on there, he said. Then he'd been posted to Mauthausen in 1939 and promoted again, this time to *Obersturmführer* (equivalent to first lieutenant in the British Army).

The way Kramer described Mauthausen you might think it was no more than a tough prison. There'd been no ill-treatment, he said, and if a guard had had cause to shoot and/or kill an inmate trying to escape, an investigation would have been conducted, not that anyone would have been punished for doing their duty. But the conditions in the camp had been reasonable. There was enough accommodation, no one was ever beaten. That was his story.

It didn't alter when he referred to his next posting, to Auschwitz, in May 1940, as adjutant to the commandant, Rudolf Höss. The prisoners, he said, were Polish, maybe 3,000 to 4,000 in number. It was a relatively new camp. Again no ill-treatment had been practised, he said. Any corporal punishment had to be authorised by Berlin. If it was approved, it had to be administered by the prisoners themselves by order of *Gruppenführer* Richard Glücks, head of the concentration camp system under Himmler's overall command. Deaths in the camp were from natural causes, perhaps thirty a week. He would see the reports from the medical staff. The bodies of those who died, he said, were burnt. 'The ashes were sent to the relatives if they required them.'

In November 1941, he'd returned to Dachau for a few months ('a very good camp', Kramer said) and then on to Natzweiler in France, where he was appointed commandant in October 1942. The promotion through the upper ranks demonstrated his value to the system. Despite his senior command position, he revealed less about this camp than the others he'd served in. He didn't know whether French nationals had been there, for instance. He didn't know if prisoners had been sent to Strasbourg for medical experiments, though it was 'quite impossible that experiments of any kind' had been carried out inside the camp. And he had no idea whether any British inmates had been held there either.[61]

Kramer did remember other details, however.

Generally speaking when corporal punishment was administered the number of lashes given varied between 5 and 25. The number was laid down in the order coming from Berlin. Twenty-five was the maximum. The doctor had to be present when corporal punishment was administered. I cannot recollect where a prisoner was unable to stand his punishment and fainted. If such a case had arisen it would have been the doctor's duty to interfere as that was why he was there. The punishment was administered with ordinary wooden sticks, 3 or 4 feet long and about as thick as my thumb. The sticks were made of solid wood as you find them in the woods around the camp. The punishment was administered by another prisoner who was chosen at random and in the following manner: the prisoner was made to bend down over a table and the lashes were given on his backside, without his clothes having been removed previously. I never had any difficulties with prisoners who had to administer this punishment. They were given the order and they complied with it. If they had refused to comply with the order I could not have punished them for this refusal. The orders from Berlin were that so many lashes had to be administered by another prisoner but the order did not say what should be done if one of the prisoners refused to beat one of his comrades.

Only one hanging had occurred during his time as commandant and that had been after a direct order from Berlin, he said. A Russian. No other executions had been carried out. He'd never heard of punishment cells. Everything had been under his command and he would have known if anything untoward had been happening.

Kramer returned to work under Höss in Auschwitz in May 1944. He'd been placed in charge of one of the camps within Auschwitz, which by then had grown to immense proportions. Kramer had commanded Auschwitz II-Birkenau and had the hospital and agricultural camp under his control. The deaths here were of a new order. Between 350 and 500 a week. They'd been sick people who'd been either ill or old. He said, 'The death rate was slightly above normal due to the fact that I had a camp with sick people who came from other parts of the camp', and of course the prisoners had to work hard. If anyone died, a proper procedure would be followed.

> I carried out inspections of the bodies of people who had died through natural causes in my capacity as Camp Kommandant when I was wandering round the camp. Whoever died during the day was put into a special building called the mortuary, and they were carried to the crematorium every evening by lorry. They were loaded on the lorry and off the lorry by prisoners. They were stripped by the prisoners of their clothes in the crematorium before being cremated. The clothes were cleaned and were re-issued where the people had not died of infectious diseases. During my inspections I never saw prisoners who had died through physical violence. When a prisoner died a doctor had to certify the time of death, the cause, and the details of the disease. A doctor signed a certificate and sent it to the Central Camp Office. These certificates did not go through my hands. The two doctors worked daily, from 8 o'clock in the morning until 8 or 9 at night. All efforts were made by these doctors to keep the prisoners alive. Medical supplies and invigorating drugs were applied. Two different doctors took charge of my part of the camp every day. I remember one very well because he had been the longest period in my particular part of the camp and he had also served under my predecessor, Hartgenstein. I do not know how long he had been there. His name was *Hauptsturmführer* Mengele.[62]

Kramer was lying. Not in everything he said, but in much of the detail. Despite the admission of high casualties in the camps where he'd served, he hadn't touched upon the true cause of death for the vast majority of his prisoners. Captain Stewart asked him about gas chambers at Auschwitz and Kramer said he'd heard the allegations of mass executions, but they were all untrue. As for his tenure at Bergen-Belsen, where finally he'd been sent in December 1944 as commandant, he said he'd been told many Jews there were to be 'exchanged' for German nationals held abroad. Bergen-Belsen was to be a camp for 'sick prisoners' from all the concentration camps in northern Germany.

Then his story became little more than a lament: for the few months he'd been in command the numbers of prisoners increased dramatically, he said, so much so that his administration had stopped keeping records. Trainloads had appeared, but no extra food or provisions. The death rate reached 400–500 a day. He'd warned his superiors of the catastrophe unfolding, but, he said, he'd been powerless. Cannibalism, suicide, sickness, spotted fever: they'd cremated the dead until the coke ran out. Then they'd resorted to mass graves.

'When Belsen Camp was eventually taken over by the Allies,' Kramer said, 'I was quite satisfied that I had done all I possibly could under the circumstances to remedy the conditions in the camp.'

Kramer's simple denial of responsibility, his calm assurance that he was but a functionary within a legitimate penitentiary system, did not convince the investigators. Despite their lack of personnel, the No. 1 War Crimes Investigation Team at Bergen-Belsen were already drawing together statements and taking affidavits that directly contradicted Kramer's account. Inmates were telling appalling stories of Auschwitz as well as other camps. They recalled seeing Kramer in Auschwitz taking part in the 'selections' of newly arrived Jews: those fit for work were marched off to the barracks, those deemed 'useless' were herded to the gas chambers where they would be killed immediately.

There was more. Captain Fox interviewed Renée Erman, who'd been arrested in France in 1943 and sent to Auschwitz.[63] She'd worked as a nurse in the experimental laboratory under SS Dr Weber, who'd carried out various experiments on women prisoners. When he'd finished with them, she said, they'd been sent to Birkenau, 'where a selection was made to find those fit for work'. If not fit, they went to the gas chambers. She knew about other doctors: SS Dr Schumann, who'd sterilised young Greek girls, subjecting them to strong X-rays, and operated on them to remove their sexual organs. Erman had seen some of these girls in her block and she'd seen them die of the operation. Then there were SS Drs Wirths and Clauberg, who'd both experimented on women, performing operations without anaesthetic, removing wombs, testing for something, Erman wasn't sure what.

Investigators found another survivor, Dr Charles Bendel, who confirmed the stories.[64] He was a Romanian doctor who'd been living in Paris when arrested for failing to wear the Star of David on his coat as required under the Nazi-imposed regulations. First taken to the French camp at Drancy, he'd been transported to Auschwitz in January 1944. By February, he'd been allocated to work in the Roma enclosure of the camp in Birkenau, where he'd encountered SS Dr Mengele. He said Mengele had carried out research on twins, testing them for all sorts of reasons. Mengele would kill them to observe how they died and conduct yet more experiments on the corpses.

Perhaps incomprehension prevented the investigators from pursuing the detail. Perhaps Bendel couldn't recall much of the activities of Mengele. Perhaps it had little relevance for the potential Bergen-Belsen trial given that Mengele wasn't one of those in custody. Perhaps they were overwhelmed. But the stories were not unique. Major Bell took a deposition from Reina Abas, who'd been at Auschwitz. She told him of a special block in the camp where she'd been taken, confirming the story of the twenty Greek girls aged between fifteen and twenty who'd been experimented upon, sterilised, their wombs removed for tests, she said. Margarete Berg from Prague told Bell that she'd seen one SS man, Walter Kümmel, drown two newborn babies at a 'camp near Hamburg'.

On 23 June, a member of the War Crimes Team, Captain Alexander Forbes, took another deposition, this time from Stanisława Michalik from Poland. She'd been at Ravensbrück. When taken to the camp's hospital in January 1942, she'd seen terrible things and heard terrible things: women had had their legs operated on. Some had died. When she'd been called back to the hospital the following year, even though perfectly healthy, she'd been given a bath, then her legs were shaved and injected with an anaesthetic. The next morning she'd woken in great pain. Her legs were bandaged. Discharged weeks later, unaware of what had been done to her, her legs continued to hurt, and she couldn't walk properly. Three years on, having been transported to Bergen-Belsen when they'd closed Ravensbrück, she was still suffering.[65]

The medical practices may have been abhorrent, but it was the organised extermination of Jews at Auschwitz-Birkenau that dominated the tales of many survivors. Again and again they described the 'selections', how transports of Jews would arrive at the camp, the

SS would choose who was fit for work and would 'select' those who were to be exterminated.

When Captains Alexander and Fox saw Dr Klein in his decrepit state, confronting him with the allegations, he was ready to confess. He told them that, whilst a GP in Romania in 1943, he'd volunteered for the SS and been sent to Auschwitz, where he worked with the likes of SS Drs Wirths and Mengele. It'd been their job, all of them, he said, to pick out those unfit or unable to work when the transports arrived. Children, old people, pregnant women, the sick, these were the ones who were gassed. He knew what would happen to them. But he was following Dr Wirths's orders. He didn't, he couldn't, protest. There were brothels in the camp and he would have to select girls for this 'job' too.

Klein's statement ended: 'I realise that I am as responsible as those from the top downwards for the killing of thousands in these camps, particularly at Auschwitz.'[66]

It was enough to challenge Kramer and unpick his statement.

But even as the dimensions of atrocity grew, the enormity uncontainable, no one in higher office back in Britain saw its detection as a priority. The investigative unit in Bergen-Belsen remained under-strength and without the resources promised.

15.

There was something very British about the way Leo Genn and his team approached their task. A blackly humorous, complaining, self-deprecatory, slightly louche, determined culture set in, as far as I can tell. They called themselves the 'Crime Club' and designed a little motif of a skull and crossbones to decorate their occasional home-made dinner menu cards. The camaraderie was quick to be forged, a besieged team having to battle army red tape and a lack of comprehension of their work at the War Office. They organised parties in the mess to interrupt the boredom, occasional 'swans' to European cities. When Leo Genn left the team at the end of October to be demobbed, they clubbed together to compose comic songs about everyone. The verse for Gerald Draper, one of the lawyers at JAG instrumental in many prosecutions, read:

> *The Crime Club loves death sentences ... you can see it in their dials*
> *So they expend their efforts in designing lovely trials*
> *They always try their criminals, unless the blighters die*
> *But when Gerald asks them questions, well there's no one left to try.*

The chorus:

> *Good folk, bad folk, everybody come,*
> *Investigate the criminals and make yourselves at home,*
> *Bring a pair of handcuffs and reflect upon the floor*
> *On singular atrocities you've never heard before.*

Waggish and gruesome: how else could they have coped?[67]

Some of Genn's theatre friends visited Bergen-Belsen and played a matinee for the troops. Sybil Thorndike and Laurence Olivier performed Bernard Shaw's *Arms and the Man* (I found it difficult to imagine the appeal of such a bittersweet play) and made a trip to the camp. Thorndike was badly affected, as one might expect (she would never forget that day, she would say later). But for all the diversions, Genn's mind was on his investigations rather than looking after his thespian colleagues. His interim report in June 1945 reads like that of a lawyer preparing a case for the local magistrates' court in the shires of England.

Though the evidence was being accumulated with greater efficiency now, Genn wasn't convinced it could be used to condemn those he held in custody. Underpinning his anxieties was an ambivalent appetite for Justice Jackson's premise that membership of the SS and other criminal organisations would be enough to establish guilt. For many British critics, Jackson's position was predicated on a falsity: Jackson had told President Truman that 'the Gestapo and the SS were direct action units, and were recruited from volunteers accepted only because of aptitude for, and fanatical devotion to, their violent purposes'.[68] However, the *Times'* correspondent in the British zone voiced doubts, and reported in the middle of June a different perspective:

> The suggestion that all members of the SS should be treated as belonging to a common conspiracy is not wholly acceptable, because in the closing phases of the war many soldiers were drafted into it willy-nilly: but much could be said for this procedure being applied to the guards of concentration camps and to the notorious 'Death's Head' battalions which invariably had their barracks at these places and were recruited from trained brutes. As it is, individual cases have to be prepared against all these minor war criminals, and though the fact of having been a camp guard is regarded as *prima facie* evidence, it is not always easy to find the necessary witnesses.[69]

Membership of the SS might provide a starting presumption of guilt, but it wouldn't be enough, at least not for the fair-minded British lawyers. Some other evidence was deemed necessary to prove personal responsibility. It was the quality of this proof, or often the lack of it, that worried Genn. 'Many of the witnesses were unversed in British ideas of evidence,' he wrote, 'and were, on some occasions, found to have little clear idea of the difference between evidence which was hearsay and direct evidence which depended on what they had themselves seen or heard, and were found to be proffering evidence without clearly differentiating between hearsay and direct evidence.'

It was clumsily expressed, but surely he couldn't have expected much more.

'Some of the witnesses were vague as to dates and to a considerable extent, as to details,' he continued to complain. But would one killing or beating or act of cruelty stand out? he asked himself. After years of such treatment, who could remember one particular incident? They were all equally terrible, committed by a variety of SS and *Kapos*, those inmates who acted as enforcers for the SS guards. How could someone who'd been through Auschwitz *and* Bergen-Belsen remember specific occasions clearly enough to satisfy a normal criminal court?

In search of the ideal testimony, Genn and his team continued to interview as many people as they could. They particularly wanted to obtain positive identification of SS personnel who'd committed precise crimes. But hundreds of SS had served in Bergen-Belsen over the course of its operation. Hundreds more had done so at Auschwitz. Finding inmates who could remember the names and faces of those who'd abused them was demanding in the extreme.

To help them, the investigators collected a host of photographs, of SS personnel, of inmates, of German soldiers, and pinned them to the wall of the interview hut in the camp. In an effort to appear 'fair', they included innocent men and women and even pinned up a blurred newspaper photograph of Field Marshal Montgomery, as a 'joke', Major Champion would say later.[70] Every witness who was questioned was asked to survey the wall and identify anyone they recognised as someone who'd committed an act of violence. One inmate picked out Montgomery as an SS brute. I imagined the British officers in the Crime Club would have laughed at that in the mess.

16.

At the end of July 1945, the officer in charge of administration of the British 21st Army Group occupying north-east Germany wrote to the Secretary of State at the War Office.[71] He said, 'It will be appreciated that it is impossible to deploy two small teams to cover the whole of the British zone and that to deal adequately and rapidly with all the alleged war crimes and atrocities now awaiting investigation in the zone calls for very greatly augmented investigation forces.' A third team had been authorised, but hadn't yet been gathered. And the two teams that had been formed were still lacking key personnel. Interrogators were desperately needed.

Despite these problems, the War Crimes section had opened more than 700 case files, taken between 300 and 400 statements at Bergen-Belsen, had sent 506 wanted reports to CROWCASS and had forwarded 231 cases to the Judge Advocate General's Branch to prepare for trial. The Bergen-Belsen case was top priority, with pressure being exerted from London to get proceedings started as soon as possible. But they were committed to pursuing every allegation. Parallel investigations started by the No. 2 War Crimes Team in Neustadt on the Baltic coast 150 miles north of Bergen-Belsen had to be pursued and were, if anything, revealing an even more complex inquiry.

4

Neustadt

1.

I'd prefer to think it was foolishness rather than hubris, travelling to Lübeck Bay with the idea that I might discover traces, clues that would reveal what had happened there nearly seventy years before. But the long list of dead on the rolls of honour in the Neuengamme KZ memorial building demanded some effort, an attempt to solve the mystery of whether any crime had been committed on 3 May 1945 and if so, who was responsible. There was a museum in Neustadt town and various memorials along the waterfront and that was where I planned to start, though I had no hard information about their location. I trusted they would be easy to find.

The bay can be a desolate sight. When the haze floats in from the Baltic and the sun's light diffuses across the water, horizon and shore merge in a miasma of brightness. Shielding your eyes helps little. Visually, the sea and land are one.

I don't know whether it was the light or simply my lack of map-reading skills, but I quickly became disoriented as soon as I entered Neustadt from the main Hamburg road. The small fishing port spreads itself around two headlands connected by a narrow bridge. You arrive in the town from the west; the traffic is channelled across the bridge and then directed up the low hill to the centre. The bay isn't visible from there, only a rather tawdry harbour with a few vessels moored and little indication that the town has much of a relationship with the sea any more. You have to guess where the open water could be. As you drive in amongst the shops and houses, the streets become narrower and more intricately laid out. There are few signposts and little encouragement to stop to find your way; one-way streets and No Parking signs dominate the central part of town. It's a struggle to find a place to pull over that isn't covered by warnings of fines or tow-away zones.

I was looking for the Cap Arcona Museum first, named after one of the ships attacked by British Typhoon fighter-bombers. The museum advertised on its website an exhibition on the ship's sinking and the events that transpired in the bay. Little information was provided about its contents or even how one might find the museum's location. Just an address and a few old photographs of the ship on its side with black smoke pluming from its decks. The tourist office's website didn't mention it at all, which was perhaps understandable once one knows the full story.

When I finally managed to find a parking space and started to get my bearings by walking towards the town centre (that, at least, was signposted), I realised I'd inadvertently parked within yards of the museum. Directed through an archway that was part of the old town gate tower, I caught sight of a small board attached to one of the gateway walls. It was in German and proclaimed the *Städtisches Museum*, Town Museum. To one side of the gate tower was a modern glass door. It was locked. Cupping my eyes to the glass, I could just about make out a notice that declared the opening times: 3 p.m. to 5 p.m. in winter. It was 11 a.m. I would have to wait another four hours.

For a few minutes I toyed with the idea of giving up, going back to Hamburg and looking at some other site. But I was reluctant to let it go so easily. If I left I would feel as though I'd joined the many who never quite cared enough about the thousands killed here that day in May 1945. Wandering around the tower, I looked into a few of the windows and saw a glass case with a large model ship inside. Little else was on display that I could see.

While I waited, I decided to look around the town and the surrounding area for vestiges of the disaster. A memorial was supposed to be out by the bay, a few clusters of graves along the shoreline too. I'd intended to do this anyway, although I'd hoped to get a better understanding of the geography of the disaster before searching for the memorial sites scattered about the district.

The map I'd printed off wasn't very helpful. It lacked detail and I found myself driving rather aimlessly away from the town along a minor road that kept close to the water. I knew the main monument was on the beach, but had no idea exactly where. There were no signposts. The road petered out and then veered back inland into an affluent area of suburban houses. I finally spotted a road named Cap-Arcona-Weg. It headed back towards the bay. I didn't think the local authorities would be so insensitive to name one of their streets after such a catastrophe unless the victims were honoured at its end.

The road took me to the coastline, to a small car park and a little pier, with a few shops and a row of holiday homes facing the beach. There was no sign of a memorial. I turned right and walked away from the houses along a cycle path set a little way back from the coast. After a hundred metres or so I came across a garden enclosed by a stone wall. An iron-grilled gate led into a rather sorry-looking assemblage of shrubs. In the middle was an ugly stone plinth. It was like a tasteless and oversized 1960s fireplace. The figure '7000' was carved in the middle (the number estimated to have died in the bay), an inverted equilateral triangle above (the colour-coded symbol sewn onto the jackets of concentration camp inmates) and the letters 'K-Z' beneath with the date 3.5.1945 under that. Two Christian crosses decorated the nearest side panels of the stone monument, which mystified me. By common account many Jews had been on board the ships. Then two more stone slabs recorded the nationalities of the victims (from American to Ukrainian). On the concrete ground before the memorial a slab was inscribed in German, roughly translated: 'We remember the 7,000 victims of the Nazi dictatorship who were killed in Neustadt Bay including many trade unionists: never again fascism, never again war.'

No one was about. The stone was weathered and needed some attention. The shrubs could have been pruned too. It was a dour place, bordering on the inconsequential. I could imagine amblers and cyclists idling down the pathway taking no notice of what lay there. It was hidden from any but the more inquisitive visitors. You had to be looking for the memorial, to be making a determined effort to find it.

I'm not entirely sure what obligation a people have for remembering atrocities committed by their own countrymen in their midst. Even so, I thought this memorial was the least that could have been erected. Those who'd died here deserved more. It was a sad place and not because of the memory it served. It didn't look as though anyone cared. But perhaps that's unfair. For all I knew, the inhabitants of Neustadt honoured the victims properly when anniversaries came around. Some would say that would be enough.

The question of collective guilt, though, remains relevant for the German people, for the whole German nation. No matter that several generations now separate the present from the Nazi era. At the level of international politics it's still raised at odd and often inconvenient moments. When the Polish Prime Minister wanted to obtain greater voting influence in the European Union in 2007, he mentioned Germany's responsibility for the carnage Poland had suffered during the war.[1] It might have been particularly tasteless to remind everyone that, but for the slaughter of millions of Polish citizens, the population of his country would have been significantly larger today, thus entitling Poland to additional representation on decision-making bodies, but Jarosław Kaczyński was echoing the popular belief that Germany hadn't yet paid for its Nazi past, for the crimes prosecuted at Nuremberg and elsewhere. And as I was writing this passage in February 2015, I saw the news that the newly elected Greek Prime Minister, Alexis Tsipras, had announced that he had a 'moral obligation' to claim reparations from Germany in the amount of €162 billion for the damage done to his country and 'all European people who fought and gave their blood against Nazism'.[2] Some crimes will not be forgotten.

Even with the time it took to find the Cap Arcona Memorial I still had a few hours before the museum would open. I wasn't hungry so I drove back into the town to look around the centre. The place was very quiet. It was a Friday, but there was little evidence of any great activity, as though it had closed for the weekend already. I started to worry that the museum staff would think it pointless to open its doors. After all, who would notice?

To kill more time, I went back down to the little harbour, then across the bridge that joined the two sides of the town. There was supposed to be another memorial close to the local sports ground. If anything, this was more obscurely positioned. It took me half an hour to notice that there was any commemorative site here at all. A desultory patch of rough grass on a slope of conifers behind the sports fields hardly alerted the casual passer-by. Only if you followed a winding path up the small hillock would you notice several brass plaques laid in the grass. Each one displayed a name and the date of death. To one side of the path was a large memorial stone with an inscription that I couldn't decipher.

By the time I returned to town, the museum was open. I entered through the glass door, thankfully open, and talked to the woman at reception. I bought a ticket for the museum. I wandered about exhibits on the history of Neustadt with its artefacts from various periods, from the Stone Age onwards. There was nothing about the war and no mention of the *Cap Arcona*. After a couple of floors of this I gave up and returned to the entrance desk. I asked the woman where the Cap Arcona Museum was. She told me to follow her. We trooped up a couple of flights and then through a corridor of the old building before coming to a solid white door. A small makeshift sign was affixed to the door saying 'CAP-ARCONA MUSEUM: GEÖFFNET'.

Contrary to the sign, the door wasn't open. The attendant produced one of those large medieval-type keys, big enough to use as a weapon if need be, and unlocked the door. She pointed inside, motioned for me to go through and then left.

Once through the door, a spiral staircase took me down into a couple of small rooms within which were a number of cabinets. There were many photographs, a few items from the ships and the prisoners who'd died on board. It was, to my mind, a feeble attempt to honour those who'd perished in the catastrophe or to explain how it had happened. No doubt well-meaning, its location and relatively superficial display did nothing to explain the disaster nor who was responsible for such massive loss of life.

I picked up some pamphlets and leaflets that were lying on a table. Most were in German. They weren't that helpful even when I managed to translate them later. But one, in English, was intriguing. The author was Wilhelm Lange, a local historian, and he'd written a short account explaining the events of 3 May 1945.[3] Quickly flicking through the pages I saw that Lange had written, 'Right up to the end of the war the Nazis succeeded in hiding the horror of the concentration camps from the public.'

I stood in the dingy museum and wondered about the implications of this assertion. It seemed to me that a subtle message was being rehearsed: if people outside the camps had no knowledge of what was happening inside, then you couldn't hold them responsible. Ignorance may not be a total defence for the ordinary citizens of Germany (they may have blinded themselves from the truth, for instance, choosing not to see the abuses committed by overtly Nazi compatriots), but it was probably enough for a general pardon. Then all guilt would belong to the small clique of men and women who were serving in the camps, the Nazi officials, the Gestapo and those who shot and tortured and gassed and let die the inmates. I didn't know whether it was conscious or unconscious, but reading the booklet, and others I've come across in German museums, the language made me think the acts of remembrance might also, perversely, be a way of forgetting. The art of camouflage or hiding in plain sight, perhaps.

With little to learn from the museum, I flicked through the rest of Lange's pamphlet. It told a compressed tale of the prisoners from Neuengamme and Stutthof, another KZ in Pomerania, being loaded onto ships anchored off the town of Neustadt, and the unfortunate attack by British aeroplanes that killed so many people. A straight-forward tragedy. But then a few details made me pause. It said a Swedish Red Cross representative called Dr Hans Arnoldsson had been in Neustadt at the time of the attack and knew about the ships and their passengers. He'd apparently negotiated for the release of some prisoners to his care and was trying to arrange the surrender to the British of the remainder on board. Arnoldsson also knew that various vessels in the bay were to be targeted by air strikes. The advancing British troops were close to Neustadt on 3 May and, fearing that another air attack was imminent, he contacted British Army Headquarters to warn them about the KZ inmates still on the ships. He reportedly spoke to two British officers who agreed to inform the relevant authorities. This was on the day of the disaster, Lange wrote. Exactly when wasn't clear. But the pamphlet said the air raid took place anyway and British Typhoons bombed the ships in the harbour, killing most of the prisoners on board.

There was no doubt where Lange saw the blame lying. It wasn't with the British despite their apparent knowledge of the ship's cargo. He wrote that the Nazis were responsible for laying a 'treacherous trap for the Allies to attack these targets and annihilate the prisoners'. The SS didn't allow white flags to be hoisted on the ships, he said. The SS and SD (Security Service) then murdered inmates who swam to the shore. They were the ones responsible, acting in accordance with Himmler's orders designed to keep the secrets of the concentration camps hidden: kill all the inmates and no one would be able to tell the story. And Lange wrote that after the air attack panic broke out in

Neustadt 'and the German departments could not organize a rescue operation to save those who were fighting for their lives at sea'. When the British finally entered the town at 4 p.m. on the 3rd, though 'shocked to find so much misery' among those who had survived, 'there were no reprisals'.[4] 'Helping the survivors from the ships was the first priority. People from Neustadt had to feed and to clothe them. All those in need were given accommodation in civilian and military hospitals.'

As a brief coda to the story, Lange wrote: 'Most of the survivors of the disaster returned to their countries as soon as possible without worrying about the part the Germans or the British had played in this tragedy. Today there are 14 large cemeteries along the bay of Lübeck to remind us of the tragedy and every year services are held in memory of the 7,000 concentration camp prisoners who died on 3 May 1945, victims of a tyrant's war and an evil war.'

Was there really no appetite for any continuing introspection from *either* side of the conflict, no desire to find out who should be held accountable for so many deaths? No blame on the British, no blame on the citizens of Neustadt, perhaps no blame on the population of Germany as a whole; an intimation, even, that there had been a joint humanitarian reaction, as though the ships had been sunk through some natural catastrophe? The suggestion was that any deeper respon- sibility lay solely with the Nazis, with Hitler, the tyrant who'd unleashed an evil war, and with those secretive and exclusive organ- isations, particularly the SS, who'd followed him.

The pamphlet was a form of remembrance through commisera- tion, for the British as well as the Germans. We'd suffered together, it implied.

I didn't believe that. There had to be more to the story than regret. But it wasn't to be found in Neustadt.

2.

Colonel Jack Christopher entered the town of Neustadt on 4 May 1945. He made his way to the Marine barracks at the U-boat school and found hundreds of living-dead, crowded into the school buildings, emaciated and diseased. The conditions were so bad and the people he discovered so decrepit, he believed he'd stumbled across a concentration camp. It was perhaps an easy mistake to make. With the reports of Bergen-Belsen and Buchenwald and the other camps being widely and vividly publicised, Christopher could be forgiven for thinking here was another terrible example of Nazi atrocity. The fury was patent in his report. He described conditions at the barracks as 'terrible'. 'Large numbers lay dead or dying of starvation in a big shed. Several women and children were already dead lying in filthy straw mixed up with those still alive when I arrived. The stench was indescribable.' Christopher wrote, 'There was no sanitation, everywhere there was dirt, filth, and disease.'[5]

The men and women gathered in the Marine school were in fact the survivors of the ships that had been sunk the day before. Dressed in their striped uniforms, little more than rags now, they were the few who'd escaped the fires and the freezing water and the indiscriminate shooting on the beaches when they swam ashore. As Christopher talked to them he learned that they'd endured overcrowding and starvation on board the ships for days before the British bombed them, and before that a long march from Neuengamme KZ or transport on crammed barges from Stutthof KZ (near Danzig) after those camps had been evacuated. Their resilience must have been extraordinary. Or they were simply lucky. However they'd ended up in that U-boat school, they were the small remnants of many thousands who'd suffered in multiple and differing ways over years. Their collective experience and condition provoked anger.

When Luftwaffe Field Marshal Erhard Milch was captured near Neustadt that day, the fury erupted in a very personal, almost petty way. Brigadier Mills-Roberts, commanding No. 6 Commando Unit, to whom Milch surrendered, had been one of the first to enter Bergen-Belsen a few weeks before. He was apparently still shaken by what he'd seen. As the Field Marshal presented his baton in the traditional act of senior military submission, Mills-Roberts allegedly took it from him, shouted something like 'You're all guilty' and broke it over Milch's head. The Field Marshal was then escorted by Christopher, now the Area Commander, to the U-boat school to see the condition of the camp survivors. Christopher impressed 'very forcibly upon him our disgust at these atrocities'.[6]

Undoubtedly, here was a crime or series of crimes worthy of investigation. Someone had to be made accountable for the murder of the seven thousand. Someone had to be punished. But it was complicated. Colonel Christopher did his best to unpick events, although he was neither a detective nor a lawyer. Even so, within a week he was able to report on the most significant aspects of the crimes as he saw them. It was evident to him that various atrocities had been committed. Not only were the prisoners crammed into three ships in the bay, which were subsequently bombed and destroyed, but those who managed to escape into the water were left to drown. He reported that three German motor launches available to put to sea 'only rescued SS men and sailors'. The rest of the survivors were ignored. And of those few hundred who made the shore, '150 were shot immediately'.

Christopher also discovered that a separate outrage had occurred not long before the RAF attack. Three huge river barges with about a thousand prisoners from Stutthof concentration camp on board had arrived in the bay after a week of torturous conditions, little food and hardly any water. Many had died during the voyage and their bodies had been dumped overboard. The barges had then been left near the anchored ships without guards in the early hours of 3 May and had drifted to shore during the night. As those on board jumped into the shallows, SS men appeared and shot dozens of them. Christopher 'saw about 100 bodies, old men, women, and children lying on the beach having been shot in the face at close range'.

From the journeys endured to reach the bay, to the air attacks which claimed so many lives, to the aftermath when German troops indiscriminately shot the survivors, Christopher had uncovered a complex knot of atrocity that encompassed a panoply of war crimes.

3.

Whilst the terrible deaths of thousands of camp inmates were being uncovered in Neustadt, Lieutenant Charlton of the 53rd Reconnaissance Regiment entered a small village outside Hamburg. He'd been ordered

by his commanding officer to investigate reports that another concentration camp had been found at Neuengamme.[7] The Bergen-Belsen
investigators had already put 21st Army Group on notice that a huge
camp operated there, having heard of its existence from survivors they'd
interviewed.[8] Charlton must have feared that he would find similar
scenes of death. But when he came to the north end of the camp the
place was deserted save for a civilian policeman. Prompted by the arrival
of the British Army unit, two men appeared. They said they were
former internees of the camp. Charlton asked them to show him around.

The camp was surrounded by watchtowers and barbed wire. More
wire divided up the various compounds inside. They entered the barrack
huts first, which were clean and empty. They moved on to the medical
experimentation centre, as the ex-prisoners called it. To Charlton it
appeared like a 'butcher's shop'. The interior had 'a stone floor, tiled walls
and a large concrete slab in the form of a table raised off the floor'. All
they found, though, were some rubber gloves and what he took to be a
'preserved human heart in a bottle'. The room smelled of disinfectant.

The internees showed Charlton to a small block consisting of
four or five cells and then to the crematorium. This too was clean
and orderly. In the room next to the furnaces Charlton found fifty
urns containing ashes. Each was stamped with the date of birth,
date of death and name of the deceased. In the corner was a large
pile of similar but unused urns.

Charlton and his guides toured the camp, the many huts, the factory,
staff living quarters 'luxuriously furnished', the brickworks, which
appeared only recently abandoned but were in excellent working
condition, a small arms factory, and the camp commandant's house.
Evidence of extermination and torture and death wasn't obvious.
Only the stories of the two internees revealed anything about the life
that had been lived here. The fate of the thousands of other inmates
was a mystery.

Charlton reported on what he'd found. It would be for the war
crimes investigators to take the matter further. In the meantime, the
camp had been left so accommodating that the British immediately
recognised its potential as an internment centre for all those SS men
being rounded up across the region. A concentration camp for concentration camp guards.

4.

Knowing that the inmates of Neuengamme had been evacuated before the Allies could reach them, any investigation of atrocities had to follow the survivors. The War Crimes Investigation Teams posted out to Germany were now split. No. 1 Team under Lt Col Genn was stationed at Bergen-Belsen. That was their focus, though they, with No. 2 Team, were also engaged in the investigation of nearby Sandbostel, a known prisoner-of-war camp to which was attached a compound of several thousand political prisoners, dumped on the camp commandant by the SS in the final weeks of the war, inmates from other concentration camps, mostly Neuengamme. The Guards Armoured Division had to fight to liberate Sandbostel, entering the camp on 29 April to find the British and American POWs reasonably well cared for, but the other inmates in the attached enclosure in a terrible condition. That part of the camp was a replica of Bergen-Belsen, though on a smaller scale. Mass executions had taken place. About 600 prisoners had purportedly tried to break out of the camp and had been slaughtered and buried in a mass grave ten days before the British troops arrived.[9] Even without the shootings, diarrhoea was 'universal' and deadly. The huts were found polluted by faeces; no food was available, a stagnant pool the only water supply.

One of the British officers made the decision to use local German civilians to help clear the place up. Sixty or seventy young women were gathered in the local town of Delmenhorst and brought to the camp without being told what they were to do. In the camp were many corpses, deposited in a large pit in the centre of the compound and dusted with lime. The women helped with the burial and then with caring for the prisoners who were still alive. German men were drafted in to dismantle the huts. The Royal Army Medical Corps (RAMC) and the Friends Ambulance Unit came to tend to the desperately ill. Typhus was the fear. Thousands of prisoners had already died of the disease.[10] Another thousand or more succumbed soon after the liberation.[11] Matters were so chaotic that the medical units at the camp couldn't even keep track of the living; Father Dewar-Duncan of No. 10 Casualty Clearing

Station wrote later that some patients would occasionally disappear from their sick beds never to return.[12]

Though not quite on the scale of Bergen-Belsen, the conditions and the suffering were similar. Here, though, no SS senior officers had been arrested. The prisoners had seen all the SS leave on 20 April. Identifying and then tracking down any culprits would be difficult. The lawyer Captain Stewart, who'd also been working at Bergen-Belsen and had taken Josef Kramer's statement, analysed the investigation reports. He concluded that the senior Nazi commanders in the area who'd ordered the transfer of prisoners from Neuengamme to Sandbostel 'must have realised what state the prisoners were in' and must therefore bear some responsibility for their condition. But Stewart acknowledged that establishing a culpable chain of command in such a horrendously chaotic environment would be hard.

If the team at Bergen-Belsen was struggling, so too was the one at Sandbostel. Both were under-strength. Bergen-Belsen had an official interpreter, though they were making use of a number of ex-inmates who spoke multiple languages. No linguist had been sent to Sandbostel. Only one or two 'specialist investigators' were with either team and they were still awaiting photographers and medical orderlies to collect and assess evidence. The 'shorthand writers are apparently the greatest problem', it was reported in the middle of June. 'It is essential for the proper working of these teams that they should be really first class stenographers capable of high speed and accurate work.'[13]

The lack of personnel of all descriptions meant that the investigation teams had to be selective in what they could do. They were still reacting to reports received by British Army Headquarters rather than establishing a clearly structured and functioning organisation. It was then that news arrived of a mass of concentration camp survivors found in Neustadt.

Major Noel Till was the man assigned to investigate the series of events that connected Sandbostel to Neuengamme and ultimately to the water and seashore at Neustadt. He was a member of No. 2 War Crimes Investigation Team and was sent into now British-occupied Schleswig-Holstein.

Till was a solicitor from Yorkshire before joining up, and from his notes and reports in the War Crimes Team files, I gathered he was straight-talking and prone to irascibility. Whether as a writer or interrogator, he rarely missed the opportunity to let his reader or witness know what he thought. His records of his team's investigations are riddled with asides that showed his tetchiness. Those who directed his tasks from above would be the targets for his ire. He would complain that his team had been interrupted in its work. He would complain that they had been given insufficient time. He would complain that he'd been forced to send his men to examine other investigations, leaving him with just one other officer to complete his work. His words would be infused with dissatisfaction and frustration. At one point he would apologise that 'the investigations have not been as thorough as the importance of this case warrants'. He didn't doubt, though, that he and his team had done a reasonable job. He was simply an exasperated professional prevented from performing his duty properly.

By the time I'd examined some of Till's letters and reports, I thought I'd gained a slender insight into his character, enough to think he was important in understanding the nature of British justice as well as the mystery of the *Cap Arcona* investigation. It was a fallacy of course. How could I know any man simply through the notes he recorded many years ago?

He intrigued me nonetheless and I set out to find out more about him. By then I knew his middle name (Oughtred) from seeing his full signature on a couple of official statements. It was unusual enough to make the search easier. When I browsed the obituary and announcements columns of *The Times* I found a few references: the birth of a son in 1937, an engagement of an elder son, Patrick Field Till, in 1963, the death of a wife, Marion Christine, in 1990. And then I found an announcement of Noel Oughtred Till's death on 18 January 1993 'peacefully at Orchard Court Nursing Home'.[14] For a moment I was disappointed. I'd had unrealistic visions of Till still being alive and talking to him about his investigations at Neustadt. It was a ridiculous hope given that by then he would have been well over 100 years old.

Perhaps as a substitute I searched the web for his son, who also had an unusual middle name. Entries appeared under the Law Society's register, which meant he was a solicitor like his father. That made sense to me. He was listed as having been admitted to the roll in 1960. He was still practising as a locum in a firm in North Yorkshire. That would make him in his late seventies, which would be about right. Besides, I couldn't imagine there would be two men with the same name and the same professional and county connections as the son I was looking for. I noted down the law firm's details and though it was late on a Friday afternoon I dialled the number. There was no answer. I resolved to phone again the following week. I wrote the number on an A4 piece of paper and fixed it to my wall with a drawing pin. Each day, I would look at it and think that I would ring the following day. But for weeks, months, I couldn't do it.

I read the papers of Noel Till's investigations instead.[15]

5.

The first person to be interviewed by Till's team was a young man, seventeen and a half years old. Phillip Jackson was a godsend for the investigators. He spoke English, was an American citizen, and was already working as an interpreter for the British medical team in Neustadt who were caring for the KZ survivors in the town. And he was one of the victims, not only of the bombing in the bay, but of Neuengamme and before that the Gestapo and SD in France. His account brought together the complex strands that Till had been ordered to investigate. It provided clear evidence of the various crimes committed. He gave his statement on 25 May 1945, only a few weeks after the disaster in the bay.

Jackson said he'd been living in Paris with his parents when the war broke out. His father was an American who'd practised as a surgeon at the American Hospital in Neuilly-sur-Seine. His mother was Swiss. He said that his parents had been heavily engaged in the Resistance. Their apartment on the avenue Foch was used as a postbox for messages. In May 1944, the Germans arrested all three of them. They were handed over to the Gestapo in Vichy and separated. Jackson said he spoke to other inmates in the cell where he was held who told him they'd been whipped and tortured. He saw one of his cellmates flogged. He too was whipped for failing to stand to attention. Jackson said conditions were brutal.

After three weeks he and his father were transferred to what he described as a concentration camp at Compiègne. It was in fact a military base used as a major transit camp for Jews and political prisoners in France to be transported to Auschwitz and other camps in Germany and beyond. That was the last time he saw his mother, he said. From Compiègne he and his father had been transported by train to Neuengamme.

Phillip Jackson's statement then went on to reveal the world and personalities and conditions of that camp. The statement was vivid in its detail.

> We were taken out in batches of a hundred and taken to some showers where we were deprived of our clothes and everything else we wore or carried, such as hernia belts, rings, watches and everything. Our heads and the remainder of our bodies were completely shaved. Then we had a bath, after which a most minute search was made of our naked bodies with lamps. Then we received a most miscellaneous collection of very old clothes, not even fit for a beggar to wear, and a pair of wooden shoes.

He explained how little food they were given each day, 'about one quarter of a 3lb loaf of black bread and one litre of cabbage or swede soup per person'. The accommodation was meagre too. 'Normally we had 500 men sleeping in one block, two to a bed, but often this would increase to 700. Conditions of living were absolutely foul – the stench was awful at night when all the windows were closed.'

Jackson knew some of the camp personnel by name. *SS-Obersturmbannführer* Max Pauly was the commandant. Jackson said he was the man responsible for all the deaths and the foul conditions. But his greater condemnation was directed at the *Lagerführer*, *SS-Obersturmführer* Anton Thumann.

> He was constantly going round the camp beating and whipping the prisoners and letting his large unmuzzled dogs loose on the prisoners. I saw this happen many times. One day when we were marching back

to the camp I saw him punch my *Kapo*, namely 7083 Fritz Schon, a German political prisoner, several times in the face because he said our column was not marching in step. He always attended the hanging of people and read the sentences and gave the order to hang.

Others were as bad. *SS-Oberscharführer* Willy Dreimann was in charge of the blocks where the prisoners were housed.

His hobby was riding around the camp on a bicycle with a leather whip beating the prisoners as he went. He was a sadist in every respect. He always attended all the hangings. On these occasions the prisoners were made to take their clothes off before they were hanged, and he used to shout 'Get a move on – the quicker you are, the quicker you will be dead' or words to that effect. I heard that sometimes these people were not killed outright, and afterwards Dreimann would go to the mortuary and strangle the bodies with his own hands.

Major Till must have read this and worried. His legal training would have told him the 'I heard that ...' was hearsay, it wasn't reliable, he wasn't an eyewitness.

Fortunately, Jackson's evidence was more robust when he talked about his departure from Neuengamme. He said that he and his father along with hundreds of other prisoners from the KZ were put on a train on 21 April 1945. They passed through Hamburg and arrived in Lübeck the next day. Most inmates were disembarked and taken away, but Jackson and his father, being a doctor, were left on board the wagons looking after the sick. They spent nearly ten days in that train, Jackson said, as the prisoners were too ill to move. They soiled themselves where they lay.

On 1 May, the sick prisoners still on the train were finally loaded onto a ship, the SS *Thielbek*, Jackson said. The only ones left behind were twenty typhus cases. The ship set sail at 2 p.m. on the 2nd, arriving in the bay off Neustadt in the evening. Nearby at anchor were the ocean liner SS *Cap Arcona* and the SS *Athen*. Jackson said the prisoners were packed in the holds. They had 200 grams of bread and half a litre of soup per day. The conditions were appalling. Then he related what had happened on the day the RAF attacked.

A small launch came alongside giving the orders from the British to report into harbour. The SS *Athen* went into port, not in obeyance of this order, but to pick up some more prisoners. At 1500 hrs Typhoons appeared in the sky over the ships and dropped eight bombs between the *Cap Arcona* and *Thielbek* which was evidently a warning for the ships to obey the order to go into harbour which they did not do. White flags were hoisted in lieu of the Nazi flags. About 15 minutes later Typhoons attacked first the *Cap Arcona* which blazed immediately all over, and sank onto its port side. I could see the decks black with people who did not jump.

The bombers returned to attack and sink the *Thielbek*. 'There were hundreds of people struggling to get on deck,' said Jackson, 'there was absolute chaos.' He was lucky.

I was on deck and I waited for about five minutes while the ship was sinking to see my father. I did not see him and so jumped overboard. Being a strong swimmer I reached one of the three German launches sent out and was taken on board. Once they knew that the people swimming around were prisoners, they merely circled looking for the officers and men of the ship's company and the German guards, they could have picked up hundreds of prisoners but they failed to do this. I even saw them push away prisoners who were trying to get on board.

Eventually the launches went to the shoreline where, Jackson said, 'about 100 prisoners were unloaded and were put against a wall of a nearby shed. We thought by the conduct of the German officers and seamen that they were going to shoot us.'

The execution didn't happen. It was only a threat.

Jackson's father wasn't one of the survivors. Jackson never saw him come on deck or jump into the water.

After a few hours lined up on the shore, the small party of survivors were told they were to be put on trucks and sent to Neustadt, where the English were waiting. Transported to the Marine barracks in the town, Jackson finally saw British troops.

About 5,000 prisoners were on the SS *Cap Arcona*, and 2,000 on the *Thielbek*, Jackson told the British investigators. He estimated that only about 500 escaped. Of these, he'd heard 150 had been shot by the SS when they'd managed to reach the shore.

Jackson's account of the bombing and its aftermath raised questions. Was he right that the bombers had dropped a warning cluster? Had white flags really been hoisted? And how did he know how many were on board the ships?

The lines of enquiry took Till in many directions: back to the camp at Neuengamme; out to the bay where German sailors had refused to rescue any of the survivors other than the SS guarding the ships; and along the seashore where prisoners may have been executed.[16]

6.

The evidence Major Till collected from Phillip Jackson served a double purpose. It not only helped to explain some of the events of 3 May, but it also brought the conditions at Neuengamme KZ into focus. Though the British forces in Hamburg were beginning to learn of the camp's history, the vast majority of those who could testify as to the specific atrocities committed there had been transported to Neustadt. Enough inmates had survived to identify SS men and women responsible. Jackson was one, and he gave the investigating team reason to look for more evidence. It might not have been like Bergen-Belsen, with its piles of corpses, but it was a brutal and deadly concentration camp nonetheless.

Another material witness then appeared. Again it was someone whom any investigator would recognise as both competent and credible. Charles Kaufmann was a doctor of medicine and an eye specialist who had survived the sinking of the *Cap Arcona* and had been placed in charge of the temporary hospital at Haffkrug, a few miles south of Neustadt. He'd already assisted the investigation by identifying one of his SS guards from Neuengamme.

His was a bitter story, perhaps more frightening than Jackson's. It began with his betrayal in Chalamont, where he was arrested in 1944 for tending to members of the Maquis, the French Resistance.

He said that five members of the *Milice*, the hated French militia formed by the Vichy regime in 1943 in collaboration with the German occupying forces and often proving more brutal than the Gestapo, willing to use torture and assassination against their countrymen, informed on him to the SS.

Like Jackson, Kaufmann was taken to the transit camp at Compiègne and from there transported in a cattle truck to Neuengamme. The ritualistic dehumanisation began on arrival. He said they were all crowded into the cellar of one of the blocks. The SS appeared and called for the priests to make themselves known. Several of them came forward and they were beaten with rifle butts, pistols, rubber hosing. Kaufmann knew one of them as Father Jacques from Bordeaux. Their torture was terrible, Kaufmann said. He believed they were taken from the cellar and then sent to Dachau, the camp favoured for arrested priests.

Being a doctor, Kaufmann was enlisted into the hospital staff once installed in the camp. He benefited from privileges and no longer lived in the main compound. But he saw things that reflected the depth of brutality in the KZ nonetheless.

The hospital, he said, was divided into four barracks. The first was for the *Kapos*, those inmates who worked for the SS. One of the barracks was 'respectable'. The other three 'were butcher's shops', the living lay with the dead, 'incredible filth, complete lack of treatment'. The German orderlies, who knew nothing of medicine, were Kaufmann's bosses. Kaufmann said *SS-Sturmmann* Rheinke gave fatal injections to patients, beat the sick remorselessly and 'always volunteered to assist at the hangings'. *SS-Rottenführer* Jäger was no better. Then there was a *Kapo* called Mathis Mai, a German political prisoner who was compelled to join the SS in 1944, Kaufmann said. This man 'voluntarily carried out unsuccessful operations which caused the deaths of hundreds of people. He was not qualified to act as a doctor.' Kaufmann said Mai would be asked by the SS to select patients to receive fatal injections.

Koebbels was also a *Kapo*. He was worse than the SS, 'if that was possible'. He'd been in prison since 1933. And there was Louts, who was 'a madman and a sadist'. He would 'walk into a crowd of prisoners and beat them until he became exhausted'. And Werner, another political: Kaufmann saw him bludgeon a prisoner to death with a soup ladle.

Two German doctors received Kaufmann's greatest scorn. The man in charge of the hospital, Dr Alfred Trzebinski, was most responsible, he said. Kaufmann estimated that 85 people a day had died there during his stay. Perhaps 40,000 in total, he said, though no clue was offered as to how he'd calculated the figure. And there was also Professor Heissmeyer. 'I have seen Heissmeyer perform some of his inhuman experiments, and in particular seen him inject tuberculosis into patients.' It was an indication that something sickening had been taking place at Neuengamme.

If Kaufmann's testimony stretched credulity, it wasn't long before the investigators had corroboration. On 23 May, Major Hill, a solicitor like Noel Till, interviewed another survivor from the disaster who supported and amplified Kaufmann's account. Tadeusz Kowalski was a doctor from Poland who'd been in Auschwitz and then transferred to Neuengamme in 1943. Such movement was not unusual in the absurd market of inmates that existed within the KZ system. Prisoners were constantly shifted from camp to camp. Kowalski said men and women without any medical qualifications were appointed to 'take care' of the sick. He spoke of SS-Obersturmführer Jäger, who'd learned surgery through practice not tuition. In one case at Neuengamme Jäger had wanted to carry out an appendix operation on a patient. Nothing was wrong with the inmate, but Jäger gave the patient an anaesthetic anyway, Kowalski said, then made a 'cut much too big and after making a search with his hand in the body' couldn't find the appendix and walked away. Another medic was left to sew the patient up.

According to Kowalski, Jäger would frequently try his hand at some surgery with catastrophic results. One prisoner needed a small incision into an infected hand wound, but Jäger was so clumsy he cut one of the main arteries. Unable to stop the bleeding, Jäger solved the crisis by amputating the patient's arm.

But it was the general approach to treating the sick which led to the most deaths. The standing order was that if a prisoner was 'too feeble to work' then 'he must die'. Jäger's method was to examine any prisoner reportedly too ill to work and then 'inject them with phenol or benzene'. They would die in a matter of minutes. He was assisted in his work by a couple of SS orderlies: Willi Bahr and August Beining, Kowalski said. They would kill between twenty and thirty men like this every couple of days.

Professor Heissmeyer was again identified as experimenting on prisoners supposedly in the name of medical research. He would inject bacteria taken from tuberculosis sufferers directly into the lungs of healthy patients to see what would happen. Over weeks he would X-ray the men, charting the development of the disease. Some were hanged and then dissected. Kowalski said these experiments were also 'carried out on 20 Jewish children from 4 to 15 years old'. He said they had glands, lymph nodes, taken out for examination. They were all driven away by the Gestapo with the doctors shortly before the camp was evacuated. Kowalski didn't know where the children had been taken.

All told, about 4,000 people had died in the hospital, Kowalski estimated. Many sick inmates were sent on to Bergen-Belsen or 'other extermination camps'.

7.

The flow of accusations continued as more witnesses were interviewed. Each had some terrible story to recount of treatment at one camp or another. It provoked a response back at army HQ, where some panic set in. On 8 June, the commanding officer of the British VIII Corps pleaded: 'This HQ has been inundated with reports of atrocities [from Neustadt]: some of these are accompanied by statements, many have no supporting evidence, and all of them require investigation. JAG Branch is at present giving advice on the evidence produced but owing to pressure of normal British court martial work, and smallness of staff, is quite unable to carry out investigations itself.'

Till and his team continued regardless. The stories of savagery wrapped up in the pretence of medical care in the Neuengamme 'hospital' troubled the investigators, echoing discoveries at Bergen-Belsen and reports of the experiments and treatment carried out by Josef Mengele at Auschwitz. Similar stories were heard from Dachau and Buchenwald. They didn't monopolise their attention, however. Major Till's instructions were to follow the evidence where it took him, not to be influenced by the first terrible accounts to come his way. Conditions at Neuengamme may have been particularly contemptible, but this didn't deflect him from pursuing *any* other complaint, no matter how insignificant in comparison.

It's probably too harsh to say the young Jewish girl Cila Sokoliska was a 'victim' of this approach. Then again, it's also hard to explain why she should have received such attention in the early days of Till's investigation. In one of his first interim reports to his superiors, she received more consideration than any of the so-called doctors or guards or SS officers at Neuengamme, more too than the attack against the ships. Maybe he saw in Cila something so tragic that she was worthy of his scrutiny. He could have ignored her. Instead, he treated her case with as much dedication as he applied to any of those SS men and women against whom the most appalling allegations were being made.

Cila Sokoliska was a name Till heard mentioned as soon as he began to interview a different cohort of survivors from the bay. Mostly women, these came from another large concentration camp. Stutthof KZ was on the Baltic coast, east of Danzig. For most of its existence it had been the hub of a system of labour camps. Towards the end of 1944, it changed character with a great influx of Jews as they were transferred from ghettos in Kaunas and Vilnius and Riga. Later still, Hungarian Jews arrived from Auschwitz and the camp became awash with inmates. With the Russians advancing quickly in January 1945 an evacuation of the camp began in line with the policy that no concentration camp prisoner should be allowed to fall into enemy hands. By April, those 3,000 or so inmates still left at Stutthof main camp were marched to the port at Danzig and put on huge river barges. Many women were amongst them and they were to be trans-ported west along the coast.

On 29 June, Major Till questioned some of the women who'd made the journey. Dora Rabinowitz was twenty-two, Jewish and from Memel in Lithuania. In 1941, she said, she and her family had been

forced into the ghetto prepared by the Germans for Lithuanian Jews
in Schaulen. The ghetto was liquidated in June 1944 and the survivors
taken to Stutthof. It was another of those epicentres around which
dozens of sub-camps were clustered. Like Neuengamme, its regime
was vicious and designed to kill off those prisoners who could serve
no purpose. And, like Neuengamme, its personnel were dedicated to
brutality.

Till asked Rabinowitz about her time in Stutthof. She described
how they dug anti-tank ditches. They lived in tents and, with the
onset of winter, worked outside without coats or stockings. Was she
badly treated? Till asked.

Yes.

By anyone in particular?

Yes, Hans Graf from Danzig, a member of the SS.

Till wanted to know about others, about the SS women in
particular. What were they like?

'They were worse than the SS men,' she said. 'I have seen SS
women beating children to death.'

Till asked for the names of these women. 'The worst was the chief
SS girl, called Sorakap.' It was a nickname. Dora didn't know her real
name, but could describe her as pretty, with brown curly hair, brown
eyes.

'I have seen her beating a man to death,' a man found in the
women's camp and whom Sorakap had set about with a rubber
truncheon.

Her treatment of the women was consistently cruel. She would
make them strip and stand naked outside for hours on end whilst she
beat them.

Till asked about the SS men. Rabinowitz talked about those at the
ghetto in Lithuania. *Obersturmführer* Krause. He was especially bad,
she said. He was in charge of killing the Jews. Of the 180,000 in
Lithuania when the Germans came, only 8,000 were left once Krause
had completed his work. He was the man responsible, she said. At
Stutthof KZ, *Oberscharführer* Voth was in charge of the Jewish section
of the camp.[17]

'He was a sadist. Every morning we had to stand at six o'clock on
the *Appellplatz*. He came at seven or eight.' He would inspect their

barracks. If they weren't clean they would go without food for two days.

Rabinowitz was appointed as one of the women block police, similar to a *Kapo*, an overseer in one of the offices. Till wanted to know whether that meant she had to beat people. Yes, but it could be avoided, she said. She was given a leather belt to hit people with, although she admitted it wasn't obligatory to use it.

Till pressed her. He was on the scent of some trail. 'Some *Kapos* and other people in such positions as yours say that it was quite impossible to keep discipline unless they had beaten people.'

'It could happen,' said Dora. 'Once I was obliged to beat a little girl.'

Till ignored that and didn't ask for details.

'As a rule you found it was not necessary?'

'It wasn't necessary at all.'

'Wouldn't a *Kapo* get into trouble from the SS if he didn't carry out a good many beatings?'

Dora's answer was ambiguous. She seemed to be saying that beatings weren't expected, didn't come with the job, although the prospect of violence was ever-present.

Till had a reason for this line of questioning. He'd heard the name of another young woman in the camp whom other witnesses said had been particularly keen on beating fellow inmates. Her name was Cila Sokoliska, also Jewish. Till asked Rabinowitz whether she knew of her.

Yes, she was in charge of the potato-peeling party in the kitchens. Had she seen her beating anyone? No, but she saw that everyone was afraid of her. Was she a friend of another *Kapo*, a man? Yes. Did she know anything about this friendship? She only knew that they ate together and cooked together. They stayed together. Was she more or less living with this man? Having relations with him? Till asked. I suppose it was true, Rabinowitz said.

The matter seemed important to Till. Sleeping with one of the *Kapos* was an indication that she'd collaborated with the enemy.

Major Till's examination of another witness elicited a more condemnatory reference to Cila. Seventeen-year-old Nelly Schonfeld had come to Stutthof in 1944 having first been at Auschwitz. She said Stutthof was worse. She had known Cila well.

'What was Cila like?' Till asked.

'She was very bad. She was beating everybody for no reason at all.'

'Do you think Cila was better, as bad, or worse than most *Kapos*?'

'She was generally very, very bad,' Schonfeld said. Cila had no need to beat people. 'She just wanted to show her strength.'

Till asked whether Cila beat some people more than others.

'She mostly beat Hungarians.' Hatred was common between the Poles and the Hungarians, which Schonfeld didn't understand. 'We are all Jews,' she said.

Whatever the reason, she told Till that she'd been beaten by Cila daily.

'She beat me with a rubber stick.' It was 80 centimetres long, about three fingers wide.

Over the coming days, Till asked more questions about Cila Sokoliska. Lea Dolin, a thirteen-year-old Latvian girl, and her mother Dora, Relli Kaen from Romania, Elvira Jonas, Cescha Diner: they all gave evidence as to Cila's propensity to beat prisoners.

Finally, Till questioned Sokoliska herself. On 30 June 1945, he brought his interpreter and shorthand writer to the displaced persons camp at Neustadt and subjected her to lengthy cross-examination. It was transcribed and typed up for the files.

Cila was twenty years old and had been in the hands of the Germans since their invasion of Poland. First in the ghetto in Vilnius, then in the Riga concentration camp before being taken to Stutthof in September 1944. She contracted typhus, received no treatment, but managed to recover. She was taken to the 'potato *Kommando*', a work party assigned to peel potatoes.

'Then one day an SS guard came along and told me: "You will watch now that these women peel potatoes."' That was the beginning of her role as *Kapo*.

The male *Kapo* in charge, another inmate, was called Heinrich. Major Till wanted to know about this character's relationship with Cila.

'Is it true that you became friendly with him?'

'He was not bad to me, although he beat me now and then. It's true that he gave me things to eat because I cooked for him.'

'People have suggested that you were his lover; is that true?'

'He was a man aged 60!'

'It's been suggested by several witnesses that you had a baby in the camp.'

'Yes, that is true. That was after the typhus.'

'What happened to that baby?'

'The child died.'

It was a perfunctory, punishing line of questioning. Till didn't let up.

'Who was the father of that baby; do you know?'

Sokoliska didn't react to the suggestion implicit in the question, other than to say, 'A Polish prisoner. He was a Polish POW, an officer who was also in the camp.'

By then Till must have realised that newborn children were unlikely to survive in the KZ. Any 'care' that babies required would be anathema to the whole concept of the *Lager*. It would have meant recognising the delivery of a human being. And inmates, generally, and Jews in particular, were not regarded with such generosity. They were nothing, beneath human, *Untermenschen*. How could a child be expected to live in such conditions, without proper food or nourishment? How could a mother, denied these things too, look after a baby? Though some young children did survive in the camps, it was a rarity.

Till didn't even ask what happened to Cila's child, how it had died.

'Now,' he said, 'what have you got to say about these accusations that you were always beating people?'

And Cila just told him that that was how it was. She never beat anyone without a reason. She used a rubber truncheon given to her by the male *Kapo*. 'When he gave the order that such-and-such a woman had to be beaten I had to do it.'

Was it impossible to carry out her duties without beating people? Till asked.

'Yes … it was impossible to give an order without implementing it with beatings.'

Many people had testified that she was cruel, Till told her. Why was that? Why had so many people made these allegations?

She didn't know. But, she said, 'After the birth of my child I became tubercular. I was sick with tuberculosis.'

'Is that any excuse why you should beat people?' Till asked.

'No, I am not saying that … I have only beaten them when I was forced to, when I had to … After I had the child I went for work, then I became sick … one day I had a nervous breakdown. That was when I was told by a woman doctor I was suffering from tuberculosis.' And, she said, people turned against her. They thought she was of a different class and began to dislike her. That's why they had picked her out now to accuse.

Till asked about her family, as though finally feeling sympathy for the Jewish girl who'd been in German concentration camps since she was sixteen or seventeen.

'I know definitely that my mother is not alive … When the ghetto was liquidated we were about 10,000 in a big square. 1,800 young women were picked in order to be sent to the concentration camp at Riga. What happened to the older women and the children I can imagine. My mother and all my relations were with them.'

And as though he had to pursue this young woman to the very end, Till asked, 'Is it not true that you more or less sold yourself to the Germans because you were having such a terrible time and you wanted to save yourself?'

'It wasn't a question of selling oneself. Nobody asked whether he wanted this type of job or not. Nobody asked me whether I wanted it.'

Much more was to be said, about her survival from the sinking ships in Neustadt Bay and the SS killings afterwards. But Till had to return to her guilt at the close of his questioning. He couldn't let the young woman rest.

'Are you sorry now, when it's all over, that you acted as you did?'

'Yes,' Cila said, 'that is one of the reasons why I am still so sick.'

A month later, Noel Till submitted his interim report on the Neustadt investigations. Twenty-two exhibits accompanied a long list of persons suspected of committing war crimes. Amongst them were the doctors who'd experimented on the Jewish children and killed off the sick with lethal injections of phenol: Professor Heissmeyer and *Rottenführer* Jäger, the commandant of Neuengamme KZ, Max Pauly, along with the sadistic second in command, Anton Thumann, and the hospital orderly, Willi Bahr, who'd injected the phenol into countless inmates, were all on that list. These men were responsible for thousands of deaths. Yet of the twenty-two exhibits ten contained accusations against the young Jewish woman Cila Sokoliska. He devoted a passage of analysis to her case too.

Summarising the evidence from the witnesses still in the displaced persons compound, Noel Till wrote about Sokoliska, 'There was a considerable amount of feeling – both "for" and "against" – and the question was therefore thrashed out at some length.' But he decided that 'by no stretch of the imagination could this girl, who had been coerced into being a *Kapo*, be said to have been acting "in support of Germany"'. Rather than lay any charges against her, he said he'd handed her over to the Polish Jewish Elder of the displaced persons camp. No mention of the child she'd borne and none of what had happened to her at the hands of the Elder afterwards. Till concluded his report with some justification for his action. Was it also some attempt at atonement?

'I felt that whilst there is undoubtedly evidence on which a jury could convict, on the other hand, no judge would wish to inflict further punishment on this young girl who has already suffered so much and who, if she does not die soon, will suffer from TB she contracted during her captivity, for the rest of her life. I strongly recommend that no action be taken in her case.'

That anyone would think otherwise, that anyone would compare Cila's case with those hundreds of SS guards, doctors, administrators who ran Neuengamme camp, who undertook those experiments and killed inmate after inmate, is hard to believe. And in hindsight, it's hard to stomach.

After reading the records and transcripts, I remembered the number I had for Noel Till's son. Should I ring after all and ask about his father, the kind of man he was, whether he'd related any of his stories from his wartime investigations, whether he'd mentioned Cila or the *Cap Arcona* or anything about Neustadt Bay? He might be able to shed light on matters that had become increasingly important to me. But having avoided ringing over many months for a reason I couldn't articulate or even intuitively understand, something continued to hold me back.

And then, one Tuesday afternoon I came back to my office from a meeting, saw the number on the paper I'd pinned to the wall, picked up the phone and dialled. It rang several times and then a female voice with a strong Yorkshire accent answered.

I asked to speak to Patrick Till. He wasn't there, she said. He only worked on Mondays and Fridays.

I said I would call back.

8.

Even as I was reading the files on Sokoliska and Till's inquiries I knew I was being deflected, perhaps just as Till had been. Something about Cila's case distracted me. It registered a discordant note about the British investigations, hinted at some flaw or misjudgement.

And yet I had sympathy for Noel Till. Many people clearly had cause to complain about Cila's conduct at Stutthof. Some of them had suffered brutally at her hands. They must have hated her. Amidst a place defined by cruelty, they'd seen one of their own, another Jew, another *Häftlinge*, mete out punishments without compunction. It was a point Till was keen to emphasise during his questioning: had others in Cila's position been less willing to hit out? If so, then Cila had exercised a choice: she had chosen to inflict pain on those around her, perhaps for personal gain and favour, perhaps sadistically. And that made her culpable, one of the SS by association, one of the enemy. In the eyes of a lawyer looking to pursue those guilty of crimes, Cila was an accused. She had become one of the abhorred, indistinguishable from the German guards and overseers. But she hadn't killed anyone as far as the evidence told. She'd treated women terribly, but none had died at her hands.

Was that the difference, the circumstance that allowed Till to absolve her in his own mind? She was not in the same category as the compliant inmates, the German political or criminal prisoners who'd become *Kapos* in Neuengamme. Even so, he clearly found it a moral dilemma, enough to explain very carefully his decision not to recommend charges against Cila in his report.

I wondered whether this was a quandary troubling other investigators in the War Crimes Investigation Teams, as the role of the *Kapos* came to light in all the camps. It didn't appear so. Several were in custody at Bergen-Belsen and most were under consideration for prosecution alongside their SS masters and indistinguishable when it came to alleging guilt.

The history of the *Kapo* within the KZ system has provoked considerable unease. For here were individuals who were victims themselves, inasmuch as they were prisoners like everyone else in the camps. That was part of the malevolent logic that contributed to the whole culture of the KZ. Place the vulnerable in positions of power with the promise of better treatment if they did as they were told and severe punishment if not, and suddenly the discipline becomes a matter that can be left in the hands of human nature.

It's hardly surprising then that the rank-and-file inmates would have hated the *Kapos* who acted as the SS's enforcers. Who would not? As the direct physical link with continual beatings and punishment, they had to be detested by those whom they tortured every day. In Buchenwald the investigators learned about the particularly heinous contribution of several *Kapos* in the killings of prisoners. One named Gross was described as a Jewish professional criminal who had helped select Jewish workers for execution. Gross was killed in the camp by his fellow inmates, so it was reported.[18] One of the authors of the Buchenwald report, Eugen Kogon, was himself a political prisoner from Austria and in Buchenwald throughout the war. He gave a nuanced description of the *Kapos* and the block orderlies appointed to be in charge of labour details and day-to-day barrack discipline respectively. Both had authority to maintain order.

'There were certain prisoners of low character, of course,' he wrote, 'who shamefully misused this authority. It is true that they were often under considerable pressure from the SS. Many of them, regardless of the colour they wore and even in the Jewish barracks, were unable to withstand the temptation to brutality and corruption.'[19]

The SS appointed those who 'knew how to wield a club, though the SS often enough let them feel the end of it themselves'. On the whole the *Kapos* were a 'horde of brutes' though there were exceptions. But no matter what base traits these men and women displayed, was their behaviour conditioned as much by their own suffering as their innate tendencies? Kogon wrote about the general deterioration of the prisoners when inside the camp, whoever they were. He said, 'The change in mentality was by no means a simple matter of good or evil, conceived as standards of value. Both aspects pervaded it. Its main characteristic was a process of regression to a more primitive state ... This regression with its opposites of good and evil pervaded every mental quality. Some grew hard in order to be able to help, just as a physician, in his capacity as a man, has feelings and yet, in his capacity as a healer, has none. Others developed a cruelty that ranged from repressed sexual impulses all the way to sadism.'[20]

Viktor Frankl, a survivor of Auschwitz and noted psychiatrist, wrote in his memoirs that 'the baseness of a prisoner who treated his own compatriots badly was exceptionally contemptible'.[21] But he still acknowledged that life in 'a concentration camp tore open the human soul and opened its depths'. Was it 'surprising that in those depths we again found only human qualities which in their very nature were a mixture of good and evil'?

To what extent then could these men and women be held responsible for their actions? I don't doubt that one could answer this in many ways, using many different arguments, legal or moral. Primo Levi, though, questioned the prudence of moral *judgement* except, perhaps, by 'those who found themselves in similar circumstances and had the possibility to test on themselves what it means to act in a state of coercion'.[22] He relied on the old saw that 'power corrupts', something which was accentuated for the *Kapo* in the unnatural environment and life of the camp. They had unlimited power to impose violence, he said, at least until 1943, when the desire to retain a functioning workforce suddenly became important for the Nazi war effort and indiscriminate punishment was reduced. And in his estimation this power attracted certain types: the common criminal who saw the *Kapo* position as an 'alternative to detention'; political prisoners who had been broken over years of life in the *Lager*; 'Jews who saw in the particle of authority that was being offered them the only possibility of escaping the "final solution"'. Many, Levi said, sought the position because they were sadists or were 'the oppressed who were contaminated by the oppressors and unconsciously strove to identify with them'.

But if the role of *Kapo* attracted a variety of characters, how could you know the kind who was in front of you? How could Major Till have known, even if he'd had the luxury of time to truly investigate psychologically whether Cila Sokoliska was a sadist or an unconscious mimic of her oppressors or simply a young woman reduced to a state of emotionlessness in her struggle to live? If she'd been given, rather than sought, the position, which was her story, would that have made a difference? Levi said that all *Kapos* 'gave beatings: this was an obvious part of their duties, it was their more or less accepted language; after all, it was the only language that could truly be understood by everyone in that perpetual Babel'. The beating, the strike with fist or club or truncheon, 'was understood as an incitement to work, a warning or punishment, and in the hierarchy of suffering it had a low rank'.

Where did this leave Cila? One thing upon which Levi was adamant: to confuse the *Kapos* 'with their victims is a moral disease or an aesthetic affectation or a sinister sign of complicity'. It would suggest that however much one might want to understand why Cila acted as she did, this couldn't preclude judgement.

Maybe Noel Till thought the same. Maybe he first saw in Cila that creature who would take advantage of power bestowed on her in inhuman circumstances for her own benefit and that she should therefore face the consequences. Maybe he identified her as the epitome of innocence corrupted, where innocence was no defence when it finally gave way to base behaviour.

Whatever Till's reasoning may have been (and who can tell from an official report and scraps of letters and jottings and interview transcripts?), something in the woman he cross-examined must have told him she was not *culpable*. Though he didn't discount punishment, leaving the matter to others, he didn't want the legal process to be instigated. In that, he exercised a judgement where judgement was impossible. Why he spent so much time on the matter mystifies me, though. But his deliberation has to be valued. Whether it was replicated in all the other camp investigations conducted seems unlikely.

The *Kapo* was as much a target for prosecution as the SS guards and officers.[23]

So rather than question how Noel Till could have taken Cila Sokoliska's behaviour so seriously, it might be more appropriate to ask: how could he not? Such matters weren't an issue for the Nuremberg Trial to come. It was only mentioned in the context of the morally indefensible method of maintaining discipline through forcing camp inmates to control and punish themselves. The *Kapo* system was described as an indication of the evil intent of the camps: to make the prisoners complicit in their own extermination. That didn't erase the need to assess culpability on the ground.

9.

Cila Sokoliska may have been a shamed witness, shamed by her malleability, but what she had to say about the final moments of her own captivity was not ignored by Till. It confirmed other strands of his investigation that linked the KZ at Stutthof to the Neustadt chaos.

'What happened when you left Stutthof?' Till asked Sokoliska.

'We came in a ship.'

'What sort of ship was it?'

'It was a barge.'

'How many barges were there?'

'Three. There were two barges and one ship.'

'How many would there be in each barge?'

'Nine hundred.'

'Do you know how many there were in the ship?'

'I should think more than a thousand.'

Till asked her what the voyage had been like. She said it'd been very bad. 'During seven days we received only one issue of bread. We had sea water to drink and many people became sick from that … There were many who died and were thrown into the sea.'

When they'd arrived in Lübeck, she said, they'd heard the British were near.

How must she and the other *Kapos* have felt at this news? Would she have dreamed of liberation or feared it? But how could you fear something that would bring relief from your own torment even if it meant the possibility of retribution?

The British hadn't come then, the rumour was inaccurate, and the barges had put out to sea.

'One evening we saw that the SS who were our guard and the captain of the barge, with his family, were taking the lifeboats from our ships, lowering them into the water and leaving us. That was about 10 o'clock at night.'

Cila went on, 'We were not far from land ... about three to four kilometres ... We could see land.'

With the SS gone, the inmates tried to get to shore. Some lifeboats were left on board and some of the Norwegian prisoners, a sea captain among them, launched them and began to pull the barge towards land. By 4 o'clock in the morning they were about 100 metres away.

'The tide was still in and the Norwegians tried to put the people ashore in the small lifeboat, five or six people at a time. Then I saw how the Russians took boards off the ship and made a sort of float.'

'Did everybody get off the boat?'

'No.'

'What happened to the people who were left; do you know?'

'Those who were able to get ashore during the night were all right, but towards 8 o'clock in the morning the SS and naval personnel came.' Some clambered onto the barge that had washed onto the shore. 'We saw the SS and the marine guards standing on the deck of the barge. I saw how they shot into the little lifeboats ... They also shot the people who were not able to walk on land themselves because they were too weak.'

'Where were you when you saw this shooting take place?'

'I was on shore lined up.'

Till didn't ask for more details. Her account chimed with others and perhaps he'd already made the decision that she wouldn't be useful as a witness.

I couldn't find any further mention of Cila Sokoliska in the Neustadt investigation files and I don't know whether she survived for very long beyond the war. I don't know what the Jewish Elder decided should be her punishment either. All I know is that she didn't feature as a witness in any of the subsequent trials that the British held. Her evidence was tainted, and her evidence was ignored. Instead, she disappeared into that small group of survivors, forgotten and never honoured on some memorial along the waterfront.

On the Friday after my failed attempt to speak to Noel Till's son, I rang his office again. The same woman answered as before. I asked to speak to Mr Till. She told me he wasn't in. I asked when he might be back. He's had an accident, she said. She wasn't sure when he would return. I could ring the following week to see if there was any news.

10.

If Sokoliska faded from the records, Dora Rabinowitz, for a time a *Kapo* of a kind herself, did not. She spoke English and seemed dependable enough to be employed as an interpreter in the displaced persons camp in Neustadt. Unlike Cila, she acknowledged the difficulty of her role in Stutthof. She acknowledged that she'd hit someone, but had avoided violence where she could.

Dora was easy to trace. It didn't take me long, even though she'd changed her name when she'd married after the war. Like Cila, she'd been diagnosed with tuberculosis whilst being cared for by the British and was treated in the medical facility at Neustadt. She met a British soldier there called Frank Love. He began to visit her regularly during her recovery. In January 1946 they were married. Dora then worked for the British Army for a time and was employed by the newly formed United Nations relief organisation, staying in Hamburg to set up a home for Jewish child survivors in the suburb of Blankeness, not that far from the Neuengamme camp. Her project aimed to look after Jewish children who'd been hidden from the Nazis, survived the war and now needed some permanent home. She managed to help hundreds of youngsters. For years after they organised regular reunions. They called themselves 'Dora's children'.

Dora and her husband moved to South Africa in the 1950s, where she worked as a teacher. Much later they came to Britain and settled in Colchester, Essex. She worked at Greyfriars Community College and only retired in 2002 when her husband died. She continued to talk to audiences both in Britain and South Africa about her experiences during the war, forging a link with Essex University's history department. The university awarded her an honorary doctorate in 2009. She told her audience in her acceptance speech: 'And what can you say other than never give up, not for yourself, not for anybody else, there's always something you can do.'

I don't know whether she ever spoke about the moral complexities of her role in Stutthof. She may have admitted to beating a young girl to Major Till, but no malice was apparent in the act, no ideologically inspired hatred for the girl she said she'd hit, no evil intent that could be extracted from her testimony or her demeanour. And no one had made any complaint against her either. I feel uncomfortable even mentioning the testimony she gave back in May 1945. But Primo Levi was in favour of honesty and acceptance of the ambiguous position in which all inmates were placed during their time in the KZs. They occupied a 'grey zone', he said, and those of us who look on their actions and what they said of their experiences should not judge them. Still, she said what she said and she did what she did. Every year Essex University awards a prize in her name. She died in 2011.[24]

In June 1945, Dora Rabinowitz gave evidence to Noel Till just as Cila had done. She also told him about the journey from Stutthof to Neustadt on the barges, providing a first-hand account of the camp evacuations that brought so much death and suffering during the last phase of the KZ system. She confirmed the absence of provisions, of food or water, the deaths from drinking sea water. Till was dumbfounded. Despite all the terrible stories he'd heard already, he couldn't quite believe it. Dora said they were in the barges for eight days without anything and Till said, incredulously, 'You mean positively without anything at all?'

That he should be so bewildered after seeing so many malnourished and dishevelled survivors I find odd now.

'Only the sea water.'

'Did anybody drink the sea water?'

'Yes.'

'What happened to them?'

'Half of them died on this ship.'

'Do you mean that seriously?'

'Yes.'

When they arrived in Lübeck, the SS guards disembarked, Dora said. During the night the prisoners worked to pull the barge she was on to shore. When the barge grounded, most of the prisoners jumped into the water and waded or swam to the beach. Many were left behind, too weak to raise themselves. Those who did make it to land weren't in much better shape. They were starving and parched. With dawn breaking they were found by local villagers wandering about the gardens, searching for food. They'd eat anything, roots, raw potatoes, anything.

No pity was shown. The sight of those emaciated skeletons elicited fear, not sympathy. Villagers telephoned the local police. Calls were received in the town about marauding convicts.

Then the SS arrived. The straying prisoners were rounded up by a detachment of police and navy men, Dora said. They were taken to Neustadt.

'What did they do with the people left on the barges?' Till asked.

'Shot them.'

It was that blunt.

'How did they do that?'

The police and navy men went out to the barges and shot them. Simple. She saw everything from the shore.

Was anyone shot on land?

Those too weak to walk to Neustadt were killed where they lay.

And then?

They had been taken into Neustadt only to board another ship. That's when the British bombers had attacked. They'd been taken off the ship and were being marched through the streets when their German guards had suddenly thrown away their weapons and darted into houses. The British tanks had arrived.

Till brought the interview to a close. Later in September 1945 he went to see her again. This time she was more specific about those responsible for the killings she'd seen. She placed the blame on the

Marines who came with the police to round up the prisoners who'd managed to get to shore and look for food. When the police officer in charge had given the order for the barges to be cleared, she said the Marines hadn't hesitated. They 'were young fellows and very keen ... they at once rushed onto the barges and shot not only those who were too weak to get themselves off the barges but also those who had got into the water and were doing their best to reach the shore'. She reckoned that seventy people were executed in this way. And the killing didn't stop. If you fell down and couldn't carry on, the police or Marines would shoot you. They weren't drunk. They were enjoying it. She had tried to help an old man. Another policeman had refused to shoot anyone, throwing away his ammunition. He'd come to help her and told her to get the old man's wet clothes off and grab some dry ones from a dead prisoner. As she was doing so, another police officer struck her across the head with his rifle. It dazed her, she said, so much so that she couldn't help anyone any more. The old man wasn't mentioned again.

Dora Rabinowitz's recollections suggested that a separate atrocity had been committed on KZ prisoners just *before* the SS *Cap Arcona* had been bombed. The barges which she and Cila Sokoliska and nearly a thousand others had been aboard had been moored near the ships that would be attacked on 3 May, but they had reached shore several hours before the Typhoons carried out their strike. It was at that earlier time that the weakest survivors had been shot.

Gradually, Till formed a better sense of what had happened that morning. He interviewed a thirteen-year-old German boy called Helmut Moller, who lived in a village along the coast near Neustadt. His house was very close to the sea. He could look out across the water from his bedroom window. He remembered the morning of the 3rd very well.

'I heard footsteps just as it was getting light and looking out of the window I saw people who I took to be prisoners. A neighbour came and told us to keep the doors locked as they were people from a concentration camp.'

Helmut couldn't have been too afraid, because at 7 a.m. he went into Neustadt for some shopping. On the way, he saw prisoners lying on the ground or walking aimlessly about the lanes.

'When I got to the bridge,' Helmut said, 'I saw two groups of men marching. One group was SS and police mixed and the other group Marines ... they were marching towards the foreshore.'

Helmut said he finished his shopping and returned home. The very normality of that behaviour, surrounded as he was by the walking dead from the barges, seemed bizarre to me. More so given what happened next. On his way back, he said, 'I saw a Jewish woman, dead, with her head burst open. I went straight home and there were three other bodies lying outside. Other bodies were lying about.'

He said, 'Stragglers continued to come past the house and some laid down on the grass. Near the house by the harbour entrance I saw a prisoner leaning against a tree. One of the guards shot him.'

Witness statements rarely expose the emotion that lies hidden beneath any story. They're usually drafted by lawyers who are more concerned with matters that can be proved, not feelings that can be doubted. But this boy's account wasn't as anodyne as it read. Its direct and terse nature was more powerful than hysterical hyperbole. That it should have come from a teenager (was he in the Hitler Youth, was he feeling the patriotic need to join the fighting as so many young boys were throughout Germany, rushing to its defence following the call from their Führer?) lent it added weight. The investigation team must have thought so too. With all the evidence accumulated, the shootings on the shore were now labelled a 'massacre'. It was enough to sustain interest in the investigation for another two years, though none of that effort would come to anything. Neither Helmut Moller nor Dora Rabinowitz was ever called to tell their story to a court of law.

11.

Even though the conditions in Neuengamme, the massacre of the prisoners from Stutthof on the shores of Neustadt Bay and to a lesser extent the individual culpability of Cila Sokoliska, one of many *Kapos*, took up much of Till and his team's time, the bombing of the ships by the RAF hadn't been forgotten. The sheer number of casualties demanded attention. If the prisoners had been placed there with the intention to put them in jeopardy, then that had to be some kind of crime.

The starting presumption of the investigation was that the attack amounted to a mistake on the part of the RAF brought about by the callous negligence, perhaps even wilful design, of the Nazis in charge of the ships. Colonel Christopher, who was one of the first English officers on the scene to discover what had happened, made no comment about the RAF's role. He drafted a simple statement of fact that the ships had been attacked. There was no criticism in the observation. His disgust was directed at the way in which the SS had refused to rescue the prisoner survivors and had shot many of those who'd made it to shore despite the cold and their injuries.

Major Till was less sanguine about the bombing. He'd discovered from his interviews that several thousand camp prisoners from both Neuengamme and Stutthof had been distributed across ships in the bay. The SS *Cap Arcona* held the most, as many as 5,500 according to one statement, but at least 4,000 according to others. The ship was crowded and at first the Captain, Captain Bertram, had objected to having them on board. He'd been ordered to take the prisoners and told that they would be transported to Sweden as part of a deal between the Swedish Red Cross representative, Count Folke Bernadotte, and Himmler. About 2,000 prisoners, mostly the sick, partly under the charge of Dr Jackson, Phillip's father, were put on the SS *Thielbek* in Lübeck and then towed out into Neustadt Bay. They left behind 182 bodies to be buried in the town cemetery.

Another ship, the SS *Deutschland*, was in the process of being converted into a hospital ship. Some witnesses suggested to Till that a couple of thousand other prisoners had been on board, but that had yet to be verified. And one more vessel, the SS *Athen*, carried another 2,000 prisoners and had been moored at Neustadt dock.

Till sketched a timeline of events. On 2 May 1945, the British entered Lübeck. Waiting for them was an International Red Cross official, Paul de Blonay.[25] He knew about the thousands of KZ prisoners on board the various vessels in the harbour. De Blonay told

Major Till that he'd spoken to an English 'brigadier', possibly Major General George Roberts, and informed him of the ships and their human cargo that day. He'd assumed the details had been passed on to RAF intelligence. According to Till's report one of his team of investigators, Lieutenant Ansell, had already spoken to an RAF intelligence officer who'd admitted he'd received a message about the prisoners and the ships in the bay on 2 May, but due to some oversight the information hadn't been passed on to the RAF squadrons operating in the area.

Till's report outlined what had happened the next day, 3 May. He said that at 14.45 hours eight RAF Typhoons based at Hustedt attacked the ships with rockets and bombs. The *Cap Arcona* was hit first. 'The ship caught fire almost immediately and after a very short time the ship was ablaze. The order to abandon ship was given.' None of the fire hoses were workable, and no lifeboats could be deployed. Captain Bertram hoisted a white flag. And the badly holed ship turned onto its port side and settled in the water.

Soon after the *Cap Arcona* had been targeted, the Typhoons turned on the SS *Thielbek*. That too was hit and sunk within a matter of minutes. The SS *Deutschland* was also destroyed. Only the SS *Athen* was left, docked in Neustadt harbour though already abandoned by the guards and crew.

Between the three ships there were some 7,000 or more prisoners out in the bay. The vast majority died in the holds, where they'd been imprisoned for days. They had no time to free themselves and make it on deck let alone to dive into the water. Some managed to escape. A few hundred ended up in the sea struggling to survive.

It was a terrible vision conjured by Till's report. I imagined he must have been deeply affected by it.

In the week after hearing of his accident, I rang Till's son's office number again. The woman recognised my voice. She apologised and said Mr Till still hadn't returned. She wasn't sure when he would be back. He'd fallen down some stairs and was recovering at home. Leave it a week or two and ring back by all means, she said. Hopefully there would be better news then.

I put down the phone. I was angry with myself. For a year I'd avoiding ringing that number. Now I feared I'd lost the chance to speak to Noel Till's son. He was in his late seventies after all.

12.

It wasn't until I heard the slightly high-pitched and rather plaintive speech of Piet Ketelaar that the catastrophe in the bay became more than a few rough statements and the product of my imaginings.[26] I couldn't tell either his age or his nationality from his voice. The accent that disrupted his English sounded Scandinavian: many 'sh's and hard 'ch's marked his speech. To me, sitting in the Imperial War Museum research room a few months after my visit to Neustadt, the effect was hypnotic. I was listening to a tape of his interview with the temperature outside hitting a rare 30 °C that summer, so I was already in something of a soporific state. It didn't take long before the voice ceased to be irksome and became puzzling instead. I wondered: how could this man speak so softly and calmly about such experiences?

The recording was made in 1987 as part of the museum's programme of capturing the voices of people who'd been in the war. Thousands of these sound archives exist, interviews with anyone, it seems, who had something to remember about conflicts since 1914. The museum is slowly digitising the recordings, but Piet Ketelaar's is still available on old-fashioned cassette tape. Snapping the controls, winding back and forth to catch all that Ketelaar was saying, was a physical as well as audio experience.

I was listening because Piet Ketelaar had been on the SS *Cap Arcona* before it was bombed. Only for a short time, but enough to witness the conditions on board. He was one of those transported from Neuengamme to Lübeck in cattle trucks at the end of April and loaded onto the ship from the SS *Athen*.

A member of the Dutch Resistance, Ketelaar said he hadn't been in Neuengamme very long, a couple of months at most, when the camp was closed down. Not that he was expected to survive even that long. Arrested in the Netherlands at the end of 1944 whilst with a small band of Resistance fighters, including his brother Jan, he was proclaimed a 'Torsperre' by the Germans. Literally 'gate-barred', it meant he was condemned, a man denied the prospect of ever leaving through the gates of the KZ: he was supposed to perish for his treachery to the Greater Reich. It was yet another demonstration of the absurdity of camp-speak, given that the treatment of all inmates had little to do with notions of 'release' or sentence served.

That special denial of hope, of course, was forgotten when the camp was shut down and all the prisoners marched out, though Ketelaar took the precaution of shedding his jacket with the markings that indicated his condemned status. By chance he happened upon a coat worn by one of the Danish inmates, people who, along with the Norwegians, were treated with greater favour than the other camp occupants as a result of a Red Cross initiative. It didn't save him or his brother from being packed into the trucks for transportation to the Baltic coast.

Jan had been shot and wounded when the two brothers had been captured and was slowly dying. Piet looked after him as best he could, he said on the tape, but the lack of food and water meant his brother had little chance of recovering.

When they reached Lübeck they were driven out of the trucks and loaded onto the SS *Athen*. The ship was filthy, Piet said, indescribably filthy. It must have been bombed, he said, its condition was so bad.

Despite his own frail health, and after months of little food and extreme hard work in the camp, Piet tried to care for his brother, laid out on the deck of the ship, to fetch him water, but nothing was available. Prone, near death, his brother closed his eyes. Thinking him dead, a couple of guards grabbed his arms and legs and carried him off the ship to throw him into a large pit at the quayside. It was a mass of wasted bodies, Piet said. 'I didn't believe he was completely dead,' though he was so close to death perhaps it made little difference. Beneath Piet's voice I could hear something that spoke of a pain that wouldn't go away. Did he blame himself for failing to protest, for failing to stop them, for failing to make one last effort to keep his brother alive? I thought it would be the harshest life sentence imaginable if that's how he'd felt.

Piet was a survivor and perhaps all survivors suffer guilt at surviving. He said he wouldn't give up or give in. Though his constitution was degraded by starvation, weak to the point of transcendence from the moment, he simply would not be undone.

The SS *Athen* steamed out into Lübecker Bight and towards the huge ocean liner moored in Neustadt Bay. As Piet spoke, he seemed to remember the moment with extraordinary clarity. He talked about the wonderfully fresh sea air, the sense of emerging from the filth of the dock and the camp, the freedom.

When they came alongside the *Cap Arcona*, the prisoners were transferred onto what had once been a cruise ship, now stripped of all its luxuries. It was already 'bulging with people', Piet said. Strangely, he saw no guards, no guns, no SS. He heard some German voices as he passed the open door of a cabin, but there was no one to control the thousands of KZ inmates. Piet wandered about the ship, below decks, where the Russian prisoners had been pressed into the holds, and back again where he could breathe. He lay down for the night. With no food he continued to deteriorate. In the morning, the tannoy announced that any Dutch or Belgians on board had to leave the ship. No explanation was given for the choice of these nationalities. He never understood the reason for the order, Piet said. He was transferred to the *Athen* for the short journey back to Neustadt harbour. By the time they made it to the small fishing town and moored alongside the dock, the RAF had begun its attack.

When I first saw the name *Cap Arcona* mentioned in the museum's catalogue, cross-referenced with the taped interview of Piet Ketelaar, I thought I would learn something about the terrible injustice of that moment. I thought he would utter some cry against the pitilessness of the attack, its redundancy in terms of the war. Perhaps I wanted confirmation that here was a tragedy that deserved recognition, some investigation. I was disappointed. The interviewer asked Piet what he thought of the bombing. And Piet said, 'It didn't register.' He said they were 'all laconic about that sort of thing. Tough luck. One of those things that happens in war.' That was all. He didn't linger to look, he said, as the bombers attacked. He didn't think about it. His brother was dead, people had been dying around him over the last few weeks, during the trip by cattle truck to Lübeck, waiting without provisions or medical aid at the dockside or on board one ship or another. The bombing was just another deathly intervention, another cause of fatality amongst multiple causes.

But he said he was so weak and sick that many things didn't truly register then. He wasn't thinking or acting rationally. The only enduring sensation was his determination never to give in or do something stupid that would lead to his death. When the bombers attacked, the SS and Marines melted away and the prisoners on the *Athen* took advantage of the mayhem. They found boxes of tinned food stored under tarpaulins on deck. Piet said he had no idea why they were there. Few if any guards were around now to stop the prisoners from smashing their way into the tins and eating the contents. Within minutes people were dying from the sudden gorging. Piet knew not to make the same mistake. He decided to get off the ship. He slid down one of the mooring cables and fell into the arms of two British soldiers. They were crying, Piet said, tears running down their cheeks as they looked at the hundreds of emaciated and dying prisoners on the quayside and falling off the ship. But they didn't stop to help Piet. In his mesmerised and weakened state, he set off into the town. The townsfolk locked their doors. No one came to help. And he saw many terrible things, he said, including a *Kapo* held down and branded on his back by two prisoners with a red-hot iron bar. Somehow, and his memory was understandably blurred, he found his way or was guided to a temporary hospital. His one intention was to get home, he said, back to the Netherlands. Allied soldiers had arrived, but there were so many people in a state of malnourishment, disease and decay that chaos was inevitable. In the so-called hospital, Piet lay down amongst the sick but was given nothing. He had to find his way to a tap to drink some water; no food was brought that he could remember.

It was at this point that his voice communicated disappointment or maybe even anger. He said over and over again how he wasn't given anything, wasn't helped. He admitted that 'mentally you go' when you are as sick as he was, with delirium setting in. He remembered, nonetheless, that, still half naked in his KZ rags, without shoes or coat, he was loaded onto a lorry and driven to Lüneburg Heath. After spending a night there, he was put on board a Dakota aircraft. The flight was to Brussels, he was told. When they arrived, he was simply left to walk into the city with the other prisoners who'd been transported with him. By this stage he was very sick. He'd contracted fleck typhus, no doubt from the lice that infested the inmates, the disease that killed so many at the end of the war. The death rate was anything up to 60 per cent if untreated with vaccine. In the camps swollen with prisoners, unfed, unwashed, unwatered, the chances of survival were small. It was typhus that killed Anne Frank and thousands of others in Bergen-Belsen.

Piet ended up in a hospital and was put in isolation, where he experienced hallucinations. But he possessed a core resilience that kept him alive. He held on, somehow surviving, never giving in to despair, an attitude that had preserved him even during the worst of times in Neuengamme, on the *Athen*, in Neustadt and now Brussels. He gradually recovered and went home.

Piet Ketelaar wasn't interviewed by Major Noel Till or any of his team as far as I could discover. There was no mention of his name on the list of witnesses annexed to Till's interim or final reports on his investigations into the Neustadt Bay disaster. Even though his English was good, Piet probably wasn't in a fit state to give evidence whilst he was still in Neustadt hospital. By his account he must already have contracted typhus. The disease has something like a ten-day incubation period after an infected louse has bitten its host, though the symptoms of fever and nausea and headaches would have been unrecognisable amidst the other ailments of the KZ prisoners. He would have been a figure in a landscape of suffering that the British encountered when they entered Neustadt. What reason would there have been for him to be picked out, let alone questioned about his experiences in Neuengamme or during the attack on the ships in the bay?

But Ketelaar's reminiscences have value in the story of the British investigations. They reflect on the arbitrary nature of the enterprise. Those who were interviewed about their experiences were mostly selected by chance. The circumstances didn't allow for deliberate, measured, comprehensive and scientific inquiries. With so many crimes committed against so many individuals by so many perpetrators, the stories of one man were pretty much irrelevant. A representation of a crime was all that was needed. Once an account had been extracted from a witness considered reliable and credible, there was little impetus to look further.

13.

When I opened the box of papers, left to the Imperial War Museum by Lieutenant Colonel Savile Champion, delivered to my desk on a steel trolley after I'd listened to Ketelaar's tape, I found a series of letters and orders written to Major Till all dated the same day, 11 July 1945.[27] This was also when I discovered that Champion had been promoted and appointed to lead No. 2 War Crimes Investigation Team whilst still working with Lt Col Genn at Bergen-Belsen.

Despite the new posting, Champion maintained his involvement in the Belsen case (it was only on 28 July that he would cease his work there). Bergen-Belsen wouldn't let him go that easily. It was, after all, the most symbolic concentration camp for the British, given that they were the ones to liberate it. It was 'theirs' to pursue, as a marker of British, as opposed to Allied or American, justice.

That didn't mean the other atrocities could be ignored, though there must have been a battle for Champion's attention. In the first letter to Major Till, Champion wrote, 'Dear Till ... The position with me is very difficult, particularly as Col Genn is now in England on a conference, and as you will know, the Belsen trials are nearly front page news.' He asked Till to get in touch as soon as he returned from a field trip to Norway investigating the killing of seven British soldiers, one of the cases that took Till away from Neustadt.

Along with Champion's demand for a meeting were letters somewhat chastising in tone. Till had been left with the Neustadt-related matters and by extension the Neuengamme KZ case. Champion had looked at some of the depositions provided by Till's team and he wasn't happy. He wrote that 'the depositions should be on the face of them reasonable; otherwise in court – or shall I say in a British court – they would throw them out and acquit the prisoner'. Champion identified one particular statement and said it was 'not only valueless to the prosecution but the greatest possible asset to the defence'. He reminded Till that he needed to collect corroborating evidence. 'It is one of our most important duties not to submit any deposition the truth of which we are not satisfied with:

i.e. some form of cross-examination must be applied.' Given that Till was a qualified solicitor, this was like telling him he was ignorant of the most basic principles of legal practice.

Till's written response ignored the barbed nature of his commanding officer's comments. He adopted a peculiarly jocular tone. The letter he sent was more akin to a holiday postcard than an official report from a subordinate. It managed, nonetheless, to convey something of the chaotic and whimsical nature of the investigation. Till wrote, 'We have returned at last from our investigations into the incident of 7 British Naval Personnel; eventually we ran to earth our most important witness holidaying in the midst of the Norwegian Mountains and we have had a magnificent trip which has been well worthwhile from the results as well as the enjoyment point of view.'[28]

'I'm sorry to hear you have been suffering from Belsenitis and hope you are now fully recovered.' Till said he was typing this letter himself, which 'accounts for the various %2888844£@ etc'. He then continued with the story of his Norwegian trip: 'The car has behaved very well except that we had a puncture.' He apologised for the flawed depositions. 'I quite agree that they are in need of drastic amendment.' He gave some excuse about how a junior had taken the statements, which had then been sent on without him looking at them. He stood up for his own professionalism, though: 'I carry out my investigations without any prejudice (as far as is humanly possible) either for the prosecution or the defence.' Then came the serious element, which, given the report he would produce months later when irritated by the interruptions to his Neustadt investigations, was the first sign of a developing resentment. 'When I left I was hot on the chase of people responsible for shooting people from the barges as they landed and forming the crews of the launches who shot survivors in the water. I will pursue these criminals with the utmost vigour.'

This was the point for Till and many other investigators: they were on the trail of criminals. They weren't concerned with the wider picture of holding the Nazi regime and all its inhuman practices to account. The original brief they'd assumed was narrow, even if back in London the British War Crimes Executive was preparing the more sweeping evidence for use at the Major War Criminals trial due later in the year. I say 'assumed' because there was no proper guidance or training or instruction provided to direct the investigative operations in a coherent manner. Men like Till and Champion and Genn and the others in the investigation teams had come to Germany knowing little other than what had been reported in the press both over the war years and recently with the liberation of the camps. Initially, they had to construct cases with no formal protocol or guidance in place.

Circumstances changed in the middle of June when formal authority for prosecuting Nazi war criminals was finally issued to the British forces. It came in the form of a royal warrant, which decreed that military courts were to be established for the prosecution of any violation of the laws of war committed after the outbreak of World War II.[29] Normal court martial procedure would apply. The judges would be British officers. If the accused were from any particular branch of the German forces (army, navy, air force) some attempt would be made to have officers from the equivalent British services on the panel: it was thought British airmen would better understand the behaviour of German airmen; British sailors, German sailors; British soldiers, German soldiers. A president and two others would be appointed for any hearing, one of whom should have some legal qualifications, or if that weren't possible then a Judge Advocate would be selected, a lawyer who would guide the court advising on the law and generally ensuring that the trial was conducted properly. The royal warrant also provided direction for the type of evidence that could be presented. Normal domestic rules governing criminal trials would not apply. Instead, the court could hear any statement and read any document (which appeared authentic) if it would help them reach a judgment. The judges were merely obliged to give due weight to the evidence presented. Hearsay would not be as convincing as direct eyewitness testimony, but could be considered.

One component of the warrant reflected the legal preparations underway for the Major War Crimes trial to come. It echoed an element of Justice Jackson's draft plan for a grand trial. 'Where there is evidence', it said, 'that a war crime has been the result of concerted action upon the part of a unit or group of men, then evidence given upon any charge relating to that crime against any member of such unit or group may be received as *prima facie* evidence of the responsibility of each member of that unit or group for that crime.'

The British may have adopted this measure as policy, but there would be resistance in practice. The problem was the lack of definition. Did it apply to membership of the SS as a whole, or of the guard detachment of a specific concentration camp, or a particular unit of SS guards within a compound, or a group within a group? The lack of precision opened a prosecutorial doorway, but for those preparing the cases little advice was given as to how they could pass through it.

I doubt that the royal warrant helped Till and his team in their investigations. As he told Lt Col Champion, he remained hot on the trail of criminals like some Dorothy L. Sayers sleuth. He'd already found and arrested two senior members of the Neuengamme SS (Anton Thumann and Willy Dreimann) and knew there was much left to do. The demands of good evidence, as his CO had reminded him, required Till to construct the best case he could. With so many victims still alive, a vast supply of testimony could be called on. And with each deposition he took from a witness, more accused were identified. By August, he had a list of forty-four individuals implicated by the statements and affidavits taken so far.

The scheme set out by the royal warrant may have been fine for prosecuting SS men for specific and obvious war crimes: killing prisoners on the beaches of Neustadt Bay, for instance, or abusing them in Neuengamme KZ during the war. But did it help in the case of the sinking of the ships? Had a war crime even been committed? And if there had been a crime, which side was culpable? The German officers for placing the inmates in harm's way? Or the British for bombing ships displaying white flags?

Lt Col Champion issued a Directive for Action concerning the sinking on 21 July. He was not about to place any blame on the RAF. Nor was he confident that the senior German command held any responsibility for the tragedy. He wrote that he was satisfied about the main crime of Neustadt: the murder of the inmates on the barges and the shooting of survivors from the bombed ships who'd been washed ashore after the *Cap Arcona* had gone down. There was no doubt that these were breaches of the laws of war. He instructed his team to get on with issuing arrest warrants and finding and taking into custody those responsible. Major Till had provided a list of names, mostly low-ranking SS guards from Stutthof.

None of this suppressed Champion's curiosity as to the circumstances of the RAF attacks. Amongst his private papers, I came across various notes he'd recorded.[30] One page of typed remarks was devoted to the ships sunk in the bay. Against the *Cap Arcona*, the following entry appeared:

> ? Painted battleship grey and flying German flag – ? what German flag – conflict of evidence as to whether white flag hoisted and German flag struck – Captain Bertram's evidence – no steam up, therefore impossible to move … ? action after warning bombs – ? action and seamanship after being struck.

Champion was searching for some kind of answer. He added a few handwritten remarks in the form of a brief timeline:

> 3 May   14.45 *Warning bombs. Arcona and Thielbek hoisted white flag*
> *but Swastika remained flying*
> 15.00 *Attacked – no effort of crew to extinguish fire.*

The Directive for Action reflected Champion's uncertainty. He demanded a 'report from the RAF, including whether they had had any information as to internees being on board, whether the white flag was flying on the *Cap Arcona* and was seen and, if so, instructions as to what was to be done with any ship flying the white flag, and whether any order was given and, if so, by whom, for the ships to put in to Neustadt Harbour, and details thereof'.

Despite the apparent desire to search for the truth about the bombing, Till was given little time to follow any leads. On 7 August he and his team were informed they had to drop all the Neustadt investigations and track cases of the murder of British airmen shot down over enemy territory instead. He was allowed two more weeks to finish his inquiries, though he managed to return to the case on 7 September for another short stint. Even then he would only be provided with one assistant and a fortnight to complete all his investigations.

In this short period and with the limited resources available, Till could achieve little. The case was too complex. Few people could tell him how the ships came to be bombed. Ironically, it wasn't the Royal Air Force who were most helpful in his inquiries. The bulk of the information he gleaned came from the *Cap Arcona*'s captain, who'd been arrested soon after the British took Neustadt and had been in custody ever since.

Captain Bertram was seen as something of a 'good man' by Till and the British team. He told Major Till a long story. He was a commercial seaman, not a member of the German military fleet. It was only at the very end of the war that his ship was 'chartered' by the *Kriegsmarine*, the German navy, in an oddly proper form of commandeering given the desperate circumstances. Bertram claimed he was only acting according to orders received from the ship's owners. Even then, his position as ship's captain gave him an authority that could withstand the SS – up to a point. He had a crew of seventy-two men, but, whilst anchored in Neustadt Bay at the end of April, no fuel.

When the SS *Athen*, with 2,000-odd prisoners on board, moored alongside the *Cap Arcona* in the middle of April 1945, Bertram said he was instructed to take them as 'cargo'. At first he refused on the grounds that the ship had no means to defend itself, knowing full well that it would be unsafe to take thousands of passengers onto a sitting target, open to attack by air or submarine, and without the capacity to move out of danger. Neither did he have sufficient lifebelts for so many people. There were only enough for the crew. Nonetheless, he was persuaded to take the prisoners, those who were still alive. After transferring its human cargo, the *Athen* then steamed off to throw into the sea all those who'd died on board. No rites were performed.

Bertram said his obstinacy was met with official disdain. The *Kriegsmarine* told him he had to take more prisoners, that the ship had been transferred to the *Reichskommissar für die Seeschifffahrt*, the State Commissioner for Maritime Transport. The ship's owners told Bertram he had no choice but to accept them. He still refused. The SS *Athen* turned up again and on 26 April Bertram was handed a written order that unless he took the prisoners he would be arrested by the Gestapo.

Still resisting, he said, he travelled to Hamburg for a meeting with Max Pauly, the commandant of Neuengamme, and General Abraham, Lieutenant General in the *Waffen-SS* and chief of staff to *Gruppenführer* Bassewitz-Behr. Bertram wanted to know why all these thousands of prisoners had to be put on board ships. What did the authorities want to do with them? Save them? Kill them? Bargain with them? Were they left on board deliberately exposed to RAF bombs so that their execution would be effected by the British? Or was the intention to scupper the ships with the prisoners on board in fulfilment of Himmler's orders that no KZ inmates should fall into the hands of the enemy?

Bassewitz-Behr and the others fed him a story that the prisoners were to be taken to Sweden. They were intended to be part of a transport of KZ prisoners to Scandinavia. Other similar missions had already been arranged by Count Folke Bernadotte and the Swedish Red Cross in the previous couple of weeks with the express consent of Himmler.[31] The *Cap Arcona* was to perform a similar mission.

Till was confused by this tale of mercy Captain Bertram relayed. He didn't believe there was any 'intention that these prisoners should be taken to Sweden'. Why should he, when he'd heard and seen so much evidence of total callousness and cruelty and indiscriminate murder by the German authorities and personnel at every level? But there was no proof one way or the other.

By the time Major Till was forced to stop his investigations and submit a final report in September 1945, when he was taken away from Neustadt, all he had was the tantalising explanation offered by Captain Bertram. None of it was substantiated. Till left a recommendation that the matter be clarified by asking Count Bernadotte himself or Dr Arnoldsson, the Swedish Red Cross representative who was in Lübeck during those manic last few days of war.

In the absence of any hard evidence, Till believed that 'whatever the ultimate intention, these prisoners were in fact placed on large undefended ships in the middle of a bay, with no adequate life-saving appliances, at a time when all shipping round the coast of Germany was being constantly attacked by the British RAF'. That was done, he argued, either with 'deliberate hope that they would be exterminated by the RAF' or 'with such total disregard for their safety that the act becomes an act of manslaughter almost akin to murder'. Those responsible he identified as the most senior commanders of the region: *SS-Gruppenführer* Bassewitz-Behr, his chief of staff General Abraham, *Gauleiter* Kaufmann and Neuengamme KZ's commandant, Max Pauly.

But the matter wasn't pursued with any enthusiasm. To prove responsibility in a court of law they would have to show that the SS leaders planned to sink the ships in one way or another and planned for the deaths of all those on board. That would impose a heavy evidential burden for any prosecutor. Maybe it wasn't considered worth the effort.

14.

It's not clear to me how much communication existed between the lawyers in Britain and the teams of investigators in Germany. I doubt that the flow of information was that effective. At the same time as Till and the War Crimes Teams were embroiled in multiple inquiries across the British zone, the American in charge of prosecuting the Nazi elite, Justice Robert Jackson, and his band of lawyers were in London attempting to finalise arrangements for the trial of the Major War Criminals. Though there may have been a desire to work in cooperation with their allies, Jackson prepared as though the US would act alone. He and his staff drafted a memorandum for further action. They identified the probable defendants (Hitler, if found to be alive after all, Goering, Himmler, mentioned even though known to be dead, and 'others') and organisations that should be indicted too (the SS and Gestapo, senior members of whom could be brought to represent the organisations as a whole). They also named the charges: a common plan to dominate Europe, which involved deliberate atrocities in its construction and execution; an illegal war of aggression; war crimes in breach of accepted international laws.[32]

Although it provided a framework around which could be draped the evidence that the Americans believed would be needed, it was an unsophisticated document. Exceptionally, and in one of its first appearances, the word 'genocide' was used, drawing on Raphael Lemkin's persuasive justification for his neologism.[33] Proof of the 'destruction of racial minorities and subjugated populations' by starvation, lack of clothing or shelter, warmth or medical care, forced labour and sterilisation or castration, would establish that atrocities had been committed.

Whatever the detail of the charges, the American lawyers recognised the need to do something quickly: 'Time is of the essence,' the memo said: 'a good case ready for trial at an early date will be far preferable to a perfect case unduly delayed.' Any tribunal should accept all evidence that helped prove guilt regardless of whether or not it would be admissible in domestic criminal proceedings. Judges must take note of 'facts of common knowledge' and make 'reasonable presumptions'. For all the rhetoric, the full scope of 'fair trial' was not to hamper action.

The American memo was passed around the Allies at a hastily convened international conference in London, which opened on 26 June 1945, bringing together government lawyers from Britain, France, the USSR and, of course, the USA. It accompanied a draft protocol establishing a mechanism for prosecuting both so-called major *and* minor Nazi war criminals that Justice Jackson had presented to his President in San Francisco and shared amongst the other powers earlier in the month. The memo and draft protocol provoked each of the other three nations to query Jackson's plan. Even though the British were friendly to the Americans, they too had their questions and comments. Every representative had something to say, to amend, to clarify, all founded on different ideas about the purpose and operation of a grand trial. The British saw little value in using any tribunal as a way of establishing new principles of international law. What was the point when it would only complicate proceedings? Why not, instead, rely on laws that nations could accept as already in existence, with the notion of war crimes head of the list? The Russians were more critical, more politically minded: they saw the 'trial' as a process of confirmation, where the Nazi leaders, condemned without reservation in the Moscow Declaration of 1943, would be judged as to the extent, not the fact, of their guilt. Equally, they didn't appreciate the logic of charging German organisations such as the SS and Gestapo: they had been disbanded immediately by the occupying powers. Why raise the question again by indicting these groups and suggesting, if only in principle, that they might be acquitted?

Not for the first nor the last time, and as though determined to give credence to the worst stereotypes about prevaricating and pedantic lawyers capable of arguing interminably over every detail, the conference quickly became a bear pit. The participants spent the next month quarrelling. They hammered at the provisions of Jackson's original document. It was a sluggish process, exacting, irritating and divisive, as though a rehearsal of Cold War tensions to come. Justice Jackson was by most accounts 'prickly' and unwilling to cede anything to the other Allied countries.[34] His position was strengthened by the knowledge that US forces had most of the captured senior Nazis in their custody, had the resources to undertake a massive trial, and had control of much of the German government documentation that would be necessary to secure convictions. The Americans didn't need the other powers to fulfil their mission to bring the Nazi leadership to account. Of course, the same couldn't be said for the huge number of individuals responsible for committing the regime's atrocities across the KZ system and occupied Europe in general: many remained at large, and proof of their crimes depended on local witness testimony. But Jackson was less concerned with these 'minor' offenders. His eye was on the great hearing when the whole Nazi regime and era would be condemned through law.

Despite the animosity, despite the sophistry, despite the politics, agreement on the details of the US plan was finally reached. At the summit conference in Potsdam at the beginning of August, the victorious powers confirmed their intention to 'bring these criminals to swift and sure justice'.[35] The US, Britain and the USSR announced their 'hope that the negotiations in London will result in speedy agreement being reached for this purpose', regarding it as 'a matter of great importance that the trial of these major criminals should begin at the earliest possible date'. A list of defendants was promised by 1 September.[36]

Undoubtedly prompted by the political statement from Potsdam, the Russian delegation now accepted most of the requirements of an

Anglo-American 'fair trial' model (where the defendants would receive notice of the charges against them, would be able to cross-examine witnesses and would be able to take the stand in their own defence). They also gave way to the Americans' wish to have the first tribunal held in Nuremberg (in the US occupation zone) rather than Berlin: it had a symbolism that appealed to the lawyers – it was the city where the 'Nuremberg Laws', constructed to give official form to the persecution of the Jews, were pronounced in 1935. If law was to be the instrument of retribution, where better than the place where law had been malevolently subverted?

On 8 August 1945, a couple of days after the US dropped its atomic bomb on Hiroshima, the London Conference concluded with the signing of an agreement and a charter for the International Military Tribunal to be held in Nuremberg. The agreement confirmed there was to be a 'trial of war criminals whose offenses have no particular geographical location'.[37] It left open the right of the occupying powers to prosecute other war criminals within their zones or return suspects to nations where their alleged crimes had been committed. The prospect of further trials at Nuremberg of high-ranking Nazis was also acknowledged, at least in principle, though as yet no concrete plans for additional hearings had been made. It was proving difficult enough to organise the first one.

The charter set out the form and procedure for the tribunal. It was supposed to be 'just and prompt', presided over by one judge from each of the four powers (the US, Britain, the USSR and France), with the jurisdiction to try major war criminals of the European Axis countries, who bore individual responsibility for committing crimes against peace (waging a war of aggression or in violation of international treaties), war crimes, and crimes against humanity (murder, extermination, enslavement, inhumane acts against any civilian population before or during the war).

'Leaders, organizers, instigators and accomplices participating in the formulation or execution of a common plan or conspiracy to commit' any of these crimes, it said, 'are responsible for all acts performed by any persons in execution of such plan'. Acting on orders would not absolve any defendant of responsibility (though might be considered in mitigation of punishment). The tribunal could declare a group or organisation as criminal and, where it did so, 'the competent national authority of any Signatory shall have the right' to bring to trial under its own jurisdiction any individual for membership of such a group without having to prove the 'criminal nature' of that group. In short, Justice Jackson had achieved everything he'd wanted.

There was only one problem. The definition of 'crimes against humanity' included a semicolon: the original wording agreed and signed said:

> murder, extermination, enslavement, deportation, and other inhu-
> mane acts committed against any civilian population, before or during
> the war; or persecutions on political, racial or religious grounds in
> execution of or in connection with any crime within the jurisdiction
> of the Tribunal, whether or not in violation of the domestic law of
> the country where perpetrated.

This tiny insertion of a grammatical device implied two separate forms of crimes against humanity: the first related to acts committed against any civilians either during or *before* the war – this would catch the actions taken against German nationals as well as everyone else in occupied Europe. The second element of the clause then covered persecution connected to the other two crimes to be prosecuted: namely war crimes and crimes against peace. That would encompass all the acts of genocide and killing undertaken in foreign territory occupied by the Germans.

The Soviet version of the document did *not* have a semicolon. In its place was a comma. The difference in meaning was substantial. For a lawyer. With a comma, all crimes had to be coupled with war crimes or crimes against peace (aggressive war, in other words). That implied that internal persecution of Jews and the 'cleansing' of German society of those un-Aryan elements wouldn't be included, as they were *not* undertaken in the context of war, but only internal repression.

By October 1945, the four powers agreed to accept the Soviet version as the correct one. The comma was inserted in an official alteration to the charter.[38]

With this pedantic but vital change instituted, the Allies now had to build a case. And choose from those they had in custody who would be brought to the tribunal as the accused.

15.

If the royal warrant hadn't assisted Major Till in Neustadt, Lt Col Champion in Bad Oeynhausen, Lt Col Genn in Bergen-Belsen, or the other investigators and prosecutors of the British Army operating in north-west Germany in the summer of 1945, would the Nuremberg Charter, now proclaimed to the world, help? A few of the lawyers at headquarters who were in the midst of preparing the Belsen case might have been interested in the wording of the final document, but in truth, their reference point could only be the royal warrant. That was the authority that lay behind the British-run trials in gestation, not the London Agreement or the Nuremberg Charter. The latter were of a different order, though they shared some of the terminology, at least as regards the definition of war crimes and the idea that individuals could be held responsible for the actions of a group of which they were a member.

There might have been some comfort in the new charge of 'crime against humanity' but, as it didn't appear in the royal warrant, it couldn't be used as the basis for a direct indictment against any defendant. Despite all the original rhetoric of retribution as a single process, where major and minor figures were to be pursued with equal fervour, the British made little of any overlap. The two procedures had already begun to divide. And though a man such as Josef Kramer, commandant of Bergen-Belsen at the war's end and erstwhile commandant of Auschwitz II-Birkenau, where the massive slaughter of Jews was conducted, surely qualified as a major culprit of atrocity, there was no appetite or intention to take him to Nuremberg, to house him with the Nazis held at Mondorf, and to prosecute him at the proposed tribunal. Nor was there for Neuengamme KZ commandant Max Pauly or any other concentration camp commandant who'd then been captured. The Allies were prosecuting these men in their own way according to their own legal frameworks.[39]

It's hard to imagine much general fascination for the minutiae of the Nuremberg Tribunal's legal construction. If the politicians were to be believed, people only wanted to see retribution and punishment dished out speedily. What was it to the general public whether the crime of aggression was a new form of international law or that individual Nazi government leaders were not to be allowed immunity merely because of their appointment as ministers of state, or that men like Goering and Hess and von Ribbentrop couldn't rely on a defence that they were only following the orders of their head of state, Adolf Hitler? None of this would have inspired any great enthusiasm.

The Times greeted the announcement of the London Agreement with muted respect. There was no editorial critique, simply a demand that proceedings begin as soon as practicably possible and endorsement of the choice of Nuremberg, the place 'where every September the National Socialists used to gather by the hundred thousand to glorify German might'.[40]

Though the location and nature of the trial was known, demands increased to translate the charter into an indictment against specific individuals and organisations of the Nazi regime. It was decided to fashion this pre-trial document expansively and record details of the charges to be brought against the German leadership (those selected from the persons now held in custody). Although the British and Americans would have been happy with a simple charge sheet, providing details of the evidence to be brought against the accused later (in the form of documents or witnesses), it was agreed that an indictment more recognisable in Continental European legal systems would be produced. Narratives for each of the crimes were to be drafted, fleshing out their context and details of their commission. Though not intended to be comprehensive, these would set the parameters for the tribunal, giving a flavour of the evidence that would be produced. The full extent of the case against the accused would be there for the world to view before one word was uttered in the Nuremberg courtroom.

The various elements of the indictment were divided amongst the legal teams from the four Allied powers to draft. There were to be four counts:

Count One: the accused were party to a common plan or conspiracy to commit the crimes set out in the Nuremberg Charter. The Americans took responsibility for preparing this part of the case. As it had to draw in all the alleged crimes committed, it gave Justice Jackson control over the whole prosecution, his intention from the beginning. Telford Taylor, one of Jackson's senior colleagues, would write many years later that it 'bid fair to swallow the greater part of the entire case'.[41] It would encompass not only the grand strategy of war devised and executed by the Nazi leadership, but also the long story of Hitler's rise to power and exercise of absolute control over Germany prior to 1939. All other counts were to follow in its slipstream.

Count Two: crimes against peace. Only a statement of the wars begun by Germany and the international treaties it breached in the process was necessary. The British took on this task.

Count Three: war crimes. More complex a prospect, encompassing an almost limitless range of breaches of the laws of war that required detail to show their nature and extent. Although the evidence from the concentration camps already offered a wealth of information to lay before the tribunal, the investigation of the whole KZ system as well as thousands of individual allegations of ill-treatment and murder had hardly begun. There were also all the accusations relating to slave labour, plunder, repressive measures throughout occupied Europe. Any narrative of this charge could only be representative, an effect that was emphasised through the Allies splitting responsibility between the French, who would produce the information relating to crimes committed in the west of Europe, and the Russians for the case in the east. The demarcation line was drawn north–south through the centre of Berlin.

And then Count Four: crimes against humanity, also to be the preserve of the French and Soviets. Evidence under war crimes could be repeated here verbatim though with especial emphasis on the extermination of the Jews.

The framing of the charges was a political decision and set the structure for the whole tribunal. But there was more interest in *who* was to be prosecuted than for what. On 30 August 1945, the promise to list the defendants at Nuremberg was made good. Twenty-four were named by the Chief Prosecutors, as they had now become, from the four nations. It was confirmed in November that the Polish, Czech and Yugoslavian authorities wouldn't be allowed a presence within the prosecuting team – the four were to keep everything between themselves.[42]

The intended accused had been identified quite quickly, although not without disagreement. The crucial factor was whether they could reasonably be considered part of the conspiracy under Count One. Proof was needed of their integral participation in the plan to commit a war against peace, war crimes and crimes against humanity. Of those in custody, some fell into this category with ease. As prominent and recognisable leaders of the Nazi party, Goering, Hess, von Ribbentrop and von Papen named themselves. There was no difficulty with Robert Ley, the German Labour Front leader, Julius Streicher, responsible for the anti-Semitic magazine *Der Stürmer* as well as leader of the Nazi party in Franconia, or Alfred Rosenberg, Nazi ideologue and Minister of Eastern Territories. Ernst Kaltenbrunner as most senior representative of the SS and Gestapo now that Himmler was dead, Hans Frank, Governor-General of Poland, Wilhelm Frick, Minister of the Interior, and Wilhelm Keitel, chief of Hitler's military staff, were also familiar personalities and their nomination as putative accused was welcomed in the press too.

Questions were posed, though, about the military men on the list. 'Are these generals then war criminals or have they been merely "stooges" in the hands of their political masters?' the *Manchester Guardian* asked.[43] Though hardly a significant challenge to the tribunal, the query reflected an enduring ambivalence about prosecuting the German military: it might set a precedent that no armed forces personnel would appreciate. But Alfred Jodl, Doenitz, Raeder and Keitel were on the list and seen as too important to leave out. They represented the complicity of the German military, their failure to stand up to Hitler and their willingness to engage in total war. There was sufficient indication too that the army and navy had accepted too readily and carried out orders that every reasonable military commander would know were criminal. These generals and admirals *had* to appear at Nuremberg.

The British might only have had full responsibility for preparing the case relating to the crimes against peace, but the British War Crimes Executive was still heavily involved in the gathering and analysis of evidence for all counts of the indictment. From its formation it reported regularly on progress towards providing the documentary material to be used against the Major War Criminals. Official papers, reports, signed letters, communications, orders: these were their priority, not witness testimony. Though the latter might be produced for effect, it would be the heft of all those documents that provided proof of guilt.

The BWCE received information daily. The committee assessed and analysed the documents appearing from across Germany, and thousands of incriminating papers were boxed up and deposited in Church House in London, ready for analysis and to be fed into the draft of the indictments under preparation. It was necessary to exemplify the scale of crimes, demonstrate individual culpability and adequately shock the world on its publication. No one had attempted anything like this before, and it had to be done within weeks.

16.

I left Neustadt at dusk, but not before driving around the shore to the town marina. This was where the German troops who'd been sent to round up the survivors had been stationed and where many of those half-drowned concentration camp prisoners had been brought back to be kept under guard until the British arrived. Nothing remained of that time, no buildings, no memorials, not a single marker that I could see. Just pleasure yachts, moored in neat rows.

I stood on a jetty and listened to the lonely, solemn, irritating sound of tackle jangling against masts in the sea breeze. And I wondered what those last days of the war must have been like for the inhabitants of this town. They'd been largely untouched by the fighting up to that point, far from the Eastern and Western Fronts, far from strategic targets subjected to bombing. A quiet coastal town that had harmed no one and had seen no one harmed – until that day in May 1945 when the prisoners washed up on their beaches and searched for food in their gardens. I found out later from the investigations that had been conducted by Till and his team that many townsfolk had panicked when they saw the concentration camp prisoners dressed in their striped clothing. They'd called the police, demanding protection, fearful of what these wraiths from the sea might do, what they might steal. Compassion didn't seem to feature in the reports I read from those who'd been there. But I supposed after a decade of persistent propaganda warning the country about antisocial elements, about criminals, about the Jews, about the internal threats to Germany, the people of this remote town might have been unable to discriminate. I imagined there would have been people here who'd helped or at least who'd avoided contributing to the suffering. There had been no resistance to speak of when the British troops arrived. But it would never have been, will never be, enough.

Was that how Noel Till felt after spending so much time delving into all this shame?

A couple of weeks after learning about the accident to Till's son, I rang his law office again. I figured I would hear bad news, but thought I needed to end this hope for enlightenment about the tragedy in Neustadt Bay. The same woman's voice and my question again: can I speak to Mr Till?

Yes, hold on. And she said she'd put me through.

The unexpected transfer put me off kilter and I could feel my throat constrict with nerves. Perhaps that's why it was a wretched conversation. Wretched for me, that is. Patrick Till *was* Noel's son, but he could tell me little. He'd been ten, he said, when his father had returned from the war. Not much had been said then or later about the investigations. There had been mention of much driving around the country looking for witnesses and suspects but nothing specific that he could remember. I pressed a little, but he seemed reluctant to share any memory or detail and barely responded to my increasingly vapid questions. There was one thing he could remember, though, he said, but it wasn't to be repeated. I listened and the anecdote didn't surprise me, but it had nothing to do with the disaster in the bay, Cila or Dora or any of those other witnesses or atrocities Till had investigated during the summer and autumn of 1945. All it did was provide a tiny and insignificant fragment that helped me understand the character of the man a little better. It made me wonder whether we make too much of other people's pasts. What might seem full of meaning and importance in retrospect can often be mundane and inconsequential in the eyes of those who were there.

I finished the call, thanking Patrick Till for his time, apologising for disturbing him at work. For a while afterwards I thought about his father. I regretted that I'd failed to discover more about the man and his investigations, what he might have thought about the terrible tragedy of Neustadt Bay. Some history is simply beyond reach.

Perhaps it didn't matter much. By the time Major Till left Neustadt and Germany, attention had shifted elsewhere. In September 1945, the trial of Commandant Kramer, the 'Beast of Belsen', and the forty or so other defendants was due to begin a hundred miles south, in another pretty country town occupied by the British.

5

Lüneburg

1.

Cemeteries are curious places for me. Ever since my grandfather showed me lovingly around the churchyard at All Saints' Church in Newland in the Forest of Dean, a spectacular and verdant plot that far exceeds the needs of the tiny village which it serves, I've never feared graveyards, memorial grounds, any place where the dead are gathered and remembered in stone and painting and garden feature. Often, they reveal more about the living who tend them, live close by them, than those who are buried there.

Lüneburg's Zentralfriedhof is a wide expanse of land bounded by Soltauer Straße entering the town from the south, pleasant modern housing along Oedemer Weg to the north and Heidhamp to the west. The map printed on a large sign at its main entrance shows the cemetery as a triangular patch of woodland cut through by a maze of pathways that link little clustered memorials within the trees.

Apart from the grandiose gravestones of the rich townspeople, the cemetery has several groves where German war dead have been buried or remembered simply by some obelisk or plinth or thick stone block. The First World War memorials are the most visible, the most unashamed. Though World War II casualties have been inscribed onto the rolls of honour here and there, tacked onto the remembrance stones, a timidity of purpose accompanies the additions. I wondered if the authorities debated whether it was right to pay respect to those who'd died in the service of the Nazi state. There must have been some reticence, some worry that one or more had taken part in the pervasive crimes then coming to light.

The war graves looked shabby and untended in the April sunshine of a Saturday afternoon. Most of the individual stubby crosses, which recorded the name of the fallen soldier and no more, were reminiscent of the Iron Cross medal of the German military rather than some

Christian symbol. They were laid out in beds of creepers that had spread around and over the stone faces. Many were completely obscured.

As I walked along one avenue I found myself contrasting the way in which respect for the dead was displayed here with that at home and in the beautifully tended Commonwealth War Graves plots around Europe and the world. In Britain, every hamlet, village and town has its war memorial, usually well cared for, but here they didn't seem to bother too greatly. Did the shrouds of ivy and plants signify shame?

Perhaps. There was much to be ashamed about. And I thought that the trials held by the British in those months after the end of the war were intended to reinforce, perhaps induce, that sensitivity.

Heading out of the cemetery and towards the old centre of Lüneburg I looked for some plaque or notice commemorating the town's role as home to the first significant war crimes trial by the British in 1945. I couldn't even find the building where the trials had been held. At the time I visited, I hadn't known the address, stupidly hoping there would be directions and signposts somewhere in the town. I found nothing: no marker, no waymark, no memorial. It was becoming a common experience.

When I looked at the website of the local tourist bureau all I could see was praise for Lüneburg's fortune in escaping the war unscathed: it's now a 'lovely place to shop', the old cobbled streets lined by gabled houses and boutique cafés and fashion stores. Why would you want to spoil all this with refracted sights of an unpleasant past? Perhaps allowing the building where so much viciousness was spoken of to be assimilated into the urban landscape, much like the graves in the Zentralfriedhof, was a reasonable policy: let the marks of the past disappear, let them be overgrown, it's better that way.

I settled into one of Lüneburg's pleasant coffee bars, a poor substitute for the old courtroom I'd hoped to see, and thought about how my search for some traces of a time long buried beneath economic prosperity and political alliance was proving difficult. I wondered about the vagaries of official history too. What's remembered is so much a matter of chance, or so it first appears. Bergen-Belsen was the British trial of the century, held in this unspoilt town. It was the British trial of the Holocaust, the first occasion when the Nazi extermination of the Jews through industrial means could have been, should have been, the subject of specific and prolonged exposure. And yet the process never quite assumed that character then, nor has it since. The case is rarely referred to as anything other than the 'Belsen trial'. It isn't often known as the Auschwitz–Belsen trial even though the prosecution would make it clear from the beginning that the Polish extermination centre at Birkenau was a central element of the charges against many of the SS men and women accused. Instead, the trial is associated more with the black-and-white films of liberation, the moment when British troops encountered the pit of Bergen-Belsen.

Some of this is understandable. Time didn't allow for sustained reflection before the case was heard. The pressure to prosecute as quickly as possible, to ensure that the public would see a vigorous and swift retribution following the pictures and newsreels of Bergen-Belsen, meant that all the investigators and lawyers were operating under extraordinary burdens. They were given only a few weeks when the demands of the law required months if not longer. It was a tension (between the political need and the legal) that was never resolved and which paved the way for much criticism.

On my return from Lüneburg I went back to the National Archives at Kew. I read through the Belsen trial files kept by the British authorities. It took some time. There were many boxes full of typewritten transcripts, exhibits, general court correspondence. They recorded every word of those proceedings and as I scrutinised them the trial assumed a voice just as a stage-play script might do. It was an act of theatre and here were the lines and the directions. With some irony I later found a memo in a War Office file devoted to the administrative arrangements for the trial which addressed the question of where the proceedings could be held: the memo by a Major Harris said they'd first considered the huge castle at Celle, but the only room large enough was the Schloss theatre: it was dismissed as a suitable venue with a terse comment, 'theatrical atmosphere felt to be undesirable'.[1]

2.

The Old Gymnasium at Lindenstraße 30 was only a few hundred metres from the town cemetery, along Soltauer Straße. An ugly twin-towered brick building (from what I could tell from the photographs taken at the time), it was identified as acceptable for the hearing by the British Army, who'd occupied the town and made it the headquarters of 21st Army Group in April 1945. Inside was a large hall to accommodate the multiple defendants, their many lawyers and a huge audience, though building works were necessary to convert it into something that would look like a court. No one wanted this to be a hidden affair. It had to be public and open and capable of alerting the world to what had been done at Bergen-Belsen.

The Americans had yet to begin their set-piece war crimes trials, so it was the British who were the first to stage proceedings that tackled the worst of the atrocities committed by the Germans. Bergen-Belsen, or rather the truncated 'Belsen', was synonymous with the horror of Nazi barbarism. Though Buchenwald and Ohrdruf and the euthanasia centre at Hadamar had been discovered earlier and their terrifying secrets revealed in the press, the British were determined to bring the Bergen-Belsen personnel to trial before people could forget what had happened. The public were fickle, anyway, tired of blood and massacre, tired of war and everything associated with it. If the rhetoric of justice was not to lose its veneer then an immediate demonstration of the evils perpetrated and punishment for those responsible was necessary.

No one objected to the timetable publicly, though the lawyers must have doubted the value of such extraordinary haste. They knew that to present a proper case and mount a suitable defence, mimicking the best traditions of criminal justice, they needed time. As it was, the attorneys who represented the defendants were only appointed a few days before the trial. Within that period they were supposed to prepare their clients and identify and bring to court any witnesses who might aid their defence.

Major Thomas Winwood had the task of defending Josef Kramer, now called as of rote the 'Beast of Belsen' even though his tenure as commandant in both Natzweiler and Auschwitz II-Birkenau lasted much longer and, in the case of Auschwitz, involved the deliberate extermination of hundreds of thousands of people. Winwood was also responsible for representing three other accused, including the camp doctor, Fritz Klein. It was a heavy load for one lawyer. Either of those SS officers could have eaten up all the short time available to prepare a case. But Winwood wasn't intimidated and protested little. He later wrote a short memoir of his experiences at the trial, which betrayed the amateurism inherent in the appointment of defence counsel.[2]

In the early summer of 1945 [he said] I saw a notice from the Headquarters of the British Army of the Rhine requesting the names of serving officers qualified as barristers or solicitors. I had qualified as a solicitor in 1938 and ignoring the first rule of Army life – 'never to volunteer' – I sent in my name. Some two months later I was ordered to report the following day at RAF HQ in Celle.

The next day I was greeted by a Staff Officer who told me, 'Well, as you are the first to arrive, you had better take the first four on my list.'

Only then was Winwood told he was to defend the Bergen-Belsen camp commandant. He had thirty minutes to read the papers before seeing his clients, seven days before the trial was due to begin.

Twelve defence lawyers, all British officers appointed in similar cavalier fashion, looked after the interests of the forty-two accused. They tried to coordinate their defences but, as Winwood recalled, they 'had little time to formulate a coherent defence policy beyond agreeing that we would put forward a joint objection to the jurisdiction'.

On 17 September 1945, the case opened and was fêted in the world's media. It would be the first opportunity to see justice administered against the Nazis whilst everyone waited for the Nuremberg proceedings to begin. Newspaper correspondents had already been briefed on the characters they would see on trial, some of the wickedest individuals imaginable, men *and* women, and portrayed as sadistic, unfeeling brutes.

The courtroom constructed in Lüneburg's large gymnasium hall allowed for numerous reporters and observers to squeeze in opposite the bank of defence lawyers and behind them, the massive three-tiered dock where the accused would be seated. A public gallery could hold four hundred people and it was full too. Some brought binoculars to get a better view of the participants.

A series of photographs published in the *Illustrated London News* showed the prosecution team sitting in a dignified line behind a table covered with files and papers.[3] The names ascribed to the men were wrong: Leo Genn was on the left of the picture, sitting next to Captain Stewart. Colonel Backhouse, the lead prosecutor, was on the far right.

THE PROSECUTING COUNSEL AT LUNEBERG: (L. TO R.) COLONEL T. M. BACKHOUSE, MAJOR H. C. MORTON-BEALE, CAPTAIN S. M. STEWART, AND LT.-COLONEL L. CONN. COLONEL BACKHOUSE DETAILED ATROCITIES UNPARALLELED IN HISTORY.

The paper had pictures of the defendants too: Josef Kramer leaning forward in the dock, smiling and chatting with his British attorney, Major Winwood. And there was a fetching shot of Irma Grese, accused Number 9, looking icily beautiful.

The show began.

No one could deny the theatricality of the event, despite the precautions. It was a strange combination of military precision, a court martial operated in accordance with army regulations rather than new international legal directives, and the ceremony of criminal law. The Deputy Judge Advocate, Carl Stirling, the lawyer who was to guide the judging panel of army officers throughout the case, to interfere where necessary, to sum up evidence at the end and generally oversee proceedings, was dressed in black robe, white winged collar and wig. Advocates stood when they spoke and faux politeness prevailed.

As the defendants were marched in to take their seats, shuffling along into the three rows of benches within the wooden dock, with numbered cloths hanging around their necks, any idea that this was an occasion of immense and national reckoning was diminished, perhaps erased. It quickly became apparent that the ordinariness of proceedings dictated the style: the defence lawyers steadfastly refused to recognise the world outside the legally confined room and the case opened not with a fanfare of condemnation, but with applications of legal technicality, all raised on behalf of the defence. Major Cranfield, acting for Irma Grese (the SS woman guard who more than anyone would capture the press's attention), spoke for the defence lawyers en masse and immediately made some practical requests: whilst noting (not complaining about) the limited time he and his colleagues had had to prepare, he said they should be provided with an expert in international law so that they could challenge the whole basis of the charges against their clients; and he wanted the prosecution to bring witnesses to the court whom he and his colleagues had named in a long list. Captain Phillips, who acted for four of the lesser accused, asked for separate trials, claiming it was wrong that one set of defendants were charged with crimes committed at Bergen-Belsen only (including his clients) and another lot were charged with crimes committed at Bergen-Belsen *and* Auschwitz. Phillips was concerned that evidence brought about the latter camp, evidence that would demonstrate the policy of mass and deliberate extermination of a people, would prejudice the panel's view of those who'd only served at Bergen-Belsen, a different type of camp where death was more a matter of neglect (or so it would be said) than measured slaughter.

There was a great difference, he said, enough to warrant separate hearings to avoid prejudice.

Colonel Tommie Backhouse, the chief prosecutor (a barrister from Blackburn and a member of the Judge Advocate General's Branch during the war, now officer in charge of the War Crimes section of the British Army of the Rhine), responded by suggesting there was nothing to choose between the two camps. 'The individual methods of ill-treatment sometimes varied because ... every known method of ill-treatment was used at one or other of these camps. Nevertheless, the same people were acting as concentration camp guards in one and went to the other and acted as concentration camp guards there. They ill-treated people, and literally the same people at Auschwitz as the people they ill-treated at Belsen.'

Was this dissembling? 'Ill-treatment of people'? And the *same* people? Could that really have been the core of the prosecution's case, the appropriate language to describe the evidence to be presented? If it was an understatement then it was ill-conceived. Reading through the trial papers, I suspected caution had infected the prosecution lawyers' work. This was a unique moment after all. No one had undertaken anything like this before. They might have thought that by choosing a restrained terminology of wrongdoing, the defendants would have less chance to raise a reasonable doubt concerning their guilt. For all the pictures of piled corpses, it was still hard to believe or comprehend the prolonged and industrialised and centrally controlled form of killing that had occurred in Auschwitz. By presenting a charge of lowest common denominator (concerted ill-treatment rather than 'extermination' or 'mass killing' or even 'murder') the chances of the guilty going free were much reduced. Hannah Arendt, the renowned German political philosopher, would ask later, 'What meaning has the concept of murder when we are confronted with the mass production of corpses?'[4] So too might the prosecution lawyers have wondered how to capture the totality of crimes committed by the accused over a period of years and in two by now notorious camps.

The prosecution's case was forged from Lt Col Genn's initial investigation report and recommendations. Genn sat next to Backhouse as he delivered his opening speech, having returned to assist in the completion of his work, back from Britain where he would shortly resume his successful acting career. Captain Stewart was there too, the team looking like a row of forties film stars, which of course Genn was fast aspiring to become, having already appeared in Laurence Olivier's *Henry V*. They'd agreed that the best approach, the safest, was to condemn the individuals by their association, their connivance with an abusive design, criminal by the standards of the laws of war. They'd agreed to fuse the evidence on Auschwitz and Bergen-Belsen in one trial. What was the point, after all, of prosecuting Kramer and Klein for their deeds at Bergen-Belsen: to seek and surely obtain their death sentence, and then open another case in relation to the evidence they had about Auschwitz? The Russians as occupiers and the Poles as a sovereign people had geographical jurisdiction over Auschwitz, and under the terms of the Moscow Declaration of 1943, Kramer and the others would then have to be extradited to them to prosecute. The opportunity to see Kramer and the others hang for the horrors of Bergen-Belsen wasn't to be given up so easily. Besides, as Backhouse had said, so many accused had served in both camps and so many inmates had been held in both as well. It would be absurd to ignore that evidence when the world wanted to know what these men and women had done, what evil system had been invented. But if the intention was to unpick the wickedness not only of the individuals but also the regime that served up Auschwitz and Bergen-Belsen, then there were some odd omissions in the charge and in Backhouse's introduction. There was no mention of the plan to exterminate the Jews. There was no mention of the philosophy or ideology that was the foundation of the policy. There was no mention of the years of persecution that ran through the period of Nazi rule, from before that date, from the 1920s when Hitler and his party took shape. There was no mention of when persecution was transformed into the deliberate annihilation of whole peoples. There was no mention of the Gypsies either, the Roma and Sinti who had a camp of their own within Auschwitz. There was no mention of any of this.

Why did the prosecution avoid this hinterland of criminality? What were they afraid of? Or were they largely ignorant of the complexities and magnitude of the extermination the Nazis had carried out? The trial was hastily arranged after all and the evidence accumulated was local: witnesses were those who had been found alive in the camp on liberation and seemed credible men and women. No attempt was made to construct a documentary presentation of Nazi rule. Only a few papers were presented. Unlike the tribunal being prepared in Nuremberg, where documentation was the mainstay of the case, the crimes addressed at the British Belsen trial were contained and very personal. Did it matter whether the individual SS personnel accused were acting as parts of the Auschwitz machine when witnesses could point at them and tell the court that this man, this woman, wielded a whip, crushed an inmate, beat another to death, routinely set vicious dogs on prisoners, stood at the ramps at the railway sidings inside the entrance of the camp and selected thousands in person to be taken to gas chambers for killing?

Perhaps it did. The Belsen trial would be the only British or American trial that directly examined individual deeds at Auschwitz. None of the other extermination camps, Treblinka, Sobibór, Belzec, would figure in the Western Allies' cases explicitly. Being in the east, these places were the preserve of the Polish and Russian governments. By drawing the two camps of Auschwitz and Bergen-Belsen together, through its personnel and victims, the prosecution claimed that a policy of extermination defined a systematic criminal practice and the accused were acting together to see that system fulfilled.

The phrase used was 'concerted action': the defendants as a unit operated to commit war crimes. That was the charge. The defence lawyers tried to analyse the words. One even pulled out his *Little Oxford Dictionary*. Captain Phillips for the defence said that 'concerted action' implied 'a certain amount of common intention or common action between various people to contrive, to premeditate and to plan'. He argued the prosecution couldn't prove this. Where was the evidence? Colonel Backhouse said it lay in their conduct: all the kitchen SS and *Kapos* behaved with equal despicability towards the camp's inmates, all the SS guards and *Kapos* on trial exacted similar punishments, all the SS and *Kapos* looking after the medical care of the prisoners inflicted more injuries, conducted experiments, saw to it that people were killed rather than attempt any cure; together this had to suggest concerted action. If they all behaved in the same way then they must all have been following a single design: and that was enough to prove the charge.

However persuasive this argument was, by definition the plan extended far beyond those on trial in Lüneburg. The accused were minor players within an epic story. Proving they and they alone were acting in 'concert' would be a falsity just as much as claiming their deeds in Bergen-Belsen should be examined in isolation. With the proceedings yet to begin at Nuremberg, the Belsen trial had nothing to which it could anchor itself. Only the general outrage of years of war as covered in the newspapers and Pathé film clips provided a backdrop. It was a bind which the prosecution lawyers couldn't escape.

The military panel considered the request by the defence for separate trials. And then denied it. There was to be no derailment of proceedings at the first juncture, whatever cogent legal arguments were raised.

3.

A few hours were lost before the defence lawyers' initial applications were dismissed, then Colonel Backhouse was finally allowed to introduce the case.

He embarked on a torpid tour through the technicalities of the charges laid against the accused, whom he referred to as 'members of the staff' of either Auschwitz or Bergen-Belsen or both. He quoted the royal warrant, articles and paragraphs at a time. He explained that they were not concerned with abuses committed by Germans on Germans, only Germans against Allied nationals. That was all the laws of war were capable of covering. It took him some time before he peppered his speech with invective against the accused and the system they served. He told the court that the thousands of verified deaths in Bergen-Belsen before and after liberation were the result not of criminal neglect but of deliberate and wilful killing. He introduced the camp at Auschwitz as particularly despicable. He described the 'selections' where those arriving in cattle trucks would be separated as soon as they were hauled off the trains: to one side, the fit and potentially useful labourers; to the other, the sick, the old, the young, the majority. He numbered those killed in the millions.

But a trial is an intimate event even when performed in public and even when weighed down by legal technicality. The accused have to be identified, given a personality. Despite the numbered cards around their necks, the defendants had to be brought to life: the principle of individual responsibility demanded it. Colonel Backhouse introduced the accused like a cast of characters in a drama, using the numbers on the small white squares that marked the defendents as a guide. The star villains came first.

No. 1 was Josef Kramer, commandant at Auschwitz and commandant at Bergen-Belsen. Backhouse told the court it would hear that Kramer joined the SS as a volunteer, and had been a concentration camp official ever since. It may be, he said, that evidence will be put before you of incidents at other concentration camps *if* the defence persist in their suggestion that what happened at Bergen-Belsen was accidental and not part of an organised series of events.

Then there was Dr Klein, a Romanian, a volunteer in the *Waffen-SS* since June 1943, serving in the camps since December of that year. You will hear witness after witness tell how he selected victims for the gas chamber at Auschwitz, Backhouse said. You will hear that he makes no secret of it.

Next, Weingartner, *Blockführer* of one of the women's camps at Auschwitz, a thousand women under his orders. He continued the same work when he was transferred to Bergen-Belsen.

Kraft was an SS guard at Auschwitz and Bergen-Belsen who oversaw the bread and ration store. Then Hössler, Auschwitz too, *Lagerführer*, senior SS officer under the commandant, joined the SS because he was out of work, and served in concentration camps throughout the whole of the Nazi era. In charge of the women's camp under Kramer. After he left Auschwitz he went to another camp called Mittelbau-Dora, and from Dora to Bergen-Belsen, where he became *Lagerführer* of No. 2 Camp.

Bormann, female, was in charge of the clothing store first and later the working parties at Auschwitz. You will hear how she amused herself by setting dogs on women and taking part in the selections for the gas chambers, Backhouse said. You will hear that when she came to Bergen-Belsen she was in charge of the pigsty.

Elisabeth Volkenrath: at Auschwitz she regularly took part in the selections for the gas chamber; cruel. At Bergen-Belsen Kramer placed her in charge of all SS women. You'll hear of her many brutalities.

Herta Ehlert, SS guard. She claims to have been a conscript, spending a career in various concentration camps before eventually arriving in Bergen-Belsen after a spell at Auschwitz. She was the second in command of the women, and like so many others will say the conditions were a disgrace, but, of course, everybody other than herself was to blame.

Then there was Irma Grese, commandant of working parties, and, for a time, in charge of the women's punishment quarter at Auschwitz too. Some will say she was the worst woman in the camp. Not one type of cruelty which you will hear of was beyond her, Backhouse said. She regularly took part in the selections for the gas chamber, made up punishments of her own, and when she came to Bergen-Belsen she carried on in precisely the same way. She too specialised in setting dogs on people. She had made three statements. You will see how they vary. Do not believe a word she says in her defence, Backhouse warned. Irma Grese became the press's favourite because she was blonde, with more than a hint of sexual titillation accompanying the report that she was Kramer's lover.

Ladislaw Gura, a Bergen-Belsen *Blockführer*, against whom evidence of at least two murders would be brought. Schreirer, Heinrich, commander of Block 32. Then, again, you will hear of his regular cruelty.

Those were the SS members from Auschwitz. Three other women were charged with crimes committed at that camp: Ilse Lothe, Hilde Lohbauer, Stanisława Starostka, but these weren't SS guards. They were prisoners, each a *Kapo*, each cruel and wicked, deeds without name, secret, black and midnight hags all, Backhouse might have said.

And then he came to Bergen-Belsen and the kitchens. If you want to imagine how despicable were the conditions and the treatment of the inmates then you will hear about the actions of Klippel, Flrazich, Mathes, Pichen, Barsch, Ida and Ilse Förster, Haschke, Lisiewitz and Hempel, Backhouse said. They behaved callously towards the inmates, proof of concerted action to harm the prisoners. Men and women of terrible character. With faces to match.

There were some others, the rump, SS *Blockführers* Otto and Polanski, administrators Schmedidzt, Egersdörfer, Opitz, Charlotte Klein, Bothe, Frieda Walter, Fiest, Sauer, Hahnel, Kulessa, Ostrowoski, Stärfl and Dörr and more *Kapos*: Burgraf, the almost Neanderthal-looking Erich Zoddel, Schlomowicz, Aurdzieg, Roth, Koper.

Erich Zoddel

No details of their crimes yet. These would come. It was enough to look upon their faces lined up in the dock to understand their wickedness. My God, the prosecutor seemed to say, they look evil, don't they?

As far as the charges against them were concerned, the panel of officers, and perhaps the audience too, had only to be convinced that criminal conditions of abuse existed in Bergen-Belsen and in Auschwitz, and the prosecution would have proved their case against each and every offender.

By the end of the first day, Backhouse had introduced each of the forty-eight defendants by name and outlined their association with particular crimes. Only once was the word 'Jews' used and that only in the context of saying, 'You will hear that 45,000 Greek Jews were taken to that camp [Auschwitz], and when they were evacuating the prison only 60 were left.' Otherwise the victims were not categorised. *Why* these people were killed in this way was unexplained.

No one in the press reflected on the omission. 'Beasts of Belsen Taste British Justice' was the headline in the *Daily Mail*.[5] Edwin Tetlow, special correspondent, who'd been with the troops when they entered Bergen-Belsen, followed this up:

> Josef Kramer, the 'Beast of Belsen,' and his 43 associates from Belsen and Auschwitz concentration camps sat for hours like so many pale, grave-faced automata under the floodlights in a converted military gymnasium here today. Their mass trial as war criminals, a spectacular curtain-raiser to the coming proceedings at Nuremberg against [Goering] and the rest of the Nazi big-fry, had begun.

Indeed, Justice Robert Jackson was just then calling a press conference to announce that the Nuremberg trial would begin by the winter and to confirm that the twenty-four major Nazi figures already identified would be the defendants.[6] But for now, after Kramer, Irma Grese was the biggest draw. In one sense she was *the* attraction. Tetlow couldn't help but convey her appeal. 'She was the handsomest person in court,' he wrote, 'even without make-up, though there were faint, dark circles under her hard grey eyes.' Then in bold print:

> She had carefully brushed and groomed her hair for today's first appearance and she had given herself a splash of colour by putting on a light blue blouse beneath her drab grey-blue tunic.

The character of reporting didn't improve. On 25 September, Tetlow wrote:

> Witness after witness is now being called upon to walk up and down before the dock and identify as many of the prisoners as he or she can. Something approaching fear is beginning to show in the pale tight-lipped faces of some of the women as they are picked out again and again.
>
> But Irma Grese, the sullen blonde, remains unaffected as she stares out the witnesses and contemptuously obeys the court's command to stand up and sit down in her turn. Kramer, too, is unmoved still. In fact, he often smiles as an accusing finger is pointed straight as a die at him.[7]

The Times was more reserved. It avoided dramatic banner headlines. 'Colonel Backhouse, for the prosecution,' it reported, 'began quietly to retell with additional dreadful details the story of the two concentration camps, [and] though the story was well known to everybody present and to most of the civilised world outside, it had not lost its power to conjure up horror, pity, and anger.'[8] Auschwitz was named and so was Irma Grese, though without the titillation that permeated Tetlow's accounts, the paper avoiding any sexual connotations. Instead, it gave its readership a sober and accurate rendition of the first day's proceedings.

4.

Defence lawyers often appear as heroic figures when it suits dramatists and novelists. The maverick but brilliant attorney who takes a hopeless case and defends the seemingly guilty is a stereotype adored in films and fiction. He or she is the embodiment of justice. The character of Atticus Finch in To Kill a Mockingbird perhaps best exemplifies the noblest traditions of those who practise law. It's a romantic picture, of course, but weighted with those profound values that are supposed to define British (and American) justice. Prime amongst them is the belief that everyone is entitled to have professional representation in court. The principle is ingrained in law school teaching.

Several years ago I was in the US, in Virginia. Through some convoluted route that isn't relevant to this story, I was visiting a team of lawyers. They were capital defenders. Their sole job was to represent people on death row, people who'd already been convicted of a capital crime, a particularly horrible murder usually, and had been sentenced to death. Those American states, like Virginia, that practised the death penalty nonetheless had sophisticated and long-drawn-out appeal systems that afforded the defence lawyers plenty of opportunities to challenge the verdict or the penalty.

I arrived in a town in the Appalachians in late March. It was a raw day and between the frost and the leafless forested hills I felt uncomfortable even before entering the office of the attorneys I'd come to visit. I suspected I would encounter something deeply challenging to my cosy life and my equally cosy principles. That turned out to be true. Before the introductions were cold I was asked to look at the crime scene photographs of a triple murder. The attorneys were representing the man who'd already pleaded guilty to the crime. Their client had been sentenced to death. They were concerned with his appeal. As I clicked on each image on the office computer screen, images which showed the bodies of the victims lying in their blood, in the middle of their home, their lives ended in immediate and cursory fashion by the man they thought to be their friend, a man who was disturbed, ill-educated, with a troubled and gun- and alcohol-riddled history, I couldn't quite understand what I was supposed to feel. Being adamant that the death penalty was wrong, no matter what the circumstances, was enough to make me think the attorney deserved my support. But another voice asked: did that really require the most expert services that could be afforded? Did the self-confessed killer merit a brilliant lawyer who might be able to twist the system to his advantage?

My attorney host sat down with me in his office after I'd viewed all the photographs. 'Horrific, aren't they,' he said, and he asked me what I thought. There was no point in dwelling on the terrible circumstances of the killing. The sequence of events had already been explained to me. So I said I admired the attorney for what he was doing. I was against the death penalty too, I said, and it was right that the accused should be given every assistance. The attorney shook his head. 'It's not about that,' he said. 'Whether the death penalty is justifiable or not isn't the issue. If we ever became associated with that debate we'd be lost.'

The attorney explained his philosophy. His guidance came not from opposition. If anything the system was to be upheld. He might disagree with its operation and its penalties but it didn't matter. 'One of my most difficult tasks,' he said, 'is trying to persuade the defendant to appeal. Most just can't face the prospect of life in prison. That's their only alternative and it terrifies them.'

'How do you get them to change their minds?' I said.

'We have to show them that they still have a life they can lead, even in prison. I don't know whether they're convinced. But we usually get them on board.'

Perhaps I should have asked not how but *why* they persuaded these people to fight their sentence of death. I imagine the answer would have been that life is sacred, and that the system shouldn't be allowed to end it without resistance. Whether that was the same thing as being against the death penalty, I'm not sure.

A few years later I spoke to one of the leading mitigation lawyers in the US, a remarkably vibrant and determined man called Russell Stetler, whose role is to coordinate advice to attorneys across the States representing inmates on death row. He said something that chimed with the sentiment of that Virginian attorney who'd shocked me with his images and, if I'm honest, his approach. Stetler said, 'Everything I and my colleagues do is premised on one belief: that someone is more than the worst thing they've ever done.' And that meant even the most heinous offender should be heard, perhaps understood and given the chance of redemption.

Thinking about those men and women sitting in the dock at Lüneburg, all those accused whose testimonies I'd read (and there are hundreds) from courtrooms across Germany, in Hamburg and Wuppertal and Hannover, I wondered how much I could give credence to the sentiment: they are, were, more than the worst thing they'd ever done. And thus they are, were, deserving of representation by a skilled advocate. I wondered, too, whether Major Winwood and Major Cranfield and the other defence lawyers believed the same. Did they defend those people, who as far as I could tell had spent years doing the worst things they'd ever do or anyone could ever do, for such principled reasons?

On 25 September 1945, the *Daily Mail* published a letter in its 'Brickbatz, bouquets, and viewpointz' section from a Miss Turnbull of Berwick. She had been moved to write on the horrors of Bergen-Belsen which she'd heard about over the radio and in the newspapers and said primly: 'It is extremely surprising, therefore, to read that British officers are apparently willing to "defend" those guilty of, or responsible for, those atrocities … simply because the "Belsen beasts" have chosen them.'

The editor responded: 'Indignant reader Turnbull should remember that Belsen trial serves secondary purpose as example to Germans of democratic legal process. Long proud tradition of British justice is that accused persons have right to choose their defenders.'

Curt prose it might have been, but it also reflected the fundamental principle I encountered in Virginia. Some criticism was directed at the lawyers defending the Nazi war criminals (Thomas Winwood expressed surprise and I think sadness at the attacks made against him in his all too brief and unpublished recollections which I read amongst his papers), but it wasn't prevalent in the British press.

That might have had something to do with pressure being exerted from the War Office. Towards the end of the trial, a memo was issued from the army in Germany which noted 'the disparaging remarks' appearing 'about the defending officers'. It requested the President of the Court to make a public statement affirming that 'NONE of the defending officers volunteered to defend any of the accused', 'no option was given to any of the officers as to whether they would undertake the defence or not', and 'the case has been tried in accordance with the principles of British justice, one of which is that an accused person should have every reasonable facility for putting up his defence'.[9] If these retributive trials were to define the difference between 'us' and 'them', between the Allies and the Nazis and all they stood for, then fairness had to be maintained and that meant representation by a skilled lawyer. I had to remind myself of that many times. Major Winwood and the other defending lawyers tested that proposition to the limit. Not by the fact of their representation, but by their willingness to adopt *any* argument in defence of their clients. Major Cranfield, representing Irma Grese, made a suggestion that seemed petty, ill-judged, fundamentally insulting to the obvious crimes of the Nazi concentration camp system. He said that the camps were 'legal institutions' under German law. *The Times* reported the argument's conclusion: 'A German working there could not be expected to deny his own law or to judge the camps by the standards of international law',[10] and thus couldn't be guilty merely by reason of service. The newspaper didn't condemn the argument, it merely repeated it. Cranfield's lawyerly point incensed many. Later, commentators used it to doubt the integrity of proceedings, an indicator of how proper process had overshadowed justice. An insult to the memory of the victims.

Defending the indefensible may be inherent in the principle of fair trial, but once adopted, only counter-argument and perhaps established rules of procedure can properly intervene to limit the scope of the defence. Whether it was palatable or not, those acting for the perpetrators on trial were free to defend as they saw fit. And they hammered at each and every prosecution witness, claiming fabrication, mendacity, distortion, exaggeration. If witnesses hadn't seen the events they were testifying to directly, then they were attacked for relaying hearsay. All standard legal tactics.

It was a very blunt instrument, nonetheless. And given that the prosecution was trying to establish that a criminal regime existed and bringing evidence of the culture and environment at Auschwitz and Bergen-Belsen, the testimony followed suit. Often, it was simply vague. How else could it be when a victim witness had seen abuse and death day after day after day? Every suffering merged into one long, torturous experience. Moonlit sharpness of memory was rare. And any imprecision provided even more ammunition for the defence.

5.

Like many of the prosecution witnesses, Dora Szafran was young, twenty-two years old, Jewish and from Warsaw. She'd been arrested on 9 May 1943, was taken to Majdanek to begin with, then transferred to Auschwitz in June of that year before finally being transported to Bergen-Belsen in January 1945. When Col Backhouse asked her why she'd been arrested by the Germans initially, Major Cranfield objected. He said the question was irrelevant, not a part of the charges and it might prejudice the defendants. Witness after witness, he said, had been asked the same question.

And indeed they had. Anni Jonas from Breslau, arrested and sent to Auschwitz in 1943; Sophia Litwinska, from Lublin, arrested and sent to Auschwitz in 1941; Ada Bimko from Sosnowitz, sent to Auschwitz 1943; Ilona Stein was from Hungary and transported to Auschwitz in June 1942; Hanka Rozenwayg lived in Vokhin, Poland, before being arrested and shipped to Auschwitz in the summer of 1943; Lidia Sunschein; Estera Guterman; Paula Synger; Ruchla Koppel. Each had been asked by the prosecution why they'd been taken away by the Nazis. And each one had said, 'Because I am Jewish.' Cranfield's objection was that the reason for their arrest would reflect badly on the accused, would suggest that the defendants were conspiring in the persecution of the Jews and were therefore integral to the systems of hate and extermination that infected the whole Nazi state. Given that Backhouse could barely bring himself to mention the Jews in his opening statement, at the very moment when he had the ear of the world's press, that he chose *not* to highlight the persecution of the Jews as a major part of the prosecution's case, it was odd that the matter was filtering into proceedings in this backhanded way. Was he trying to condemn by inference?

Of course he was. That was why the defence attorneys objected. But if so, it seemed a little strange to be coy over this aspect when every other systemic abuse was accentuated so as to reinforce the charge that the defendants were part of a single evil enterprise.

Major Cranfield's objection was quickly dismissed, though, and Col Backhouse took the opportunity to say that his case was founded on the principle that the laws of war required no detainee to be ill-treated because of their religion. And he asked again, 'Why were you arrested?' and she replied, 'Because I am a Jewess.'

Szafran showed to the court a large and deep scar on her arm. After she was tattooed on arrival at Auschwitz one of the *Kapos* had struck her. But this was incidental to her evidence. She told of the 'selections' for the gas chambers. They were carried out, she said, by Kramer, Klein and Dr Mengele. Grese was there too, she said, pointing to them as she was allowed down from the witness box to parade in front of the dock and scan the ranks of accused. She could identify Johanna Bormann as well, the woman SS member who she'd seen setting her dog, she thought an Alsatian, on an inmate who'd been unable to keep up with a work party, pushing the dog to tear at the victim's throat. She didn't know whether the prisoner had died.

But the bulk of her evidence focused on the 'selections'. She heard the shouts and shrieks of those sent to their deaths. She said Kramer beat people so often that she'd lost count of the number of times. Grese too, using a stick, a riding-crop type of implement, she was not quite sure. Then, whilst at Bergen-Belsen, she said she'd worked in the kitchens. She saw another of the accused, Karl Flrazich, an *SS-Rottenführer* (who one inmate, Frenchman Raymond Dujeu, described by contrast, in a short deposition taken by Major Smallwood early in the investigation on 8 May 1945, as an 'exception to the ordinary guards and always kind and never beat anyone'), fire out of the window of the kitchen at the prisoners the day before the British liberation, killing several, maybe as many as fifty, she said. There were no reasons for the shooting as far as she could tell, unless it was revenge.

The cross-examination began. Major Cranfield requested permission for the witness's scar to be inspected by a medical officer. Did he think she was lying? Did he think that he could make her look foolish by showing that her wound might have been caused other than how she'd told the court? The request was granted and a British Army doctor called upon by the defence advanced to the witness box and examined Szafran's scar. He then retired (to consider his opinion?) and for the moment the scar was forgotten. The witness was left to answer questions from the defence lawyers.

Major Winwood was first in line. He challenged Szafran's memory and her veracity. His aim was to establish that his client, Josef Kramer, hadn't taken part in any beatings, that he was an honourable soldier forced to do a job against his wishes, but who'd undertaken duties at both camps with as much care for the prisoners as he'd been allowed. The witness was adamant she'd seen the commandant at many selections. Winwood didn't challenge her, as though he'd accepted that he could only defeat the evidence of gassing through legal argument. There was no point in suggesting Kramer hadn't been there. Kramer had already confessed to his presence on the Auschwitz ramp where Jews had been subjected to selection for the gas chambers on disembarking from the trains. In September, a couple of weeks before his trial was to begin, Lt Col Genn had taken another statement from him. Instead of denying any knowledge of mass killing, he confessed liberally.

> The first time I saw a gas chamber proper was at Auschwitz. It was attached to the crematorium. The complete building containing the crematorium and gas chamber was situated in Camp No. 2 (Birkenau) of which I was in command. I visited the building on my first inspection

of the camp after being there for three days, but for the first eight days
I was there it was not working. After eight days the first transport, from
which gas chamber victims were selected, arrived and at the same time
I received a written order from Höss, who commanded the whole of
Auschwitz Camp, that although the gas chamber and crematorium were
situated in my part of the camp, I had no jurisdiction over it whatever.
Orders in regard to the gas chamber were, in fact, always given by Höss
and I am firmly convinced that he received such orders from Berlin.
I believe that had I been in Höss's position and received such orders, I
would have carried them out because even if I had protested it would
only have resulted in my being taken prisoner myself. My feelings about
orders in regard to the gas chamber were to be slightly surprised and
wonder to myself whether such action was really right.

The qualified confession was enough for Winwood to focus his
cross-examination on Szafran's memory for specific instances of
violence allegedly committed by his client. He had to present a picture
of a man uncomfortable with his role, who'd only looked on and
hadn't joined in with the violence. It was a hopeless task.

Had she seen Kramer beat anyone?

Yes.

Could she describe any such occasion?

In Auschwitz, she saw a prisoner lose her shoe just as they were
passing out of the gate in her work party. Kramer beat her with a
stick as he was standing by the gate.

When was this?

End of 1943, beginning of 1944.

And in spite of the distance of time, you can still remember the
full details of that one incident?

Yes. Emphatically. She could not possibly forget, she said. And
Major Winwood sat down. Maybe he was satisfied that the story
hadn't revealed anything more ghastly than a beating.

The other defence attorneys probed her stories too. They asked
for more and more detail. The exchanges were painful in their dissec-
tion. The account of Johanna Bormann setting her dog on a prisoner
was Major Munro's concern. Bormann was his client. She was fifty-
five years old and had joined the SS in 1938. Her first major

concentration camp posting had been to Ravensbrück. By 1943, she'd been transferred to Auschwitz II-Birkenau. Like so many others, she'd found herself evacuated to Bergen-Belsen in the early months of 1945, where her job was to look after the pigsty. She was thin, her cheeks depressed. Photographs of her taken on her arrest showed a woman who looked mean-lipped and pinched. But, then, what picture of any accused presents a comforting and pleasant face?

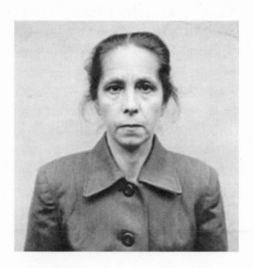

Munro wanted to know from Szafran how many people had seen the incident with the dog, how far the witness was from the incident, and then he attempted to push a different version of the story, a wholly benign interpretation.

'Is it not the case,' Munro asked, 'that the dog escaped from the guards' control?'

Szafran said, 'I saw it with my own eyes, and the woman boasted about it to an *Arbeitsführer* afterwards.'

'Is it not the case that the woman who was attacked broke the ranks?'

'It was already in the *Lager*, and I mentioned that the woman had a swollen leg. She lagged behind and that is what happened to her.'

'Is it not the case that the woman who had charge of the dog tried to stop it from attacking the other woman?'

'When the dog went for the woman's clothes she rebuked it and urged it to go for the woman's throat.'

'Is it not the case that the woman who had charge of the dog put her hand on the throat of the other woman to shield it against the attack?'

'As I am saying for the third time, she commanded the dog to go for the woman's throat to choke her to death.'

For those few minutes when the various questions were being put all context was lost. The camp and its barracks and *Appellplatz*, its work parties and barbed wire, its stench and roughness, its timeless violence, all were momentarily dispatched and the only things that existed were the question and the answer. Give more detail, describe more clearly, unpick each statement, each scarred memory, and if the witness can't do this with fluency and total recall then doubt is cast by faulty recollection.

Major Cranfield asked Szafran to say more about the stick she said Grese used to beat inmates: describe the riding-crop, he asked. It was made of leather, she said. But yesterday she couldn't remember the stick was made of leather: why not?

'I put it to you,' said Cranfield, 'that you're hopelessly confused about this beating.' She'd been colluding with other witnesses, hadn't she? And Cranfield finally came back to the scar on her arm. He said she should have gone to the camp hospital to get the wound treated, that the scar wouldn't have been prominent if she'd sought medical attention. Cranfield implied that the Auschwitz hospital was like a doctor's surgery: if not inviting and comforting then at least able and ready to administer health care. Had he not been listening to the evidence?

By the third week of the trial, irritation infected the courtroom and those who observed the proceedings. 'The wheels of the law are grinding exceeding small,' said the *Manchester Guardian*.[11]

6.

Reading trial transcripts is a painstaking process. It has to be. But it's an imaginative one too. You can't help but infuse the words with voices, with character. For all the potential for variety of human life that this implies, the Belsen transcripts, or at least the questioning at Lüneburg, relentlessly minute and focused, was depressingly familiar. I'd come across the same line of enquiry many times. The 2006 court martial in Britain of seven British troops for the ill-treatment of Iraqi civilians in an army base in Basra depicted in *A Very British Killing* hardly deviated in style or content. Remarkably, though perhaps for some reassuringly, given the institutionally asserted enduring quality of 'British justice', the tactics and language were almost identical: disregard the context, the defence attorneys would say, fix your eyes on the lies instead, on the exaggerations and inconsistencies. That was the tactic in 1945 in Lüneburg and it was the same sixty years later in Bulford court martial trial centre in Wiltshire.

Was the comparison valid?

When I read Winwood's and Cranfield's and the other defence lawyers' cross-examinations, I thought it might be. Not because of the content but rather because of the style of lawyerly performance. It was ripe for parody. When Slobodan Milošević, Serbia's erstwhile president, was accused of crimes against humanity and genocide committed in the wars in Kosovo and Bosnia and Croatia during the early 1990s, and stood before the International Criminal Tribunal for the Former Yugoslavia at The Hague, he decided that he would take that defence lawyer role for himself. He delighted in sitting alone at his desk, earphones strapped across his head, files before him, a panel of judges to his front, several ranks of prosecution lawyers to his flank, entering this valley-like arena as though he were a heroic defender of a nation. It was an image the world could see and Serbia could see, the proceedings streamed on TV channels as it developed into an epic soap opera. He used the opportunity to cross-examine witnesses as a political *coup de main*, striking at 'the West' with each spearing question. Or at least, he appeared to do so by the wit of his questions and the sharpness of his recall and the audacity of his posture (he refused to stand up when addressing the court as all the other lawyers in the room were required to do, and he insisted on referring to the senior judge only as 'Mr May' instead of 'Your Honour', thus adopting and resisting the polite conventions of this theatre at the same time).

Milošević became so successful in the drama that the prosecution had to intervene. They applied for some witnesses to be exempt from his cross-examination. Two women raped in the conflict, whose written testimony, given at another trial, had been presented to provide the court with evidence of sexual violence amounting to crimes against humanity, should be protected from the defendant's questioning, the prosecution argued. The judges agreed. Cross-examination 'should not be permitted mechanically and as a matter of course'.[12] Provided the rights of the accused were protected sufficiently, the veracity of the witnesses' evidence having already been adequately tested in the previous proceedings, there was no need to subject them to the trauma of living through their ordeals again.

That aside, and it was an exception, Milošević played the court with bombastic ease. His demeanour and delivery must have been stimulated by all those clever lawyers he mimicked or mocked. With one anonymous witness, referred to as Number 1011, who made a statement about an action in the war in Brčko and was brought to the trial because his evidence was contentious and the defence were entitled to test it, Milošević picked at him for hours. He called him 'Mr 1011'.

'You say that the war in Brčko began in the night of the 30th April and now you say that it began on the 4th May. You say actually in your statement that it was on the night of the 31st April. The 31st of April does not exist.'

Milošević wouldn't let the idiotic little error drop. He referred later to the war that began on 31 April, deep sarcasm permeating his questions. And he continued to hunt down little mistakes whenever he could. It was precise and sort of clever, dissecting each witness with the same intense and well-briefed scrutiny. A 'tour de force', some would call it, though it was more a 'tour d'imitation', a mockery of the British lawyer's art. With the chief prosecutor of the case being a British QC of long standing, Geoffrey Nice, the synthetic was matched against the real in every session. But Milošević didn't fare badly by the comparison. Was he an inspired advocate who could have been a brilliant barrister? Or was the lawyer's job easy to replicate for a politician well versed in antagonistic debate?

Milošević's trial was 'fair' by most accounts and that was how an advocate was supposed to behave in a fair trial. Whether Bergen-Belsen, Nuremberg or The Hague, we have one form to fit all circumstances. If that invites mockery, as Milošević was wont to do and others have too, then that's unfortunate. Perhaps it doesn't matter whether defendants can exploit the form of trial for their own amusement. A more pertinent concern might be that the form is flawed *if* its purpose is to discover the truth of a person's suffering and an accused's guilt. Milošević wasn't subverting the process: he was simply playing the game. His might have been a pedantic and irritating performance, one which any good professional lawyer might ridicule, but he was acting little differently from those lawyers at Lüneburg casting every doubt they could on the testimony of all witnesses brought before the court. It might be fitting for a solitary crime, where the evidence is tested to establish what happened and who was culpable. But with witnesses brought only as representatives of thousands of victims, with a whole institution of abuse under scrutiny, with dimensions of harm transcending any one moment, extending across years and locations and casts of perpetrators, was it appropriate? Was it fair to victim, witness and accused alike?

7.

There was an evident problem with the Belsen proceedings. It stemmed from the inadequacies of the investigation. Though hundreds of witnesses had given their testimonies to the British investigators, once interviewed no one kept close track of their movements. Bergen-Belsen camp remained alive, with tens of thousands of survivors recovering but also desperate to leave. Who would want to stay in that hell-hole?

Over the four or five months from liberation to the trial good witnesses had been allowed to disappear. Many had left, to return to their homes. They'd scattered across Europe, to Prague, Hungary, France, too far to chase after and bring back to Lüneburg.

After presenting all his 'live' witnesses, Colonel Backhouse wanted to ensure that all the evidence collected from the investigation was put before the court. He gave assurances that he'd done his best to bring the witnesses to the hearing, but it hadn't been feasible in many cases. He still wished to rely on the evidence in their original sworn statements. The prosecution team had compiled a thick book of witness depositions, dozens of them, and he wanted the court to accept them as further evidence against the defendants.

One of the defence lawyers, Captain Phillips, objected. 'In our submission the whole of the evidence contained in this book is completely unreliable, thoroughly slipshod, and incompetent.' It was worthless, he said.

But Carl Stirling, the Deputy Judge Advocate, ruled that the book of statements would be admitted, though the court would have to weigh the value of each witness account with caution, and they would have to be read out aloud to the court, one by one, so everyone could hear. The defence could object to any part and then they'd see whether to accept the statement or not.

And so began a long recital. Fortunately, many of the accounts were brief. Ridiculously so, again reminding the court that the initial investigation was deficient. Dora Almaleh's was the first. It had been written down by Major Champion, then second in command to Lt Col Genn, now leading No. 2 War Crimes Investigation Team. This was its extent:

1. I am 21 years of age and because I am a Jewess I was arrested on 1 April, 1942, and taken to Auschwitz Concentration Camp where I remained until I was transferred to Belsen in November, 1944.

2. I recognise No. 2 on photograph 22 as an SS woman at Belsen. I knew her by the name of Hilde. I have been told now that her full name is Hilde Lisiewitz. One day in April, 1945, whilst at Belsen I was one of a working party detailed to carry vegetables from the store to the kitchen by means of a hand cart. In charge of this working party was Lisiewitz. While I was on this job I allowed two male prisoners, whose names I do not know, to take two turnips off the cart. Lisiewitz saw me do this and pushed the men, who were very weak, to the ground, and then beat them on their heads

with a thick stick which she always carried. She then stamped on their chests in the region of the heart with her jack-boots. The men lay still clutching the turnips. Lisiewitz then got hold of me and shook me until I started to cry. She then said, 'Don't cry or I'll kill you too.' She then went away and after 15 minutes I went up to the men and touched them to see if they were still alive. I formed the opinion that they were dead. I felt their hearts and could feel nothing. They were cold to the touch like dead men. I then went away, leaving the bodies lying there, and I do not know what happened to them.

3. I recognise No. 1 on photograph No. 5 as an SS man at Belsen who was in charge of the bread store. I have now been told that his name is Karl Egersdörf [er]. One day in April 1945, whilst at Belsen, I was working in the vegetable store when I saw a Hungarian girl, whose name I do not know, come out of the bread store near by carrying a loaf of bread. At this moment Egersdörf [er] appeared in the street and at a distance of about 6 metres from the girl shouted, 'What are you doing here?' The girl replied, 'I am hungry,' and then started to run away. Egersdörf [er] immediately pulled out his pistol and shot the girl. She fell down and lay still bleeding from the back of the head where the bullet had penetrated. Egersdörf [er] then went away and a few minutes later I went and looked at the girl. I am sure she was dead and men who were passing by looked at her and were of the same opinion. The bullet had entered in the centre of the back of her head. I do not know what happened to her body.

Sworn by the said deponent Dora Almaleh at Belsen this 13th Day of June, 1945.

(Signed) Dora Almaleh.

Captain Brown was Karl Egersdörfer's lawyer. He objected to paragraph 3 being admitted. He said the general charge against his client was for war crimes committed against Allied nationals. He said the victim described in paragraph 3 was Hungarian. A war crime could not be committed by a German against a Hungarian, he said. They had been on the same side.

In reply, Colonel Backhouse argued that Hungary ceased to be allied to Germany before April 1945 and had then joined the Allies to 'some extent'. Besides, he said, he was trying to show how people were treated at Bergen-Belsen generally. Whoever was injured or killed was immaterial: it was enough to know that this was the nature of the regime. The paragraph was allowed to stay, though as the witness wasn't there, she couldn't be cross-examined. There lay a deep flaw in the prosecution's preparation.

Egersdörfer was forty-three years old. He'd joined the SS in 1941 and had been sent to work in the cookhouse in Auschwitz. He was there nearly four years. Given that the prosecution had said, at the beginning of the trial, that the whole operation of the kitchens and stores was an affront to humanity, a means of perpetuating the suffering of the inmates with callously inadequate distribution of food, the general torment that each so-called 'meal' would represent for every inmate, one might have thought his position alone would have condemned Egersdörfer. But the case against him would come down to *this* affidavit of Dora Almaleh, nothing else. No other statement or witness would be brought against him. This one moment of violence was attributed to him and described by a witness who wasn't in court. And Egersdörfer would deny any ill-treatment, let alone murder. The court would acquit him. Despite the prosecution's claim that he was part of the KZ machine and that this affidavit said he'd killed someone unlawfully, some corroboration was needed. Someone had to stand up and say: 'I saw him kill someone, beat someone.' But that wasn't to happen in Egersdörfer's case.

There were nearly a hundred or so other depositions like Dora Almaleh's.

8.

Nineteen days had passed by the time all the prosecution witnesses had retold their stories and the depositions and statements had been read out to the court. It was then for the defence lawyers to frame their arguments. They and the watching press and locals, who'd come to hear what could possibly be said to excuse any or all of the accused, waited on Major Winwood as he was invited to make his opening address on behalf of Josef Kramer. He was also the lawyer for the doctor Fritz Klein, *Blockführer* Peter Weingartner and *Lagerführer* and cook Georg Kraft. But Winwood's advocacy for these three other men would have to wait. Kramer came first. He was the most important figure, after all.

Winwood must have known that each word he uttered would be scrutinised and reported around the world. He must have known that all he would say would reflect upon him as well as his client. Did he care? Or did the shield that lawyers think protects them as mouth-pieces for those whom they represent extend to him too? His speech wouldn't be long by lawyers' standards and he must have anticipated that the journalists present would repeat only those parts that stood out amidst the grey gloom of boredom that had inhabited the Old Gymnasium in Lüneburg for nearly four weeks. (Any interest of the local population had apparently already been exhausted – the *Daily Mail* said that only thirteen Lüneburg Germans had stayed throughout the afternoon session on 4 October, chatting amongst themselves, yawning and reading the local newspaper.)[13] Despite this, Winwood erred.

By now it was clear that the defence were relying on the supposed 'German' culture and law of blind obedience to excuse everyone on trial. It was the foundation of his case, Winwood said, that Kramer was a member of the National Socialist party, was a member of the SS and, he said, was a *German*.

'I would ask the Court when the time arrives for them to find their way through the maze of evidence before them to grasp that phrase: Kramer is a German, in the same way as Ariadne when she was making her way through the labyrinth.'

The classical reference disappeared rapidly, but the tenor of argu-ment was consistent. The German state, the German law, *was* the Führer. Obedience was absolute and that principle was enshrined in the law, in the oaths that Kramer was required to take when joining the SS, in the being of every German at that time. Winwood quoted from the Nuremberg Laws, he quoted Alfred Rosenberg (whom he and the other defence attorneys had visited in Nuremberg prison to confirm that no individual could feasibly deny the authority of the regime), Rudolf Hess, Robert Ley, all in custody a few hundred miles away waiting on their appearance at the Nuremberg trial, and of course Hitler himself, to confirm total obedience as a way of life and state. If Winwood was to be believed, there was no room for moral, let alone legal, choice. Kramer was a slave to the regime. He had to obey.

The line of argument became stretched when 'the chimneys of Auschwitz', as Winwood called them, were the result. Kramer wasn't just a German watching on as the state carried out its policy of liquidating the Jews: he was the commandant of the extermination centre at Birkenau that was run to fulfil, to define, to refine that policy. He was at the core not the periphery. In his desperate attempt to overcome such a prejudicial realisation, Winwood made a ridiculous slip.

Commenting that Germany hadn't invented the concentration camp (he reminded the court of British actions in South Africa during the Boer War and in Egypt, probably elsewhere too), Winwood said that the 'object of the German concentration camp was to segregate the undesirable elements, and the most undesirable element, from the German point of view, was the Jew'.

Oblivious to the sudden opening of ground before him, he pressed on:

> The type of internee who came to these concentration camps was a very low type and I would go so far as to say that by the time we got to Auschwitz and Belsen, the vast majority of the inhabitants of the concentration camps were the dregs of the Ghettoes of middle Europe. There were the people who had very little idea of how to behave in their ordinary life, and they had very little idea of doing what they were told, and the control of these internees was a great problem.

Winwood hadn't finished. He couldn't avoid the subject of the 'gas chamber'. Instead he maintained the theme of obedience. And for this Winwood had to find someone, virtually anyone, to whom he could point as having a superior or more responsible position that would allow Kramer to claim subservience. So he turned to Rudolf Höss, the commandant of Auschwitz No. 1 (Birkenau was Auschwitz No. 2). Höss, he said, was in overall command of the whole complex.

It was he who'd ordered the selections and the gassing of those chosen to die. Winwood said:

Now to return to the gas chamber. It existed, there is no question about it. There is very little question about its purpose, its purpose being to remove from Germany that part of the population which had no part in German life. The way it was done, we have heard from several witnesses, was by selections, selections which took place at the station when the transports arrived, and we have heard also of selections which took place later on inside the camp. These selections were ordered by Höss and later by the commandant who relieved him. They were presided over – and this is the Defence's line – invariably by a doctor. All doctors in Auschwitz were under the direct control of Auschwitz No. 1. The head doctor and all the other doctors lived in Auschwitz No. 1, and all hospitals in these areas and all doctors, and everything connected with the hospitals, was directly under Auschwitz No. 1. Present at these selections were certain SS people. There were large numbers of transports coming in, and it is quite obvious that a certain amount of control was needed. When one thinks that a lot of these people knew what they were coming to Auschwitz for, I think it is fair to say that a good deal of control was needed when they arrived.

It so happened that these transports came in to Birkenau. They came into Birkenau, Auschwitz No. 2, because in that camp was situated the gas chamber. That was a misfortune for Kramer, because he held that job, was commandant of that part, and as commandant he will tell you that he received instructions from Höss and that he was responsible for law and order on the arrival of the transports and for the control during the selections. There have been allegations against Kramer and against various other people belonging to the camp that they took an active part in those selections, and there have been allegations that they themselves actually chose victims for the gas chamber. Kramer will tell you that he never once chose a victim for the gas chamber. He will tell you that he took no active – if by 'active' is meant helping – part in choosing people for the gas chamber. He will tell you that a physical selection was done by doctors to decide which people were capable of working for the German Reich, and that would only be done by doctors.

So, there was the defence for his time at Auschwitz: Kramer had been unlucky. Unlucky to be sent to Auschwitz rather than the Eastern Front as he'd desired. Unlucky to be given command of a whole camp within the gigantic and dispersed compound. Unlucky that his camp should have included the gas chambers and crematorium. Unlucky that he should have had the job of overseeing the selection of new arrivals to die or to live a little longer to work. Unlucky that some of those who'd arrived, knowing what was in store, resisted their fate and, therefore, had to be 'controlled'. Unlucky. Höss was the man responsible, the doctors were responsible, by implication even Dr Klein, who served with Kramer at Auschwitz and came with him to Bergen-Belsen, whom Winwood was also representing and who sat next to Kramer in the dock. (Of course, Winwood had a similar defence prepared for Klein: he would say briefly and simply in a couple of days' time that though Klein had been one of the doctors who'd made the selections, 'those capable of work and those incapable', 'there was no question of not carrying out that order; there were lots of other doctors there who would have done it if he had refused and been sent to a gas chamber himself'.)

That was Winwood's line. Even allowing for the benefit of hindsight, it's difficult to believe he could have thought this was sensible. The language, the inferences, the argument, were an affront.

The executive committee of the Board of Deputies of British Jews protested as soon as they heard reports of Winwood's speech. So, too, the World Jewish Congress. Winwood 'besmirches the memory of millions of men, women and children who died under unspeakable horrors, or were murdered for no other fault but that they were Jews', the Board of Deputies telegraphed the President of the tribunal, Major General Berney-Ficklin. They said his remarks were 'an insult to Jewry', 'vile and clumsy'. 'The unwarranted slur cast by the defending officer on countless Jewish dead and their surviving brothers and sisters all over the world is a gross violation of British fairness and transgresses the just limits of British advocacy,' the telegram added.[14]

I wasn't able to discover much of Major Winwood's career or life after he'd finished the Belsen trial. Unlike many of the lawyers involved, who cropped up in the obituary columns or became senior members of the Bar or the legal profession, Thomas Winwood returned to country practice as a solicitor in Britain. I knew he was a partner in a firm of solicitors in Salisbury. I knew he died in Bournemouth on 18 September 2005 and that various papers of his relating to the trial were deposited with the Imperial War Museum, mostly annotated transcripts from his infamous trial appearance. Other than that, nothing. Perhaps he found no difficulty in telling clients and friends and colleagues that he was once the Beast of Belsen's attorney. But I wondered whether he might have been somewhat circumspect after the statements he'd made in Kramer's defence. Would he have felt shame at his callous assertions? Probably not. The short recollections I was able to read merely alluded to the derision he received from some quarters. The only explanation he mustered was predictable as the defence lawyer's mantra: I was my client's mouthpiece. I was speaking for him.

9.

If Major Winwood's defence of Kramer was hopeless for the Auschwitz charge, the same could not be said for the Bergen-Belsen element. He'd already set out in his opening address the line he wished to follow: that Josef Kramer took command of the concentration camp for only a short period when no one could have done anything to alter the terrible conditions there. With increasing numbers of prisoners being foisted onto the commandant each day, the position would have become untenable for anyone.

Kramer claimed that he'd done all in his power to alleviate the situation. A letter was produced. It was from Kramer to his superior in Berlin, *Gruppenführer* Richard Glücks, who was the Reich Inspector of Concentration Camps, the man in overall charge of the KZ administration. Dated 1 March 1945, the letter supposedly supported the defence's argument. Winwood described it as the 'very kernel of Kramer's defence'. Though he couldn't with any authority say it was genuine (there were suspicions that Kramer's wife had provided the copy), he intended to rely on it as if it were.

Even if a fabrication, the letter registered the voice of a man who'd been at the forefront of Nazi atrocity. The language alone betrayed the deeply ingrained sentiments of the system.

Gruppenführer [the letter began], it has been my intention for a long time past to seek an interview with you in order to describe the present conditions here. As service conditions make this impossible I should like to submit a written report on the impossible state of affairs and ask for your support.

You informed me by telegram of February 23, 1945, that I was to receive 2,500 female detainees as a first consignment from Ravensbrück. I have assured accommodation for this number. The reception of further consignments is impossible, not only from the point of view of accommodation due to lack of space, but particularly on account of the feeding question. When SS *Stabsarztführer* Lolling inspected the camp at the end of January it was decided that an occupation of the camp by over 35,000 detainees must be considered too great. In the meantime this number has been exceeded by 7,000 and a further 6,200 are at this time on their way. The consequence of this is that all barracks are overcrowded by at least 30 per cent. The detainees cannot lie down to sleep, but must sleep in a sitting position on the floor. Three-tier beds or bunks have been repeatedly allotted to the camp in recent time by Amt. B. III, but always from areas with which there is no transport connection. If I had sufficient sleeping accommodation at my disposal, then the accommodation of the detainees who have already arrived and of those still to come would appear more possible. In addition to this question a spotted fever and typhus epidemic has now begun, which increases in extent every day. The daily mortality rate, which was still in the region of 60–70 at the beginning of February, has in the meantime attained a daily average of 250–300 and will still further increase in view of the conditions which at present prevail.

Kramer outlined the irresolvable problems he faced, the failed delivery of winter supplies being the most immediate. He didn't have enough potatoes, enough turnips, enough bread. Even when he received a consignment he didn't have boilers sufficient to service the kitchens.

The incidence of disease is very high here in proportion to the number of detainees [Kramer supposedly wrote to his superior]. When you interviewed me on December 1, 1944, at Oranienburg, you told me that Bergen-Belsen was to serve as a sick camp for all concentration camps in North Germany. The number of sick has greatly increased, particularly on account of the transports of detainees, which have arrived from the East in recent times – these transports have sometimes spent eight to fourteen days in open trucks. An improvement in their condition, and particularly a return of these detainees to work, is under present conditions quite out of the question. The sick here gradually pine away till they die of weakness of the heart and general debility. As already stated, the average daily mortality is between 250 and 300. One can best gain an idea of the conditions of incoming transports when I state that on one occasion, out of a transport of 1900 detainees over 500 arrived dead.

The sewage system couldn't cope. He begged:

I am now asking you for your assistance as far as it lies in your power. In addition to the above-mentioned points I need here, before every-thing, accommodation facilities, beds, blankets, eating utensils – all for about 20,000 internees.

As for 'the Jews', as Kramer put it, he had 7,500 whom he requested be removed from the camp.

The removal of these internees is particularly urgent for the reason that several concentration camp Jews have discovered among the camp internees their nearest relations – some their parents, some their brothers and sisters. Also for purely political reasons – I mention in this connection the high death figure in this camp at present – it is essential that these Jews disappear from here as soon as possible.

It wasn't clear what 'disappear' meant in the circumstances.

Perhaps surprisingly, given the terminology he used, the emergence of the letter served Kramer reasonably well. It confirmed Winwood's contention that Kramer had done all he could to alleviate suffering and to protest against the further influxes of inmates from across and beyond Germany. The first charge against his client was that Kramer was 'responsible for the well-being' of those at Bergen-Belsen, had ill-treated the inmates, causing the deaths of certain Allied nationals. If it could be shown that he neither directly assaulted nor ordered the killing or beating of anyone, then Winwood needed only to prove that Kramer intended to fulfil, and had done all he could to fulfil, his obligation as commandant towards the well-being of those at Bergen-Belsen, but was prevented by others or circumstances from doing so.

The wording of the indictment prompted a defence of 'good intentions'. Again it was flawed by lack of context. Reading the letter again, I didn't feel as though human beings were the subject under discussion. A chicken farm, perhaps. But a place where people were contained and their lives respected? Without the slightest expression of compassion, with only the tenor of administrative burden, the letter should have been as condemnatory as Winwood believed it to be exculpatory.

During the examination by Winwood that followed, Kramer was allowed to further his claims of righteousness. He said, 'In March on my own responsibility I distributed more potatoes than the ration system would have allowed me to do.' He said, 'From the larger concentration camps, Sachsenhausen, Buchenwald, I received telegrams one or two days before the arrival of the prisoners. As far as the other transports were concerned, the vast majority, thousands of people, the only notice I received was when somebody at Belsen station phoned me up and said: "You can expect a transport for your camp in about half an hour's time."' After an outbreak of spotted fever was found in February, he closed the camp, but Berlin refused to acknowledge the command. He said transports from evacuated camps kept arriving. He'd been impotent in the face of the deluge.

Later, when Kramer neared the end of his testimony, the Deputy Judge Advocate interrupted to ask Kramer what his attitude was to the Jews sent to the camps he commanded. It was a timely reminder. Kramer replied: 'I had nothing to do with the reasons why these people were sent into my camp. I was there and I received them.

Why they were sent to me I do not know. It had nothing to do with me. Whether it was a political enemy or a Jew or a professional criminal had nothing to do with me at all. I received the bodies, that was all.'

The denial of complicity in a policy of extermination was replaced by an admission of indifference to the humanity of those over whom he had exercised control. Bodies? Not people. Corpses indistinguishable from consignments of wood or any inanimate material. That was Kramer's position.

In completing his opening address, Winwood had apparently intended no irony as he'd said, 'When the curtain finally rings down on this stage Josef Kramer will, in my submission, stand forth not as the "Beast of Belsen" but as "The scapegoat of Belsen", the scapegoat for the man Heinrich Himmler whose bones are rotting on Lüneburg Heath not very far from here, and as the scapegoat for the whole National Socialist system.'

10.

The cross-examination of a defendant is the moment when a trial comes alive. On the twentieth day of the Belsen proceedings, 9 October 1945, Kramer was in the witness box.

Colonel Backhouse began with one of those questions that advocates should avoid.

'Do you believe in God?'

It was a despairing beginning, a precursor not to some existential and moral enquiry but to an accusation that the defendant had a propensity to lie on oath. Kramer's first statement to Lt Col Genn had denied that there were gas chambers in Auschwitz, something Kramer retracted later. Now Kramer explained that he'd been bound by an oath of secrecy and this had prevented him from telling the truth about the extermination of the Jews and the mass executions. He'd felt no need to be honest when captured. He hadn't known then that the statement would appear in his trial.

Backhouse said the statement was made on oath. If Kramer believed in God then that oath should have been sacred: that was the implication. Given all that the court had heard so far, Kramer's ability to lie in contravention of any vow to God seemed of such minor importance as hardly warranting notice. And yet, as I found later, this was not the last time such a line of questioning would appear in concentration camp cases. As if God had anything to do with the Nazi regime.

It took a few minutes before Backhouse moved on from this irrelevant exchange. His next line of questioning related not to Auschwitz or Bergen-Belsen, but to Kramer's time as commandant of Natzweiler-Struthof. Though not on the charge sheet, his stint there was pertinent and, as he confessed to his attorney, Kramer was sensitive to its inclusion, particularly as he'd been personally responsible for the gassing of prisoners there so that their bodies could be used for medical experiments. Were the gas chambers in Natzweiler constructed by his order? Backhouse asked.

Yes, said Kramer.

Did he deliberately gas eighty prisoners there?

Yes, on a command from Himmler. A special transport. The bodies were to be sent to Strasbourg University after the killing.

And he simply followed those orders?

The highest military authority commanded him – think what they would have done to him if he'd refused.

Did he actually force these people into the gas chambers himself? Yes.

Yes. No equivocation. Bold, bland, blind. Read that 'yes' and the human condition – about which so much has been written, debated, pondered – splinters and fractures. One affirmation by a man who said he was obliged to follow his orders.

I couldn't tell whether Colonel Backhouse thought for a moment about this 'Yes'. Had he paused? I didn't think so.

With some speed, Backhouse moved from Natzweiler to Auschwitz. He asked what purpose the gas chambers served there.

Kramer didn't know.

Wasn't it part of a doctrine of the Nazi party, a party Kramer had joined, to exterminate the Jews?

Kramer didn't know: he didn't talk about such things.

Wasn't it part of policy to exterminate all intelligent Poles?

He didn't know.

How many people were killed in those chambers?

He didn't know.

Did he remember the transports arriving?

They came in day and night.

Did he remember the crematoria couldn't keep up?

Yes, they had to dig trenches.

Wasn't this mass murder?

No, it was the execution of orders.

Did he remember all the witnesses who'd appeared here and said they saw him making selections at Auschwitz, taking part in the beatings of the prisoners arriving and being divided?

They were lying. There were never any beatings anyway, at either Auschwitz or Belsen, not when he was present.

The quickfire questioning was soon completed. Two hours, no more. Backhouse could do little to pierce the cloak of admission, denial and excuse. Kramer had to rely on his dogged observance of all superior orders as his defence or he would be hanged. It was as simple and as complex as that. A scapegoat for Germany, Winwood had said. Or a Beast, as the press would have it. Was there any real distinction?

The Times noted Backhouse never succeeded 'in shaking Kramer's quick-witted composure. He answered questions about the deaths of thousands of people without faltering or change of tone.'[15]

That insouciance alone condemned him.[16]

11.

I thought I might learn something about the mentality of those who ran and served in the concentration camps before I began reading Backhouse's cross-examination. It was one of my aims when I started investigating this story of retribution that spread across so many trials and tribunals with Nuremberg at its supposed core. Imagining the courtroom scene, musing over the words and sentences, finding something profound within the utterances that would help understand the character and mentality of the perpetrators of great wrongs, of the survivors, of the men and women who took on the role of investigator and prosecutor and judge: that was my plan.

Of course, I knew the phrase 'cross-examination' pulsed with the theatrical. All courtroom dramas love that controlled sparring which typifies the encounter between lawyer and witness. It's supposed to be the moment when the guilty are revealed through the power of intelligent questioning, picking apart the very bones of a person's character and truthfulness. The process of cross-examination is infused with the notion that the truth will be uncovered.

The reality in Lüneburg was less edifying. Perhaps I should have guessed. Most cross-examination is tedious, slow, repetitive (you have to pause after each answer so that the judge or jury members can note down what has been said). As a means of understanding a person's condition, it lacks grace and subtlety.

Nonetheless, reading the cross-examination of Kramer I wanted there to be a confrontation that might have made sense of this man's actions. I wanted to read how he could have presided over, taken part in, watched on, lent a hand or a boot or a stick as witnesses claimed, actively organised a systematic, drawn-out shredding of the lives of others. There were some insights into Kramer's mind. But if you wanted to confront the worst thing he'd ever done it would be hard to separate the building and operation of the gas chambers at Natzweiler, where he stood outside listening to the cries of the eighty prisoners dying inside, from those terrifying daily 'selections' on the railway ramps of Auschwitz, where he said he merely observed the choices made by the doctors. Did those little confessions, which weren't intended to confess to anything, merely describe and reiterate his impotence in the face of orders or disclose something more significant? Where were the moments of normality in those years of KZ service? Where were the stories of human existence, of a life spent in cohabitation with others that didn't lead to some deliberately imposed suffering? The good lawyer would tell me that the courtroom is not the place to conduct psychoanalysis. But buried within the proceedings were small clues. In most respects other than his 'job' (it feels wrong to give the post of commandant that innocent-sounding credibility of a 'job') Kramer presented the trappings of normality. Wife, children, pets, a newly born baby he hadn't been able to see until halfway through the trial. Nothing remarkable before or after the worst things he'd ever done.

Major Winwood brought Frau Rosina Kramer to make that point. Asked to testify as to her husband's anxiety for his prisoners in Bergen-Belsen, she said, 'He told me his duty was to take care of them and this is what he has been doing the whole time, night and day. I remember he came once between duty hours and spoke with me and my children, that was his all, his own treasure, and he said: "If I could find anything so that those people should not lie on the bare floor," and then he gave orders to see that some fern plants should be collected so that these people should have something.'

Colonel Backhouse wasn't moved. His cross-examination of her recalled that she and Kramer had spent time at Auschwitz together. And he asked: 'You knew about the gas chambers, then, did you?'

'Everybody in Auschwitz, the whole area, knew about it,' Frau Kramer said.

Backhouse asked, 'Your husband realised that it was very wrong that these people should be killed, did he not?'

'Yes, naturally.'

Natürlich. Naturally. Whichever language it was in, did the word rescue or condemn the soul of the commandant? If the killing of the Jews at Auschwitz could be understood so easily, so naturally, as wrong, what redemption was possible? Maybe there *was* reason for Backhouse to press Kramer about his belief in God after all. It might have been the first foray into salvation. But who could really believe that?

Outside the courthouse, as Frau Kramer was escorted from the building after giving her evidence, a Polish woman, a prosecution witness, reached out and slapped her face. The authorities hurried the commandant's wife away. A shout from the crowd: 'Your husband killed my husband *and* my children.'

12.

By mid-October 1945, once the interest in the Beast of Belsen had dissipated, the media turned their eyes to the grander event waiting in the wings. The press were becoming aware of rifts between the Allies and their approaches to the major trial at Nuremberg. They'd been informed that the lawyers from the Soviet Union, France, the US and Britain would meet in Berlin and one item on the agenda was the location of the trial. The Russians wanted it to be held in Berlin even though Nuremberg had already been earmarked by Jackson and endorsed by the others on the prosecution team. It was an argument that provoked speculation in the press. The *Manchester Guardian* reflected that it was a 'small point, so trifling, in fact, that its mere raising after once being settled arouses impatience'.[17] It suspected that behind the spat 'lies a more serious division between the Western Powers and Russia over how these trials should be viewed', and that the Russians weren't interested in strict legal process. Moscow radio was reported as having announced that the 'chief criminals "must be destroyed"', indicating their expectations. 'Our representatives will have clearly in their minds', *The Times* assumed rather pompously, 'that they are establishing a legal and not a political tribunal.' The process underway at the Belsen trial may have been 'as tedious as the evidence is revolting, but the Court's painstaking records will stand scrutiny in the future. Hasty trials urged on by political pressure would seem unsatisfactory now and odious to posterity.'

The concern with how future generations would judge the war crimes trials underway and the major one to come at Nuremberg wasn't merely press interpretation. It was a message that had been stressed by Justice Jackson and the American administration in general. They didn't believe this was just another trial. It should have been the first of many, prosecuting hundreds of the top-ranking Nazi figures. But the experience of working with his Allied counterparts had induced cynicism in Jackson. He didn't trust the Soviets in particular to carry through further proceedings once the initial batch of Nazis was dealt with.

Preparing the ground for the US to undertake proceedings regardless of Allied support, a law was drafted that would eventually be
signed by all four major powers in December 1945. Control Council
Law No. 10 would allow for the punishment of persons guilty of war
crimes, crimes against peace and against humanity. For the British, it
was more extensive than the authority given initially to the military
authorities through the royal warrant, and it primed the ground for
each occupying power to do as it pleased. The era of inter-state
cooperation cutting across ideologies had almost ended, though not
just yet.

Despite the petty dispute about the place of trial, the powers had
finally composed an indictment against the Nuremberg defendants. It
was lodged with the Nuremberg Tribunal by the committee of Chief
Prosecutors at a ceremony in Berlin on 18 October 1945. Most press
reports seemed to think it did justice to the magnitude of the crimes.

The four counts were fleshed out from the sketch produced a
couple of months previously when the London Agreement had been
finalised. Count One now stated that all the defendants, without
exception, including the named organisations, 'participated as leaders,
organizers, instigators, or accomplices in the formulation or execution
of a common plan or conspiracy to commit, or which involved the
commission of, Crimes against Peace, War Crimes, and Crimes against
Humanity'. A panoply of iniquities was set out: the wars of aggression; the systematic breach of the rules of warfare; inhumane acts
against civilian populations before and during the war; 'persecutions
on political, racial, or religious grounds, in execution of the plan for
preparing and prosecuting aggressive or illegal wars'. The Nazi party
was the fulcrum upon which all this occurred, the indictment said,
inciting others to join its illegal adventures. A description of how
total power was maintained followed. Fourth on the list was the
implementation of 'their "master race" policy'. And here the brief
story of the Holocaust, yet to be named as such, was told: the
'disfranchisement, stigmatization, denial of civil rights, subjecting
their persons and property to violence, deportation, enslavement,
enforced labor, starvation, murder, and mass extermination'.

Details of the other counts supported this primary charge of conspiracy. Aggressive war; war crimes listed in all their grotesquery:

shooting, hanging, gassing, starvation, gross overcrowding, systematic under-nutrition, systematic imposition of labor tasks beyond the strength of those ordered to carry them out, inadequate provision of surgical and medical services, kickings, beatings, brutality and torture of all kinds, including the use of hot irons and pulling out of fingernails and the performance of experiments by means of operations and otherwise on living human subjects ... deliberate and systematic genocide ... the extermination of racial and national groups, against the civilian populations of certain occupied territories in order to destroy particular races and classes of people and national, racial, or religious groups, particularly Jews, Poles, and Gypsies and others ... pseudo-scientific experiments (sterilization of women at Auschwitz and at Ravensbrück, study of the evolution of cancer of the womb at Auschwitz, of typhus at Buchenwald, anatomical research at Natzweiler, heart injections at Buchenwald, bone grafting and muscular excisions at Ravensbrück, etc.), gas chambers, gas wagons, and crematory ovens.

There was no attempt to graduate through levels of depravity, rather a serving of horrifying examples at random to demonstrate that barbarism was endemic.

Finally, there was Count Four, crimes against humanity, the extermination of the Jews paramount, other persecuted groups receiving little attention: the Roma, the disabled, homosexuals, Jehovah's Witnesses. General accusations were levelled ('Jews were systematically persecuted since 1933 ... Since 1 September 1939, the persecution of the Jews was redoubled: millions of Jews from Germany and from the occupied Western Countries were sent to the Eastern Countries for extermination ... As the Germans retreated before the Soviet Army they exterminated Jews rather than allow them to be liberated ... Many concentration camps and ghettos were set up in which Jews were incarcerated and tortured, starved, subjected to merciless atrocities, and finally exterminated') and specific ('60,000 Jews were shot on an island on the Dvina near Riga ... 32,000 Jews were shot at Sarny ... thousands of Jews were gassed weekly by means of gas-wagons which broke down from overwork'). Several separate incidents were mentioned without date or any other specificity.

The purpose of the document was both to shock and to prepare the defendants as to the nature of the charges against them. Each of the accused was named and identified with one or more of the Counts.

Gustave Gilbert, a US Army psychologist, who was assigned to observe the defendants now transferred to the prison specially constructed for them in Nuremberg, wrote in his diary about the reactions to the indictment of the senior Nazis standing accused.[18] The soldiers amongst them displayed shock, according to Gilbert. *Generaloberst* Jodl was reported as saying, 'The indictment knocked me on the head ... The crimes are horrible beyond belief, if they are true.' 'The charges in the indictment are terrible,' Keitel said.

They began to rehearse their defence. Admiral Doenitz: 'None of these indictment counts concerns me in the least.' Keitel: 'What could I do?' He was but a 'mouthpiece to carry out the Führer's wishes'. Jodl: 'I had no idea at all about 90% of the accusations ... I don't see how they can fail to recognise a soldier's obligation to obey orders.'

The other defendants were variously resigned, dismissive, distraught, outraged, confused. Goering acknowledged the inevitability of the victors judging the vanquished. Frick, the Minister of the Interior, said the indictment rested on fictional conspiracy. Von Ribbentrop believed the wrong people had been accused. Kaltenbrunner denied his guilt: he said he was being dragged there because Himmler wasn't able to answer for his crimes. Speer accepted the necessity of the trial so that common responsibility for 'such horrible crimes' could be assigned. Hess said he couldn't remember anything.

Whatever evidence the indictment presented, it was clear that it could only be a tiny fraction of that which would need to be brought before the tribunal. The Belsen trial alone confirmed that, with its weeks of testimony dragging on into winter.

13.

Once Frau Kramer had left the courtroom in Lüneburg the quick descent into tedium began afresh. Each defendant was brought into the witness box and repeated the same argument: they were not guilty of specific acts of violence alleged against them; if they were at Auschwitz, they were only following the orders of their superiors in the selections for gassing; and when at Bergen-Belsen they were overwhelmed by the conditions as much as the inmates had been.

The predictability challenged the trial's capacity to do anything other than undermine any hope that posterity would value this process, at least as a means of understanding how the extermination of peoples could so easily have been pursued. It felt more of a trudge through necessary but unsatisfactory routines. Even the defendants displayed the hallmark of the bored: inappropriate laughter. When Peter Weingartner, Defendant Number 3, the Yugoslav carpenter conscripted into the SS in 1942 to serve in Auschwitz as a guard, then *Blockführer*, appeared on the stand, the other accused watching him from the large enclosure giggled at his dim-witted answers. His counsel, Major Winwood again, said of him that 'his mentality and temperament are, to say the least, not quite normal', that 'his nerves and temper sometimes overrode his reason'. The other accused laughed at his idiotic performance under questioning. It was enough to wonder whether such a man should have been on trial at all, though he looked the image of brutality from his photographs. His features may or may not have counted against him. He would be found guilty and sentenced to death in any case.

At the other end of the spectrum, Dr Klein was clearly intelligent, but his admissions about the gassing selections were simple and brutal. As one of the doctors at Auschwitz he'd been ordered to divide transports arriving in the camp. He said he had to decide who was fit for work and who wasn't. Children under thirteen or thereabouts were considered automatically part of the latter.

And those not selected as fit for work? Klein said he'd had no influence on this, but he knew some of them were sent to the gas chambers. He said he didn't approve, but protest was useless. When it came to Belsen, he maintained he'd advocated for disposal of the piles of rotting bodies accumulating in the camp and improvement in the water supply. He gave the impression of a humanitarian, a medical doctor with the welfare of his patients his utmost and Hippocratic concern.

Unlike with Kramer, Colonel Backhouse's cross-examination was direct.

Did Klein realise that the killing of people in the gas chambers was murder?

Yes.

The people who were declared unfit for work were simply destroyed?

Yes.

Those who were fit for work were beaten, starved until their time for the gas chamber came?

He hadn't seen any of that, though he treated some people who had been beaten in the hospital.

Was he aware that experiments were carried out at Auschwitz?

Yes.

The questioning took no more than twenty minutes. Detail now seemed to be considered unnecessary. Once the admissions about the process of selections and the end for those selected was established, there seemed to be little else to say.

Only with Irma Grese did a frisson of interest pass through the courtroom. She was the only possible connection with sex, and thus the stuff of life rather than death, that the observers from the press could imagine in this grim catalogue of atrocity. Major Cranfield took her through her story in the *Konzentrationlagers*. They discussed the whips she'd carried at Auschwitz. She admitted she'd used them, but denied individual cases when it was alleged she'd beaten inmates. She was only twenty years old then, she said.

When Colonel Backhouse cross-examined her, he seemed fascinated by her age. She was only eighteen when first taken on the staff at Ravensbrück KZ, she told him. Though the regime was severe, she said, she'd never struck anyone.

When she moved to Auschwitz her duties included commanding a gardening detail. She told Backhouse about the work, innocuous by her account, picking out weeds, but she had no dog and no stick.

Suddenly, Backhouse asked, 'I suggest to you that when you went out with these working parties you made a habit of beating women and of kicking them and you enjoyed it?'

'That is a big lie,' Grese answered.

He accused her of having fun hitting her prisoners, of choosing heavy boots for that purpose, having a whip made out of plaited cellophane at the factory, and beating people to the ground and then laying in with her boots. He accused her of being part of the selection process. She agreed she'd been with Dr Mengele, though said she had no idea about the gas chambers, why the selection was being made. And she denied she would hit people to the ground and drag them back to the selection ramp if they tried to run away. She admitted that she had to strike some prisoners but it wasn't ill-treatment.

Grese listened to the accusations against her. The women who said she was always cruel? She accepted none of it. And the *Daily Mail* reported that she'd raised her voice to a scream to say she'd *never* shot anyone.[19]

Backhouse's questioning was more detailed than for Klein or many of the other defendants. It reflected the interest in Grese, in the detail of her life in the camps. Though even that was beginning to wane. The press had little more to say other than that she'd been seen sobbing for the first time, four weeks into the trial. For a moment, she was transformed from beast to young woman. But only for a moment.

Without time for pause, the forty or so other defendants then presented their defences. Some were concentration camp prisoners themselves, turned into *Kapos* in the KZ system and seen as worse than the SS by some inmates. Ilse Lothe, for instance. Two or three witnesses had spoken against her. But the charge was the same as it was for Kramer or Klein or Grese or the other SS: by taking the role of *Kapo* she'd become part of the Auschwitz regime, indistinguishable from the SS members who'd commanded her and punished her too. The defence said the three women who'd testified against her, who'd spoken to the British investigators in June, had conspired to have her picked out for the trial, that their statements were suspiciously similar, that they'd fabricated their accounts. Lothe denied all allegations and claimed she was as much a victim as those who'd informed on her. She didn't even know them, she said, knew nothing about the incidents they mentioned. Ultimately she would be believed by the court, believed enough to cast doubt on the specific allegations of brutality.

There were others like Lothe. Inmates supposedly turned into agents of violence for their SS captors. No fewer than a dozen accused were *Kapos*, men like Ignatz Schlomowicz, a veteran of the KZ system. Since 1939 he'd been in many of the notorious camps: initially arrested by the Gestapo in the Netherlands, he'd been imprisoned in Oranienburg, Groß-Rosen, Auschwitz (where he'd survived one of Kramer's selections on arrival and worked in the Buna factory), Hannover, Mauthausen, and finally Bergen-Belsen about eight days before the British troops appeared. He'd survived all those years, survived typhus after his liberation. And the reason he was in the concentration camps? He was Jewish.

Colonel Backhouse tried hard to pierce Schlomowicz's story. The defendant insisted that although he may have been a *Kapo* in Hannover, in Belsen he was simply one of the *Häftlinge* like every other Jew there. He hadn't hit anyone despite the allegations made by a couple of fellow inmates. What was different about him compared to the millions of other victims? Why was he on trial at all?

14.

After seven weeks of testimony, the Deputy Judge Advocate, Carl Stirling, brought the proceedings to a close. He had to summarise the evidence for and against each of the accused, directing his analysis at the panel of military men who had to decide their guilt. It took him over two days. He began almost sheepishly. And in so doing, he cut through to the heart of the British interpretation of a fair trial.

This trial has taken a long time. I think at the outset there were a number of people who thought and hoped that this was to be a sort of pageant in which these people in the dock would play their part and whatever was seen, whatever was heard, in this court they would go to their ultimate fate. But, gentlemen, that is not so. The powers which brought you here decided that these people should have a trial in accordance with the law and though they may not have appreciated that it would take so long they must have appreciated that it would take a great deal of time.

If you have a reasonable doubt in regard to any one of these accused, it is your duty to record a finding of not guilty. On the other hand, if the Prosecution have established their case to your satisfaction, and have excluded a reasonable doubt by producing that judicial certainty which excludes such a doubt, then, gentlemen, it would be your duty to convict and to mete out that stern justice which a conviction on charges of this kind not only requires but demands.

Then, once he had painstakingly proceeded through all that he'd noted over the weeks, detail by detail, he left the panel to make up their minds. It was 10.57 a.m., Friday, 16 November 1945. No more than six hours later the decisions had been made.

Kramer: guilty.

Klein, the doctor: guilty.

Weingartner, the laughably stupid one: guilty.

Grese, the blonde beast: guilty.

Lothe and Schlomowicz, the *Kapos*: not guilty. Twelve others also acquitted and released from the concern of the court.

It was not the guilty verdicts that surprised. It was the acquittals. Suddenly, with the declaration that a whole cohort of defendants had been released, found innocent of all charges as far as the public could see, the trial as a process of retribution, supposed to channel the fury at the Nazis and all their servants, had become an ambiguous undertaking.

Georg Kraft, SS conscript from 1943 who'd served in Buchenwald, Dora and Belsen; Josef Klippel, SS camp guard since October 1943; Karl Egersdörfer, SS member at Auschwitz; Walter Otto, SS too, Auschwitz and Bergen-Belsen. Not guilty. The judgment said: simply because you worked in the concentration camps, even though you served in one of the notorious death and labour camps for years, you won't be condemned out of hand; you might even be deemed innocent.

No reasons were given for the decisions. It was clear that the acquittals arose because the prosecution had failed to provide sufficient evidence against those particular defendants. Take Egersdörfer: an affidavit alone purported to condemn him. No witness had appeared in person to say he'd abused anyone, either at Auschwitz or Bergen-Belsen. Even though he was in the kitchens of these camps for years and undoubtedly served up the cruellest and meanest provisions, the court wouldn't convict him. It seemed, after all the rhetoric that instituted the war crimes trials, it wasn't enough that a defendant was a member of the SS unit which made the working of the camps possible, who contributed to the operation of a place designed to kill and torture and treat with total disregard any inmate's humanity.

Whilst those acquitted were taken away, the guilty had to be sentenced, but only after the defence attorneys spoke in mitigation. Undoubtedly, Major Winwood's task was difficult, having the two most senior SS men to defend. In the spirit with which he'd so far approached his role, he spoke with little discretion.

He said of Dr Klein:

He is a professional doctor and an elderly man. It has been said that he sent thousands to their death in the gas chamber, but every man or woman who Dr Klein chose as fit for work was saved from the gas chamber, and he or she was granted a lease of life. Surely, Sir, a man of this type could do no more for the internees by taking part in selections than by leaving the selecting to the more brutal and more advanced SS men. I would ask the Court when considering his sentence to look on Dr Klein as a man who, to a certain degree, actually saved people from death.

Kramer, he said, 'has put himself before you as a true German who carried out an order because it was an order. He may have wondered himself whether it was right or not, but his own personal feelings or qualms faded into insignificance besides the fundamental German principle that an order is given to obey.' Winwood drew a comparison with what was about to happen at Nuremberg. Was the court to sentence these 'minor war criminals' to a punishment which couldn't be exceeded for the 'major'? Was Kramer to be treated the same as Goering?

Major Cranfield was more sensitive in his pleas. Irma Grese's age and innocence were the qualities he stressed: could she be responsible for all the actions attributed to her? Could a girl so young be said to be truly culpable? he asked.

The pleas were ignored. On 17 November 1945, Kramer, Klein, Weingartner, Grese and seven others were sentenced to death by hanging. The others found guilty received prison terms from life to one year.

15.

Setting off on a walk along the paths of the Bergen-Belsen site, which drifted through the birch trees and out amidst the uneven and coarse ground that had once supported the barracks and enclosures where thousands upon thousands succumbed to disease, starvation and brutal treatment, I remember thinking about the trial. Did it accomplish anything? Did it bring retribution upon those who deserved punishment? Did it reveal their character, the reason for their actions? Did it help understand why this place, those deaths, that suffering, occurred? Did it achieve anything other than to demonstrate retribution through the sentences of death handed down? When I read the Deputy Judge Advocate's summing up, I doubted the value of the procedure in answering any of these questions. Carl Stirling, with the veneer of fairness imbuing every sentence, presented a strange mixture of personal opinion, recounted fact and rebelliousness. He didn't express the political lines laid down in Washington and Whitehall that were supposed to establish the rationale and necessity of war crimes trials. His was a legal pronouncement. It lacked ... empathy? Compassion? Or was it context? I'm still not sure of the right word.

He began, as the charge sheet required, with Auschwitz. Not the whole history of that place, only the years 1942 to 1943, when Josef Kramer was commandant of Birkenau. Stirling said to the officers on the panel who were to pass judgment,

> The German state set up the camp of Auschwitz and it now becomes your duty in the light of the evidence you have heard in this court to decide what took place in the war years from 1942 until 1943. I think you will be satisfied that to Auschwitz were taken by force innumerable people for the purpose of providing man power and women power for the German military machine, and I think you will be satisfied that among those who were taken, without any excuse, without any right, and against their wishes, were a number of Allied nationals.

I wondered how, after the stories that had been heard of the selections, the gas chambers, the experiments, the degradation of human beings for the sake of nothing save the satisfaction of a caprice, Stirling could say no more than this as a prologue to his advice.

Stirling *did* make one reference to the gassings.

> If you are satisfied that Allied nationals were taken in the way which has been described to you, and that they were put in a gas chamber because they were of no use to the German Reich, is that or is that not a violation of the customs and usages of war? Gentlemen, it seems to me that you will be entitled and well entitled to say that it was.

'No use to the German Reich'? Was that the perceived reason for the extermination of the Jews who were driven from the train trucks onto the platform ramp and pushed one way to work and the other to die? Was there nothing else to say?

There was, though Stirling used the law to say it. Concerned with the defence that the accused were only obeying orders and that this might absolve them of responsibility, he advised there was precedent that members of an armed force may be bound to follow legal orders. But they couldn't escape liability where the act both violated a clear rule of war and outraged the 'general sentiments of humanity'. And he said:

Do you think when people have been dragged away to Auschwitz and have been put in the military machine, and have been gassed and killed without any trial, because they have committed no crime except that of being a Jew or being unwanted by the state, that that is not a clear violation of an unchallenged rule of warfare which outrages the general sentiments of humanity?

It was no more than a passing mention of the Jews, one that wasn't to be repeated. The context was replaced by fascination for fact, or at least fact as presented in the testimony heard in the courtroom. Stirling said,

There is a tremendous general body of evidence going to establish that at Auschwitz the staff responsible for the well-being of internees were taking part in these gassings; that they were taking part in improper, unlawful beating; that they were taking part in Appelle; that they were taking part in the use of savage dogs; that they were over-working and under-feeding the internees; and maybe that there were even experiments imposed upon people, so called in the interests of science, against their will.

He said it was a matter for the panel to decide whether any particular defendant was guilty of involvement in this 'general crime'. He said that 'at Auschwitz there had grown up a practice or a course of conduct under which internees, including Allied nationals, were being treated in such a way that they were of no value at all as human beings'. He said Bergen-Belsen was similar, though 'substituted for the gas chamber you have what the prosecution allege to be a state of wilful or culpable neglect whereby thousands of innocent people lost their lives'. Neglect? The law defined the charge. It didn't also have to define the summary Stirling gave.

He turned to the affidavit evidence, the mass of written testimonies of survivors whose accounts had been taken down by Lt Col Genn and his team in the aftermath of liberation. Many witnesses had dispersed across the European continent. God knew what had become of them. The prosecution didn't. How should all those affidavits be considered? Stirling said, 'They are dangerous material.' He said,

> We all know how people will tell you things in the smoke room and how they would quickly retract them if they had to appear in a court and be cross-examined. I have the greatest faith in cross-examination. I have been brought up to realise what a potent weapon it is in discovering the truth. That, of course, has been denied the defending officers. Consider these affidavits and the way in which they were taken, especially on the question of identity. You need no words from me to realise that you must be most careful in dealing with those affidavits, and I am sure you will find it is difficult to act upon just one or two unless they are supposed in material particular showing that they are really worthy of credence and belief.

Cautious and proper, all in accordance with the standards of British justice. Later, at the end of his summing up, dealing with each of the accused and the evidence against them, Stirling identified the 'golden thread' familiar to all British criminal courts: it is the duty of the prosecution to prove the guilt of the accused; if there is reasonable doubt from the evidence presented, then the accused must be acquitted. He said, 'The principle that the prosecution must prove the guilt of the prisoner is part of the common law of England, and no attempt to whittle it down can be entertained.' It defined the whole trial. For good or ill. British justice applied with little regard to the extraordinary context.

If the politicians and most senior lawyers of America and Britain had thought these hearings would provide a lesson for history, would open to scrutiny the soul of those who had overseen wickedness few could comprehend, would provide a precedent for the remainder of the minor proceedings, the Belsen trial must have been a disappointment. It was a very peculiar process.

6

Dachau

1.

The visit to Nordhausen was a diversion. I was still thinking about the Belsen trial, what it said about the quality of British justice, the people brought to answer for the worst of crimes and those who investigated and prosecuted them. But ignoring the parallel work of the Americans and, of course, the overshadowing Nuremberg proceedings about to begin, would have been a mistake. I knew the British plan for achieving retribution couldn't be understood without some sense of what was happening elsewhere.

Mittelbau-Dora, outside Nordhausen, was one of the other major camp centres the American troops had liberated during their ferocious push into the heart of Germany. The journey there didn't feel any great distance, though with multiple roadworks on the autobahn it took three and a half hours by car, travelling south with the weather getting colder the further I drove into the Harz Mountains.

In April 1945, it was a route (though going the other way) that thousands of concentration camp inmates had been forced to take with their SS guards. Whether marching by road or packed into trucks and transported by rail, many travelled the 200 kilometres to Bergen-Belsen to escape the oncoming forces of the US Army. Deaths were commonplace along the way, victims of that last, desperate, chaotic and murderous exodus of camp survivors, whipped from place to place like an army of aimless vagrants, executed if they stopped to rest or fell exhausted at the roadside. Most at the Mittelbau-Dora KZ complex had already been brought from Auschwitz and Groß-Rosen, enduring the dangers of Allied bombing as well as the abuse from their own guards, when those camps had been evacuated in the face of the Soviet Red Army's advance into Poland and Prussia.

I turned off the main road from Nordhausen and followed the familiar brown signs that mark the concentration camp memorials across Germany. The entrance to Mittelbau-Dora could have been mistaken for a private farm. There was no grand edifice, as at Bergen-Belsen and Buchenwald, only a cattle truck on a short length of rusted track. The narrow road curved into pasture with a modest hill line to the right and open fields to the left. I drove for another kilometre and parked by the roadside in sight of a large white-panelled modern building sitting incongruously up a small incline overlooking a flattened expanse of ground that sheltered amidst a crescent of hills. This was the exterior camp, an overflow for the prisoners. The original *Häftlinge*, those brought in at the end of 1944, had been housed in tunnels.

When I'd read the transcripts of the Belsen trial I came across many witnesses and a few defendants who'd been moved to Bergen-Belsen KZ from Mittelbau-Dora: they said all the SS administrative staff had been transferred along with about 15,000 prisoners, adding to the catastrophic overcrowding. *Obersturmführer* Franz Hössler, for instance, had been at Mittelbau-Dora since January 1945, having served at Auschwitz before that, where he'd taken part in the selections for the gas chambers with Kramer; Hössler was one of those sentenced to death at Lüneburg.

Mittelbau-Dora was an arms production camp: its purpose was to manufacture V2 rockets, Hitler's so-called Vengeance weapon that was supposed to force victory at the very last moment. To escape Allied bombing, the rockets were to be built within massive tunnels dug into the hillsides. As I looked around the camp, I couldn't see any sign of an entrance to some vast underground complex. Then a small desultory group of visitors wrapped up in padded coats and scarves appeared from the modern building on the hill, walking towards me along the path. I waited until they came closer and then caught the eye of the woman leading the party, whom I took to be the guide. She was young, no more than mid-twenties, and seemed to know my enquiry even before I said anything.

'If you want to see the tunnels you can join us if you wish. You won't be able to enter otherwise. No one can go in without a guide.'

Her English was perfect.

'But,' she said, 'the tour is in German.'

I said it didn't matter and followed on behind the group. We were led away from the camp, back along the entrance road, to an obscured path that curved in towards the hillside and ended in a fence and metal gate. Beyond was a tunnel entrance blocked up by a concrete wall, a metal door in its centre.

The guide unlocked the door, telling us that the original entrance had been blown up by the Soviets. Visitors hadn't been encouraged in those days. A new entrance into the underground complex had been built later, after the reunification of Germany in the early 1990s. As she poised to push the heavy door open, the guide said, 'You only enter at your own risk, OK?' It was the only English she used for the entire tour.

Inside, despite the guide's irritating adherence to the rules of her tour (I didn't think it would have cost her much effort to say a few explanatory words in English for my benefit), it was as though I'd entered a different dimension. More than with Buchenwald and Neuengamme and Bergen-Belsen and Flossenbürg, I felt the corporeal experience of those who'd been forced into these camps.

Immediately within the entrance was a rack of heavy-duty torches. The guide picked one up, switched it on and then beckoned us to follow towards another door. This opened into complete darkness. She stepped forward and pulled at a lever on the wall. A row of ceiling lights, dim and yellow, came on in a line disappearing into the distance. I could see no end, only the roof lights hanging, their light pale in the gloom.

The guide began to walk on and for about five minutes we followed her in complete silence, strung out behind, shuffling a little because we couldn't quite see where we were putting our feet. Her lamp lit up the tunnel, which was cut roughly into the rock. The floor was uneven and damp. After a while, I could see the tunnel opening into what appeared to be some kind of cavern. When we arrived, and the guide switched on more lights on the wall, we could see it was only another tunnel, running at right angles to the entrance shaft.

It felt icy, breathing in the slightly fetid air of the tunnel. More lights went on. There was another tunnel to our left, its end out of sight, much higher than the one we'd just walked through. The guide gathered us around a strange structure of metal tubes, about three centimetres in diameter, several metres long, criss-crossing each other, bending slightly here and there, some ending abruptly, hanging suspended on wires from the ceiling. It looked like a modern sculpture. The guide explained that this was a representation, a model, of the tunnel system we had entered. And in understanding this, equating the point on the tubes with where we were now standing and where we'd walked from the entrance, I realised that the tunnels were immense, stretching deep into the hills. The camp outside was nothing in comparison.

I understood enough of the guide's talk to know that the original inmates had been brought here to live and to work. The sleeping quarters were inside the hill, amongst the manufacturing plant for the V2 rockets, and some prisoners stayed for months without seeing daylight. Conditions had been terrible. With the ear-cracking noise of the production, the dust from digging and dragging heavy loads, the smell of gas and faeces of the prisoners who had to relieve themselves in buckets or by the edges of the tunnels, disease and accident and intensely arduous labour cut the workers down. Thousands had died in the tunnels or had been shipped out as broken beings to die elsewhere in the camp system.

When the guide moved on, deeper into the tunnels, the oppressive cold and damp became more intense. A long steel walkway raised off the tunnel floor had been constructed to view some of the interior chambers. Piles of rocket parts and tubing littered the ground, nose cones and engine housings. As we walked along, I caught a glimpse of a row of broken toilet bowls in a partially bricked-up cave to the side of the main tunnel. I was at the rear of our small party and stopped to look. I had to crouch a little to see into the latrine room. I didn't know whether these were for the guards or the prisoners. I thought about the people who'd used them. I thought about the natural function they would have performed, the urine and excrement, the daily ritual, the sudden dysentery. No one could have escaped that.

I hurried to catch up the group, unwilling to be left too far behind. We rounded a corner and the walkway stopped, a couple of metres above the ground. Beneath was an oil-sheened lake spreading into the darkness of yet another tunnel siding. Through the minimal lighting reflected off the water's surface, I could just make out more rusting hulks of metal underneath. The water was completely still, like a sheet of Perspex.

The guide kept talking, but I stopped trying to make sense of what she was saying. It all sounded a little academic anyway, divorced from the surrounding blackness and devoid of feeling. The numbering of the dead, the statistics of their suffering, the sorrowful stories: none penetrated the dark beyond the lamplight. All I could think about were those toilets, that row of bowls, cracked and dirty, half hidden in a rough recess, but so familiar and basic and human; they provided an absurd connection with their users, the prisoners, as I took them to be, who lived here. In some odd way I now find difficult to explain, those toilets were the only real thing I saw in those tunnels.

It was getting dark when we finally came out of the tunnel complex. There were a few 'goodbyes' and some polite chatter but most of the group were reserved and content to slouch off to their cars. The guide was jollier. She waved to a couple walking down the hill from the exhibition centre. They too were wrapped up in heavy coats and big woollen scarves. It was very cold now the sun had gone and they didn't stop, other than to greet their colleague and sweep her away with them, walking together along the road towards the town. They'd finished their work for the day. Tomorrow they'd go through the same routine, delivering the same patter about the deaths and violence.

I watched the guides go and wondered what it must be like to tour this place every day recounting the history of brutality perpetrated by their own people. Did it make them angry? Or had they become inured to the human suffering they had to speak about? The woman who'd led my party had delivered her talk without any ostensible emotion. Maybe she'd had to learn a script.

2.

On 11 April 1945, American troops entered the city of Nordhausen, uncovering hundreds of dead and dying left at the sub-camp of Boelcke barracks. With bitter irony, and not for the first or last time, the casualties were the result of a British bombing raid. The RAF had flattened an area outside Nordhausen on 3 April. The barracks hadn't been marked with red crosses or anything to distinguish them from normal industrial or military use and they'd been targeted without any knowledge of their occupants. Rather than tend to the injured or bury the dead, the SS guards, who'd been able to make use of their air raid shelters, had evacuated the camp after the raid and left behind anyone who couldn't walk. Then the US tanks arrived.

Over the next few days, the Americans caring for those who'd survived the carnage at Boelcke heard about the underground camp at Mittelbau-Dora. They heard that secret weapons were produced there. They followed the road I would take nearly seventy years later, their minds not entirely on saving the inmates. The missile technology hidden in the tunnels was a significant attraction. And as Nordhausen and this region was marked for occupation by the Soviet Union, part of the preprogrammed-carve-up of Germany between the victors, the US forces had to act quickly to extract every piece of material that could prove useful for their own military purposes. The removal was part of a vast coordinated plan to acquire as much German technology and intelligence as possible, both in terms of hardware and of the scientists who'd designed and built it. It was quite a scramble. Engineers and scientists working in various sites on the V2 and other secret weapons were captured and taken into custody. Men like Arthur Rudolph, one of the production managers in the tunnel complex of Mittelbau-Dora, who with many other rocket engineers was soon transported to the US to become integral members of the Apollo space missions. Little thought was given to the role these people played in the perpetuation of conditions that purportedly killed 20,000 forced labourers in those subterranean works. Justice was always expendable, it seemed, when it came to 'strategic interests'.

Despite the partial blindness towards culpability, the US military leadership was already encountering so many examples of camp atrocity that the public fervour to pursue those responsible and bring them to trial in parallel with the British and other Allies became increasingly evident in the month of April. By the time the survivors of Nordhausen and Mittelbau-Dora were photographed and presented to the press as more examples of Nazi wickedness, they'd already discovered Ohrdruf, Buchenwald, Dachau and many sub-camps dotted about the southern German landscape. A determined effort was made to gather evidence, witness testimony from survivors, and arrest those suspected of involvement in the KZ system. In July 1945, orders were issued that military commanders could proceed with cases against suspected war criminals other than those who held high office (the latter were to be handed over for the major criminal trial planned for Nuremberg later in the year).[1] As with the royal warrant authorising British trials (which triggered the procedure for Belsen), the Americans were now legally able to push ahead with their own prosecutions. Military commission courts, akin to the courts martial instituted by the British, were supposed to respond quickly to the terrible evidence emerging from the liberated concentration camps in the US zone.

In the case of Mittelbau-Dora, a team of investigators had completed a report on the camp, and identified those to be regarded as suspects, by the end of May 1945.[2] They wrote that thousands of forced labourers had been treated appallingly. 'A complete indifference to the welfare of the prisoners was exhibited by their guards and custodians,' they reported. They'd uncovered a whole system of sub-camps where the underground workers had been housed. 'At the time of the liberation hundreds of bodies to which death had come from starvation and bombings were strewn about Boelcke Kaserne,' they wrote. 'These bodies were emaciated, and bony prominences of the skeletons were conspicuous under the skin. These bodies were laid in rows in various conditions of decomposition. A pile of naked bodies, the result of one day's deaths, was found under the stairway at the Boelcke Kaserne camp.' But the conditions throughout the years of operation were known to have been deadly too. Men had been worked to death, executed on the slightest pretext or left to die should they be unable to work.

Of those SS deemed responsible, some had ended up in Belsen after Dora was evacuated and were prosecuted at the Lüneburg proceedings in the autumn of 1945, though only in relation to their crimes committed whilst serving in Auschwitz or Bergen-Belsen. Many other accused and witnesses were now in the Soviet zone, but cooperation with the Russians quickly became impossible. Letters weren't answered, arrangements for extradition of individuals to the West, as it was now, weren't fulfilled, so that it wasn't until 1947 that a Mittelbau-Dora trial with nineteen defendants was held at Dachau KZ. Four were acquitted and the others sentenced to varying terms of imprisonment. Only *SS-Obersturmführer* Hans Möser was given the death penalty. Möser's execution was carried out in November 1948. The rest were all out of prison within a few years, the last in 1958, released as part of the reintegration of West Germany into the Western Alliance.

On the face of it, and as far as I could see from the US case reports and trial transcripts available, American justice didn't seem to have differed that greatly from the British efforts typified by the Bergen-Belsen trial and Neustadt investigations.[3] But unlike the British, who fanned out investigators across their sector, gathered suspects at different holding centres and brought trials in numerous locations (usually close to where the crimes had been committed), the Americans centralised their operations. Initially, they formed their headquarters in Wiesbaden, near Frankfurt, the 3rd and 7th Armies retaining occupational responsibility in the US zone. By June 1945, nineteen American War Crimes Investigation Teams were operating, compared to the two sent out by the British, and the decision was made to bring all suspected 'minor' war criminals found by US forces to one site pending trial. Dachau was identified as the place where the accused Nazis would be imprisoned (more than 15,000 of them) and also where their trials would be held.

It was a symbolic (as well as practical) choice. Whilst the British were using grand public buildings for their showcase trials, places that civilised the process, echoed the sounds of Crown courts in England, and arguably made distant the stories of atrocity told, the Americans brought attention to one of the centres of the whole SS and KZ system. Dachau was the first major camp constructed under the Nazis and provided a model for all other massive KZs throughout Germany and, later, occupied Europe. Having the trials there was a constant reminder of the abysmal nature of the camps for all those brought to trial: months after the liberation the place still reeked of death and decay.

The location was not the only dissimilarity with the British programme. A much more steely and pragmatic approach appeared to have been taken to legal procedure. Though defence lawyers (US military personnel for the most part appointed to represent the accused) would object to prejudicial and arguably unfair processes, just as Thomas Winwood and his colleagues had done at the Belsen trial, the objections were uniformly and sharply dismissed. There was little breast-beating on the part of the American Judge Advocates before deciding that normal rules of criminal proceedings back in the US could be bent, and whatever was necessary was done to secure convictions in the messy and evidentially hazy circumstances of prosecuting camp personnel. In the summer months of 1945, the US authorities established principles of prosecution that would govern their concentration camp trials. They were broader than their British counterparts. The definition of 'war crimes' of which enemy nationals could be charged included 'offenses against persons or property which outrage common justice or involve moral turpitude'. The last phrase owned a beauty all its own. It could address any depravity without the need for precise definition. And 'common justice' enabled a subjective interpretation that also liberated the prosecutor and court from having to find some precedent for condemning a particular act.

Despite the resources and organisational qualities of the Americans, not everything they did was superior to the British effort in those early months. The Hadamar case in particular suggested an uncertainty at the heart of the US prosecutions: it raised the question as to whether they were prepared or able to confront the depth of depravity to which the Nazi regime had sunk.

Hadamar was an asylum outside Wiesbaden. American soldiers had found the medical institution populated by human wreckage. Patients were lying barely alive and barely tended, in wards that only pretended to look after the mentally ill. It was soon established that Hadamar was one of the euthanasia centres, part of the notorious T4 programme (named after the address of its operating institution at Tiergartenstraße No. 4 in Berlin) devised to remove from German life those who didn't conform to the Aryan model of humanity. Lethal injections were employed to kill over 15,000 people during the asylum's operation (although estimates of the number of dead at the time and since have varied enormously).[4] Initially, the mentally ill were the targets, although political opponents were sent there too. The graveyard in the grounds was full of the victims, mostly German nationals, though Russian and Polish slave workers deemed too sick to work were brought here from 1944 and murdered as well. The former weren't the concern of the Americans, legally speaking. Their deaths could only be introduced into a prosecution tangentially, proof of the intent and purpose of the institution. The main charges had to relate to the killing of Allied nationals. That was the restriction formulated before the end of the war by those lawyers meeting in London. The US team therefore prosecuted the administrative head of the asylum, Alfons Klein; two male nurses, Heinrich Ruoff and Karl Willig; the doctor, Adolf Wahlmann; and several other staff in October 1945, all charged with the killing of 'human beings of Polish and Russian nationality, their exact names and number being unknown but aggregating in excess of 400, and who were then and there confined by the then German Reich as an exercise of belligerent control'.[5]

It hardly conveyed the depth of offence. War crimes, not crimes against humanity. All the prosecutors could do was note the policy of extermination of the 'insane'. They were not required to analyse the programme that gave rise to this policy or its application in Hadamar. As a later American summary of the case repeated, 'it is not deemed necessary to do more than state the above facts as a prelude to the important elements of the present case', namely that Allied nationals were killed unlawfully after June 1944. The prosecution extracted from the defendants an admission that they gave fatal injections to the Poles and Russians because they were 'incurably ill from tuberculosis' which suggested that euthanasia was an accepted practice in the Nazi regime. Some exhumed bodies hadn't displayed the disease, but this was hardly the point.

After seven days in court, Alfons Klein and the two male nurses were sentenced to death. It was a quick and positive result. The convictions encouraged the other American trials under preparation in Dachau to go ahead though it didn't attract significant public interest. As with the Belsen trial, any exposure of the barbarism of the Nazi regime – the warped policy of 'purifying' the German people, German blood, by extermination – was to be left to Nuremberg.

3.

At the Bergen-Belsen memorial, I'd worried about the potential for a macabre tourism that could develop around the concentration camp sites. When I travelled on from Mittelbau-Dora to Dachau, mindful I was entering the American territory for retribution, that feeling grew. The camp outside Munich had attracted a more obvious commercialism. Companies advertised walking tours around the city: beer and brewery in the morning, Hitler's Munich in the afternoon, Dachau concentration camp the next day: *our guides are happy to accept tips if you wish to show your appreciation but please do not do so within the memorial grounds*. You can even get a discount on a Munich World War II combo. Private tours available: prices vary.

Simply walking about the compounds, watching the tour guides and their parties, the danger of turning the camps into an 'experience' snapped at me: Dachau as 'The London Dungeon' or some other such *Horrible Histories*-type encounter. But everything was respectful where respect was possible. There were no undignified representations of suffering. The exhibits in the old maintenance administrative buildings did not offend. They were centred on the people who'd been in the camp, taking you through their daily routines, the circumstances of their deaths. Biographies of some of the prisoners were displayed, telling you about their lives before and, for those who'd survived, after their time in the camp. Nothing within the prodigious compound (the site stretches to all points) was out of place or invasive or irreverent. Still I couldn't dispel the thought of a dangerous slippage from actual to feigned horror, Dachau as another optional tour amongst the pleasant sights of bygone Munich with its own tram stop and parking complex, fury consigned to the moment of reading the exhibition literature, then back to the beer cellars and comfortable hotels of the city. The irony that I too could be so accused didn't escape me.

But perhaps I was being too puritanical. Perhaps this was the fate of all atrocities in time. What is the lifespan of anger at pogroms and massacres from ancient days to modern: the sack of Troy, the slaughter of the Carthaginians, the massacre of Huguenots, the genocide of Armenians, too many, in truth, to list and each still capable of robbing you of sleep? Wasn't it better that the places of slaughter be noticed even as tourist attractions rather than allowed to merge into the periphery of cities, unadvertised and forgotten? The commercialism might be distasteful, but it was important to access the sites of past wrongs. For some, the trials conducted after the war were supposed to serve that purpose too. The scheme of justice undertaken by the British and Americans was not only to punish individuals but to memorialise the terrible crimes committed so that they wouldn't be repeated, so that people, the Germans included, would hear about the evils of the Nazi regime, recognise them as abhorrent and guard against their recurrence.

Similar sentiments were reiterated more recently when the appetite for international war crimes trials resurfaced after the late 1980s and the end of the Cold War, for those held for the atrocities committed in the Former Yugoslavia, Rwanda, Sierra Leone, Cambodia, East Timor. Each time the avowed intent was to use the trial process as some kind of authoritative recounting of what had happened and who'd been responsible. And yet, reading through the files and accounts of British trials conducted away from Nuremberg, discovering the multiple crimes prosecuted and the many perpetrators responsible, I doubted that was truly feasible. The fact that I was able to read about them may have suggested otherwise, but once amongst the detail I wondered again whether the Belsen trial had produced anything other

than a sensationalist and an inevitably sketchy representation of
Auschwitz, Bergen-Belsen and the general KZ system. Reports on the
fatal instruments of these camps abounded, but very little was said to
fix the facts of the past so that no one could doubt the extent and
nature of wrongs done.

The main American trials that began at Dachau in the autumn of
1945 were little different. If anything, they were less disposed towards
memorialisation. The political desire was to see them completed
'successfully' within the least amount of time possible. The Dachau
KZ case began a couple of days before the Bergen-Belsen verdicts
were pronounced. On 15 November, proceedings opened with a
similar number of defendants (forty) and similar stories of what had
been found when the camp had been liberated (a train of closed cattle
trucks in the camp siding full of emaciated corpses). Though the
British press took some notice of the trial, attention was mostly
reserved for the lurid details of medical experiments (prisoners were
'put in giant bell-shaped caissons and subjected to varying air pressures after which most were dead or dying', The Times noted).[6] There
were no day-by-day detailed reports. Given the attention that Dachau
had received before the war, an iconic example of Nazi Germany's
repressive regime, I found this surprising.

The US War Crimes group accused all defendants of acting 'in
pursuance of a common design to commit acts hereinafter alleged
and as members of the staff of the Dachau Concentration Camp, and
camps subsidiary thereto'. They did 'wilfully, deliberately and wrong-
fully aid, abet and participate in the subjection of civilian nationals'
and of 'captured members of the armed forces of nations then at
war with the German Reich, to cruelties and mistreatments including
killings, beatings and tortures, starvation, abuses and indignities, the
exact names and numbers of such victims being unknown but aggregating many thousands'.[7] The accused represented a spectrum of
rank: nine men who'd served as either camp commandant or deputy,
medical orderlies, Blockführers, an officer in charge of supplies, and
three prisoner functionaries, Kapos.

Evidence was brought over the next month to prove the inhuman
conditions. The defendants denied specific charges or explained or
excused them. As to the general charge, they claimed they'd had no

choice but to carry out the orders given to them, ultimately flowing from Himmler and Berlin.

The defences failed.

The Dachau trial was over within four weeks, and apart from the odd detail of horror, the verdict was the only item of significant interest to the British press: of the forty defendants thirty-six were sentenced to death. If establishing a record of atrocity for current and future generations was the aim, then little was achieved other than that men were deemed unfit to live. Besides, by the end of November 1945, Nuremberg now held the reputation as the repository for memory: little space remained for the multitude of other cases then being pursued, whether British or American.

4.

Whatever justice was being done in Dachau camp, in Lüneburg, in the makeshift courtrooms constructed in Celle, Wuppertal, Hamburg and across Europe, was ancillary. Even though these places were where the victims had an opportunity of speaking and confronting their abusers, where some of the killers and torturers and vivisection-ists and selectors on the ramps had to answer for their actions, it was to Nuremberg that political and public attention was directed.

By mid-November 1945, after all the arguments, after the backroom negotiations, after the political deals, the mistrustful conferences, the petty manoeuvring, the legalistic discussions, the naming of the defendants, the accumulation of evidence, the detailing of the indict-ments, the construction of the courtroom, the gathering of the lawyers and witnesses and defendants and translators and newspaper reporters from around the world, the International Military Tribunal at Nuremberg was ready.

Not everything was resolved: the witnesses to be brought, the evidence to be shown, remained work in progress. Some issues were highly controversial. Amongst the papers of General Donovan, a senior member of the US legal team and, during the war, head of the

Office of Strategic Services, precursor to the CIA, I found a note written on 6 November 1945 to Justice Jackson, the Chief Prosecutor, saying, 'The Katyn forest murder of 925 Polish officers may present a difficulty in the trial. The defence may wish to make an issue of this and produce witnesses who will testify that this murder was done by Russians.'[8] It was quite an understatement both in terms of numbers killed and the impact it would have had if Soviet culpability in those murders had been acknowledged. The Russians had indeed executed more than 20,000 Polish officers when they'd carved up Poland with the Germans in 1940, but had gone to elaborate lengths to blame the Germans ever since. The 'secret' was kept from the public by all the Allies, the Americans and British going along with the fiction that Katyn was another example of German atrocity. They were intent on avoiding any destabilisation of the tribunal and its presentation as a just process.

Even with such difficulties, the trial of the twenty-four named accused formally opened at the Nuremberg Palace of Justice on 20 November.

No one expected anything other than a spectacle and that was what had been prepared.[9] The venue was more like a gladiatorial amphi-theatre than a courtroom. A wall had been knocked through to make room for the press and public galleries. There were ranks of lawyers, scribes, translators working in booths, ushers, uniformed guards, clerks, a small team of American psychologists and psychiatrists to watch and sometimes to report. The defendants sat in one large box, the dock, without those ignominious numbered white squares around their necks that were favoured at the concentration camp trials. The judges faced them. There were four, one from each of the prosecuting nations: General Nikitchenko (Soviet), Francis Biddle (American), Henri Donnedieu de Vabres (French) and Geoffrey Lawrence, the British President of the panel.

The reading of the indictment set the trial proper in motion. As with all documents from then on, it was read out slowly and in full, simul-taneously translated so that no one could claim anything had been slipped into proceedings without due and proper consideration.

The United States of America presented the first count; Great Britain the second, read out by Sir David Maxwell Fyfe; France and the Soviet Union the third and fourth through Pierre Mounier, Charles Gerthoffer, Lt Col Ozol and Capt Kuchin (it was a long and detailed read). Between them it took all day. As the indictment had been made public already, boredom set in. British newspapers had been struggling to maintain their interest as it was. The *Daily Mail*'s main article, written by journalist Rhona Churchill, led with descriptions of the accused rather than the substance of the charges.[10]

'Looking, with a few notable exceptions, for all the world like a bunch of City clerks sitting on a double railway station bench patiently waiting for the fogbound 8.10, twenty of the top ranking Nazis today awaited their judges in the crowded court-room of the International Military Tribunal.' At 10 a.m. proceedings started, but Churchill's interest was in the behaviour of Rosenberg (he bites his nails), Keitel (sitting 'stiffly correct and Junkerlike'), von Ribbentrop (wearing dark glasses, which when removed showed 'two small eyes reddened by weeping'), Goering ('looking one moment like a cheeky schoolboy, the next like a spoilt baby').

Elsewhere, the paper gave a profile of the British judge serving as the President of the tribunal, Lord Justice Geoffrey Lawrence, whom its correspondent described as 'Nemesis', a man who 'demands not only evidence but – when he can get it – absolute and personal conviction'. *The Times* summarised the events of the opening day of the 'Great Nuremberg War Trial': 'The whole of the day was spent in reading the indictment in four languages', twenty-four thousand words over five hours, during which Hess read a 'Bavarian novel', whatever that meant.[11] The paper looked forward wistfully to the next day, when the accused would enter their pleas and Justice Robert Jackson, the Chief Prosecutor, would deliver his opening speech, 'of which great things are expected'. A strong sense of rage was waiting to be released.

On 21 November everyone gathered in the Nuremberg court again (though defendant Kaltenbrunner was in hospital having suffered a brain haemorrhage, Robert Ley was dead, having committed suicide, and Bormann was presumed dead and buried in Berlin somewhere). The accused now had to plead 'guilty or not guilty'. Lord Justice Lawrence made clear to the defence lawyers that no other words were permitted; it was a simple choice that must not be accompanied by any statement. The lawyers were given fifteen minutes to make sure the accused understood. Then one by one the defendants were brought from the dock to stand in front of a microphone facing the bench of judges. Goering was first and immediately tried to read a statement. Lawrence swiftly silenced him. Guilty or not guilty, that was all they wanted to know. 'I declare myself in the sense of the indictment not guilty.'

Hess came next. He said simply, 'No,' and Lawrence commented drily, 'That will be entered as a plea of not guilty,' much to the amusement of the audience in court. Lawrence wasn't intending to be funny and silenced the audience too. The rest followed and in one form or another said 'not guilty' to the charges against them.

With that formality over, Justice Jackson's moment of fulfilment, perhaps his reason for being on this earth, began.

5.

Occasionally over the past hundred years or so speeches have marked an era, a moment, a movement. Many have achieved iconic status after the event. I imagine that no more than a handful of orators have known without any doubt that their words were destined to be that significant. They might have hoped them to be so, may have planned it that way. But Jackson *knew*. He could have been in no doubt that his was a speech for history as much as it was for the judges on the bench before him. His first words set the tone: 'The privilege of opening the first trial in history for crimes against the peace of the world imposes a grave responsibility.'

He had been planning this moment for weeks if not since the day of his appointment by Roosevelt the previous April. Every sentence recognised its audience as extending far beyond the geography of that Nuremberg courtroom and far beyond the times he was living in. His speech was more than an introduction to the case and the evidence. It was a manifesto for outlawing war and holding the leaders of a state

responsible for terrible deeds committed under their regime. He knew
that every word would be recorded and replayed and analysed and
used as precedent for future reference. That must have been his hope
as well as realisation. Perhaps that ambition became lost in the mire
of terrible deeds then related, but it remained there for anyone to
study. It provided the basis for the whole prosecution and indicated
how Nuremberg was very different from every war crimes trial before
or after. I thought this evident in the carefully crafted prose of his
opening sentences.

This inquest represents the practical effort of four of the most mighty
of nations, with the support of seventeen more, to utilize international
law to meet the greatest menace of our times – aggressive war. The
common sense of mankind demands that law shall not stop with
the punishment of petty crimes by little people. It must also reach men
who possess themselves of great power and make deliberate and
concerted use of it to set in motion evils which leave no home in the
world untouched ... In the prisoners' dock sit twenty-odd broken men.
Reproached by the humiliation of those they have led almost as bitterly
as by the desolation of those they have attacked, their personal capacity
for evil is forever past. It is hard now to perceive in these men as captives
the power by which as Nazi leaders they once dominated much of the
world and terrified most of it. Merely as individuals their fate is of little
consequence to the world. What makes this inquest significant is that
these prisoners represent sinister influences that will lurk in the world
long after their bodies have returned to dust. We will show them to be
living symbols of racial hatreds, of terrorism and violence, and of the
arrogance and cruelty of power. They are symbols of fierce nationalisms
and of militarism, of intrigue and war-making which have embroiled
Europe generation after generation, crushing its manhood, destroying
its homes, and impoverishing its life. They have so identified themselves
with the philosophies they conceived and with the forces they directed
that any tenderness to them is a victory and an encouragement to all
the evils which are attached to their names. Civilization can afford no
compromise with the social forces which would gain renewed strength
if we deal ambiguously or indecisively with the men in whom those
forces now precariously survive.

The symbolic value of the defendants was laid out for the court and the world to understand. As individuals they mattered less in the scheme of proof of criminality than the regime they represented. For all the claims of individual responsibility, which their presence confirmed, their true purpose was as exemplars.

But Jackson didn't forget the demands inherent in his conception of a trial. The accused might have been the living embodiment of the Nazi movement (not, said Jackson, the German people), but they had to be treated 'fairly'. He accepted that they were innocent pending the prosecution proving their guilt and he accepted the burden of that proof. The case wasn't about single atrocities, but a common plan and conspiracy to commit crimes against peace, to perpetrate war crimes and crimes against humanity. That had been set down in the indictment and Jackson proceeded to articulate the basic facts with his own flourish of interpretation.

By the time he'd finished, no one doubted the quality of the speech or its importance. For that alone Jackson would be given credit, even though later he'd become a strange, brooding figure who some saw as a disappointment when it came to the direct cross-examination of individual defendants. But for Jackson those first lines of his presentation suggested he was less concerned with the personalities than the system that the Nazis had constructed. That was the real evil, not those dissolute characters crushed into the dock. He knew, though, that there was a craving for people to be exposed and disembowelled. Detailing the myriad atrocities could never be enough. They had to be draped around these men in the dock, associated with them to the point where they became synonymous. Only then could retribution *and* punishment function as entwined concepts. Someone had to take responsibility.

6.

Once Jackson's speech was done, the prosecution began to present details of the evidence. The American legal team were first, dealing with the charge of conspiracy. They made it clear that the case was

to be proven by documents; witness testimony might support the
central claims but the evidence would be written: letters, reports,
communiqués, minutes, texts that had been discovered in the captured
German archives. Though not comprehensive, there was sufficient
to prove the charges, the American lawyers said.

The strategy of laying before the court mounds of documents
irritated the President of the tribunal, Lord Justice Lawrence. He
worried that few of the documents had been made easily available
to the defence attorneys, in contravention of the fair trial requirements
that the Americans had been so keen on promoting. The frequent
interruptions by Lawrence to ensure the defence were in receipt of
everything they needed undermined the momentum established by
Jackson's speech. It confirmed that adherence to procedure would
dictate the pace of the trial, just as it had in the Belsen case a few
weeks earlier. Whatever the political preference, this was not going
to be a drama pitched for the demands of an impatient audience.

Anything that deflected from the reality of outrages committed by
the German nation challenged justice rather than fulfilled it. But the
absurd performances of the accused, whose every gesture provided
entertainment for the press to report amidst the dry rendition of
documentation, highlighted how the solemnity of law was in danger
of being subsumed as another theatrical event. Ironically, an attempt
to redress the balance, made at the end of November, rested on the
skills of Hollywood movie-makers. It was a pivotal moment.

A film of what had been found at the concentration camps liberated
by the US and British forces was shown to the court by the prosecution on 29 November 1945, a week into proceedings. A number of
cinematographers had been involved. Lt Col George Stevens, a
Hollywood director, Hollywood legend John Ford, who'd directed
John Wayne in ground-breaking westerns in the 1930s and early 1940s,
and others had shot and then edited a one-hour-long movie. Lt Kellog,
another film veteran, who had worked at 20th Century Fox since 1929,
was brought to testify that the film hadn't been retouched or tampered
with and was a faithful representation of the 80,000 feet of film taken
(only 6,000 feet was used). Assurances were given that the out-takes
consisted of the same types of images; the edited version did not
distort what had been recorded by the film-makers, Kellog confirmed.

The film was (and is) a direct confrontation: for the court, for the defendants, for any audience, ultimately for the world. It resurrected the crimes and made them immediate and timeless. Watch it now and the first scenes show the discovery of the concentration camps, Ohrdruf and Buchenwald and Bergen-Belsen and Dachau and Nordhausen, where the mounds of corpses appear in every lingering and panning shot, making redundant the efforts of prosecutors to describe and understand the conditions found in those places. The film shows bodies burned, fused to the ground, lying in front or in the middle of barbed wire. It shows a few survivors in cots with terrible sores or wounds or in a decrepit state: no respect for the victims as their skirts and shirts are lifted for the camera. There are smiling faces of those alive and on stretchers. Then Ohrdruf, Eisenhower's visit and hundreds of US soldiers touring the camp, bodies decaying and heaped upon each other in huts, someone demonstrating how punishments were carried out on a form of rack. There are more dead, mouths agape, cheeks hollowed, charred remains of people burned on a pyre of railway sleepers, Eisenhower grim-faced, local Germans brought to witness, transported into the camp in the back of US trucks, lining up and being told by a young US officer that they will see everything in the camp, then being forced into the barracks full of rotting corpses, lined up again and shown more of the dead. Then Hadamar: a grave-yard of thousands in the grounds and the bodies exhumed to determine the identity of the dead and perhaps how they died, an autopsy conducted before the camera on the grass beside the graves, physical evidence for the trials to be held of those who ran this euthanasia centre. Some survivors in hospital beds in the 'wards' have their limbs revealed to demonstrate how emaciated they've become. More camps follow, Münster and Breendonck, Belgium, where demonstrations of punishments and weapons used by the SS guards are re-enacted. There's no break from the horrific: Nordhausen and weeping inmates, barns full of men barely alive, dead ignominiously carried from the rubble to be laid out in lines for the camera; Hannover, Arnstadt, Buchenwald: German civilians from Weimar brought to the camp, lots of smiling faces as though they are being given a day out before they're shown a lampshade made of human skin, shrunken heads, obscene drawings: a woman faints, another looks sick. An inmate appears whose toes

have been amputated, or so it seems. The civilians file back out of the
camp without the bravado they exhibited on their way in. Mauthausen
next. An American serviceman, Lt Jack Taylor of the US Navy, speaking
to camera about his time as a POW in the camp, the starvation, beatings, the killings. Thirty-eight minutes into a film that will last exactly
an hour, presumably the length of time that the producers believed
would be the most effective, the time after which they must have
calculated the audience would cease to look, camp ovens are shown
with skeletons inside. Piles of bone ash left as damning residue. Then
Dachau from the air, the enormous site, row after row of barracks in
illustration of the scale of incarceration, 30,000 prisoners within the
series of long huts stretching away and around the parade ground.
Back to Buchenwald and more rooms with corpses, lingering footage
of their nakedness as local citizens are taken through the camp as
elsewhere. A shot of a gas chamber and a tin of Zyklon B, the poison
used to kill so many people, labelled clearly and left on the ground.
Naked male survivors, no dignity for those in the eye of the camera.
And Bergen-Belsen with a British officer speaking about what he's
seen. Josef Kramer appears and other SS members (is that Dr Klein?),
hounded to bury the dead. A small bulldozer attending to those corpses
too liquefied in their decomposition for the SS men and women to be
able to separate and carry to one of the limed pits.

   And then the movie, for that is what it is, a Hollywood movie, ends.
   The film portrayed a tiny fragment of the atrocities committed
across the years of war and Nazi rule (and even then only at the
moment of liberation by US or British troops) and spoke not at all of
the systematic extermination of the Jews and Gypsies and Slavs and
others, though the piles of bodies provided enduring images otherwise only imagined from the dry documentary evidence read out by
Justice Jackson and his colleagues. But it seared into the minds of
everyone who saw it, pitching them close to the dead and close to
the crimes that lay at the heart of the prosecution. Whatever the
politicians may have wanted to achieve through this trial, the concentration camp film attested to a deliberate and very personal brutality
separate from, though inextricably linked to, the offence of making
war. The film was an artful distortion, a blunt instrument for focusing
minds, a medium that could not do justice to the weight of claims

made against the Nazis and Germany too. It achieved its purpose nonetheless: to shame, to shock, to justify.

When I examined the Nuremberg transcript I saw no record of any words having been spoken in the court immediately after the film was shown. President Lawrence and the rest of the judges apparently left the chamber without comment. What could they say? The *Manchester Guardian* reported, 'The air of remoteness that has hung over the Nuremberg trial with the unravelling by the United States prosecution of the historical threads of the vast conspiracy now became stark reality.'[12]

I watched the film a number of times. It's easily accessible on the web. I recognised the camp at Buchenwald from my visit. The barracks no longer exist, but the entrance to the main prisoners' compound and gate are still standing. So too the crematorium, the ovens, the paraphernalia of the camp preserved in the exhibitions. Little has changed. I recognised the camps at Nordhausen and Dachau and Bergen-Belsen too. All the scenes from those places testified to the horrors as no witness could have possibly done. But I also thought the film was cruel, using victims with no regard for their suffering or their dignity. One scene showed a man demonstrating how his crotch had been split by his SS tormentors, who'd apparently grabbed his legs and pulled them apart in some latter-day re-enactment of a medieval torture. A long shirt covered his genitals for the most part, but not effectively. He was one victim of torture prepared to replay his suffering. I wondered how he was chosen, why he was edited into the film. Were the skills of Hollywood brought to bear, not to fabricate or entertain (I didn't believe that would have entered their minds), but to arrest attention? It didn't seem to me to represent the truth of the crimes being prosecuted or the guilt of those accused. The scenes shown were almost arbitrary. The form didn't establish responsibility or even the slightest connection between the defendants and these crimes. Perhaps it wasn't intended to. Instead it provided a visual reignition of the initial outrage which was already dissipating as the wearisome proceedings continued. Where the opening of the case relied on dull accounts of historical events, the film catapulted the tribunal and those watching back to those moments of disgust in April 1945. It was a reminder, a clever tactic. An artifice, one way of averting the gaze from the peccadillos of the defendants, who were becoming caricatures of pompous or eccentric politicians and military leaders, and back to the soul of the case. Not for the first or last time, the concentration camp was made the symbol of Nazi injustice.

I questioned, nonetheless, if the film had succeeded in achieving the aims of the prosecution. Perhaps, I thought, it also perversely provided a subliminal defence for the German population as a whole. For if the Nazi leaders were shown to be shocked by the images from the camps, to be *surprised* at the true human cost of their decisions and actions, then didn't that reinforce the claim of ignorance for every other German? Leave aside those who served in or for the camps, everyone else could point to Goering and the others and say, 'If *they* didn't know, how could we?'

The *Daily Mail* reported, 'The Nazi war criminals today were stripped of their bravado, their cynicism, their indifference when they saw the Belsen and Dachau concentration camps horror film, and were reduced some to tears, some to perspiring horror.'[13] Perhaps a better indication of how the accused responded came from Dr Gustave Gilbert, a US Army psychologist, who was one of a team assigned to monitor the mental health of the accused. He was in the courtroom and watched the reactions of the defendants as the film was played.[14] Gilbert wrote in his diary that the defendants variously displayed utter confusion or disgust or frantic torment. As the dock was lit by spotlights, a 'security measure', with the rest of the hall in darkness so the movie could be seen properly, Funk 'brushed away the tears from the puffy pockets under his eyes'. Doenitz was 'apparently shocked, but fascinated', before 'putting on his dark glasses' and ignoring the screen.

Gilbert went to see the defendants in their cells later that night, talking through their responses to the film. He didn't take notes during these visits, but wrote down what he remembered as soon as possible afterwards. If accurate, his account demonstrated how hollowed out the accused had been by the screening. Each one voiced their ignorance and astonishment. Some disbelieved, some found excuses, some denied any association, others were possessed by a sudden realisation of their fate. Goering was described as upset that the day had been spoiled. It had all been going on quite pleasantly for him until that moment, he told Gilbert. He'd been enjoying himself.

I knew, though, that Goering and others had already been forced
to watch part of the film when they were in Ashcan, their hotel prison
in Luxembourg. It was part of the entertainment laid on by their
gaoler. Was the film, then, really that much of a shock to the defendants? Gilbert's records supported the appearance of ignorance at the
detail and extent of the camps' horrors nonetheless.

And what of the German public? In his opening speech, Justice
Jackson accepted the proposition that the German population wasn't
on trial, wasn't being held responsible without distinction. And the
film supported the contention that the German people didn't know
about the atrocities in their midst. When the camera lingered on all
those smiling civilians marching towards the camps only to be transformed into haggard observers of the lines of cadavers, wasn't that
proof of their obliviousness?

Then I reminded myself of that map in the Flossenbürg KZ
museum. Hundreds of camps were located throughout Germany.
They were not all isolated. Many were in the towns and cities or
within their outskirts. Prisoners were forever moving between them.
Vast armies of labour performing every function of production.
Trainloads crossing the country. General ignorance about the final
conditions in Bergen-Belsen and Dachau and the others might have
been real, but wilful myopia would have been necessary to miss the
presence of all those who were suffering around them. And of course,
none of the film had anything to say directly about the complicity
needed to exterminate the Jews, homosexuals, political opponents,
the mentally ill. They couldn't have disappeared without people
noticing, without people helping, without people turning their backs.
That would be an absurd claim.

7.

The film may have been the moment of direct connection between
Nuremberg and the British and American prosecutions across
Germany, but it was only an interlude. Perhaps understanding that

only the bizarre, if not comic, would divert attention away from the horrific images left in everyone's minds from the film the day before, Rudolf Hess, once Deputy Führer, mocked the gravity of proceedings by delivering a confession the next day, 30 November 1945. Since knowing he was to stand trial, he'd maintained that he suffered from complete amnesia about everything that had happened before he'd deserted Germany in 1941 to fly to Scotland. But as discussions took place in court about whether he was fit to stand trial at all, following an application by Hess's lawyer that he wasn't, and it appeared that he might be excluded from proceedings, he suddenly performed a volte-face.

Hess was allowed to speak to the tribunal. He stood and said, 'Henceforth my memory will again respond to the outside world. The reasons for simulating loss of memory were of a tactical nature. Only my ability to concentrate is, in fact, somewhat reduced. But my capacity to follow the trial, to defend myself, to put questions to witnesses, or to answer questions myself is not affected thereby.'

Hess could hardly have chosen a statement more likely to prove his insanity. But the tribunal took him at face value and dismissed his attorney's motion, pronouncing that Hess should remain on trial.

The newspapermen and women were overjoyed by this moment of 'excitement'. The psychiatrists and psychologists from the Allied nations had been made to look foolish. Hess's attorney was reported as saying, 'He is not crazy, but he is definitely a psychopathic case.'[15] Proceedings were quickly developing into an epic opera, prompting emotions from pathos to bathos, solemnity to absurdity, in the space of twenty-four hours. Whatever the intentions of the judges and prosecuting lawyers, it was an entertainment.

Even so, the legal proclivity for tedium remained unavoidable, and over the next few weeks before Christmas 1945, the trial moved back to the mundane as the charge of conducting aggressive war required exacting attention to be paid to political manoeuvring and diplomatic exchanges. It was to be the British who would take over this element from their American colleagues.

Sir Hartley Shawcross, the British Attorney General, stood up on 4 December 1945. The opening of *his* speech was bewildering:

The British Empire with its Allies has twice, within the space of 25 years, been victorious in wars which have been forced upon it, but it is precisely because we realize that victory is not enough, that might is not necessarily right, that lasting peace and the rule of international law is not to be secured by the strong arm alone, that the British nation is taking part in this trial. There are those who would perhaps say that these wretched men should have been dealt with summarily without trial by 'executive action'; that their power for evil broken, they should have been swept aside into oblivion without this elaborate and careful investigation into the part which they played in bringing this war about: Vae Victis! Let them pay the penalty of defeat. But that was not the view of the British Government. Not so would the rule of law be raised and strengthened on the international as well as upon the municipal plane; not so would future generations realize that right is not always on the side of the big battalions; not so would the world be made aware that the waging of aggressive war is not only a dangerous venture but a criminal one.

Col Telford Taylor, one of the senior American prosecution lawyers, described Shawcross's assertion as 'hollow'. That was an understatement, given how difficult it had been to persuade the British to accept a trial rather than summary execution for the leading Nazis.

'Human memory is very short,' Shawcross went on with unintended irony. He was referring to the tribunal's purpose as a record of wrongdoing so that people shouldn't forget the crimes committed by the Germans, but it was equally applicable to the sudden finding of virtue in the British approach to retribution. After that, his speech was a protracted journey through the wars fought and treaties broken by the Nazi state in its attempt to conquer Europe, and unobjectionable for all that.

Only when the prosecution finally returned to the concentration camp system and the extermination of the Jews and other peoples a few days later was interest rekindled. Thomas Dodd, the American lawyer charged with presenting this count, wove together the stories of the camps, the persecution of the Jews, the oppression of opposition, the sustained programme of gassing as a means of extermination, into a long, convoluted narrative. It took him and his colleagues two days. In the middle of the presentation, another (though much shorter) film was shown, this one taken by the SS, he said. There was no definite proof as to when or where the movie was shot, but most likely it was during the 'extermination of a ghetto by Gestapo agents, assisted by military units'. The prosecution asked the tribunal to note particular scenes and frames as they watched the short film.

Scene 2 – A naked girl running across the courtyard.

Scene 3 – An older woman being pushed past the camera, and a man in SS uniform standing at the right of the scene.

Scene 5 – A man with a skullcap and a woman are manhandled.

Number 1 – A half-naked woman runs through the crowd.

Number 15 – Another half-naked woman runs out of the house.

Number 16 – Two men drag an old man out.

Number 18 – A man in German military uniform, with his back to the camera, watches.

Number 24 – A general shot of the street, showing fallen bodies and naked women running.

Number 32 – A shot of the street, showing five fallen bodies.

Number 37 – A man with a bleeding head is hit again.

Number 39 – A soldier in German military uniform, with a rifle, stands by as a crowd centres on a man coming out of the house.

Number 44 – A soldier with a rifle, in German military uniform, walks past a woman clinging to a torn blouse.

Number 45 – A woman is dragged by her hair across the street.

The new film lent visual substance to the language of the documents and letters that referred time and again to the genocidal intent in the Nazi movement. But it was a gesture rather than a moment of epiphany. The documentary detail was where the Allied prosecution saw the devil lying.

A captured series of teletype messages and photographs and statistics collected into a booklet in 1943 by Jürgen Stroop, *SS-Brigadeführer* and Major General of Police in Warsaw, recounting the extermination of the Warsaw Ghetto and presented to the tribunal, was particularly damning for the accused.[16] It formed a centrepiece for the prosecution's attempt to show the mentality that had infected the Nazi regime.

The notion of a crime against humanity was substantiated with each sentence:

> The resistance put up by the Jews and bandits could be broken only by relentlessly using all our force and energy by day and night ... The Reichsführer SS issued through the higher SS and Police Führer East at Cracow his order to complete the combing out of the Warsaw Ghetto with the greatest severity and relentless tenacity. I therefore decided to destroy the entire Jewish residential area by setting every block on fire, including the blocks of residential buildings near the armament works. One concern after the other was systematically evacuated and subsequently destroyed by fire. The Jews then emerged from their hiding places and dug-outs in almost every case. Not infrequently, the Jews stayed in the burning buildings until, because of the heat and the fear of being burned alive, they preferred to jump down from the upper stories after having thrown mattresses and other upholstered articles into the street from the burning buildings. With their bones broken, they still tried to crawl across the street into blocks of buildings which had not yet been set on fire or were only partly in flames ...
>
> One day we opened 183 sewer entrance holes and at a fixed time lowered smoke candles into them, with the result that the bandits fled from what they believed to be gas to the centre of the former Ghetto, where they could then be pulled out of the sewer holes there. A great number of Jews, who could not be counted, were exterminated by blowing up sewers and dug-outs ...
>
> Only through the continuous and untiring work of all involved did we succeed in catching a total of 56,065 Jews whose extermination can be proved. To this should be added the number of Jews who lost their lives in explosions or fires but whose numbers could not be ascertained.

Little needed to be said about the dehumanising language, the pervasive sense of almost religious zeal in conducting the operations against the 'Jews', the complete disregard for human life.

The defendants may have looked astounded, but the prosecution case was not concerned with individual responsibility alone. As with the Dachau and Belsen trials, now completed, collective responsibility for the system, conspiracy if you will, formed the kernel of the charges. The defendants were just as accountable for the Warsaw liquidation as Himmler or any of the SS officers involved, whether or not they were aware of the details or had seen the messages in Stroop's report.

As though determined to maintain the distinction *and* connection between the revelations of atrocity here at Nuremberg and the Allies' investigations and trials elsewhere, Thomas Dodd confirmed that 'Individual prosecutions are going on, going forward before other courts, which will record these outrages in detail. Therefore, we do not propose to present a catalogue of individual brutalities but, rather, to submit evidence showing the fundamental purposes for which the camps were used, the techniques of terror which were employed, the large number of victims, and the death and the anguish which they caused.' In other words, the trials away from Nuremberg were supposed to be dealing with the personal barbarities, those seen in the two films that had been shown and apparent in the emerging documents painstakingly read out by the prosecution.[17]

It was true up to a point, or so it seemed to me. The American prosecution of Dachau personnel was just then being completed. Every defendant was found guilty on the basis that their duties 'were such as to constitute in themselves an execution or administration of the system'. From *Kapo* to commandant, all were guilty. None could defend themselves against the accusation that they were part of the cruel system. And on 13 December 1945, the same day as the Dachau trial pronounced the conviction of all forty defendants, Josef Kramer, Fritz Klein, Irma Grese, Franz Hössler, Johanna Bormann and five others condemned at the Belsen trial were hanged in Hamelin gaol.

Taking a break from Nuremberg, just before New Year whilst the main trial was in recess, Dr Gilbert, the prison psychologist, travelled to Landsberg, where the Dachau defendants waited for their execution. He interviewed some of them just as he had the Major War Criminals. The Dachau men 'run almost the whole gamut of intelligence', he recorded in his diary, 'from dull-witted brutes like Viktor Kirsch to brilliant doctors like old Klaus Schilling, who killed hundreds of Dachau inmates in malaria experiments'.[18] Some of the convicted told him that they shouldn't have been held responsible. Everything they'd done had been in accordance with orders.

Gilbert had little time for them: he described how one junior SS officer 'blubbers in self-pity' as he railed against the 'big shots' in Nuremberg: these were the men who should suffer, the condemned man said.

8.

I'd hoped the Nuremberg trial record would reveal some of the character of those senior men accused, perhaps in turn shedding more light on the minds of the so-called 'minor' war criminals. But I was disappointed again. The transcript told much but didn't penetrate that far. Even the diaries and memoirs of those present at the trial I found to be of limited value.

Gustave Gilbert's account, often referred to as a primary source, was particularly unsatisfactory. I couldn't say whether Gilbert wrote the truth of all his encounters and conversations and, though there shouldn't be any doubt (otherwise his integrity would be impugned and I have no reason to do that), his preference for taking notes only *after* his conversations, rather than during, must raise the question of his powers of recall, or at least the precision of his quotations. Gilbert's diary certainly makes for an extraordinary read, a book unlike any other I have encountered: part memoir, part sustained psychological analysis, part travelogue of sorts, part commentary, part history of the events both within and behind the main stage of the trial. But frequently his entries tell you more about Gilbert himself than those he was charged to observe. He infected virtually every reported conversation he had with the defendants with some damning, sarcastic, irritating intervention. He couldn't help himself from ridiculing the accused, trying to wound with his little barbed comments. The more I read the more I thought how insufferable he must have been. At one point whilst observing several of the other defendants at lunch laughing at Goering's pronouncement that they should all confine their defence to three words, 'Lick my arse', Gilbert butted in and said, 'Ah, yes, war would be a great joke, if only so many people didn't die of it.' Goering supposedly replied, 'Who gives a hang about that?' which is about all he could have said.

Gilbert's diary is peppered with his cutting remarks. Perhaps he thought of himself as tormentor as well as confessor or confidant. He reminded me of a jester, the medieval fool who had privileged access to a prince or man of state, and who had the power to mock as well as entertain, who held a mirror to the soul of those he taunted. I was driven back to the transcripts, which I took to be a more trustworthy source.

But the more I read of these, the more I thought the whole legal process was simply ill-equipped to dig deep into individual characters or into the nature of the German nation, if such a thing could be said to exist. It wasn't designed to comprehend, only to confront.

I thought the same structural inability to get to the root of Nazi criminality was evident in the other trials I'd examined by then. Discovering what made the individuals being prosecuted so brutal or callous or indifferent was never a priority or a goal. It didn't help that the unrepentant and blatant Nazi fanatic was mostly absent amongst defendants (which would otherwise have provided an easy explanation for wickedness), even though the prosecution tried to portray them as sadistic members of the SS or the Nazi party: at the Bergen-Belsen trial the defendants uniformly described them-selves as obedient workers, nothing more; soldier ants programmed to do exactly as they were told.

Many studies of the SS and other Nazi organisations that have tried to find an answer as to why men and women took part in the system of mass killing and cruelty without objecting often refer to the fanatic, the one who *believed* that what they were doing was right, was justi-fied and had value. That belief may have been based on indoctrination, it may have already existed within German culture, but the first *idea* that exterminating the Jews and anyone who supposedly threatened the German nation emanated first of all from the fanatic. Putting the idea into practice then involved others who weren't necessarily so enthusiastic: the guard, the bureaucrat, the scientist, the civilian who turned away and wouldn't look.

Few defendants at the numerous trials that were conducted by the British, and whose records I examined in some detail, truly revealed that stereotypical fanaticism. But then, why would they condemn themselves by admitting adherence to an idea that was self-evidently intended to inflict mass murder? Self-preservation would most likely override ideology. That might explain Frau Kramer's affirmation of Colonel Backhouse's statement put to her during the Belsen trial that the extermination of the Jews was obviously wrong. She'd agreed on behalf of both herself and her husband, whom she described as a caring father who loved his children and only did that horrible work because he was ordered to.

If the fanatic rarely made an appearance at these trials (and only occasionally at Nuremberg), which characters did present themselves? The individual sadist, the psychopath, another type identified with the Nazis? Irma Grese was portrayed as a woman who enjoyed inflicting injury with her specially constructed whip made of cellophane, who wore heavy boots so that her kicks at the inmates would do maximum damage, who had dogs trained to shepherd and harry and attack prisoners in her working and punishment parties. But the others? Were they sadistic or simply functionaries, the ones who helped make the system work because that was their allotted task, following orders from above? Did the trials reveal anything that would explain their actions? Did they show the presence of 'evil', that concept to which the press and the lawyers at the trials constantly referred? Were others infected by evil, like a disease? Would we even know an 'evil' person if we met one?

Many years ago I saw someone people once called evil. He was a tyrant, the dictator of Malawi. His name was Hastings Banda and he had been Life President of the country since it became independent in the early 1960s. He must have been in his nineties when I saw him. He ruled the one-party state by suppressing all opposition. His may not have been the worst of regimes, but there was enough evidence of torture in prisons, of extrajudicial killings of opponents, of brutal control over the lives of the people to warrant international sanctions (eventually) and condemnation by human rights bodies.

I was living in Lilongwe, the capital of Malawi, in 1991 when condemnations of Banda and his regime were intensifying. The world was changing and the tolerance for tyrants was, for a moment at least, reduced. One afternoon I heard he would be travelling through the city on his way to the airport for a foreign visit so I joined the hosts of citizens who lined the roads to watch him as he passed by. On the very edge of the tarmac, Young Pioneers (reminiscent of the Hitler Youth in their uniforms and absolute loyalty to the President and his party) stood as sentinels along the roadside looking bored. There was hardly any noise, no murmur of anticipation nor idle chat. Everyone was waiting silently in the heat. Groups of women in costumes of yellow or blue or red with a portrait of President Banda pictured within a large circle on the backs and fronts of their dresses danced by the side of the road. They were called Banda's *mbumba*. After many minutes of waiting I became conscious of a gradually swelling noise. A grey Land Rover drove down the middle of the road, straddling the white lines, 'Malawi Congress Party' stencilled on its side. A huge loudspeaker was fixed to the roof, braying some kind of message in Chichewa to the crowd. I heard mass applause in the distance. A few people around me started to clap as well, though I still couldn't see anything worthy of the enthusiasm. Two police motorcycles, their blue lights flashing, came into view. The Young Pioneers turned and began gesticulating frantically to the crowd. Some shouted angrily. Little Malawian flags emerged above heads. The *mbumba* began to jig. Another pair of motorcycles passed by followed by a black Mercedes. I caught the sound of cheering, a wave advancing like some ghostly sirocco. It was frightening, exhilarating, a warning to brace oneself. A black open-topped Bentley appeared, serenely inching its way along the highway. Huge and cumbersome, it was funereally slow. The crowd shrieked, the *mbumba* danced and sang maniacally, flags waved, hands clapped above heads.

And then I saw him. He was sitting in the back of the Bentley. A very old man. He wore a black Homburg hat, a black suit, black tie, Ray-Ban sunglasses. He waved a fly-whisk rather feebly. He looked puny, small and decrepit, like a frail pensioner out for a Sunday-afternoon drive in the country. I laughed.

Despite all the trappings of oppression, despite all I knew about Banda's long and sometimes bloody reign, I couldn't honestly say I saw evil that day. I would like to say I did because I believed the accounts of his despotism and it would have seemed right to have recognised it in his features. Later I witnessed the brutal suppression of a rebellion by Banda's paramilitaries, which confirmed the regime's propensity for violence, though that's another story. But at that moment he was just an old man sitting in the back of a limousine.

Evil is such a heavy, inconstant word. It's indiscriminate. Empires, regimes, institutions, individuals are denounced with the term, a shorthand for character and behaviour that is to be despised. Like other descriptors, 'mad' or 'alien', it's a way of grasping something that we do not comprehend, something which we fear and something we can ascribe to others, those creatures who are not like us. And yet 'evil' says little. It communicates nothing intelligible. Particular acts of violence, war crimes, collective systems of abuse, even antagonistic and selfish manners, are all called 'evil' if their intent or their consequences harm people, cause suffering deliberately or even negligently.

Not long after my journey to Mittelbau-Dora and Dachau, I attended a seminar given by a Dutch law professor. She looked to be in her forties I would guess, maybe older, casually dressed, as though ready to wander about the local shopping centre on a slow Saturday afternoon. There was nothing pretentious or scholarly about her demeanour. She was about to give a talk on the perpetrators of atrocities, a subject that couldn't have been more out of keeping with her appearance. The room was barely half full, no more than a dozen of us. In the corner was a youngster who could have been a first-year university student. He had headphones on and was looking at a portable DVD player. I thought how rude he was. Then the speaker said she hoped we wouldn't mind if her son sat in on the seminar. She explained that he'd heard her talk so many times before on this subject that she didn't have the heart to make him listen again.

We all laughed, of course. And as the professor began her talk, introducing her analysis of the personalities of those responsible for mass killings, crimes against humanity, genocide, I began to drift. I wondered first at how the boy had been for a moment a figure to be despised until a fragment of explanation induced complete forgiveness. And then I wondered how he could have become so bored and disconnected from the horrific stories which stippled his mother's account. Though it might have been the typical teenager's response to a parent's enthusiasm – feigned boredom, rolled eyes – it might equally have been an unmanufactured response. And I thought, with so many atrocities in the world and from history, have we reached that point when we just stop listening? We've heard it all before, countless times and in countless different forms and regarding countless different locations. The professor's list of gross human rights violations encompassed Rwanda, Former Yugoslavia, Congo, Chile, Argentina, the Holocaust ('of course'), even the horrible killings by Islamic State 'fighters' in Iraq, though she might just as easily have mentioned a host of other examples from the past and present. I might have added Malawi during Banda's regime. Then her talk shifted to the personalities of the perpetrators.

The professor's delivery was careful, with nothing sensationalist to capture our interest unnaturally, no tricks or thespian techniques. It was almost bland. She spoke of a 'typology' of offenders that she'd compiled, having studied hundreds, perhaps thousands, of individuals who'd committed these crimes. There was a PowerPoint presentation and charts appeared on the screen from time to time. One slide suggested culprits were a product of intersecting contexts: ideological, political, institutional I think were the three she mentioned. She explained how a dogma promoted widely within a state could induce hate against a group, how political conditions of tyranny might induce fear that would encourage acceptance of violence against a perceived enemy, how institutional culture (particularly of the military) could provoke general obedience no matter what the order. And within this variously constructed context, the characters of the perpetrators would be forged, so that not only the sadist or the ingrained criminal or the indifferent bureaucrat, but also 'ordinary' men and women could be conditioned to participate in (or avoid disrupting) mass killing, torture, abuse and to follow orders that they knew to be wrong. (Primo Levi thought they were 'obtuse brutes, not subtle demons', attesting to their conditioning for violence, not their inherent maleficence.)[19] She mentioned a number of psychological experiments in support of her analysis. Some people about the room nodded in recognition as she spoke of Milgram and Zimbardo. The professor spoke with mock astonishment (it had to be artificial given how long she'd been studying these matters) at the ease with which Stanley Milgram in the 1960s had been able to instruct his 'normal' New Haven participants to believe they were delivering increasing electric shocks to another person (who was actually an actor) for answering questions incorrectly. And Philip Zimbardo, who took a couple of dozen volunteers, college students, placed them in a mock 'prison', appointed half of them guards and half of them inmates and watched on as within a matter of days, the guards became gradually more and more vicious, abusing and sexually humiliating the 'prisoners'.

The experiments are famous, products of the sixties and seventies and the enduring fascination for why people commit atrocious acts, how they can turn from seemingly ordinary, kind-hearted individuals into potential killers and brutes. Milgram wrote about his experiments: 'This is, perhaps, the most fundamental lesson of our study: that ordinary people, simply doing their jobs, and without any particular hostility on their part, can become agents in a terrible destructive process.'[20]

I was worried, though. I asked the professor if her analysis might not be misguided. If she maintained that political, institutional, ideological contexts were so influential, how could she explain these experiments? The subjects were tempted to obey and abuse almost instantaneously. They either did as they were told from the start and thought they were inflicting pain or took on a role that quickly became oppressive of others and violent. Perhaps it suggested that context was one influence but so too a predisposition of human nature that was not fundamentally kindly, that was easily warped back into a primordial lack of care about anyone other than oneself. Wasn't obeying orders the ultimate in selfish behaviour, the excuse we needed to divert any suffering onto others, distant or close? And our anger directed at the bureaucrats and soldiers and civilians, men or women, who fell into committing atrocities or, at best, diverting eyes from them, merely camouflaged our own propensity for hatred and indifference? And wasn't 'evil' just another word for ourselves, the side we normally and so desperately try to keep hidden within us?

The conversation went on for a while. Back and forth, swapping ideas that perhaps the human condition is fundamentally cruel and uncaring, that for good reasons we've been socialised to suppress this, and that it takes very little for the inherent tendencies to be released and for us to return to our natural state of indifference to the pain of others. A little stress is all that is required, maybe a strong personality to lead us on.

We didn't resolve anything.

After her talk, I looked up the professor on the web and found that she led an international group of academics who studied crimes against humanity. It had been operating for eight years and produced regular newsletters. One of the series of research questions they asked was: Who are the perpetrators and why do they commit these crimes? Which organisations play a role? What kinds of ideologies underlie these crimes? What is the role of the bystanders? Why do or don't they act? An extended reading list of all those articles and books devoted to the questions followed. I realised that I'd read most of them.

I'm not sure what was more depressing: the endless academic interest in the people who commit atrocities or the fact that we seem no nearer an answer despite all this study. With so many examples, you'd think we would have a better idea by now. And this contemplation is not a new phenomenon – incomprehension, even despair, at the evil of humankind is the stuff of scripture: 'The heart is deceitful above all things and desperately sick; who can understand it?' was the Old Testament prophet Jeremiah's lament.[21]

Perhaps, though, we have become more aware and more sensitised to suffering the more distant our lives have become from its daily perpetuation. Then, when we see it, encounter its influence and its stories, we're even more horrified. Or perhaps each generation has to think of new ways to refute the evil side of humanity.

The professor from the Netherlands had set me thinking about the people who appeared as offenders in the transcripts, in the statements, in the memoirs. It set me thinking about Kramer, Grese, Klein, those others paraded every day in that Lüneburg courtroom, and those at Nuremberg too. Were they very different from those Germans who weren't in positions of authority, who watched and did not intervene, didn't even consider intervening? Were they 'evil'? Were they very different from me? If all those psychological experiments showed how the 'ordinary' person could so easily inflict pain, then what would I have done?

Whenever these questions are voiced now, Hannah Arendt's phrase the 'banality of evil' is often quoted as a description of the way in which ordinary Germans became party to a system and mechanism for the destruction of the Jews and other groups through mundane administrative actions.[22] She'd reached this conclusion in Jerusalem watching some of the trial in 1961 of one of the architects of the Holocaust, Adolf Eichmann. It seemed to me when I read her book that she believed him to be neither mad nor sadistic, but an ordinary man undertaking ordinary bureaucratic acts in the full knowledge that they would have extraordinarily terrible human consequences. 'Evil' was relevant as a word, as a concept, as the product of these actions *and* the people who contributed to it. The phrase 'banality of evil' wasn't an oxymoron in this rendition: evil was defined by its dullness, its ordinariness, there was nothing special about it and it was normal, constant, a fundamental part of being human.

I've thought of those men and women brought to trial after 1945, not necessarily the ones who would appear at Nuremberg, but the ones who served the system in the concentration camps or in the military. There were undoubtedly psychotics amongst them, but the personalities they revealed were sickeningly ordinary. It didn't mean that I thought I could do what they had done. I do not believe I have the capacity to fashion a bull whip out of tightly wrapped cellophane to hit anyone who displeases me. Nor do I believe I could give direct orders for people to be ill-treated, let alone killed. But perhaps it *did* mean I have the capacity to be cruel to the extent I could ignore my part in a chain of connected actions, or failures to act, which will cause someone, somewhere, to suffer. If that were true, I thought, I could be just as complicit in evil as anyone else.

And then I supposed the anger I felt (an emotion marked as a sin in its own right) when I read of the violence of the camps, the individual acts of brutality revealed during the British trials as well as at Nuremberg and all the other war crimes proceedings, might be a sort of primitive deflection: blaming others for blatant wrongs might be a device for failing to look within at one's own cruelties, one's own heedlessness to others in distress. I thought perhaps fury (other than of the victim) is naturally predisposed to dissipation over a short period of time because the pristine sense of virtue it requires is unsustainable. Far easier to allow indifference to settle in as shock is replaced by recognition and maybe, for the more benign, forgiveness. Only the obsessive can keep anger alive and seek retribution indefinitely.

The morning after the talk I glanced out of my office window and saw the professor leave with her son, pulling one of those trolley-cases behind her. I thought they must have stayed on campus for the night. They seemed happy. The two of them chatting between themselves, joking a little, I could tell, deciding which way to go, what to do next. It was a portrait of normality. A simple series of ordinary, peaceful acts and choices. No one paid them any attention.[23]

7

Hamburg

1.

In the spring of 2014, I was drawn back to Hamburg. The story of the British investigations revolving around the city and its suburb of Neuengamme, always running parallel to the proceedings in Nuremberg, purportedly complying with Thomas Dodd's promise of retribution for the 'minor' war criminals, was irresistible. If evil had been done here, if that word *did* serve a purpose, I wanted to find its remnants.

I took the U-Bahn to Steinstraße in the Altstadt district and walked down towards the Zoll Canal, one of the various waterways of the city centre. I was looking for an ordinary office block. It was impossible to miss.

The Messberghof is a huge brick building that overlooks the canal. It was refurbished and modernised in the 1990s, having survived all the bombing of the war. When the renovation works had been proposed, attempts were made to have some memorial noting the occupation of the firm Tesch & Stabenow, which had been one of the companies operating out of the original building during the 1930s and throughout the war. After much negotiation a small metal plaque was attached to one of the outside walls. It was unobtrusive, perhaps deliberately so, and easy to miss. Small, insignificant, it told the briefest of stories: Tesch & Stabenow occupied part of the premises and organised the supply of poison gas that was used for the murder of the people of Europe in Auschwitz, Majdanek, Sachsenhausen, Ravensbrück, Stutthof and Neuengamme. The owner and manager of the firm were convicted and executed in 1946 by a British military court, the plaque said. There was an extract from a poem about the Shoah too. The sign must be incomprehensible to most passers-by, if they even notice it.

Standing in front of the plaque I felt self-conscious, struggling with the translation. I imagined people were watching, wondering what it was that fascinated me on the wall, following my gaze. They carried on by, of course, and I didn't think they would be intrigued enough to come back later and look more carefully at the inscription. Even if they did, would it make sense to them? I doubted it. The problem with many of these memorials, which dot buildings and places about German cities, sometimes obtrusively, sometimes obscured, is that they presume prior knowledge. Perhaps the word 'Auschwitz' was enough, the common signifier recognised by everyone as a symbol of the Nazi regime. But the other names on the plaque?

It seemed a paltry memorial to me, telling the barest of accounts, insignificant when compared to the enormity of killing that was made possible, if only as part of a necessary chain of supply, from a small suite of offices within this conventional office block. Just as today the ordinariness of the place and the business facade protected it from notice.

If the memorial at the Messberghof lacked weight, the same couldn't be said for Bullenhuser Damm, the other place I'd come to see. A few kilometres separated the two, a walk that took less than an hour through depressing streets of low-level warehouses and ramshackle businesses and long, spiritless avenues where pedestrians were rare. I imagined the area had been devastated during the war and had never quite recovered a desire to regenerate as a space where people lived.

When the old Bullenhuser Damm school came into view, down a cobbled street, I thought it a charmless building, a red-brick monster not that unlike the Messberghof in its hulk and oppressive lines. It had the appearance of a grim reformatory rather than a place for children to learn.

Inside, down in the basement, there was an exhibition. It was cold and cheerless and the story it told offended every appealing notion of humanity. There could be no room for cavilling at the pertinence of fury here. For this was where the twenty children from Neuengamme KZ hospital had come, the children whom Major

Noel Till had first learned about from his inquiries at Neustadt, the children who'd suffered TB experiments at the hands of the concentration camp doctors, but whose fate was not then clear. The trails would eventually lead the British War Crimes Teams to the Messberghof and Bullenhuser Damm and back to the camp at Neuengamme. But though their knowledge of the atrocities they were pursuing must have spurred them on, their task was hindered by lack of resources and official support. Nuremberg was monopolising everyone's attention, the anger that drove the Allies' commitment to track down *every* war criminal was waning. Perhaps the administrators and civil servants had lost interest, had more pressing concerns with reconstruction and reconciliation. But from what I could glean in my searches amongst the files, hoping to understand what had happened with the investigations and trials, the British effort had begun to lose some of its vitality after the Bergen-Belsen experience. Lt Col Humphrey Tilling, who succeeded Leo Genn as head of No. 1 War Crimes Team, wrote to his old commanding officer and friend to tell him 'half the zest of the battle has gone with your departure'.[1] The story of impassioned retribution I was following had become more one of political indifference, or so I sensed.

2.

Criticisms of the process and outcome of the Belsen trial emerged soon after its conclusion, particularly when comparisons were made with the apparent efficiency of the Americans' version of justice at Dachau. Questions were raised in Parliament on Monday, 3 December 1945. Hansard recorded the exchange:

Mr E. P. Smith asked the Chancellor of the Duchy of Lancaster how many convicts of the Belsen trial were adjudged guilty of murder and did not receive sentence of death.

Mr Mathers replied: 'None of the accused in the Belsen trial was specifically charged with murder. The charges related to the ill-treatment of internees which, in some cases, caused their deaths. Eleven of the 30 found guilty were sentenced to death, but the Court did not specifically state in its findings that any of them had been responsible for causing deaths.'

Mr Vernon Bartlett: 'Is the hon. Gentleman aware that his reply shows what a farce the whole thing is?'[2]

There was criticism from Moscow too. The Red Star published its response to the trial on 23 November 1945. 'The prosecution did not perform its task,' it commented, 'as was observed by representatives of the press, as might have been expected. The accused were executives of orders given by the fascist party. The prosecution, however, said nothing at all about fascism but formulated the accusation as if the matter under consideration were a criminal affair remarkable only by reason of the number of accused.'[3]

The article went on to condemn the British court's failure to present Bergen-Belsen and Auschwitz as part of a whole fascist system. Whether politically motivated or not, the Soviets had a point.

But even before the verdict, the British government was demonstrating impatience with the whole war crimes programme. Sir Hartley Shawcross, the relatively new British Attorney General (appointed after the Labour Party's success at the July 1945 General Election) and the man who was about to lead Britain's advocacy at the Nuremberg trial, attended a meeting of the British War Crimes Executive in Church House, Westminster, in October 1945 and laid down an ultimatum: the government wanted a minimum of 500 minor war crimes cases to be tried in Germany by 30 April 1946.[4] It did not want the lengthy Belsen trial to be a precedent; otherwise the British could be committed to pursuing the Nazis for decades to come.

The arbitrary demand induced a sense of panic within the British Army of the Rhine in Germany during the autumn and winter of

1945. Major General Chilton at Field Marshal Montgomery's BAOR HQ wrote to the War Office saying that

until the Attorney General's target figure became known to this HQ, the policy was to give priority to the more serious and flagrant war crimes, and these are the cases which take time to investigate and prepare. Unless cases are carefully prepared and presented for trial, military courts will not convict and an undue number of acquittals will result. In order to comply with the instructions contained in your signal, a modification of this policy would be necessary, and it is probable that only those cases which could be most expeditiously disposed of would be proceeded with, regardless of their relative importance ... It is therefore requested that you should confirm that you accept the changed policy in principle, and that you agree that it is preferable to try a large number of trivial cases than a few involving more serious offences.[5]

The War Office wrote back, ducking the question. Selection of cases for prosecution was the BAOR's affair, it said, though it was 'undesirable to give priority to the more trivial cases to the detriment of trials concerned with serious atrocities'.[6] Promises of support were made so that *all* matters could be prosecuted. But in reality, the generosity was confined to rhetoric. An ironic (at least it reads like that to me) note was sent from the legal team in Germany to the War Office on 2 November: 'Excluding Sundays, there are now 155 days in which to reach this figure [of 500 cases], which means that approximately three cases must be completed in every working day between 1 November and 30 April.'

Group Captain Tony Somerhough, recently appointed as head of all the War Crimes Investigation Teams (WCIT) in Bad Oeynhausen, was the man charged to fulfil the British forces' obligations. Somerhough was immensely popular, and immensely dedicated to his mission. Across the few years of the British investigations, he was a central figure, resolute in the defence of his men and arguing for the resources they needed. Vera Atkins, a former member of the Special Operations Executive, who worked with the WCIT in tracking down those responsible for killing some of the women operatives sent to France,[7] would describe him later as 'quite the most brilliant man I have come across and certainly the most brilliant wit'.[8] But even with his talents and determination he couldn't conjure cases from nothing. He needed detectives and man-hunters and interrogators.

The logistical problems were matched by organisational ones. The War Crimes Teams' efforts were still chaotic, with some investigators being suddenly sent to Norway, Austria, the Low Countries, Denmark and France as well as across Germany in pursuit of some clue, usually involving the killing of British forces personnel. A Special Air Service team, which was carrying out its own inquiries, added to the mix. They had a very specific and narrow brief. In 1944, it had become common knowledge that Hitler had issued a 'Commando Order' in October 1942 authorising the 'disposal' of special forces when captured. Though the SAS was in the process of being disbanded at the war's end, some operatives (at least eighteen) remained unaccounted for. It was suspected that many had been murdered in accordance with Hitler's directive. Rumours existed of executions in Natzweiler KZ, on the French–German border in Alsace, and in Ravensbrück. The SAS, ever intent on looking after their own, weren't going to leave the matter to others.

In June 1945, the commanding officer of the 2nd SAS Intelligence Unit, Col Franks, arranged for a small team of SAS men under Major Eric Barkworth (whom everyone called 'Bill') to carry out investigations into these probable killings.[9] They worked out of a house in Karlsruhe, soon acquiring a reputation, driving into and around France, careless of approval from the French government, investigating with a tenacity that would typify their work for the next couple of years.

Barkworth's team wasn't appreciated by everyone. Lt Col A.J.M. Harris at BAOR HQ wrote in October 1945 that 'although the SAS are in many ways extremely valuable as investigators, Barkworth's material conforms to no known legal standards of proof and is very often based on pure hearsay; much of it is never reduced to writing'.[10] Harris was also upset that 'Barkworth and his party have made themselves somewhat unpopular with the French', running around the country demonstrating an attitude that 'the French regard as highly offensive'.[11] Though focused on crimes committed against the SAS, it was thought these rogue investigators should be attached to the general War Crimes Teams. They could then be brought under control and might prove useful.

Despite resistance by both Somerhough and Barkworth, it was the logical thing to do. By the end of 1945 the SAS investigators formed a separate but linked unit with noted success and skill in tracking down war criminals. For some, their talents highlighted the inability of the rest of the war crimes units to adopt anything like a professional approach to the search-and-find aspect of their work. One of the London-based War Office SAS team, Captain Prince Yurka Galitzine (the man who'd reported on Natweiler KZ's crimes back in November 1944), became so incensed by the incompetence of the general British efforts that he wrote a punishing report. Col Bradshaw of the War Office passed it on to BAOR HQ in Germany as a 'proposal'.[12] But Galitzine's paper was more a critique of the lamentable progress in bringing suspected Nazi criminals into custody. He identified the problem, as he saw it:

On 25th October 1945 some 3000 Wanted reports had been received by CROWCASS from British sources. Out of these, CROWCASS has so far only been successful in locating 1 accused. Of the 3000 Wanted by the British some 200 are detained in our custody and 1000 can be classed as 'witnesses' or wanted in respect of crimes committed against Allied National cases being dealt with by the British Authorities. It can thus be seen that at present some 1800 persons who have committed War Crimes against the British are still untraced.

Galitzine outlined the curse of bureaucratic inefficiency. CROWCASS, based in Paris, possessed a list of wanted people but according to Galitzine they had to wait for the forms relating to each captured suspect to be processed before this information was passed on to investigators. He estimated that it would take another ten months before the outstanding batch would be completed. Otherwise they were dependent on Somerhough's War Crimes Investigation Teams. Galitzine commented acidly, 'There are two such teams in the Rhine

Army working on cases in the field. In the due course of their work they occasionally manage to track down suspects.'

The difficulties were many, according to Galitzine. Thousands of German prisoners were being released by the Americans and the British, many to work in the German mines, which otherwise had lost their labour to the war, and many to the harvest in the summer of 1945. The German Army was being demobbed, and tracing anyone was becoming almost impossible. The Russians didn't reveal whom they held. Allied armies (including the French) were recruiting Germans, allowing suspected war criminals to hide in their midst. Galitzine even accused the French of being corrupt and failing to hand over suspected war criminals. For fear of being exposed as collaborators, or after receiving money, some French officials, he wrote, had either released suspects or denied their existence.

Dramatic action was needed, Galitzine said. Categorise the 1,800 wanted men and women in order of importance, treat their hunting down as an 'operation of war', employ '100 investigators fully equipped with transport, armed and under bold and enterprising direction', all with the backing of the Cabinet, set a time limit (April 1946) and make their work the highest priority. He thought using intelligence officers would be the most effective method, run from London. They would be split into two: one touring all Allied POW camps searching for criminals and the other a 'rover section' following up on known home addresses.

Group Captain Somerhough scrutinised the report. His response began dismissively: 'It is difficult to criticise this paper as it is so obviously based on a complete misconception of what machinery is in fact in existence.' He said, with anger pouring through his letter, 'There are *three* War Crimes Investigation Teams in the Rhine Army ... To say, however, that in the course of their work these teams occasionally manage to track down suspects is as untruthful as it is offensive. These teams must have arrested dozens, if not hundreds of suspects by now.' He ended, 'Need I comment any further in detail?'

But the proposal had found favour. A special search unit largely composed of the SAS operatives was formed by the end of December 1945 to support the investigators and lawyers preparing cases. The initiative, however, merely plugged one of the many gaps. The cases awaiting investigation by the British began to mount in the winter of 1945. A few may have been brought to trial in the closing months of the year but by 31 January 1946 there were 53,000 Germans in British custody, most of whom were in the 'automatic arrest' category: concentration camp guards, members of the SS, members of the Gestapo. Of these, about 2,500 were suspected war criminals.[13] It was a huge number to process.

Compared to this mountain, the War Crimes unit remained an under-resourced operation, desperately unsure about their direction; should they focus on investigating the cases with British victims or go after every concentration camp official? Investigations became haphazard, random, pursued without any apparent sensible plan. Amateurism pervaded the operation, exemplified perhaps by the appointment of Lt Col Ian Neilson to command the new No. 3 WCIT.

Neilson had been working at Bad Oeynhausen with the Air Despatch unit after the end of the war, delivering newspapers to Field Marshal Montgomery. But he'd become rather redundant. The Signals Corps had taken over most of his job. Then, as he would recall, 'I was at a party one evening and I met a chap from "A" Branch', who asked what he was doing and Neilson said, well, nothing much. They talked about what had been happening and the chap had said he might be able to help him and invited him to his office the next day at 9 a.m. By 10 a.m. 'I found myself commanding No. 3 War Crimes Investigation Unit in a field at that stage I really knew nothing about at all.'[14]

Neilson speculated that his background had some bearing on his appointment: he'd studied forensic medicine and law in Glasgow ten years previously and had begun training as a solicitor. But his studies had been interrupted by the war when he was only twenty-one and he'd joined the forces, serving with the Air Observation unit. He'd never had the chance to practise as a lawyer. And yet a quick chat and he was commanding one of the three investigation teams. It was a sign of desperation and pragmatism. However competent and skilful Neilson may have been, he was not an expert in law, medicine, detection, interrogation, case preparation or much else at that stage. But he was on site and competent. He would only stay in post until March 1946, as it was, such was the quick turnaround of personnel through demobilisation.

Though inexperienced, Neilson soon appreciated the problems. 'We needed more interrogator–catchers, we needed more transport drivers, we needed more clerks and interpreters and we had the job of catching and interrogating not only the war criminals but also the witnesses.'

Six months into the programme of retribution and the work had yet to be taken seriously.

3.

Despite all the difficulties, Somerhough was confident that the target of 500 prosecutions before 30 April 1946 would be achieved. He pointed out that as of 1 January 1946 the US had tried 100 war criminals to Britain's 94. And the Americans had 'at least 19 war crimes investigation teams to our three'.[15]

The satisfaction and optimism of the War Crimes Teams was superficial. Complaints about an absence of committed support from the British government for investigations and prosecutions had never been resolved. The amateur detective had not been replaced by a fully equipped team of experienced professional police, and people were still often working according to their own whims. At the beginning of 1946, Somerhough, together with the increasingly influential Major Alan Nightingale, sketched out how the investigation could be better organised.

Nightingale would soon become the leader of the War Crimes Teams and Somerhough's deputy (promoted to lieutenant colonel in March 1946, taking over from Lt Col Neilson). He was twenty-nine years old, had joined the War Crimes Team in July 1945 and had become a prominent figure in the original No. 2 WCIT, taking command after Lt Col Champion had returned home. He spoke French, Russian and German, the reason for his appointment in the first place. But for all his qualities, he had little if any legal training. Nonetheless, six months into the job he was considered one of the most experienced and able investigating officers. Somerhough thought very highly of him.

Together they planned that the group would be renamed the War Crimes Investigation Unit (WCIT) and split into six separate teams. Officers in No. 1 included Captains Ellis, Alexander and Murdoch and Lieutenant Glass. Nightingale would command No. 2 Team with Captain Walter Freud (promoted to major at the end of February 1946) as one of his seven officers. No. 3 was led by Major Silley with Captains Rheinberg, Harrison, Comper, Nicholson and Davies. Major Vernon commanded No. 4 with Captains Crass, Le Bosquet, Hodge and Worcester. No. 5 Team was composed of the SAS investigators, still acting independently under the control of Major Barkworth. And No. 6 was the search-and-arrest team named, I can imagine, with more than a hint of pessimism as Operation Haystack. That was commanded by Major Bramwell with Captains Nixon, Bone, Lee, Stone, Schweiger, Park, Priestley, Rantzau, Thornton and Lyon and Lt Bruce operating from their separate headquarters at 24 Lettow-Vorbeck-Straße. Many non-commissioned officers and drivers were part of the unit too, but even so it remained a ridiculously understaffed outfit given the numbers of suspects and allegations coming to light. It didn't help that both officers and other ranks were constantly being demobbed and less experienced replacements only sent after long delays.

The organisational and personnel deficiencies were illustrated in less than obvious ways. With the few people available to cover the great distances of the British zone, the War Crimes Teams had to depend on cars to reach all the crime scenes and all the places where suspects or witnesses might be found. Major Nightingale reported, 'Motor cars are being unmercifully "caned". Wolseley 18hp cars are being habitually driven at 60 mph or over, with the result that most of them have had shock absorber and spring trouble ... Mercedes are all delicate cars and need considerable maintenance to ensure a lasting performance.'[16] By the summer of 1946 the impact on vehicles seemed absurd; complaints were made from the War Office about the amount of expenditure needed to keep vehicles going: but then, they were undertaking an estimated average of 30,000 vehicle miles per week. They were writing off cars at the rate of one every three weeks or every 90,000 vehicle miles.[17]

The problems with cars continued well into 1946, a source of continuing dispute and frustration. Nightingale had to report in December on courts of inquiry into discipline of his officers and men.

There had been fifteen traffic accidents, seven losses and one misbe-haviour to deal with. The last one involved Captain Rantzau, whom Nightingale had transferred out of his unit for 'improperly associating with German females'. Nightingale had to be investigated himself as he'd lost a Kodak half plate camera. He was 'invited to pay £15' in compensation to the War Office for a replacement.[18]

But the vehicle difficulties were more a symptom of too few men chasing across too large distances than a failure of engineering. Nightingale felt strongly enough to write to JAG about the shortage of officers in April 1946. 'Owing to several factors,' he said, 'but primarily to demobilisation, the shortage of officers in this unit is now even more acute than when the Unit was first formed, and up to now no new replacements have been posted to make up these decreases in strength. As a result of this, the output of work has been seriously affected.'[19] He illustrated the problem. There should have been twenty-seven captains or lieutenants as investigators/interpreters, but he had only fourteen, of whom two were shortly to be sent home. He had thirteen cases underway of which four were 'major cases of the concentration camp type'. 'A further eight are "shelved" pending further investigations owing to inconclusive evidence or lack of accused and which, owing to the shortage of personnel, it is not economical to continue. Twenty-eight cases remain uninvestigated.' Only six officers and two staff sergeants were available to examine smaller cases after deployment of the others to the concentration camp ones.

Things weren't much better in the search team. Of the fourteen officers he was supposed to have, only nine were present. Of twenty sergeants only five were available. And he had 350 names of wanted persons of whom 74 had been located and a further 30 were being pursued. That left 250 not being searched for at all.

The response to Nightingale's pleas was dismissive. Instead of increases the War Office wanted cuts. Government finances weren't in good shape. The army was a massive drain on the country's reserves. Every unit would need to reduce its costs. No one was exempt. Group Captain Somerhough understood that cuts to the WCIU were 'abso-lutely essential and the inevitable delay in rounding up war criminals has been accepted'.[20] He agreed to a 20 per cent cut in his budget.[21] But on 30 May 1946 he wrote: 'It does not seem to be appreciated in certain branches of this Headquarters that the WCIU is engaged on priority work or that it is a highly specialised unit, consisting not of ordinary regimental officers and men, but composed of persons specially chosen for their linguistic and other qualifications, many of whom have deferred their release voluntarily in order to do this work.'[22]

Brigadier Shapcott, at the legal end of the chain in the Judge Advocate General's office in London, pleaded to Major General Brownjohn in June 1946 that no further cuts to his war crimes units should be ordered. Seven officers and thirty-three other ranks had already been removed from the unit. Shapcott noted with an obviously acerbic tone, 'War crimes trials cannot take place unless war criminals are apprehended and cases investigated.' He went on: 'The unit as you are probably aware have recently been successful in apprehending Oswald Pohl one of the more important Nazis still at large as a result of which their tails are probably well up. This however was probably off-set by the decision of the War Establishment Committee to reduce the Establishment of the unit which is I think you will agree doing a first-class job of work, albeit of a somewhat unpleasant nature.'[23]

The entreaties made no difference. A war of resources was underway. Indicatively, by August 1946 Major Cartmell would be complaining about the 'intolerable amount of work which the pathologist is required to undertake' with exhumations, identifications and professional interrogations. 'Some cases have now been held up for a period of two to three months', a position made worse, he believed, 'owing to the vast amount of medical investigations necessitated in connection with the Ravensbrück concentration camp'. Somerhough and Nightingale had to beg for no more cuts to their interpreters. As a trade-off they agreed to cut the two gravediggers and employ German labour instead.[24] It was an absurd haggling that undermined the programme of retribution at each stage.

Over at the International Military Tribunal in Nuremberg, the prosecution maintained the impression that the Allies were pursuing *all* perpetrators for the worst of crimes. In theory that was right. In practice, no one engaged in the investigations or government could have been fooled.

4.

After the exhibitions in the basement of Bullenhuser Damm School, it was depressing to read about the administrative difficulties hampering the British investigators. Depressing because it was unsurprising. Depressing because I could imagine how frustrated those men and women employed to hunt down war criminals must have been. They were face-to-face with the sickening residue of atrocity. Even if the bureaucrats and politicians back home may have had their fervour for justice tempered by the demands of economic caution, the investigators couldn't turn away from the evidence so easily. Many were Jewish émigrés who'd escaped Germany or the occupied countries of Europe before the war began and were seconded to the War Crimes unit where their language skills and knowledge of the country were essential. The victims of the concentration camps in particular weren't faceless numbers to them: they could be relatives, friends, colleagues.

Despite the likely determination of these committed investigators, this was the time, I thought, towards the end of 1945, early on in the pursuit of justice, only six months since the fighting had stopped and the reality of the Nazi regime had horrified the world, when the fury started to dissipate. I suspected the political demand to finish with war crimes cases altogether, to cut the expenditure on investigations, to respond only slowly to demands for resources, to focus mainly on offences committed against British troops, began to bite. Still the impetus to expose the scope of atrocity and hunt down those responsible hadn't yet been *wholly* suppressed, nor, I gathered, were the investigators and lawyers to be deflected so easily. Their initial resolve to follow the evidence of complicity in the massacres and exterminations remained strong. In particular, the investigations into crimes associated with Neuengamme KZ begun by Noel Till and those in No. 2 WCIT seemed typical of an ardency yet to be undone. They'd found and arrested commandant Max Pauly and his right-hand man Anton Thumann, who were leading suspects. Witnesses had come forward who could talk about Thumann in particular: he had a reputation not just in Neuengamme but other camps too. Izaak Ochshorn had given a statement that identified someone called Anton Tomann (whom the investigators believed was Thumann) as camp commandant at Groß-Rosen KZ who'd ordered the murder of every Jew who'd entered the camp. According to Ochshorn, Thumann's favourite winter sport was to dump Jews alive into a pit and have them covered in snow until they suffocated. The Yugoslav government wanted him extradited for the killing of their nationals at Neuengamme.[25] But the British had him in custody and weren't about to hand him over. He'd already confessed to one atrocity: the killing of dozens of Russian POWs one night towards the end of the war on the order of Pauly and the Hamburg Gestapo. He said, as was the common line by then, that he'd simply been carrying out his orders. The investigators had more than enough to indict him, Pauly and a number of other Neuengamme KZ guards they'd managed to round up.

It was during the piecing together of this information that other matters came to light, ones that would eventually connect those buildings I'd visited in Hamburg, the Messberghof and Bullenhuser Damm, and the main camp in Hamburg's suburbs. My obsession with Neustadt and Neuengamme encompassed them all now, tightly entwined as these places and the crimes committed there were.

In June 1945, the investigation team at Bad Oeynhausen received a tip-off in a letter first sent to the British Army authorities in Hamburg by a man named Emil Sehm. He called himself a tax adviser.[26] The letter was short, and lacking in specifics. It said:

According to my estimation I am able to supply very important information that means fresh evidence to commit war criminals for trial. The war crime I am referring to concerns an official discussion which took place between a businessman of an IG Farben sister concern with leading men of the OKW [*Oberkommando der Wehrmacht*, the high command of the German armed forces], about the application of the hydrocyanic acid process to kill human beings. Further the training of SS men to apply this process. My profession gave me the opportunity to see top secret files and that is where my knowledge results from.

It was sufficiently scant to be ignored. But Sehm wouldn't forget. He wrote another letter on 24 August 1945.[27] This time he provided more details. He said he was employed as a bookkeeper, tax adviser and accountant for the firm Tesch & Stabenow, a company specialising in the supply of poison gas. His post gave him access to confidential documents, secret papers which his employers didn't want revealed. One report he remembered well. Written by the firm's principal, Dr Tesch, it told of a conference he'd attended in Berlin during the war. Tesch had been invited because of his expertise in the eradication of parasites, bugs, lice. The report said that a speaker at the conference explained the purpose of the meeting. Execution of the Jews by shooting had become unhygienic and the SS wanted Tesch to advise on how 'Jews could be exterminated by using hydrocyanic acid', a deadly gas. According to Sehm, the report discussed how this could be achieved by using sealed barracks into which the acid gas could be released by way of plates deposited in the rooms during the night. All bodies would then be cremated. 'Dr Tesch offered himself to SS men who will be selected by the OKW and put at his disposal to train on courses for this purpose,' Sehm wrote. He said the accounts revealed that the training took place, was paid for and that hydrocyanic acid was supplied to the OKW and the SS in huge quantities.

The reality of the 'gas chambers' had already filtered into the consciousness of the investigators and prosecutors. Witness evidence had been gradually accumulating amidst the testimonies taken at Bergen-Belsen, and knowledge of extermination through gassing at Auschwitz had been spreading since the Soviets issued their reports after overrunning the eastern camps in the summer of 1944, if not before. The most impressive accounts so far recorded by the British were taken during the Bergen-Belsen inquiries.

Dr Ada Bimko had given evidence at the Belsen trial and had sworn a deposition providing a precise account of the nature of the extermination at the Birkenau section of Auschwitz.[28] She had testified that she'd seen the gas chambers complex on a day when they hadn't been in operation. At the end of her visit she'd been led to a room above the chamber.

Across this room were two pipes, each about three inches thick. I did not notice whether there were any branch pipes leading from them. The SS man told me that the pipes, which were in the floor, were

connected to the spray fittings in the gas chamber below. In a corner
of the room were two large cylinders, but I did not notice whether
these cylinders were connected to the pipes. The SS man told me that
the cylinders contained the gas which passed through the pipes into the
gas chamber.

At Bad Oeynhausen the War Crimes Team spied a connection
between the tip-off letter from Emil Sehm, the evidence of witnesses
from Bergen-Belsen and statements taken by Major Till and his
men from survivors of the *Cap Arcona* sinking, who'd talked about
the mass killing by using poison gas of two hundred Russian prisoners
of war at Neuengamme.

Major Gerald Draper (as he was at the time) of the legal corps,
though busy acting as prosecutor in other British war crimes trials
and quickly becoming a central figure in the war crimes prosecution
programme, directed the investigation. Draper was certainly a lawyer
intent on giving vent to fury against those responsible for what he
called the 'Schweinerei' (a word I also found used in Nuremberg by
Alfred Rosenberg and meaning 'scandalous doings' according to the
official translation).[29] As an officer in the Irish Guards, Draper had
seen Bergen-Belsen after its liberation and it had affected him deeply.
He'd been involved in the preparation of that trial and, according to
a friend who would write his obituary in 1989, his reading of all the
evidence left him experiencing 'disbelief at the extent of the evil'.[30]
Captain (Anton) Walter Freud and Staff Sergeant Fred Pelican of No. 2
WCIT were no less fervent in their feelings. They were assigned to
look into Sehm's claim.

5.

Captain Freud and Sergeant Pelican were an odd pairing, though
given the haphazard approach to war crime investigation appointments I'd come across perhaps that wasn't surprising. Neither was
British by birth and both were refugees from the Nazis who had

escaped to Britain before the war began. Apart from that, they couldn't have been more different.

Unlike many of the investigators and prosecutors, they wrote about their time spent in Germany after the war. Freud was the grandson of one of Europe's most famous figures: the psychologist Sigmund Freud. Born in 1921 and brought up in Vienna, Walter was well educated and well connected, leading a privileged existence. He was one of the Jewish elite in the city before the Nazi-sympathising Austrians began to clamour for *Anschluss*, union with Germany. Fearful of the future, the Freud family scattered in 1938. Walter left for London with his mother. When he turned eighteen in 1940 he was interned as an enemy alien by the British authorities and deported to Australia on the troopship HMT *Dunera*.

I came across Freud's recollections of that journey when I opened his boxes of papers deposited in the Imperial War Museum.[31] It's an odd collection, containing an array of letters and notes and photographs. One set of pictures were of the grounds of Bergen-Belsen: the pits where thousands were buried in mass graves; the crematorium; signs erected by the British telling any visitor (in English only) how many had died at the camp ('victims of the German new order in Europe'); a woman in army uniform (no name on the back); a watchtower and barbed wire fence; a group of sergeants and corporals posing as though a football team.

Amongst the papers there were also detailed notes of the treatment accorded to the 962 German and Austrian internees who'd accompanied Freud on the nine-week voyage aboard the *Dunera*. According to Freud they were all anti-Nazis, although that hadn't prevented the ship's military crew from exercising a control more suited to suspected criminals. The notes showed how disgusted he'd been at the way his fellow passengers had been treated.

Freud had managed to convey to the authorities sufficient poise and breeding during the long journey, however, to impress upon them his value as an ally rather than enemy. Almost as soon as the ship had docked in Australia, he and a number of others identified as loyal to the British had been sent back to Britain, where he'd joined the Pioneer Corps, the only military outfit (other than the secret services, where 'needs must' governed recruitment) open to enemy nationals. It was a non-fighting division whose duties largely consisted of tedious labour, digging ditches, building various army works. But his pedigree and his language skills marked him out as a man of quality and he was recruited to the Special Operations Executive. Though he went through the whole training programme and was parachuted behind enemy lines in Italy, the war ended before he could do anything destructive to the Nazi cause. In August 1945 he was posted as an interpreter to Germany and by September he was serving with No. 2 WCIT, taken on as yet another wholly unqualified detective.

Fred Pelican's history was very different.[32] He was three years older than Freud, born in Poland, close to the German border. The family Pelikan (Fred changed the spelling when he was in Britain) moved to Breslau on the German side of Silesia. Being Jewish, it wasn't a clever transfer. Come *Kristallnacht* in November 1938, the Pelicans were vulnerable. Fred evaded arrest by leaving his home and heading for Berlin, hoping to find some passage out of the country. He was aiming for Belgium but was picked up close to the border. From there he was transported to Dachau. The concentration camp wasn't yet a sealed prison and after five and a half months Pelican was released. His family had heard of his arrest and had made arrangements for him to acquire emigration papers. At the time, this was enough for many Jewish inmates to obtain their release from the camp and, at considerable expense and with considerable difficulty, leave Germany. He returned to Breslau at the beginning of 1939 and was eventually allowed to depart for Britain, originally with the intention of boarding a ship heading from Liverpool to Shanghai. It was an arbitrary destination. As long as his ticket was for somewhere outside the Reich, that was all that mattered to the Nazi authorities and was sufficient to allow him entry onto British soil.

Pelican never had to board that ship bound for China. On arrival in Britain he was housed in a transit camp and when war against Germany was declared soon after, he was allowed to join the Pioneer Corps too. By the end of the conflict he'd served in France, interrogating captured German officers in Normandy. It was natural that his fluent German marked him out as a potentially useful member of the incipient War Crimes Team. Like Freud, he was posted to Bad

Oeynhausen in May 1945 as an 'interpreter', although the term was fast becoming a euphemism for 'investigator' given the dearth of qualified personnel assigned to the new War Crimes Teams. Some training for his new role was provided, as he would recall, but it was limited.

> I went through a rapid process of acquiring knowledge of investiga-
> tion, cross-examination, interrogation and legal procedure. I was also
> shown how to handle an Army issue Rolleiflex camera. I was instructed
> how to take a legally binding sworn deposition; how to interrogate
> an accused person, preferably at night; never to use a ceiling light
> during interrogation; and how to observe changes on an accused
> person's face in course of cross-examination.[33]

All this was done over twelve days in a mansion in Wiltshire. Pelican never knew the exact location; it was kept secret from him. But, he said, this had been the extent of his preparation. How effective a training this could have been to take part in the most complex investigatory programme the British Army had ever to undertake is a mystery. It didn't concern Staff Sergeant Pelican. He was confident he could 'accomplish any task which faced me when I returned to my unit'.

In September 1945 he was working with Captain Freud and Major Draper in Hamburg.

6.

On the day after the opening of the Bergen-Belsen trial, 18 September 1945, Freud and Pelican travelled to Hamburg and interviewed Sehm, who told them that the firm of Tesch & Stabenow was still operating, selling poisonous gas to the British authorities for use in the delousing and fumigation of ships anchored in Hamburg port. Little attempt had been made to conceal the business. All the owner Bruno Tesch had changed since the war's end was the company name. It was now simply called 'Chemical Industries'.

The firm retained the offices it had occupied since the late 1920s on the second floor of the Messberghof in the city centre. Freud and Pelican visited the offices, barged in and arrested Dr Tesch, suspecting he'd been the man who'd supplied Zyklon B to Auschwitz and other concentration camps. They transported him back to their HQ at Bad Oeynhausen for interrogation by Draper.

Tesch gave little away under questioning. He presented himself as a respectable businessman, a chemist, whose knowledge of the sales of his products was sketchy. He denied any and all suggestions that he'd colluded with the SS to produce a quick way of exterminating the Jews. He denied that he'd attended any conference concerned with the subject and he said he hadn't devised methods for using his Zyklon B for anything other than the fumigation of barracks. He didn't even know if his product had been sold to concentration camps at all. But Tesch did admit to being a member of the Nazi party and a 'supporting member of the SS'. He explained he'd been affiliated to the SS Hygiene Institute in order to obtain their business.

Tesch wasn't believed, but there was little hard evidence to disprove his account. With only the word of Emil Sehm to go on, pressure mounted from the British authorities in Hamburg to let Tesch go, incensed as they were that one of their essential suppliers had been detained. So many ships required fumigation and Tesch's firm had been hired to undertake the difficult task. Draper gave way. Tesch was released and allowed to return to his firm.

It was a decision Captain Freud opposed.[34] Convinced Tesch was an arch-war criminal, he and Pelican worked hard to persuade their superiors to overturn their decision. They argued that Tesch's case was the first dealing 'not with persons directly concerned in the murder or ill-treatment of prisoners or slave workers, but with those who lent their skill and services to facilitating the gruesome work of the concentration camps and so identified themselves with breaches of the laws of war on a wholesale scale'.[35] Even though the whole Nazi extermination policy was supposed to be secret, thousands of people had to have been involved to enable it to be carried out. This was their chance to expose the sickening trade that enabled that policy to be executed.

They succeeded in their entreaties and Tesch was rearrested on 6 October. But Freud was angry. He pointed out later that Tesch would have had 'full knowledge of both the evidence of Sehm and also the lines on which his interrogation has been conducted' after his first arrest, enough to warn him and burn any papers that might condemn him. Even though Tesch had been at liberty for only a short period, five days at the beginning of October, there was time for him to dispose of damning documentary evidence. Who knew what incriminating papers he might have destroyed?

For the next two months Freud, Pelican and other members of the No. 2 WCIT pursued Tesch. But perhaps because of Tesch's ill-timed release the investigators struggled. They first had to establish the link between the firm and the supply of gas to the concentration camps. Without that evidence Tesch would have no case to answer.

All available members of Tesch's firm were rounded up. Twenty people were found by the team, including Tesch, his business partner, Karl Weinbacher, the firm's chief chemist, Dr Joachim Drosihn, and the accountant, Alfred Zaun. Questioning them revealed that 'Zyklon B' was the exclusive trade name of prussic acid gas in powder form distributed by 'Testa' (as Tesch & Stabenow was known), which had the exclusive rights for supply east of the River Elbe. The manufacturer was the company Degesch of Frankfurt, who produced the gas in varying strengths. The investigators learned that Type A was powerful enough to kill rats on board ships. Type E, stronger and deadlier, was used to fumigate a barracks, purportedly to eradicate lice. Tesch & Stabenow supplied not only the gas but also special gas masks and circulation plants with electric motors, suction pipes, pressure pipes, evaporisers – most of what was needed to operate a 'gas chamber'. The gas was produced as small, blue, pea-sized pellets and sold in various sized tins which could only be opened with a special grapple and, as the tin warned, 'by trained personnel'. There was plenty of evidence showing the firm supplied large quantities of the strongest type of Zyklon B to concentration camps. A sharp rise in profits had also occurred during 1942 and 1943, when it was known the mass gassing operations were at their most intense. The gas supplied over this period amounted to an average of one tonne a month. But nothing emerged to suggest Tesch and his personnel *knew* their product would be used for anything other than killing vermin.

Pelican and Freud raided the houses of the firm's employees. Again little of importance was gathered for any prosecution. The pursuit was not without its surprises though: in the house of the chemist Drosihn they found a huge stash of pornography. Captain Freud was impressed by the collection, which he described in his official report as 'an elaborate and quite astonishing record and summary of his sex life'. It included a host of revealing pictures and statistical details about Drosihn's erections, noting precise measurements. However sordid, it proved nothing. Speculation was all that the investigators could manage by way of incrimination. Freud assumed that everyone had been fully briefed to keep silent, and he might have been right given the time Tesch had been afforded after his initial release.

For his part, Tesch adopted an attitude of ignorance carried 'to an absurdity', Freud reported. Weinbacher, Tesch's partner, was 'blindly obedient ... has a slow brain ... an arrogant man with limited intellect'. 'During his interrogation at Altona gaol he was so insolent that special steps had to be taken by the interrogating officer', whatever that meant.

Before long, the British administration in Hamburg insisted that the firm of Tesch & Stabenow had to resume its business with or without Tesch. They needed supplies of chemical pest-control products. Alfred Zaun, the company accountant, was asked to take over the firm in Tesch's absence. He agreed, but said he needed written authorisation from Bruno Tesch to sign cheques and access accounts. The investigation team sensed an opportunity, perhaps because they were becoming desperate for any sort of information against their suspects. They organised a meeting in a room at the prison where they placed hidden microphones. Zaun wasn't told. When the two men were seated in the room, Staff Sergeant Pelican, who was to oversee the meeting, was called out. The hope was that, unattended, Tesch would incriminate himself. Much whispering was indeed recorded but no one could hear what was being said with any clarity. The sound equipment wasn't good enough to pick up their voices clearly.

Zaun was interrogated after the meeting. He was told he'd been bugged and it was intimated that they knew everything that had been said between him and Tesch. Zaun lost his nerve. He admitted, and had accounts to prove it too, he said, that the huge quantities of gas *had* been supplied to various concentration camps. He mentioned Auschwitz and Neuengamme as well as several others, though he said he'd never known the purpose of its delivery and had never questioned the enormous quantities involved. Invariably, the strength was Type E, which was to be expected given the use for which Tesch had said the product was supplied – the fumigation of barracks.

Then, amongst the mass of papers confiscated from the firm's office, Freud found some documents about a training course delivered by Tesch to SS personnel in January 1941 at Sachsenhausen KZ. Names of the SS men involved were listed. They were all of low rank: *Unterscharführer, Scharführer, Sturmführer, Rottenführer.* But a familiar name appeared amongst them, familiar, that is, to the No. 2 War Crimes Team and Fred Pelican: *SS-Rottenführer* Willi Bahr.[36]

7.

Willi Bahr was one of the names that had emerged as Major Noel Till and his colleagues had questioned the Neuengamme survivors in Neustadt a few months earlier. He'd been identified as responsible for killing hundreds of inmates in the hospital. Witnesses spoke of his barbarity.

As chance would have it, and luck was so instrumental in the hunt for war criminals in the chaos of a devastated Germany, Bahr had only just been found hiding in a cellar of one of the houses near Neuengamme camp. He'd never left the area when the war had ended. His hope had been that everything would quieten down once the British had taken occupation of the town and a few weeks had passed. Then he could surface and start his life again. But someone had spotted him scavenging for food and the British forces were alerted to this feral creature hiding beneath ground. They picked him up and informed No. 2 WCIT. Bahr readily admitted his true identity and former position.

Blindly obedient, like a simple dog, Bahr had always done what he'd been told. As an SS member he'd assumed any role, any task allotted to him. And when he was ordered to tell the truth about his exploits in the Neuengamme KZ to the British interrogators, he did so.

Fred Pelican was the first to question him. He waited until 10 p.m. ('as customary', as he put it in his memoirs) to begin. According to Pelican, Bahr didn't bother with many preliminaries. He said he'd worked in the camp hospital and then immediately confessed to killing Jews and 'Untermenschen' (subhumans) by using phenol injections. Over a period of two or three years, he said, he'd been sent inmates unfit for work for an 'examination'. Bahr said he'd made them undress, had them climb onto a table and lie face down, and then he would inject them in the neck with a petrol mixture. They'd be dead within minutes. It was a painless and humane procedure, he said to the incredulous Pelican. Bahr said he would dispose of twenty to thirty prisoners a day like this. Without the slightest trace of contrition, he told Pelican he'd probably killed over a thousand men during his time at Neuengamme.

The witness statement signed by Bahr was brutal and blithe. It didn't end with his exploits in the hospital. He had another confession to make, this time about his connection with the use of poison gas. In 1942, he'd been sent on a course at Oranienburg. It was a prussic acid training session run by Dr Tesch. He'd been awarded a certificate and shown how to apply the tins of Zyklon B for delousing operations in barracks. Back at Neuengamme he'd used the gas to disinfect prisoners' clothes. But one time in 1942, he couldn't remember exactly when, he'd been ordered to empty tins of gas into a sealed barracks filled with Russian POWs.

Bahr's testimony was the first linking a gassing of KZ prisoners, the SS personnel administering the gassing, and Dr Tesch. But it wasn't that conclusive. By Bahr's admission, his training in the use of the gas was for delousing clothes. It had never been suggested that it be used for killing human beings. Tesch had warned the SS trainees on his course about the dangerous nature of Zyklon B and how its users had to take precautions, Bahr recalled. Only once had Bahr used the gas on humans, and that was to kill the Russian prisoners. Tesch had had no involvement in that, Bahr said. He'd received his orders to kill the Russians using this method and that was what he'd done: follow orders.

Despite the questionable value of Bahr's evidence (as far as Tesch was concerned) and the weak circumstantial evidence, Major Draper at JAG believed he had enough to charge Tesch, Weinbacher and Drosihn with a war crime: that they knowingly supplied poison gas for the purpose of exterminating Allied nationals. The trial was set to begin in March 1946.

It's difficult to see now how Tesch and his two colleagues could have been prosecuted with absolute conviction. And it's hard to see how they *couldn't* have been prosecuted either. The evidence that had emerged from the Bergen-Belsen witnesses provided a picture of extermination that was visceral. The method of killing through the use of gas had already entered the public imagination. Those stories of selections on the ramps at Auschwitz II-Birkenau, the stripping and beating and the hounding of those chosen to die by a party of so-called doctors, had embedded themselves in the consciousness of those appalled by the genocidal actions of the Nazis. There was little doubt either that Zyklon B had been the product used in the gassing. Once it was found that a private company had supplied the poison in huge quantities to the camp most notorious for extermination, Auschwitz, as well as other KZs *and* a camp guard had confessed to using Zyklon B to kill prisoners, the War Crimes Team were compelled to respond. They relied on the belief that Tesch and at least some of his colleagues *must* have known that they were supplying their gas for killing people. And if they had known that, then who could doubt that they should be held to account?

The case had taken the war crimes group into deep, emotionally charged waters. By no means could the Tesch matter be considered trivial. But did the British investigators and prosecutors have sufficient expertise and manpower to do justice to its pursuit? Captain Freud and Sergeant Pelican were amateur detectives only. Though advised by the lawyer Major Draper, the lack of professional police investigators and interrogators undermined their efforts to acquire good-quality evidence.

Some years later, the man responsible for all interrogations of German prisoners of war, Lt Col Scotland, looked back on this period as a shameful one.[37] In January 1946, he established the War Crimes

Interrogation Unit at the London Cage in Kensington. It was merely a conversion of the prisoner interrogation operation he'd led there successfully, if brutally (some have alleged), throughout the war.[38] He criticised the way in which war crimes investigations had been handled in 1945. The Judge Advocate's team set up in BAOR headquarters to organise the war crimes prosecutions was referred to in dismissive terms. Scotland wrote,

> Lack of experience of AG3 [Adjutant General 3 Branch] in dealing with an operation of this kind soon became manifest and the organisation of so-called teams of interrogators who were to tour Europe and collect evidence of suspected war criminals held as PoW in the various camps on the continent of Europe proved to be a fruitless effort, chiefly because the teams did not include local language speakers. Some of JAG officers also took the view when files were sent to them that 'investigation' of the crime was a portion of their duty, this was shown, however, to be the wrong method of operation.

Neither Freud nor Pelican nor Draper (the JAG officer involved) nor any other members of the War Crimes Investigation Team working on the Neuengamme case could break Bruno Tesch or the others. They couldn't extract from him the slightest hint of a confession that he'd known or even *might* have known the purpose for which his chemical product was to be used. Even their amateurish ruse with the bugged meeting failed. But Tesch was SS (by association and membership) and he was arrogant. In the absence of more concrete evidence, they decided to proceed in any event, determined that those who'd made the extermination programme in the death camps feasible through their support and tacit approval had to be punished too.[39]

8.

Willi Bahr was a strange creature to occupy the centre of a web of atrocity. At Nuremberg, in the Allied press, amongst British and American political leaders and government functionaries, the story conveyed was of a gang of criminally twisted well-known figures who'd instigated the evil Nazi system, who'd exercised control over the country and were the most culpable for all that ensued. And yet, as I read more and more of the material collected by the War Crimes Teams, it was the lowest of personnel who, it seemed to me, characterised the quality and extent of German guilt. Bahr was nothing, but if it wasn't for him, and thousands, millions perhaps, like him, would the brutalities perpetrated have been possible? Of course not. But how could that be addressed at Nuremberg, where attention was fixed on condemning the nation's leaders?

In a world where justice was more broad-visioned, the Nuremberg court might have come to Neuengamme and to Bullenhuser Damm to see for themselves the devils in the detail. But that didn't happen. Given the enormity of destruction and death wrought by the German people across Europe, the killing of twenty young children might have seemed an atrocity eclipsed by atrocity.

Yet the search for the meaning of justice and retribution I'd begun a few years previously felt sharply focused by the exhibition at Bullenhuser Damm school. Though no more than a fragment of a story for the British and the Allies' investigations, I thought it to be vitally significant nonetheless. In the basement of that old building there was a semicircle of open boxes which was explanation enough. Each one contained a short biography. In truth, there was not much that could be said. For the lives charted there were of young children, ten boys, ten girls, none older than twelve. They'd never had much chance to *live*. What little remained of their stories was defined by their suffering, a piteous reference for any life no matter how brief.

They'd come from Poland, Italy, the Netherlands, Yugoslavia, France. All had been brought to Neuengamme KZ as subjects of an experiment. Many people knew of their presence in the camp. It wasn't a secret. One of the first witnesses seen by Noel Till's team at Neustadt, Tadeusz Kowalski, provided a statement about his time as a medical orderly in the Neuengamme 'hospital'. He'd been arrested by the Germans in 1942 for suspected opposition to the occupation of Poland. After terms in Auschwitz and other camps, he'd been transferred to Neuengamme in 1944 and assigned to the TB section of its medical facilities. At the end of December 1945 the British investigators went to see him again, alerted by Bahr and others to the treatment of the twenty children in the camp during the war.

Kowalski gave them more details and said that in 1944 twenty children 'between the ages of six and twelve years were brought from Auschwitz to Neuengamme and placed in a special block, No. 4, from which all adults were removed. Eighty per cent of the children were Polish; the others were Dutch or French. At this time Block 4 was not only for TB cases but for other cases as well. Of all those children, only one was suspected of TB.' He said Dr René Quenouille from France, a Parisian radiologist and an arrested member of the French Resistance, was charged with their care. 'I saw him with the children in the X-ray room,' Kowalksi said, 'and have also seen X-ray photos of them.' He'd been told by Quenouille that the children had incisions either on the left or right breast or on the arm, into which TB bacteria had been rubbed.⁴⁰

Infected parts of the children were cut away and tested on the orders of Professor Heissmeyer, who'd personally come to Neuengamme, collected the samples and returned to Berlin. Then with news in the middle of April 1945 that the British were fast approaching, 'all the children were taken away along with the doctors', Kowalski said. He didn't know what had become of them.

Captain Freud pursued the inquiry. Many of the SS guards and officers from Neuengamme had been captured and he began to question them. They were remarkably forthcoming. Max Pauly, the camp commandant, knew of the children and said they'd been sent to Bullenhuser Damm, a former school that had been converted into a satellite camp for the main Neuengamme compound, where prisoners had been housed so that they could clear rubble from bomb sites in Hamburg. When Neuengamme had come to be evacuated, the children had been removed to Bullenhuser Damm with the camp's SS doctor, Alfred Trzebinski. Pauly said the doctor had then killed the children by 'means of injections'.

Trzebinski was in custody in Fuhlsbüttel, the former Gestapo prison close to Hamburg airport. Freud obtained a confession from him too.

The doctor admitted he'd been called to see Max Pauly in late April 1945 and ordered to dispose of the children. Trzebinski said Pauly had told him that they had to 'get rid of unpleasant witnesses'. With three SS guards he'd loaded the children and their French carers (Quenouille and another French Resistance prisoner, Professor Gabriel Florence) onto a truck and reported to Commandant Strippel in Hamburg. He'd been directed to Bullenhuser Damm, where they'd been met by Johann Frahm, a *Blockführer*, and *Oberscharführer* Jauch.

'The children were taken down to the cellar,' the doctor told Freud. 'The nurses of the children and the grown-up Russians were taken to a separate room and hanged there.' He'd stayed with the children whilst Frahm had told them to get undressed. 'I then gave a morphine injection and they fell asleep. Then the children were hanged on hooks on the wall by Frahm.' Quenouille and Florence had been hanged as well, though without the benefit of morphine.

Freud followed the trail of culprits. Johann Frahm had been captured in October, though his initial statements only registered that he'd served in Neuengamme, first as a guard then as a *Blockführer*. He'd said he'd been in charge of the punishment company loading and unloading sand and clay into tip wagons. 'I had to drive the prisoners to work very hard because I could be observed from the house of the commandant. I admit to have beaten prisoners with my stick.' That was all.

Armed with the other confessions, Freud went back to see him. Frahm purportedly confessed everything, confirming Dr Trzebinski's account, implicating others. He said of the children, 'Those who were giving signs of life after the injection were carried to another room. There a rope was placed on their necks and, like pictures, they were hanged on hooks on the wall.' He named Jauch, Trzebinski and two other Neuengamme SS men (Adolf Speck and Wilhelm Dreimann) as the men involved.

Dreimann and Speck were also under arrest. They too were Neuengamme KZ personnel. Inmates had already named them as particularly cruel guards. Of the other suspects, the area commander, *SS-Obersturmführer* Arnold Strippel, was on the run and Heinrich Wiehagen, another SS guard who'd been in the truck that had transported the children to Bullenhuser Damm, had reportedly been killed by British troops in Neustadt Bay attempting to escape after the *Cap Arcona* sinking. However, Professor Heissmeyer, the TB expert from Berlin who'd controlled the experiments on the children, had disappeared. He would never be brought to account by the British.[41]

The multiple confessions were sufficient to prepare a trial for those complicit in the murders. But competing interests were at work. Most of those involved in the killings were also wanted for the grand proceedings being planned for Neuengamme KZ as a whole. Captain Freud was instrumental in investigating that case too. Trzebinski, Pauly, Dreimann, Speck and Bahr were key defendants: the British needed a good show after the criticism levelled at the Belsen trial. Two hearings were therefore arranged. The main camp trial to be held first in March 1946 and immediately thereafter one for the Bullenhuser Damm atrocity. Frahm and Jauch would be held back for that, though Pauly and Trzebinski would be brought as witnesses.

9.

Whilst I was reading their handwritten notes or sometimes listening to their voices on audiotapes I wondered if the investigators and lawyers had talked to each other about their cases. I hoped so. They worked together and lived together, socialising as a unit in the mess at Bad Oeynhausen when they weren't in the field, and no one who hadn't been with them and seen what they'd seen could have understood. Had they unloaded the horrors they'd discovered on each other, I wondered? How else might they have assimilated them, come to some arrangement in their minds as to the place in their lives that these nightmarish stories would occupy?

The question occurred to me when I came across another case investigated by the War Crimes Teams. In the autumn of 1945, Captain Stephen Stewart, the lawyer who'd already had to cope with some of the Belsen investigation and was soon to be given responsibility for the Neuengamme KZ trial, received a report from Velpke near Helmstedt. He was informed that during the war, the Germans had opened a home for the newly born babies of foreign slave workers, Polish women for the most part. It seemed the children had been 'forcibly removed from their mothers and sent there by order of the Kreisleiter', a local functionary. A policy of taking the babies away had been instituted so that their mothers could carry on working without distraction. The evidence suggested the home had been operated by a group of men and women who at best saw no reason to care for the babies handed to them, and at worst, intended for them to die. Ninety graves had been found near the home. The Americans had arrested both the official in charge of the home, a man called Hessling, and the *Kreisleiter* of Helmstedt.[42]

Investigations were completed and nine suspects, including the home's medical staff and women 'carers', were charged with a war crime, in that they, 'at Velpke Germany, between the months of May and December 1944 in violation of the Laws and Usages of War, were concerned in the killing by wilful neglect a number of children, Polish nationals'. The wording wasn't too dissimilar from the Belsen indictments: a simple construction that would then need to be substantiated at trial.

The enthusiasm for prosecution was tempered, however. JAG headquarters saw the list of victims and believed this was a case for the Polish authorities. Only in January 1946 did the army lawyers in London agree to a trial proceeding under British military authority. It was with the belief that the home and one of its sister institutions, at Rühen, which the Allies had also uncovered, were 'just as much extermination camps as Auschwitz and Belsen'.[43] The British assumed jurisdiction for that reason.

It sounded like a contrivance to me or at best a strange understanding of 'extermination' or mass killing. There had been no Jewish victims at Velpke. No evidence had emerged that the babies had been killed rather than let die. With the Nuremberg Tribunal revealing an account of the Holocaust and the 'Final Solution' and the Belsen trial having already relayed to the world the circumstances of hundreds of thousands of deaths at Auschwitz, it was hard to believe the War Office thought Velpke was truly analogous. But then the victims were defenceless children. They'd been starved, left to die. Who wouldn't have wanted to prosecute such a crime? As the Allies had decided that all atrocities should be tried by the country whose nationals had suffered except where they were part of a widespread plan, naming Velpke as an extermination camp served to catapult the case into the British sphere of responsibility. Even if a device,

I only had to read the statement taken from one of the mothers involved to understand the desire to prosecute.

Stefanie Zelensky was Polish, brought to Germany as a forced worker in 1940. She'd been sent to work on a private farm at Offleben. This is what she had to say:

> On 16 February 1944 I gave birth to a daughter at the farm in Offleben and the father of my child was Anastasius Zelensky who was also employed at the same village and whom I have since married. We christened the baby Natalia.
>
> I was allowed by the farmer to keep my baby 4½ months during which time I fed her and looked after her myself.
>
> About 25 June 1944 I took Natalia to the home on the order of the farmer Wagenfuhr but when I saw the condition of the other children there I did not want to leave my baby; but there was a policeman there and he forced me to leave her and took my child from me.
>
> At this time she was in good health. After 4 days I went to see my child; she was well but appeared to be very hungry and was sucking her hands. I held her for a short time and in the wooden cupboard was a bottle of sour milk.
>
> About 10 days later I went to the home again with her father and we were told by a nurse that the baby was dead. We saw Natalia and she was black and blue all over her body. A nurse told us that she had been dead for three days.
>
> As we had to return to work on the farm, it was not possible to make arrangements for her burial and until today I do not know where she is buried.[44]

The testimony was brutally brief, drafted by the British investigator, controlled and devoid of the cry of pain. But for all its coolness it was highly charged nonetheless. Was this, I thought, how the investigators and lawyers coped, by laying charges and prosecuting those they believed responsible? Just as with Bullenhuser Damm, no one could have read those details and thought retribution was undertaken only as a chore or imposed duty. Even though civil servants and politicians back in Britain may have cared little for war crimes prosecutions by now – considered costly, of dubious value compared with the scheme of rebuilding Europe, the growing antagonism with the Soviets and the decay of Empire – I couldn't believe that the investigators and lawyers prosecuting were unmoved.

And then I remembered how Lord Justice Lawrence had left the Nuremberg hearing without saying a word after the showing of the hour-long concentration camp film back in November 1945. Could that have been *his* display of controlled and unspoken fury?

10.

The Nuremberg trial may have been significant for cataloguing the grand canvas of atrocity committed by the Nazi regime, but it was mostly a detached affair in comparison with those contemporaneous British investigations. Whilst the Velpke baby home and Bullenhuser Damm cases were being prepared in early 1946, Allied prosecutors in Nuremberg were still making long-winded presentations, reading out document after document, making certain that the case against the Nazi regime and its leaders was unassailable.

The American lawyers carried the burden, with occasional forays by the British, Sir David Maxwell Fyfe, Lt Col Mervyn Griffith-Jones and F. Elwyn Jones covering matters associated with the aggressive war charge; lawyers François de Menthon and Edgar Faure outlining the case for France; and General Rudenko doing the same for the Soviet Union. Throughout January and February 1946 these prosecutors and their many assistants interspersed grand rhetoric with more specific accounts of the multiple crimes committed by the Nazi state. They also had to introduce the substance of charges specifically relating to each of the defendants. Yet more volumes of documents were collected and handed to the judges before the court was told of their contents.

Ernst Kaltenbrunner, the only one of the defendants who was in the SS, was the first to receive this treatment, on 2 January 1946. He may have been in hospital with a brain haemorrhage but that didn't delay matters. Lt Commander Whitney Harris described

Kaltenbrunner's appointment as Chief of the Security Police and SD after Reinhard Heydrich had been assassinated in Prague in 1942, propelling him into one of the most senior positions in the SS, directly under Himmler. He was responsible for a succession of crimes, Harris said: the 'murder and mistreatment of civilians of occupied countries by the Einsatz groups'; the 'execution of racial and political undesirables' from prisoner-of-war camps; ordering the taking to concentration camps of recaptured escaped Allied POWs, knowing full well what would happen to them; deportations for forced labour; the execution of commandos and paratroopers following Hitler's infamous order. Harris had a string of documents to link Kaltenbrunner with each allegation. The forensic approach was tailed by rhetorical flourish: 'Kaltenbrunner was a life-long fanatical Nazi ... Like other leading Nazis, Kaltenbrunner sought power; to gain it, he made his covenant with crime.'[45]

SS Major General Otto Ohlendorf was brought as a witness for the prosecution. Colonel John Amen of the US prosecution team and chief of the interrogation division described Ohlendorf as 'an old SS man who was thoroughly familiar with the activities of Einsatzgruppa ... in connection with the extermination of Jews and the communist commisars'.[46] He didn't look like a Nazi thug according to Telford Taylor, Justice Jackson's assistant, who described Ohlendorf as 'small of stature, young-looking, and rather comely'.[47] I had no idea what Taylor meant by that.

OHLENDORF

Originally enlisted into the SD, the SS's intelligence wing, Ohlendorf was an information officer who'd been happy to translate the rhetoric of eradicating the Jews into reality. At the end of the war he'd been arrested at the same time as Himmler and had been willing to talk when interrogated. In 1941, he said, he'd been a member of one of the SS *Einsatzgruppen* sent into Soviet territory attached to the advancing German army. They had specific instructions on how to deal with Jews and Soviet commissars: he told the court they were to be 'liquidated'. This was their mission and their orders were known to the commanding general of the army, von Manstein, as well as Kaltenbrunner.

Ohlendorf was asked by Col Amen, the American attorney charged with his examination, 'Do you know how many persons were liquidated by Einsatz Group D under your direction?'

Ohlendorf said 90,000, including women and children. But the figures for the other three groups were considerably larger. 'I was present at two mass executions for purposes of inspection,' he added. Jews were rounded up under the pretext of being 'resettled', taken to the execution ground in trucks, shot and 'buried in the anti-tank ditch'.

Col Amen drew out the details: how the victims would be shot, how their valuables would be collected, how gas vans were introduced later and how this imposed added mental strain on Ohlendorf's men with the unloading of the bodies.

Ohlendorf was a significant witness for the prosecution. He helped establish the planning of extermination as an integral element of the invasion of Russia. He helped establish that various strands of the Nazi government and military knew this to be the case. He was a traitor in the eyes of some of the Nuremberg defendants, particularly Goering, though his frankness wouldn't save him. He would face his own trial in 1947 and be convicted and sentenced to death.

According to Gustave Gilbert, the American psychologist at Nuremberg, the effect of the testimony was 'depressing' for the accused.[48] Ohlendorf had confirmed the normality of atrocity as part of the war endeavour. Unlike the concentration camps, of which all the defendants would deny any explicit knowledge as regards their day-to-day operation, and the extermination camps, which they would claim were kept secret from them by Himmler and his cronies, Ohlendorf showed how the barbarity unleashed in war in the east was known to many and was not a matter for embarrassment. As *The Times* reported: 'Ohlendorf confessed with the utmost candour.'[49] He'd also confirmed that blind obedience had induced a multitude to accede to *any* instruction, however barbaric, however inhuman. In this he was not a surprising witness: anyone who'd followed the Belsen and Dachau trials would have known that the worst of crimes had been committed without question. Josef Kramer, Dr Klein and the rest hid little because they thought they were hidden already: behind the dictum *Befehl ist Befehl* – orders are orders.

The cases against Goering, von Ribbentrop, Frank, Keitel, Jodl, Rosenberg, Streicher, Schacht, Funk, Doenitz, Raeder, Schirach, Bormann (despite the increasing suggestions he had been killed in Berlin – papers were reporting that he'd been decapitated when a tank exploded as he was trying to escape the city as the Russians entered)[50] and Frick followed over the next two weeks. The prosecution had to pin blame on each of them in turn.

11.

For all the revelations and itemised barbarities, building a scrupulously composed library of atrocity (one visitor described the contents of the document room as 'astonishing in their volume'),[51] the trial at Nuremberg descended into boredom again for many observers. It was a ritual being played out in a chamber isolated from the place and time, from the sights, sounds and smells of all those atrocious acts to which it made constant reference. The courtroom was immune to the physicality of the past. Unlike the Americans with their hearings in Dachau or the British trials held close to the scenes of crimes, Nuremberg was its own spectacle: contained by the rules and behaviours that quickly became regimented and routine. As with any repetitious procedure, participants couldn't help but be figures within a boxed landscape. Only the imagination allowed escape. The dull speeches of lecturing prosecutors must have been soporific, peppered occasionally and with accentuated effect by an encounter with a witness like Ohlendorf, an outburst from a defence counsel, the showing of a film. Keenly anticipated was the appearance of the defendants in the witness box. Their defence, their testimony, their voices and their cross-examination, the personal confrontation between accused and accuser, were crucial for the whole process of justice that Nuremberg symbolised.

During spring and early summer of 1946, running in parallel with the later stages of the Nuremberg proceedings, the crimes emanating from Neuengamme KZ would also have their trials. In the centre of Hamburg, Tesch, the Bullenhuser Damm killings and the main concentration camp case would be heard as part of a whole carousel of prosecutions. If justice was done for all those crimes first encountered by Noel Till and his fellow investigators on the shores of Neustadt Bay several months before, then this was where I thought it would be found.

8

Hamburg Revisited

1.

The Curiohaus is on Rothenbaumchaussee, a cultured, tree-lined avenue close to the centre of Hamburg. It's a grand old construction built by a successful German merchant at the turn of the twentieth century, initially as a restaurant, then converted into a ballroom. The building remains a centre for dining and dancing and company events. In 1946, it was one of the chosen locations for the British-led war crimes trials. Over the course of a few months the Zyklon B, Bullenhuser Damm and main Neuengamme camp trials were held there.

Standing outside, I found it impossible to summon up the phantoms of that time, of those cases, despite my now heightened sense of the topography of atrocity fanning out across Hamburg from Neuengamme. Though I imagined contour lines connecting the concentration camp with the Messberghof, with the school in Bullenhuser Damm, with Fuhlsbüttel prison, even out across the countryside to the bay at Neustadt, and back to this pretty mansion house, none of those places seemed related to the prosperous, commercial facade in front of me. The Curiohaus had buried its past in the sleekness of corporate entertainment. No one wanted to celebrate the location of the British war crimes trials. Why would they?

It wasn't a disappointment. I knew that if I was to satisfy my curiosity as to the nature of British justice delivered in response to all those investigations (a curiosity originally sparked by that picture of prosecutors I'd seen in the Neuengamme camp exhibition) I had to retreat to the documents, the transcripts, the written notes.

When I returned to Britain, I arranged for a prolonged stay at the National Archives at Kew, that place of quiet efficiency, conducive to study, with records delivered to a numbered locker within forty minutes of ordering, blue-jacketed stewards (as if on a sombre holiday from Butlins) watching over you, whispering in your ear should you mishandle the papers.

The contrast to the physical confrontations with concentration camp and killing ground seemed acute at first. But after hours reading about the British-led trials and investigations into war crimes and the Nuremberg proceedings running in parallel, I sank deeper into the quicksand of atrocity. The photographic evidence and witness testimony and the summaries of outrages darkened every day to the point where I could no longer focus properly. I would read until my eyes hurt and wonder not only at my capacity to absorb these stories but at how the investigators and prosecutors must have suffered from the bleakness of their task. What is it, I thought, to read account after account, statement after statement about the utmost cruelty? What is it to disinter the bodies of murdered comrades, hear the stories of the survivors? Should it provoke anger? Sadness that human beings can be so indifferent to the suffering of others? Whatever the emotions, I doubted they were positive. Even so, every file deserved scrutiny for the simple fact that the lives of men and women were in the balance.

When I took the Neuengamme files to my desk, I was surprised to find first amongst them a whole box of photograph albums confiscated by the British investigation team, page after page of snaps of laughing and posing German soldiers; one officer out for a walk with a woman and a pram, a sort of wheeled sled being pulled by a trio of dogs; a wedding portrait; a couple of soldiers sitting with beer glasses in front of them and between them a woman throwing her head back in exaggerated laughter; two SS officers, one with his arm draped over the shoulder of the other, their knees familiarly touching above the jackboots; a Christmas feast full of SS and their wives in 1944 (a few numbered in blue ink on the print, the numbers that would hang round their necks at their trial), spirits seemingly unaffected by the approaching end of the war; pictures of huts and construction workers, prisoners, a factory, an office, all lovingly labelled in German.

These were albums of happiness and normality, friends and colleagues enjoying life, in the snow, on bicycles, with their dogs, smoking cigars, marching with their units, mouths wide open singing. None were used as evidence. They were irrelevant to the proceedings, though they revealed more than any cross-examination I'd read so far.

I opened more boxes. There were several containing thickly filled lever-arched files. These were the Neuengamme KZ case transcripts.

Here, I thought, I might find the answers to questions that had provoked me ever since that first visit to Hamburg, questions which were simply factual (how had all those inmates come to be on the *Cap Arcona* and the other ships in Neustadt Bay?) or ethical (who was responsible for their deaths?) or analytical (how did those British trials relate to the grand event in Nuremberg?), perhaps even psychological (what was it that had motivated those SS who'd whipped and executed and tortured seemingly without pity?). The folders holding the thousands of pages that recorded every word of the Neuengamme trial appeared as hermetically sealed containers which, when opened, would solve these mysteries.

Then I thought how strange it was that I could place so much trust in a typewritten script merely because it was neatly stored in files with official labels on their fronts and taken from the shelves of a storeroom in a national archive. There was a story there, though. There were many stories.

2.

The fourteen accused sat in the readied courtroom, lined up in one long row, numbers hung around their necks, a small army of uniformed guards sitting behind them. The cards drawn tightly up to their collars were the means by which they were to be officially recognised, following the precedent set at the Belsen trial. It was easier that way when witnesses were asked to identify particular individuals. And it reduced these men below the status of any normal 'accused'. For all the pretence that this was another criminal trial, you'd never see such numbering back at the Old Bailey.

Carl Ludwig Stirling entered. His reputation had been growing since the Belsen trial, where he'd acted as the Deputy Judge Advocate. He would be described a few years later by Ronald Clark, the author and journalist, as having become 'that hawk nosed Dickensian Judge Advocate General who in 1945 and 1946 appeared in British military courtrooms like a shrivelling and avenging flame'.[1] I found the article amongst Stirling's private papers held at the Imperial War Museum. The passage had been underlined in blue pencil. Perhaps Stirling hadn't appreciated Clark's description, though his photographs did indeed show a balding, aloof, monocled man looking like an eagle waiting on its prey.

As with all his trials, he would maintain rigid control, a task made easier as there were no British barristers defending here, unlike at the Belsen trial. The German lawyers were a little more circumspect when it came to raising arguments in defence of their clients. Perhaps being citizens of a guilty country induced caution.

Above the Judge Advocate there was a balcony where the German civilian spectators sat and watched. As he listened to the opening of the case Stirling doodled. It was the same sketch which appeared scattered throughout his trial notes, punctuating those taken not only at Neuengamme but the other cases over which he presided. The drawing was a tiny and rough outline of a ship with a single funnel flanked by two cross rigged masts. There were a couple of protuberances from the foredeck, perhaps guns, perhaps some other form of rigging, it was hard to tell. A battleship, a cargo steamer? I had no idea. And I had no idea what it signified other than at times during these trials he was most likely bored. Which was understandable. Most legal proceedings have flashes of intensity when everyone within the courtroom will be so absorbed that they will never forget such moments. But these flashes are immersed in an ocean of monotony. Even when unpicking the extraordinary life of a concentration camp and its inhabitants the effect could be numbing.

Stirling was fresh from the Zyklon B case. That had finished only ten days before when Tesch and his manager Karl Weinbacher had both been found guilty and sentenced to death despite the absence of hard proof that either had known their product was used for gassing humans. One of the accused had been acquitted, though: Dr Drosihn. This is what Stirling had said about him in his summing up: 'He is married and he has children, he is about forty years of age. There was some little reference to a slight sexual or moral kink which the man may have had, but I think we all agree that that should play no part in the assessing of Dr Drosihn's integrity or reliability in the witness box.'[2] And indeed it seemed not to have affected the decision.

Surprisingly, nearly all lawyers present in the Curiohaus, for the prosecution or the defence, were native Germans or Austrians. There was newly promoted Major Stephen Malcolm Stewart leading the prosecution case. He'd been involved in the Bergen-Belsen and Velpke baby home cases and had now been promoted to lead the Neuengamme prosecution. You might have thought from the name that he at least would have been a stalwart British citizen. But he was really an Austrian lawyer called Karl Stephan Strauss who'd only in the very month the trial in Hamburg began been given a British naturalisation certificate following wartime service in the Pioneer Corps.[3] Like Walter Freud, he'd escaped from Austria shortly before the outbreak of the war, recognising the danger of the *Anschluss* and

Nazi takeover of his country. Rather than stay and face certain incarceration and persecution for his political opposition, a stance that would have seen him almost inevitably interned in one of the camps that he was now helping to expose, he'd left his country and made his way through Poland and eventually to Britain. Stewart was assisted by Major Wein, another legal refugee from Austria.

All the defence lawyers were German. There were none of those willing British advocates, like Major Winwood, who'd caused so much antagonism with his 'clever' legal points on behalf of Josef Kramer at the Bergen-Belsen trial the previous year. And the defendants were German too. They looked calm and ordinary. Each was accused of the same familiar charge, that they, 'between June 1940 and May 1945, when members of the staff of the Neuengamme Concentration Camps, in violation of the laws and usages of war, were together concerned in the killing and ill-treatment of Allied nationals being inmates of the same concentration camps'.[4]

It was the formula used in all the other trials that had been heard by British military tribunals over the past six months or so.

Whatever his nationality, Major Stewart began the case in English and in poetic style.

> It was a hot summery day in May 1945 when a Lieutenant in the Reconnaissance Corps drove his tank through the streets of the village of Neuengamme. He was ordered by his Commanding Officer to go and see a hutted compound in which it was believed that there were thousands of internees and thought it had been a concentration camp. When he arrived ... all he found was a black cat. Not until much later when some of the evacuated ex-internees returned and told a story and bit by bit like a jigsaw puzzle the full story of Neuengamme Concentration Camp through the years from 1940 to 1945 was put together.

He said this was not a case of 'victors' justice'. 'Nothing could be more dangerous [than] to believe this was about the winners meting out revenge,' he said, parroting the line taken by Justice Jackson in his opening speech at Nuremberg. Stewart then identified the most important elements of the crimes, all within the context of the KZ structure. He said, 'The whole system was set out to achieve a complete debasement of the individual and one in the image of God was reduced to a state where they were much nearer animals than human beings.' He mentioned the killing of the children subjected to TB experiments at Bullenhuser Damm, but kept the court's mind fixed on the law.

I know sir that it is extremely difficult to restrain one's emotions when human beings stoop to the depths of experimenting on and eventually liquidating innocent children, but I must ask you to view this piece of evidence the same as the rest of the evidence not with what may well be the justifiable anger of outraged humanity but in the cold and sober light of the law.

It was a little disingenuous. His subject matter aroused passion. How could it be avoided when listing the history of malice in such a camp? He told the court about the hospital, 'one of the foulest aspects of the whole case', and how the whole camp population of thousands would be crammed into the cellars of the two brick buildings when there was an air raid.

Can you imagine the scene? [he asked] Can you imagine the siren going and then these wretched creatures exhausted after a twelve-hour day staggering out in the dark, out of their huts being remorselessly bullied by their warders to run to the shelter and then when they reached the shelter, in the doorway falling over each other, stampeding, being beaten with rubber truncheons and kicked continuously down the stairs in the dark until eventually they reached the cellar where they were packed like sardines with no ventilation. There was something like 10,000 of them in those two cellars. It is a scene which is really too terrible to describe.

Stewart described it nonetheless. He likened it to the London Tube station disaster, raw in British imagination at least, a reference to the night of 3 March 1943, when 173 people were crushed to death in Bethnal Green Underground station as crowds poured into the makeshift shelter, seemingly panicked by the sudden firing of a nearby anti-aircraft battery, and the tripping of a woman that caused a chain reaction of people falling over each other down the long stairs. Stewart said such a crush was a nightly occurrence in Neuengamme.

Of course, the prosecutor couldn't avoid embellishment, and however much he protested he couldn't avoid the descriptions either. That was his job, to bring to life the misery and cruelty and protracted suffering of the camp. How else could he evoke the reality of the KZ if not through emotive language? He might have liked to bring it all back to the sober light of the law, but how ridiculous that was when you read his words. British criminal trials may be exercises in rational thinking, but to dismiss sentiment would be to deny the humanity that had been lost in the camps.

Stewart ended with a little story. It was another flourish that pandered to the press gathered at the back of the Curiohaus. He described how, after gassing a group of Russian prisoners one day, the SS called out the whole camp onto the *Appellplatz*. The bodies of the Soviets were dragged out on trollies and the assembled inmates were forced to sing:

> *Hail to thee, happy ambassadors,*
> *a thousand welcomes, friends, be yours.*
> *High honour to this day belong,*
> *oh raise your sweetest voice in song.*

'This is typical of the sense of humour of the people before you,' Stewart said.

At no time during his speech did Stewart mention Neustadt Bay and the ultimate fate of the Neuengamme prisoners.

3.

It would take some days for Stewart to present the many facets of brutality. He had to provide a tableau of institutional and individual abuse. He had to show how the camp was deadly, designed to be so and administered with that purpose. He had to show that the men sitting in the dock were integral to the KZ where they worked, had committed acts of violence against prisoners and contributed deliberately to the killing and injuring and ill-treatment. The Belsen trial, where so many accused had been acquitted because of a failure to prove individual culpability, had put Major Stewart on guard. Witnesses were now brought who could point at the accused with certainty and say what they'd seen them do as well as describe the cruel nature of the KZ as a whole. It would take him thirteen days.

The first witnesses were those Major Till and his team had found recovering in Neustadt soon after the sinking of the *Cap Arcona*. Albin Lüdke knew the most as he'd been in the camp since 1940. He'd observed how the conditions and treatment had deteriorated over the years. He said Defendant No. 1, Max Pauly, was a 'very bad commandant and his bad name preceded him' before he arrived in July 1942 from Stutthof KZ. Prisoners who'd served time there 'began to tremble when they heard that their former commandant was coming to Neuengamme'.

No. 2, Karl Totzauer, was the adjutant from 1944 but wasn't seen much in the camp. Only when executions took place, special executions. Lüdke was asked to remember one. In October 1944, he said, about 800 Dutch prisoners arrived. Eighty of them were picked out, had their heads partly shaven and 'were given an armlet saying "Torsperre", which means they were not permitted to leave the camp'. These men were employed weaving mats in one of the cellars. By February 1945 there were only about 60 of them still alive. All were hanged in one go, even the ones in the sick bay, brought to the execution place on litters. That was when Totzauer would come.

Then there was No. 3, Anton Thumann. He was 'a sadist in the true sense of the word. He liked to spend his time at beatings and executions, of which he was always the leader.'

All the others were described too. Each had his little violent foibles. Adolf Speck, Lüdke said, had first come to the camp in autumn 1943. His peccadillo was to be spiteful. 'There were two ditches round the camp filled with water [for fire precautions]. When the inmates came in from work and did not march properly to attention, either because they were too tired or physically not fit enough to do so,

then it was a great joke to pick out one or two or more and to throw
them into these ditches filled with water.' Lüdke had seen it happen.
It wasn't hearsay.

If these defendants were bad, Willi Bahr, Defendant No. 12, well
known to the War Crimes Team now, was worse. 'He was especially
brutal, stupid and cruel,' Lüdke said, confirming Bahr's confessed
speciality: killing inmates by phenol injection. He had seen him select
men, take them away to the hospital and 'after six or seven minutes
I saw them carried out ... into the mortuary'. He hadn't witnessed
any of the injections administered directly, but what other inference
could be made? It was the same with the murder of two hundred
or so Russians who'd been gassed by Bahr using Zyklon B. One
day in the autumn of 1942, Lüdke had been in the workshop next
door to the cells where Soviet POWs were kept. 'When I passed
the door,' he remembered, 'I saw that the door was open and a
mountain of corpses in a cramped position and of the height of
one metre 70 to one metre 80 was visible. In front of this mountain
of corpses the commandant, Pauly, was standing, and also the then
Lagerführer Luetkemeyer. These corpses were loaded on trucks.'
Everyone knew Bahr was the man who'd been the executioner.

And so he continued, itemising each cruelty he could recall, pointing
at a defendant, describing the institution of suffering within which he
had lived and seen thousands of others die.

Each defendant's counsel stood to ask him questions, seeking to
distance their client from any observed act of violence. It made for a
long and dull process, attempting to distinguish between what Lüdke
had seen for himself and what he'd heard from others. Even Judge
Advocate Stirling intervened to pin him down. Lüdke was steadfast,
giving example after example of the crimes he'd witnessed.

4.

On Wednesday, 20 March 1946, the court travelled the short distance
to Neuengamme to see the camp for themselves. Lüdke and another

witness, General de Grancey of the French Army, were the guides. Everyone was there, the accused, their counsel, everyone. They exchanged questions and statements. They toured the buildings and factories and clay pits and barracks and crematorium. It was still a prison, except the inmates were now all SS or German officials. I could imagine that tour, now that I'd seen the site. It must have taken some time given its spread. But there was much to see.

Back in the courtroom, counsel for Willi Bahr, the man who'd killed so many in the hospital and whenever ordered, made an application: 'It is my duty to ask the court to accept this plea of insanity.'

Stirling informed him that assertion of madness would be insufficient. He had to prove it, obtain expert psychiatric testimony. If that was to be his defence he had to prepare properly. That was English law.

The refusal seemed to sap the German lawyer's enthusiasm for his application. 'I myself think Bahr is not quite responsible for his actions,' he said, 'but I do not think he is quite insane; if you look at the accused you will see that he does not give the impression of a normal human being. I myself might even call it schizophrenia.' He asked for a psychiatric report, but it would come to nothing. Bahr wouldn't escape that easily and the witnesses came to tell of his role in the camp.

Joanneas Everaert was a Belgian, a twenty-five-year-old medical student arrested in July 1941 as a member of a socialist youth movement and the Belgian Resistance. He'd ended up in Neuengamme from September 1941 onwards, first working as a bricklayer and then from 1942 as a medical orderly. He'd been there until 1943 and then returned again at the beginning of 1944 until evacuation. He knew the camp doctors, Kitt and Trzebinski, and he knew Willi Bahr. He hadn't seen Willi Bahr carry out the injections on prisoners, but he'd prepared the syringes for Bahr to use, filled them with phenol or strychnine or evipan, an anaesthetic, and had heard Bahr boast of his killings afterwards.

Then there were the TB experiments on the children. Everaert knew about them too. 'At the end of 1944 I have seen 20 children arriving at Neuengamme camp. They were Jews, ten male and ten female.' Two were French, one called 'George' and one called

'Jacqueline'. He spoke with them several times. They'd been in good health when they'd arrived. But that changed with the TB experiments. He remembered Professor Heissmeyer visiting from Berlin, dressed as a civilian, spending a few hours at the camp and then leaving late in the evening.

It was the first witness evidence connecting the Bullenhuser Damm case with the main camp proceedings.

Other ex-inmates came to the court, identifying the accused where they could, distinguishing between what they'd heard and what they'd seen or experienced directly. The operation of the hospital was a key element in many of the testimonies, but the executions and general conditions in the camp were always a point of reference. It was the prosecution case that the camp had been run with an intent to eliminate the camp prisoners through work and through harsh conditions.

A small cadre of journalists and locals observed the case, but few others. There was scant press coverage. The newspapers back in Britain weren't interested, not when the Nuremberg proceedings sucked what marrow there was out of public attention. How could Neuengamme compete, a camp that hadn't been liberated to reveal heaps of corpses or packed crematoria or telltale stacks of shoes, teeth, hair, the detritus of unspeakable killing?

The writer Christopher Sidgwick was one of the few who stayed. He popped in now and then, absorbed despite the slowness of the process.[5] The 'immense detail' and the interminable double and sometimes triple translation, from German into English into French and back again depending on the identity of the witness, set a plodding pace that tested the attention of everyone. But he had a special interest. He'd visited Dachau soon after Hitler and the Nazis had come to power, when the KZ system was relatively fresh and there were doubts in the British press as to the nature of these concentration camps: were they places of torture and death or not?

Sidgwick had toured the concentration camp outside Munich in February 1935. He had published a letter in the *Manchester Guardian* reporting on what he'd found.[6] 'The faces and carriage of the men as they went past me betrayed two things,' he'd written, 'lack of sufficient exercise and a continual terror.' He'd described the poorness of the food (two beakers of 'slop' for lunch) and an officer who was 'a sadistic bully', but his only enduring complaint had been that the prisoners didn't know how long they would have to serve there. Their sentences were rarely fixed to a specified term. Otherwise, according to Sidgwick, torture was 'a thing of the past', beatings were only a penalty for attacks on the guards, and the SS warders were on the whole 'kindly, ordinary Germans doing their job as efficiently and considerately as circumstances permitted'.

Sidgwick had concluded, 'I myself could put up with [the living conditions] ... for some time,' provided he knew that they would be temporary. The few inmates he'd spoken to didn't have that luxury, but his impression at the time from both his inspection and a tour of the country had convinced him that 'the fever of persecution and intolerance in Germany will continue to diminish at the slow and sure rate already apparent'.

Perhaps he was haunted by his acute misdiagnosis when he returned to Germany in 1945. He was one of those army officers (serving in the Royal Artillery) sent to Neuengamme to help transform the old KZ into an internment camp for German prisoners of war. On surveying the place to determine its suitability, he wrote that 'standing before the deserted ovens in the crematorium, you became conscious of a primitive fear'.

> One of the oven doors stood open. Projecting into the oven was a long metal stretcher, the length of a man, and on it were still the remains of human bones, charred to a chalky-grey gravel. All round the ovens the concrete floor was crunchy with these little fragments of bone. In the corner was a pile of urns, some already in cartons addressed to civilian cemeteries. It was a straightforward mail-order business.

I wondered whether Captain Sidgwick, as he then was, had embellished what he'd seen at Neuengamme. Lieutenant Charlton, the first British officer into Neuengamme, had said nothing in his statement about any carcass in the crematorium. The description of a floor crunchy with bones was highly effective too, but it wasn't one that Charlton mentioned either. Charlton referred to the urns only.

Everything, he said, was 'clean and in good order'. Had he missed what Sidgwick said he'd discovered? Or was this Sidgwick's way of. capturing the waning interest of his readers? A little dramatic licence? The idea of having to embroider the truth of the camp seems absurd now, but then maybe commentators were struggling to maintain public disgust and horror. There had been so much after all. The facts and figures and photographs and film were everywhere. Nuremberg was replete with them. So how could people's interest be sustained without some dramatic turn of phrase that required a slight alteration of the truth? Floor crunchy with bones. Carcass left in the oven stretcher. Images to make you start, to pay attention, to think: retribution is necessary.

If Sidgwick was to be forgiven for elaborating on the truth, assuming that that was what he'd done, then I suppose he could be applauded for his confession to a different sin. He wrote in 1946, when reflecting on the Neuengamme trial, that he'd felt the 'contagious nature of hatred', a human trait that he believed had consumed the Germans who'd worked in the KZs. During the five days he'd policed the intake of Nazi suspects interned in Neuengamme, time he said he and his colleagues had spent 'hounding our prisoners', he'd become aware that his own 'regard for those men was dwindling to the same proportion as theirs had been for their victims'. It was something of a presentiment of the Zimbardo experiments to be conducted in Stanford a decade or more later, experiments that suggested few are immune to the insidious impact of power in encouraging sadistic propensities. But I'm not sure he could so easily equate what had happened in the camps, in Neuengamme, with enmity induced by control over an enemy. He and his fellow British guards hadn't worked the interns to death, hadn't set dogs on them, hadn't overseen experiments to see how TB developed in healthy children. They may have been brutal. There was evidence to show there were sadists in the British Army, men who would take the opportunity to let base desires loose. But that's not the same as signing up to a whole culture and regime designed on one premise: the dehumanisation and destruction of anyone considered an 'undesirable', a Jew, a political opponent, a foreigner, an *Untermensch*. It was different, wasn't it?

5.

The press had sought drama at Nuremberg too. That was their business: seeking entertainment amongst a decidedly unentertaining
process. A slow accumulation of evidence had drained the novelty
from proceedings by February 1946, three months into the trial. The
Daily Mail reflected: 'Time marches backwards in the court-room at
Nuremberg. Outside the world steps into the future, but here day
after day, the past is unrolled ... Already it begins to seem remote
as it plays about the half-forgotten men in the dock ... The atmosphere is at all times tense – the scene theatrical, with its lights, flags,
white-helmeted American guards, earphones, and glass-caged interpreters.'[7] They waited on the next act with impatience.

On 13 March, as the Neuengamme trial was about to get
underway, their curiosity was temporarily reignited. Hermann
Goering, the man who'd asserted moral command over the defendants in the dock, who'd imposed his personality on proceedings,
taking upon himself the mantle of senior Nazi in the absence of
Hitler and Himmler, was called into the witness box. If anything
marked the fairness of the trial, of all the trials operated by the
British and Americans, it was this ritual opportunity for defendants
to justify themselves. Goering grasped the chance with clear delight.
He must have known that his time on earth was seeping away, but
his ego wouldn't allow him to go quietly.

Over the next few days, Goering took the stand and gave fulsome
answers to questions placed by his counsel. It was an exercise in self-
aggrandisement. 'Bombastic', 'unrepentant' and an enduring loyalty
to Hitler were the initial impressions of his performance. His 'last
long speech to the world' would confirm the character of a German
patriot who would do anything that was necessary to strengthen the
state. The suppression of opposition and the founding of concentration camps were all essential to solidify power in the Führer's hands.
The end of a steel-strong Germany justified the means, the violence,
the wars. When quizzed by his attorney about 'the Jews', Goering
continued with his sweeping validation. 'There were many Jews who
did not show the necessary restraint,' he said. They had too much

power, too much influence, they opposed National Socialism. He argued if 'many a hard word which was said by us against Jews and Jewry were to be brought up, I should still be in a position to produce magazines, books, newspapers, and speeches in which the expressions and insults coming from the other side were far in excess'. The Nuremberg Laws were to 'separate the races', reduce the power and influence of Jews in public life, he said, 'until a controlled emigration ... should solve this problem'.[8] Otherwise, Goering claimed, 'the Jews on the whole remained unmolested in their economic positions'. 'The extraordinary intensification which set in later', as he described the mass extermination, was, he said, a result of one 'radical group' in the Nazi movement 'for whom the Jewish question was more significantly in the foreground'. He denied that the wars of aggression were linked to the destruction of the Jewish race. He denied that extermination had been planned in advance.

Despite this flit across the inhumanity of Nazi rule, Telford Taylor, one of the senior American prosecutors, admitted years later that Goering's performance was 'lucid and impressive'.[9] The *Daily Mail* agreed, saying he'd 'almost talked himself back into his old boisterous and defiant tone'. He 'not only had the floor of the War Crimes court all day but held his former colleagues in the dock in raptures of admiration as he boasted of his work in building up Nazi power'.[10] *The Times* said he 'was by no means without dignity and he spoke with the courage of his convictions'.[11] He was 'making the most remarkable speech of his career. His audience is the world and there is an astute calculation behind every word he utters.'[12] He was 'disarmingly frank', the paper's correspondent admitted. It was as though all had swooned before the celebrity that Goering had become. It was as though the 'excesses' against the Jews, as it was being termed by some of the defendants and their supporters, were an unfortunate and dismissible consequence of an otherwise pure intent and plan of action. Power was Goering's cause: power for the Führer and power for Germany. That was the almost statesmanlike figure he tried to present. And for many he succeeded. It didn't make him any less culpable, but it did provide a political glaze that commanded grudging admiration.

Such was the effect of the trial: it provided a platform for the defendants to rationalise everything done by Nazi Germany.

Cross-examination, the moment in every Anglo-American trial when the prosecution has the opportunity to cut through the shield constructed by the defence, was the only way of returning the mood to outrage and condemnation. But it takes skill.

Justice Jackson was the man who took responsibility for questioning Goering. It was natural that he who'd brought the Nuremberg Tribunal into being should adopt the task. Someone had to assume the burden. But he took it as a personal mission, one not to be widely shared beforehand with the whole prosecution team. It was *his* moment. He began uneasily.

'You are perhaps aware that you are the only living man who can expound to us the true purposes of the Nazi Party and the inner workings of its leadership?'

It was an exercise in mock deference. Observers tried to understand later the reasons for asking that first question. Jackson apparently wrote that he sought to flatter Goering, to draw him into a puffed-up stature so that he would confess to all crimes in a grand show of hubris.[13] Perhaps the complimentary nature of press reports on Goering's performance had irritated Jackson. Perhaps he'd wanted to humiliate the defendant, to show he was despised, a mere man who represented nothing but a corrupt and evil regime. If so, the plan failed. Sir David Maxwell Fyfe wrote to his wife about Jackson's performance: 'The oddity about his attempts so far is that they have no form and no follow-up.'[14]

Reading the transcript, you can see the meandering nature of the questioning. Nothing pierced Goering's shell. Jackson achieved little more than a repetition by Goering of his defence. The complete lack of impact caused Jackson intense irritation. Goering's ability to expound at length in reply to every question brought Jackson to the point of breakdown, it seemed. Angrily, he attempted to persuade the tribunal to order Goering to answer 'Yes or no' to questions put. He said the trial appeared to be getting 'out of hand'. It was a remarkable and ineffective outburst that the panel of judges dismissed.

But the impression Jackson gave was accurate. The trial wasn't achieving the 'justice' that the Allies had sought. It was there to be hijacked as all trials of this nature can be. Perhaps more disturbing than Jackson's inability to crack Goering, though, was his prioritisation.

Not once on that first day of cross-examination did Jackson mention the Jews and their extermination. Not once on the second day. It was only well into the third day that Jackson finally brought Goering to address the question. Why he hadn't started with that subject I couldn't tell. But even when he did, it was a laboured affair, drawing out from Goering nothing more than he'd already admitted. Maybe Jackson knew that it would be futile, that Goering would plead ignorance, reinforcing the impression that a handful of 'radicals' in the SS and under Himmler, as Goering had called them, had taken it upon themselves to kill the Jews of Europe.

Other prosecutors were given the chance to continue the cross-examination once Jackson had finished. Maxwell Fyfe was first and he immediately turned to the killing of the *Great Escape* officers, the fifty men who'd been executed after their recapture from the Stalag Luft III mass POW breakout. Though undoubtedly a matter of great public notice in Britain, the killing was hardly representative of the Nazi spectrum of atrocity. The benefit of Maxwell Fyfe's initial questioning, though, lay in his style, not its content. By detailed and pointed examination he made Goering look evasive. When finally Maxwell Fyfe turned to the extermination of the Jews, the defendant was unsettled. But the shield of ignorance that Goering had constructed remained. Maxwell Fyfe reflected on the proven millions killed in the concentration camps and asked, 'Are you telling this tribunal that a Minister with your power in the Reich could remain ignorant that that was going on?' Goering said it had been kept secret from him. And from Hitler too, he added.

Maxwell Fyfe said, 'I am asking about the murder of four or five million people. Are you suggesting that nobody in power in Germany, except Himmler and perhaps Kaltenbrunner, knew about that?'

'I am still of the opinion that the Führer did not know about these figures.'

'You did not know to what degree, but you knew there was a policy that aimed at the extermination of the Jews?'

'No, a policy of emigration, not liquidation of the Jews. I knew only that there had been isolated cases of such perpetrations.'

That admission of awareness, even of 'isolated cases', was enough for Maxwell Fyfe. It was the most that he or any attorney was able to extract from Goering.

The British press warmed to the personal nature of the encounter. The *Daily Mail* reported, 'The great battle of wits between Hermann Goering and the man he fears most in his trial here, Sir David Maxwell Fyfe, deputy British prosecutor, wound up today with the former *Reichsmarshal* baffled and beaten.'[15] 'Goering Hard Pressed by British Prosecutor', the *Times* headline read.[16] Even then, national pride had more influence on perceptions of the trial than the search for accountability.

6.

If the high political justification for what were euphemistically called 'excesses' regarding the Jews and all other victims was acknowledged, if not accepted, by Goering in Nuremberg, how could those directly engaged in its delivery excuse their part?

At the Curiohaus, the Neuengamme camp commandant, Max Pauly, entered the witness box as the first of the accused to put his defence. Just as with Goering, he was given hours to answer the questions of his counsel. He explained how he'd joined the SS, wanted to be part of an SS fighting unit in the war, but had instead been posted to the Danzig Security Police. From there, between 1939 and 1942, he'd assumed command of Stutthof KZ, built some 40 kilometres east of the city. Initially, the camp imprisoned Jews and Poles from Danzig and the surrounding country, but in 1942 it was incorporated fully into the KZ system. It was then that Pauly had been transferred to Neuengamme KZ as commandant.

Unlike Goering, Pauly played down his importance, his knowledge of crimes, denying the claims made by all the witnesses who'd appeared so far. He passed on responsibility to anyone else he could: his SS colleagues in the camp, his superiors in the Hamburg district and predictably all those powerful names in Berlin. It was another act of multiple deflection: Thumann was the officer whose cruelty defined the conditions in the camp, Pauly claimed; Dr Trzebinski was solely responsible for the killing of the children at Bullenhuser Damm;

Bassewitz-Behr had given the order to kill the inmates from Fuhlsbüttel prison as the Allies advanced; and General Oswald Pohl, the man responsible for the organisation of all concentration camps and whom the British War Crimes Investigation Unit would soon apprehend, was the one who'd instructed KZ commandants at a conference in Berlin that all prisoners should be exterminated by whatever means if the Allies invaded. And orders *had* to be obeyed, Pauly said. It was an extension of Goering's power hierarchy, measured by total obedience.

Major Stewart's cross-examination was his first in the case. As they were finding at Nuremberg, these moments defined the success of the trial, at least in so far as an audience might perceive the performance. Not that it could matter much in terms of the result, the simple announcement of guilt or innocence. But a poor interrogation by the prosecutor and the whole procedure would look shabby. It might encourage the German population to think this was a sham. They might think this was just an act of theatre and condemn the findings of the court. And where would that leave the project of retribution through proper and fair legal process?

How to start well, then? Stewart had been one of the team at the Belsen trial. He would have remembered his colleague Colonel Backhouse and his opening question to Josef Kramer. His was very nearly the same and prompted an odd exchange.

'Pauly,' Stewart said, 'I saw you swear on the Bible yesterday much to my surprise. How is that? Do you believe in it?'

'Yes.'

'Am I right in saying that all members of the SS, officers or other ranks, had to leave their church on entering the SS?'

'I joined the SS in 1931 and at that time there was no such order.' But later, when promoted, officers were expected to leave the Church, he said. This happened for him in 1934 or 1935.

'Why then do you swear on the Bible?'

'I have nothing to do with the SS any more and the SS cannot do anything about it if I want to return to the church.'

The claim was almost redemptive. A sinner repenting. And a sinner who'd never renounced his beliefs but had only hidden them. Pauly explained he'd been forced into the SS, first because he needed money and then by the dictates of party leaders. He sketched the image of a young man (he was thirty-two in 1939) who'd been compelled to do what he was told. But underneath was a moral core that had now been released.

Stewart's gambit was threatened. He had to prick this balloon of inner innocence. This was a member of a select band of maleficent figures, the KZ commandants. He couldn't be allowed *any* redemption, not here, not in the name of God. That would challenge the divine nature of justice that this trial and all the others had assumed. Stewart had to demonstrate that Pauly *wanted* to work in the camps, that he'd chosen to do so or at least had taken the role seriously.

Just as Jackson had been condemned for his opening question at Nuremberg, Stewart could have been equally criticised. Reference to the Church and Pauly's supposed refound religious conviction was an interesting way of provoking the ex-commandant. That Pauly had a defence strategy had been emphasised in the examination by his lawyer. But Stewart gave him the opportunity to repeat his claims that he was a victim himself, he'd *had* to join the SS, he'd *had* to obey their orders and he couldn't serve both God and the organisation at the same time, though beneath the black uniform he'd been a believer who'd resisted where and when he could, following commands as any underling or junior officer had been obliged to do. It may have been an unconvincing story, given the recent revelations about the absolute power over life that all KZ commandants possessed. Pauly nonetheless maintained consistently that he'd been ignorant of the whole system, that his time in Stutthof hadn't prepared him for KZ service, that he'd been aware illegal killings and ill-treatment had occurred in concentration camps, but he'd been determined not to follow suit.

Pauly was asked why he hadn't served with the *Waffen-SS* and fought in France, why instead he was placed in charge of a camp in Stutthof?

Those were my orders, Pauly said. He'd asked to fight at the front but had been put in command of the civilian internment camp near Danzig instead. Stutthof had been changed into a concentration camp only later, in 1942.

What was the difference, Stewart asked, between Stutthof the civilian internment camp which Pauly commanded from 1939 to 1942 and Stutthof the KZ from 1942 onwards?

The 'inmates were allowed to keep their own clothes', Pauly said. Was that all?

Pauly avoided answering. He became glib. 'They were behind barbed wire just in the same way.'

But their treatment?

'The laws and regulations in an internment camp were different. I certainly tried in Stutthof and Neuengamme to treat the prisoners properly.'

Turning to his term as Neuengamme commandant, Pauly said, yes, the *Reichsführer* Himmler gave authority to order capital punishment, but he hadn't made use of it. It only applied to Russians anyway, he said (as if that would be acceptable to everyone in the courtroom), and even then he'd only carried out 'executions when they were ordered by higher authority'.

As camp commandant could he order other punishments?

'Reprimands, arrest, withdrawal of a meal and withdrawal of food,' Pauly said.

What did that last punishment entail?

Missing a Sunday midday meal for three consecutive weeks, Pauly claimed rather too innocently. He portrayed a regime where punishment was infrequent, light, without violence. Only if he received a direct order from Berlin could he authorise beatings, he said.

Stewart's incredulity was met with the same response: Pauly had seen nothing and read no order which could prove he was lying.

Ridicule was Stewart's next tactic. How could Pauly argue that he was in command and yet had no idea what was happening in the bunker, in the brickworks, in the punishment companies, to which all of the witnesses had testified and the other defendants had confirmed in their statements?

Max Pauly stood fast.

Then Stewart quizzed him about his knowledge of other camps, other camp commandants. Pauly admitted he'd met Kramer, commandant of Belsen and Auschwitz, and Rudolf Höss, commandant of Auschwitz too. They would gather in Berlin when summoned to discuss concentration camp policy. None of them had told him about *their* camps, he said, although he'd heard about gassings. If he'd been required to transfer sick patients to these other camps, it was in order to have them cured, Pauly said.

'Do you really want to tell this court that after having conferences with all these camp commandants including Kramer and Höss you really believe that people went to Belsen and Lublin to be cured?'

Max Pauly portrayed himself as wandering amidst a host of cruel and despicable men without noticing. Reading the exchange with Stewart, it occurred to me that Pauly was becoming a metaphor for the whole German nation.

The crimes Stewart mentioned then became more specific. Did he remember the execution of the men and women from Fuhlsbüttel in April 1945?

Yes.

Who ordered the killings?

The higher SS and police commander in Hamburg.

Did Pauly give Thumann the order to carry this out?

Yes.

And when Thumann killed some of the Fuhlsbüttel people with hand grenades, what did he do?

Reprimanded Thumann. Severely.

And the hospital? Did he visit that place?

Yes.

Did he know about Willi Bahr and the injections he'd used to kill inmates?

He knew nothing about them.

What about the orders from Goebbels and Himmler approving the 'extermination through work' policy to be applied in the camps: what did he think of them?

He knew nothing about them either.

The cross-examination ended weakly. Faced by a wall of innocence and denial, Stewart had little to exploit. He had to rely on disbelief that Pauly could have been so blind to the deaths and brutality that the witnesses had said defined this KZ and the whole concentration camp system. Pauly was one of an elite band, men who were paraded now as the embodiment of Nazi ideology put into practice. If you were a camp commandant you had to be privy to the whole structure and policy of imprisonment and extermination. Every major KZ operated within this web. Prisoners and guards, and commandants too, moved between the main centres continually. The most senior SS officers were brought to Berlin to attend regular meetings about the organisation of the system. No one in such a position as Pauly could possibly be so ignorant of the wholesale killing that the camps oversaw.

The ever fair Judge Advocate Stirling wasn't satisfied. He was entitled to ask his own questions if he thought there were unresolved matters, often a sign that the prosecution hadn't been thorough. Stirling asked where Pauly had lived whilst serving as commandant. Inside the camp, Pauly said, ten minutes' walk to the main gate in that little white house behind one of the brick barracks. His children had joined him there from Danzig.

The mention of children prompted Stirling to talk about the Jewish girls and boys who had been experimented on and killed in Bullenhuser Damm. Pauly knew about them and had followed orders unwillingly. He'd already admitted that. Orders couldn't be countermanded by him, however unpleasant. He accepted too that the two French professors, Florence and Quenouille, were sent with the children to be executed with them.

Stirling asked him about the death rate in the camp. Pauly blamed the high number of sick prisoners transferred to Neuengamme from other places. They arrived in such a state, he said, that there was little anyone could do, though they tried their very best, he assured the court.

He presented himself as a professional, a soldier who had done his duty and had cared for his charges as much as he was allowed. There was no contrition and no acceptance of guilt, responsibility, anything that connected him morally with those whose killings and deaths and tortures he'd overseen.

7.

Pauly's defence shifted the gaze of those in the Curiohaus proceedings onto the general structures of the Nazi regime. That was his aim: to pass blame to those further up the hierarchy. Even though a camp commandant, Pauly argued that he was a lowly figure in the SS, preconditioned, as all military men were, to obey all orders. He was nothing more than a common foot soldier, nothing more than a functionary in the KZ system, who'd served his time and followed commands.

For a moment the proceedings in Hamburg and a few hundred miles away in the tribunal at Nuremberg became intertwined. On 15 April 1946, a week or so after Pauly had given his evidence, Rudolf Höss was called to testify in Nuremberg. He epitomised the dark soul of the Nazi era. As commandant of Auschwitz between 1940 and 1943 he'd administered part of the programme to exterminate the Jews of Europe and was at the top of the list of wanted war criminals. His arrest in March 1946 by No. 1 War Crimes Investigation Unit, Captain Hanns Alexander leading the operation, was a triumph. The confession that followed, with Höss revealing the innermost secrets of the 'Final Solution' and his role within it, couldn't have been better timed for the Allies in Nuremberg in their determination to *prove* that extermination, not resettlement, was the Nazi plan. The trouble was the prosecution had already rested its case by the time Höss had been captured.

To make the most of his confession, the Allied prosecutors offered Höss to the accused. Kaltenbrunner was about to present his defence and Dr Kauffmann, his attorney, needed a witness to support his argument that Kaltenbrunner had had no responsibility for the death camps or the extermination of the Jews. After being allowed by the Americans to interview Höss, Kauffmann believed that the Auschwitz commandant would support this contention. He called Höss as a defence witness and questioned him. The exchange that began Kauffmann's examination was terse, matter-of-fact.

'From 1940 to 1943, you were the Commander of the camp at Auschwitz. Is that true?'

'Yes.'

'And during that time, hundreds of thousands of human beings were sent to their death there. Is that correct?'

'Yes.'

'Is it true that you, yourself, have made no exact notes regarding the figures of the number of those victims because you were forbidden to make them?'

'Yes, that is correct.'

'Is it furthermore correct that exclusively one man by the name of Eichmann had notes about this, the man who had the task of organizing and assembling these people?'

'Yes.'

'Is it furthermore true that Eichmann stated to you that in Auschwitz a total sum of more than 2 million Jews had been destroyed?'

'Yes.'

'Men, women, and children?'

'Yes.'

Like Pauly, Höss had risen through the ranks of the SS concentration camp hierarchy. First at Dachau then Sachsenhausen. In May 1940 he'd become commandant of Auschwitz. The following year he'd been called to Berlin by Himmler.

Höss said of this meeting, 'He told me something to the effect – I do not remember the exact words – that the Führer had given the order for a final solution of the Jewish question. We, the SS, must carry out that order. If it is not carried out now then the Jews will later on destroy the German people. He had chosen Auschwitz on account of its easy access by rail and also because the extensive site offered space for measures ensuring isolation.'

Kauffmann asked, 'During that conference did Himmler tell you that this planned action had to be treated as a secret Reich matter?'

'Yes. He stressed that point. He told me that I was not even allowed to say anything about it to my immediate superior *Gruppenführer* Glücks. This conference concerned the two of us only and I was to observe the strictest secrecy.'

Glücks had been the inspector of concentration camps under Himmler. Asked what 'secret Reich matter' meant, Höss said, 'No one was allowed to speak about these matters with any person and that everyone promised upon his life to keep the utmost secrecy.'

Had he broken that promise?

Yes, he said. He'd told his wife when she'd asked him about rumours she'd heard. The *Gauleiter* of Upper Silesia had mentioned to her that Jews were being killed in their thousands in Auschwitz and she'd been curious whether it was true. He'd told her the truth, he said. But otherwise he'd divulged the secret to no one else.

What was this truth?

Höss told how his camp, isolated, surrounded by empty country-side, operated.

The Auschwitz camp as such was about 3 kilometers away from the town. About 20,000 acres of the surrounding country had been cleared of all former inhabitants, and the entire area could be entered only by SS men or civilian employees who had special passes. The actual compound called 'Birkenau', where later on the extermination camp was constructed, was situated 2 kilometers from the Auschwitz camp. The camp installations themselves, that is to say, the provisional installations used at first were deep in the woods and could from nowhere be detected by the eye. In addition to that, this area had been declared a prohibited area and even members of the SS who did not have a special pass could not enter it. Thus, as far as one could judge, it was impossible for anyone except authorized persons to enter that area.

And what happened there?

During the whole period up until 1944 certain operations were carried out at irregular intervals in the different countries, so that one cannot speak of a continuous flow of incoming transports. It was always a matter of 4 to 6 weeks. During those 4 to 6 weeks two to three trains, containing about 2,000 persons each, arrived daily. These trains were first of all shunted to a siding in the Birkenau region and the locomotives then went back. The guards who had accompanied the transport had to leave the area at once and the persons who had been brought in were taken over by guards belonging to the camp. They were there examined by two SS medical officers as to their fitness for work. The internees capable of work at once marched to Auschwitz or to the camp at Birkenau and those incapable of work were at first taken to the provisional installations, then later to the newly constructed crematoria.

Kauffmann prompted Höss to emphasise the concealment of the process.

Sixty men were always on hand to take the internees not capable of work to these provisional installations and later on to the other ones. This group, consisting of about ten leaders and sub-leaders, as well as doctors and medical personnel, had repeatedly been told, both in writing and verbally, that they were bound to the strictest secrecy as to all that went on in the camps.

Kauffmann asked, 'And after the arrival of the transports were the victims stripped of everything they had? Did they have to undress completely; did they have to surrender their valuables? Is that true?'
'Yes.'
'And then they immediately went to their death?'
'Yes.'
'Did these people know what was in store for them?'
'The majority of them did not, for steps were taken to keep them in doubt about it and suspicion would not arise that they were to go to their death. For instance, all doors and all walls bore inscriptions to the effect that they were going to undergo a delousing operation or take a shower. This was made known in several languages to the internees by other internees who had come in with earlier transports and who were being used as auxiliary crews during the whole action.'

'And then, you told me the other day, that death by gassing set in within a period of 3 to 15 minutes. Is that correct?'

'Yes.'

'You also told me that even before death finally set in, the victims fell into a state of unconsciousness?'

'Yes. From what I was able to find out myself or from what was told me by medical officers, the time necessary for reaching unconsciousness or death varied according to the temperature and the number of people present in the chambers. Loss of consciousness took place within a few seconds or a few minutes.'

Then a sudden shift from Kauffmann, one which would serve no great purpose for his client; maybe he simply couldn't listen to the deliberate and prosaic description of industrialised killing without some emotional response. Kauffmann asked, 'Did you yourself ever feel pity with the victims, thinking of your own family and children?'

'Yes.'

'How was it possible for you to carry out these actions in spite of this?'

'In view of all these doubts which I had, the only one and decisive argument was the strict order and the reason given for it by the *Reichsführer* Himmler.'

Himmler's name drew Kauffmann back to the defence of his client.

'I ask you whether Himmler inspected the camp and convinced himself, too, of the process of annihilation.'

'Yes. Himmler visited the camp in 1942 and he watched in detail one processing from beginning to end.'

'Does the same apply to Eichmann?'

'Eichmann came repeatedly to Auschwitz and was intimately acquainted with the proceedings.'

'Did the defendant Kaltenbrunner ever inspect the camp?'

'No.'

'Did you ever talk with Kaltenbrunner with reference to your task?'

'No, never.'

I watched the old film of this exchange. One of the judges tapped his pencil, took a sip of water from a beaker in front of him. Officials and lawyers around the courtroom pressed headphones to their ears. As Höss talked of the 'final solution' guards stood to attention behind him, stenographers typed away on their machines, and Höss sat small and slightly hunched, delivering his breathless evidence. Everyone looked sombre but none of the faces registered shock. I supposed they'd heard all this before. It had become commonplace, non-revelatory, even bland now in that courtroom.

It wasn't Dr Kauffmann's intention to reveal the horror of the Holocaust. His only concern was to prove that his client, Kaltenbrunner, the most senior SS officer before the Major War Criminals trial, second only to Himmler in the SS hierarchy after Heydrich had been killed in Prague, had known nothing about the extermination of the Jews. Whatever else he was accused of, this abomination couldn't be laid at his door, so the advocate claimed. Höss was supposed to confirm that the mass killing was kept tightly secret, only known by a handful of men, like Himmler and Eichmann and of course the few SS guards who had to carry out the gassing operations.

It was a simplistic representation. If Höss's wife had heard about the extermination in Auschwitz from sources who hadn't had the necessary security clearance, then the secret hadn't been that well kept. And what about all those who hadn't been killed, the other guards and SS officers, hundreds who came and went? And the same numbers who had undertaken similar extermination procedures in other camps, in Treblinka and Belzec and Majdanek and Sobibór?

Under cross-examination Höss repeated his confession, given to the Allies a few days earlier, that although he'd been required to operate in secrecy, 'of course the foul and nauseating stench from the continuous burning of bodies permeated the entire area and all of the people living in the surrounding communities knew that exterminations were going on at Auschwitz'.

How likely was it, then, that men like Kaltenbrunner could not have known about the mass killing? How likely was it, when gathered together in Berlin or Oranienburg, as they did through the central KZ Inspectorate, the concentration camp commandants, Max Pauly included, hadn't heard about, talked about, the mass killing in Auschwitz and the other death camps? How likely was it that when trainloads of Jews passed through the labour camps such as Neuengamme and Bergen-Belsen, to be shipped on to Auschwitz, that no one had understood the reason for their journey?

Further evidence given by Höss made a nonsense of the idea of covert killing on such a scale. He described the way in which Auschwitz worked beyond its role as a killing factory. He'd said in his statement to the American interrogators that 2,500,000 people had been killed by 'gassing and burning' and another 500,000 had died from starvation and disease whilst in the camp. This figure, he said, represented 70–80 per cent of the prisoners sent to Auschwitz. The rest were selected for slave labour in the concentration camp industries. Prisoners would come and go through Auschwitz. They would end up in places like Neuengamme for distribution amongst the many sub-camps for agricultural and industrial work, all for the war. They would take with them their knowledge of the slaughtering. Even if they only talked of the smell, rumours would spread. How secret then was the extermination?

But if Max Pauly somehow managed to keep his ears closed about the killing, could he really maintain his innocence over the ill-treatment within his own camp? Höss said of Auschwitz,

The internees were treated severely, but methodical beatings or ill-treatments were out of the question. The Reichsführer gave frequent orders that every SS man who laid violent hands on an internee would be punished; and several times SS men who did ill-treat internees were punished ...

If any ill-treatment of prisoners by guards occurred – I myself have never observed any – then this was possible only to a very small degree since all officers in charge of the camps took care that as few SS men as possible had direct contact with the inmates ...

In the course of the years the guard personnel had deteriorated to such an extent that the standards formerly demanded could no longer be maintained. We had thousands of guards who could hardly speak German, who came from all lands as volunteers and joined these units, or we had older men, between 50 and 60, who lacked all interest in their work, so that a camp commander had to watch constantly that these men fulfilled even the lowest requirements of their duties. It is obvious that there were elements among them who would ill-treat internees, but this ill-treatment was never tolerated ...

Of course a great deal of ill-treatment occurred which could not be avoided because at night there were hardly any members of the SS in the camps. Only in specific cases were SS men allowed to enter the camp, so that the internees were more or less exposed to these *Kapos*.

Pauly might have nodded at Höss's claims as support for his position, but even for him the evidence was self-defeating: though Höss said ill-treatment hadn't been tolerated, he and everyone else had known that it happened. Passing blame to the *Kapos* couldn't dislodge the duty of care which Höss said was supposed to permeate the camps. The same had to apply to Pauly.

Then there was the matter of the final year in the story of the KZs. Höss repeated much that the defence had said on Pauly's behalf, and had been raised in the Belsen trial six months earlier. He marked 1944 as the period when the pure order of the concentration camps, as he characterised it, broke down. He said,

When the war started and when mass deliveries of political internees arrived, and, later on, when prisoners who were members of the resistance movements arrived from the occupied territories, the construction of buildings and the extensions of the camps could no longer keep pace with the number of incoming internees. During the first years of the war this problem could still be overcome by improvising measures.

That all changed when materials for construction stopped arriving, and rations for internees were cut. The prisoners 'no longer had the staying power to resist the now gradually growing epidemics'.

The main reason why the prisoners were in such bad condition towards the end of the war, why so many thousands of them were found sick and emaciated in the camps, was that every internee had to be employed in the armament industry to the extreme limit of his forces. The *Reichsführer* constantly and on every occasion kept this goal before our eyes ... Every commander was told to make every effort to achieve this. The aim was not to have as many dead as possible or to destroy as many internees as possible; the *Reichsführer* was constantly concerned with being able to engage all forces available in the armament industry.

As the war had drawn to a close, Höss said,

The number of the sick became immense. There were next to no medical supplies; epidemics raged everywhere. Internees who were capable of work were used over and over again. By order of the *Reichsführer*, even half-sick people had to be used wherever possible in industry. As a result every bit of space in the concentration camps which could possibly be used for lodging was overcrowded with sick and dying prisoners.

It was all unconvincing. Though individual commandants like Pauly and Josef Kramer may have faced an impossible task, inundated with increasing numbers of inmates with whom they could not cope, they had been prominent in the maintenance of the system. They had been instrumental in its operation. Höss might have confirmed the unforgiving and desperate position towards the end of the war, but the existence of the system, constructed over a decade and more, made ill-treatment and death inevitable. That was the culpability that could not be shaken off across the spectrum of ranks.

8.

A different form of defendant took the stand after Pauly had finished presenting his defence. Anton Thumann was a man who had no part to play in the grand decisions which opened and closed the KZs. He'd forged a career in the camps, working his way up the hierarchy, demonstrating his willingness to use whatever violent measure he felt like employing. It was a skill valued by those senior to him. No one could ever doubt, so it would seem, Thumann's commitment to the underlying purpose of the camps.

When Thumann came to give evidence, though, he denied the portrait the prosecution had crafted. Commandant Max Pauly was the evil influence, he claimed. Despite being Pauly's deputy, Thumann said he had no power to do anything other than follow the commandant's orders. Everyone had feared Pauly, Thumann said. 'When the commandant came to the camp my predecessor would leave by the window.'

Pauly had two characters, according to Thumann, 'One a brutal one and the other the one he presented here in court.' But his brutality was mostly directed at the SS leaders, not the prisoners. It consisted of 'words'. He 'dressed everyone down'.

Thumann was not a particularly clever man. He demonstrated that quickly enough. Asked by his attorney, Dr Koenig, whether he'd signed a document declaring that he would not beat prisoners, he said 'yes' but then confessed that he hadn't obeyed it. 'Because without being able to punish them myself on the spot I would not have been able to keep the required order and discipline.' He admitted to hitting prisoners in the face, of beating with a stick 'five to twenty-five strokes', of owning a 'wolf dog' which he assured the court he'd never turned on anyone, though it would dive at a prisoner should Thumann strike him. He presented himself as a slave to the commandant and the hierarchy stretching above Pauly to the upper ranks of the SS. And he said he hated the regime under his superior. He had even applied for a transfer to the front. His commandant's approach hadn't been what he joined the SS for: 'In peace time the idea was to re-educate prisoners, and in war time they were to be included in the war effort.' He did not believe a policy of extermination through work had been created. Yes, he'd conducted executions, but every *Lagerführer* was required to do that: orders came from the *Reichsführer-SS*. Thumann had no choice but to obey. And that was what he did: carry out those orders. 'If the orders said "To be hanged" then we hanged them; if the orders said "To be shot" then we shot them.'

Reading Thumann's testimony made me think the defence of unwilling obedience was self-defeating. To be credible he had to admit that he'd carried out the most atrocious of crimes. He had to demonstrate the total corruption of his autonomy by acknow-ledging the killings and beatings as part of a daily ordering of his life. It had to extend to the execution of the children in Bullenhuser Damm. And Thumann indeed confirmed, 'I can only say that I had given the order to *Rapportführer* Dreimann for Speck and Wiehagen to arrange the convoy to transport these children to that place.'

But it was his account of the killing of the detachment of prisoners from Fuhlsbüttel on 23 and 24 April 1945 that marked Thumann. He said he'd been ordered to accept the convoy from the Hamburg prison and execute them. It was an 'untimely' duty. He was overworked. 'On that particular day 4,500 Jews were evacuated,' he said, as though describing the despatch of a consignment of boxes. Thumann accepted the fifty-eight men and thirteen women from the Gestapo's prison at Fuhlsbüttel, separated them, then fixed the execution for the following night. Then between 9 p.m. and 9.30 p.m. he'd stood at the entrance of the execution bunker and watched by lamplight as first the women were brought in their underwear, stood on chairs and hanged. The men were next. Six were executed in the same fashion without any problems. But when he went to the cells to collect the next batch, the inmates attacked him with a wooden bar from one of the cell beds. Thumann remembered it as though he were in the middle of a furious battle at the front.

> I was hardly conscious, I could just about stand. I was quite defence-less. One of the prisoners came out of the cell and attacked *Blockführer* Brems. Whether I shut the door or somebody else did I can't remember. The prisoner who had attacked Brems and given him a stab in the upper region of the chest was then shot by Brems ... The other pris-oners then barricaded the door.

Thumann called for a ladder to look through the high cell window. The prisoners couldn't be seen. They'd set themselves back in the corners. When he put his hand in and tried to shoot them, his hand was hit and the pistol fell into the cell. Thumann called for grenades. The prisoners fired several shots. A grenade was thrown in. The explosion demolished the wall between two cells. All but one of the prisoners were buried in the debris. Thumann grabbed a machine pistol, stuck it through the food hatch and fired. 'I gave every one of the prisoners a short burst as I was not quite sure whether they were dead or not.'

'Did you consider yourself justified in resorting to these extreme measures?' Thumann's lawyer asked.

'I was convinced of it in order to protect my subordinates.'

His conviction lacked substance: 'After I had finished off the male prisoners with my machine pistol I left the bunker and a short while afterwards I heard a woman scream. I went to the door and saw a woman inside in a crouched position by the door and she was yelling horribly. I was of the impression that she was injured and I shot her.'

Then he retired for the night.

The next evening, he said, he'd dealt with the rest. 'I had the prisoners undressed and I shot them myself.'

Why?

'I took the moral responsibility from the shoulders of my subordinate officers on to my own.'

There was little to add. Only that on 2 May 1945 he'd heard the firing from the front and he'd left Neuengamme. He and the commandant had travelled towards Plön, hoping to catch up with the guards and prisoners from the camp. On the way they'd heard Neustadt had been taken and so headed for Wesselburen, where the commandant's in-laws lived. Then they'd travelled to Flensburg, where Thumann was spotted by some former inmates.

Thumann's life story was almost over.

9.

I was fascinated by Thumann. I'm not entirely sure why. Perhaps it was his photograph, his face. He looked not just ordinary, but kindly. The slight upward curve at the corners of his mouth suggested a humorous man, someone wanting to break into laughter. We set so much store on facial features, judge quickly on appearances. And a glance at Thumann made me feel pity for him and his predicament. I wondered if I'd have warmed to him if I'd met him. But photographs are poor means by which to assess a person. In the flesh he might well have exuded a completely different personality. Maybe his cruelty and mercilessness would have shown in his eyes, his demeanour. How could I possibly tell?

Did it matter anyway, whether he was a pleasant man or an evil one? His prosecution wasn't based on his character, nor was his defence. He'd been following orders, he said by way of excuse. But Nuremberg negated such a plea, its fourth principle saying: 'The fact that a person acted pursuant to order of his Government or of a superior does not relieve him from responsibility under international law, provided a moral choice was in fact possible to him.'

Had Thumann a moral choice? He'd admitted as much in carrying out the executions of the Fuhlsbüttel prisoners rather than leave them to his subordinates. Whether or not he enjoyed the killing mattered little, other than perhaps when it came to sentencing him for his crimes. A sadist couldn't have expected mercy. But can you really tell the difference between a sadist and a man programmed to kill, who takes a weapon and carries out an order with efficiency and, perhaps more importantly, without apparent disgust at his own actions?

Not more than a couple of years ago, whilst I was in the middle of writing this book, the question of moral choice for a soldier became a public concern in Britain. Marine 'A', as he was identified during proceedings, was charged with murdering a Taliban fighter in Afghanistan in 2011. The enemy combatant had been wounded and lay helpless on the ground. He'd been dragged to the side of a field where Marine 'A' had shot him in the chest, saying, 'Shuffle off this mortal coil, you cunt. It's nothing you wouldn't do to us.' The killing and the words had been caught on the helmet camera of another soldier and Marine 'A' had been charged, convicted and sentenced to life imprisonment.

On the face of the reported evidence, which was the limit of my knowledge about the case, the marine had to be guilty. He'd broken one of the fundamental rules of legalised warfare: you don't kill anyone who can't defend themselves. If they're *hors de combat* then shooting them is a crime. Simple. That's the law. And Marine 'A' had a moral choice. He wasn't compelled or ordered to shoot the unarmed, wounded man. Unless you believe that the stress of intense battle and the training in violence inherent in any soldier's preparation took away the marine's free will. Then the question of moral choice becomes a little more complicated. What choice do you have when compulsion, a psychological issue, is the product of insidious, subliminal influences? Don't we give credence to the impact of many factors on the 'free will' of individuals? Don't we accept that in some situations, people act according to the dictates of education, training, mental indoctrination, conditioning, institutionalisation?

Sometimes. Those who commit a clear-cut crime may be judged sympathetically, perhaps even absolved altogether. But the occasions when this is allowed are tightly constrained. Our sympathies depend on the capacity of our imagination to think, 'Maybe I would have committed the same awful deed if I'd experienced those pressures.' I might still have to accept punishment, as the wrong remains a wrong, though the moral responsibility might have been tempered.

Marine 'A' received the sympathy of many. People spoke of the immense burden of fighting in a horrible and ruthless conflict. The Taliban weren't noble opponents: the marine's comment that this was what the Taliban would have done to him was believed, or at least believable. How many prisoners of war have been taken by the Taliban and survived? But the soldier's recorded speech degraded this sympathy. The few words he'd used as he'd brought up his pistol and fired into the man's chest raised questions. 'Shuffle off this mortal coil,' he'd said. A Shakespearean quote. From *Hamlet* and the most famous of soliloquies. But Shakespeare? A tough sergeant in the toughest of outfits, the Royal Marines? At a moment when he's supposed to be acting on impulse? Was it a joke? Who would joke at a time like that? Who wouldn't? And then there was the expletive tacked on: 'you cunt'. 'Shuffle off this mortal coil, you cunt.' Was that intended to be funny, to make the two marines with him laugh? It sounded malicious. Who has sympathy with a killing infected by malice?

Marine 'A' was found guilty despite the public sympathy he'd received, though a year after the sentence was handed down an appeal court decided that he would have to serve a minimum of eight years rather than the previously stipulated ten. The judges held that combat stress should have been acknowledged and given greater weight when the sentence was handed down. Two years off for stress? Moral responsibility moderated to acknowledge the pressures he'd suffered.[17]

10.

Even if proving Thumann was a sadist was unnecessary (all the prosecution had to do to establish the main charge was show him to be a senior officer in the camp), more was at stake than finding him guilty. Why go through this protracted process of calling witnesses, cross-examining defendants, if what was needed was only a clear identification? This man, Defendant No. 3, the man with the white card around his neck, sitting in the wooden dock, is Anton Thumann, member of the SS, *Lagerführer*, camp leader, at Neuengamme concentration camp from April 1944 until May 1945, during which time thousands of prisoners died, were executed, were treated with malice. That's all that would be necessary. Thumann's admission of his identity and role was sufficient.

In reality, it *wasn't* enough. Whatever the charge, the psychology of this trial, and every trial including Nuremberg, was rooted in the belief that the defendants had a moral choice and had failed to exercise it. The prosecution were thus compelled to prove that Thumann and all the other accused acted with malice. Despite having the choice *not* to kill and torture, they did so daily, weekly, and, for men like Thumann, as part of a career which spanned times of peace and war over many years and many camps. The prosecution wanted to show the corrupt nature of these men. To show they deserved no sympathy, because the moral choice made was to accept their duties and carry them out willingly, often with pleasure, as well as efficiency.

Major Stewart's assistant, Major P.S. Wein, took the role of cross-examiner this time. His was a very different style.

'Do you call yourself a professional soldier?' Wein asked.

'Yes,' Thumann said.

'Would not a more accurate description of your activities be a "professional gangster"?'

Even in the late 1940s the term 'gangster' was synonymous with lawlessness. *Verbrecher*. Criminal. Churchill often used the term to describe the Nazis: 'Nazi gangsters', he called Hitler and his followers.

'No, I have no reason to think so,' said Thumann.

'Tell me what you have done in the way of soldiering?'

'I have been serving on active duties for five years.'

'Where: in the SS?'

'In Dachau.'

'On your own admission you have been a hangman throughout the whole of your career, is that not so?'

'No.'

Wein read out Thumann's postings. Dachau in 1933. Groß-Rosen until 1943. Lublin (Majdanek) until 1944. Neuengamme 1944 until 1945.

Wein asked about his 'wolf dog'. Thumann first had him in Groß-Rosen. The dog came to Neuengamme with its master.

'You say he was a very well trained dog?'

'Yes.'

'So that if you struck a prisoner or beat a prisoner the dog would automatically attack that prisoner.'

'Correct.'

'Why on earth did you train your dog to do a thing like that?'

'He was not trained, that was an automatic impulse of the dog.'

'The same automatic impulse that you had to beat people?'

'Yes.'

'You *agree* you have an impulse to beat people?'

'I was responsible for order and discipline.' And Thumann said not all of the fourteen thousand inmates were 'angels'.

Major Wein wanted to know about his time at Lublin, Majdanek. It wasn't the same as Neuengamme. Thumann said Neuengamme wasn't an extermination camp. Lublin was.

'So it was well realised that Lublin was an extermination camp, was it?'

'Yes. As I said before, 10,000 to 15,000 Jews were shot.'

'That was on one particular occasion?'

'Yes.'

'That all happened on one day?'

'Yes.'

'But you were there much longer than one day, weren't you?'

'A whole year.'

'So what part in other exterminations did you take?'

'Just as in Neuengamme, I was responsible for executions and I had to carry them out.'

'But you said that Lublin was an extermination camp, unlike Neuengamme. You must have been very busy with executions?'

'It wasn't so bad.'

Es war nicht allzu schlecht. It was not so bad. Did he mean: don't worry for my sake, I wasn't *that* busy? Or did he mean, there weren't too many killings?

'How bad was it? How many were executed during the year you were there?'

'Less than in Neuengamme. Fifty to eighty.'

'Perhaps you deliberately misunderstand me. How many people were executed there?'

'About 4,000.'

'Were they Jews?'

'Yes, Jews.'

'Am I right in saying they were only Jews?'

'Yes.'

The distinction between Neuengamme, a camp for labour, and Majdanek or Auschwitz, places of extermination, seemed not to trouble Thumann. He couldn't see the problem with admitting his year in Lublin had embroiled him in the whole industry of extermination. They were Jews. That's what was done to Jews. No questioning, no concern, nothing. He admitted to being part of one day's massacre of thousands of people. He admitted he was in charge of executions. He admitted that this was his duty in Neuengamme too. And yet, he claimed as his defence that at Neuengamme, Commandant Max Pauly was so despicable and cruel that he couldn't bear to serve under him.

A deep psychotic irony permeated his testimony, to which he seemed oblivious.

Dr Koenig, Thumann's lawyer, re-examined his client, asking, 'Could you describe to the court what your feelings were when you used to carry out those executions?'

Thumann answered, 'I can only say here too that whilst I was serving in the SS I was a soldier and I have always carried out my duty, and only one who has actually gone through the experience can form an opinion of the feelings a man must have had carrying out these duties.'

Thumann's wife was called later in the day in an effort to inject some human quality into the defence. Irma Thumann was from Bavaria. She'd married Anton Thumann in 1939. They had two children, a boy and a girl, four and one. At the beginning of what must have been a peculiar married life, they'd lived in Dachau for a year. Then they'd moved to Lublin before being posted to Neuengamme. Whilst there, said Frau Thumann, she would come to see her husband in the officers' mess every day.

Did she see and speak to inmates then? Yes, though she only remembered one conversation, with a prisoner called August Meyer. He had told her that concentration camps were necessary.

Necessary?

Yes. There were a 'big number of sub-human elements', he'd told her, who needed to be controlled.

Was it likely such a conversation in the officers' mess ever took place? It sounded contrived, absurd. A fabrication designed to give her some authority of knowledge. But her evidence was that August Meyer, the prisoner she supposedly spoke to, had told her that Thumann was 'very severe and strict but he was very fair and just, and he added "of course there is such a big number of prisoners that he has to be strict to get through the work"'.

Dr Koenig asked her a more direct question: witnesses had claimed her husband was a sadist. What did she have to say to that?

Frau Thumann could only respond that 'all the time I have been with him he showed the greatest tenderness and kind-heartedness towards me and towards my children'. She had been very happy throughout her married life. And to create a picture of the man she lived with she added:

> I would like to thank my husband for every hour I was privileged to spend with him. He loved nature very much and only through his eyes did I get to love nature myself. He loved the flowers and the dogs as well and the children, and he never hit the little one and I had plenty of opportunity to observe the inmates of the camp but I have never seen my husband striking any of them. In Neuengamme I spent the whole afternoon in the office of my husband from 4 o'clock until the roll call and I have never seen him carrying a whip.

What else would you expect a wife to say? It was worthless. A pathetic attempt to provide a character reference.

And no one had mentioned a whip to her.

The tribunal had heard so much of the institutionalised cruelty of Neuengamme that it hardly mattered whether her husband was good to his dogs and his children. He was second in command of the KZ. He cannot have been blind to the atrocity of the camp. Thumann was condemned by his position and the fact that he'd developed his concentration camp skills at Dachau and Lublin and Auschwitz and Groß-Rosen. He'd been through the deadliest of camps, acquiring a reputation for extreme cruelty along the way. Neuengamme just happened to be his last posting, forced there by the closure of Majdanek in the face of the advancing Russians.

Despite the dubious value of cross-examining Frau Thumann, Major Stewart did so. It may have seemed an opportunity to unmask the indifference of *all* those associated with the camps, including the sweet wife of one of its senior officials.

He quizzed her about her daily visits to Neuengamme. He wondered whether she had a pass into the camp, but it seemed she had waltzed in each day, ushered in by the guards without any trouble or formality. That much at least was believable. No one would have troubled the wife of Anton Thumann.

Stewart asked her how she came to be speaking to the prisoner August Meyer. Where did he work? In the cookhouse, she said. Where did she see him? In the cookhouse. She ate her meals there. And did the prisoner really say that concentration camps were necessary? Yes. And that subhuman elements were there? Yes. She said, 'I had a very friendly understanding with the inmates, and I must say they were very kind and nice to me.'

Major Stewart ridiculed her testimony. He didn't have to suggest she was lying. He didn't need to. He simply had to ask a few questions and let her appear absurd. If she'd really been in the camp every day, wouldn't she have seen the ill-treatment? Wouldn't she have seen the whips and truncheons? About a half of all those who'd entered Neuengamme died there. Every day there were fatalities. People died of starvation and beatings. No one disputed that. But she was oblivious, or so she claimed. Maybe it was true that she hadn't seen her husband doing anything atrocious. But she would have seen something. What did that make her? An accomplice? Perhaps she should have been in the dock too if the principle of guilt by association was anything to go by. Instead, she appeared as a character witness.

11.

Of course, I could stop here, leave the Neuengamme trial with the arch-criminals, as Justice Jackson and the Allies had called the culprits they wanted to hunt down and prosecute. But that would be to ignore the depth of cruelty evident in this hearing. Atrocity wasn't confined to the senior officers. Retribution couldn't be either.

Adolf Speck, a name I'd seen mentioned in Walter Freud's investigations, was a *Rottenführer*, a section leader. It was a lowly position in the SS hierarchy. An underling, a grunt. On 16 April 1946, as Alfred Rosenberg, chief ideologue of the Nazi party, the man who gave expression to the anti-Semitic beliefs that purportedly justified extermination, was being cross-examined in the courtroom across Germany, in Nuremberg, displaying his intellectual prowess, such as it was,

SS-Rottenführer Adolf Speck took the stand in the Curiohaus. Dr Oestmann was his lawyer and began the examination of his client.

Speck was thirty-five years old. He was married with eight children. Originally a farm worker like his father, he'd joined the SA in 1932, though for a time his membership had lapsed. He'd lost his job and couldn't pay the subscriptions. When war broke out he'd responded to an appeal on the local radio to join the Hamburg police. He'd liked the prospect of a pension, he said. It wasn't long, though, before his unit became merged with an SS police division. And in the French and then Russian campaigns, his unit developed into a fighting group. He said he'd fought at Leningrad and was decorated. But when his three brothers had been killed, leaving him as the only surviving son, he'd been transferred away from the fighting; a little like a German version of *Saving Private Ryan*, I thought. In 1943 he'd been posted to Neuengamme and instructed in the duties of *Blockführer*, commander of one of the prisoner barracks, those long sheds whose imprint I'd seen in the grounds of the camp.

At first, he said, he'd been told it was forbidden to beat inmates. But the instruction changed immediately after training was complete. He didn't know why. And so he'd struck prisoners from then on.

In September 1943, he was put in charge of the Clinker works where they made bricks, and in December moved to the general production centre. It was tough work and he had to discipline the prisoners frequently. But, he claimed, he'd only used a cane. It had been 60 to 70 centimetres long and one centimetre in diameter. He would use it on the transport troop 'if they didn't get a move on'. He denied the accusations that he'd acted like a madman, tearing about the works, laying into the prisoners with whatever tool or instrument he could pick up. He denied Lüdke's accusation that he'd kicked a prisoner to death. He denied that he'd been responsible for other deadly beatings. He said he wasn't the 'most feared of the SS in the camp', he wasn't the murderer of the production works, as witnesses for the prosecution had claimed.

But he did admit his involvement in the transport of the twenty Jewish children to Bullenhuser Damm. He said he'd been told they were being taken to the Swedish Red Cross. All he'd done, he said, was wait in the lorry as Dr Trzebinski and Dreimann took the children inside the building. They returned about half an hour later alone, their 'duties' complete. Then they'd driven to another location in Hamburg to pick up a party of Russian prisoners. Back to Bullenhuser Damm school. Four of the Russians had been hauled out and taken away, leaving Speck, he said, to guard the remainder. Thirty minutes later, two SS men named Jauch and Frahm had come back to pick up another four prisoners. When they'd reappeared to collect a third batch, the prisoners refused to leave the lorry. And then suddenly, Speck recalled, the prisoners had made a rush out of the back of the truck. There'd been a struggle. Speck had shot one with his pistol, but some of the Russians got away. They chased after them but caught none of them.

When they'd returned to the truck, Dr Trzebinski told him to take the body of the Russian into the building and down into the cellar. There he'd seen a pile of corpses, though no children were amongst them.

Speck said, 'I left the cellar, washed my hands and returned to the lorry.'

That was his story.

Major Stewart cross-examined with evident frustration. He quizzed Speck about the transport of the children to Bullenhuser Damm school.

'Did you speak to the children?'

'No.'

'You never said as much as a word to them throughout the journey?'

'No.'

'Weren't you interested in where these children were going?'

'Thumann told us the children were going to the Swedish Red Cross.'

And as far as the Russian prisoners were concerned: did he wonder where they were going when taken inside?

'I don't know. Nobody told us.'

It was exasperating. Acidly, Stewart said, 'You may be a very stupid man, but you have been endowed by the gods with the gift of consecutive thought. Will you please use it? You knew the children were going to the Swedish Red Cross and I ask you where do you think the men were going when they were being fetched in bodies of four and taken into the house and didn't return?'

'I don't know.'

'When you saw what you so charmingly described as a heap of human beings did it become clear to you then what was happening?'

'Yes.'

'Did you realise that these people had been executed?'

'Yes.'

That was the most Stewart could extract. Questioning continued for some minutes but 'I don't know' was the most frequent of answers. Unlike Thumann, his defence rested on ignorance. Nothing happened in front of him, he saw nothing, he remembered little. Ill-treatment did not occur under his command apart from a little discipline he'd had to exert over the transport troop. And he'd only killed someone, by his own admission, when he shot the Russian escapee in self-defence.

There was little difference, it seemed to me, between this low-ranking SS official and the men standing accused in Nuremberg. Alfred Rosenberg might have been the furthest removed: he was indicted for

Developing and promoting the doctrinal techniques of the conspiracy, in developing and promoting beliefs and practices incompatible with Christian teaching, in subverting the influences of the churches over the German people, in pursuing the program of relentless persecution of the Jews, and in reshaping the educational system in order to make the German people amenable to the will of the conspirators and to prepare the people psychologically for waging an aggressive war.

It was an intellectual if long-winded charge. Rosenberg was the man who had given Nazism a pseudo-academic veneer, writing books on the Jews that sought to make credible a state policy of anti-Semitism.

When cross-examined by Thomas Dodd, the American prosecutor, he too presented a face of knowing but not partaking. There was a difference of scale, but like Speck, though he knew of 'excesses' (that description again hiding no end of malevolence), he'd distanced himself from them. He may not have been in the truck outside the execution chamber, but Rosenberg was deep within the Nazi system and knew that 'Schweinerei' happened. He presented himself as the 'benign philosopher', an intellectual Speck, if you will. Even though his official position of Reich Minister for the Occupied Eastern Territories made him responsible for the area where so many atrocities had been committed, he did not accept he was connected to them. Both men, regardless of their station, claimed they had no responsibility for any of the terrible things that had been done.

12.

If Speck was at the lower end of the SS hierarchy, Wilhelm Bahr was at its very base. His status was so contemptible that even the charge referred to him as 'Willi'. No one could interpret his role in the camp as central to its functioning. But despite his utterly inferior position, or perhaps because of it, he was crucial for the prosecution, for the whole Neuengamme case, for understanding the degradation that the KZ system imposed on all within it. He stood with Himmler as opposite bookends of the criminal enterprise that was the SS and the concentration camp network. From the practice of gassing the Russian prisoners to incidental and regular killing that couldn't even be called 'execution' if that word was supposed to convey legalised punishment, to the experimentation on prisoners, to the blind obedience to every and any command, Bahr was evidence of a people corrupted and corrupt to the core.

Bahr's lawyer had already expressed doubt about his client's capacity for rational thought. Investigators and prosecutors and defence lawyers alike saw Bahr as a man of such limited intelligence that there had to be doubt about his mental capacity. Ghoulishly stupid. But the prosecution machine couldn't countenance a defence of insanity. It was not dissimilar from the approach to Rudolf Hess in Nuremberg. There, too, was a defendant who displayed insanity at every step: Hess wouldn't appear in the witness box at the tribunal and ultimately would be condemned despite that. To acknowledge mental incapacity would have been to show leniency for a major figure in the rise of Nazism and the beginnings of war. Whatever Hess's deportment in court, however bizarre it was, the presumption had to be that he was sane, that all these crimes were committed by sane men and women even though they made no sense.

Willi Bahr's actions defied the notion of sense, though. He had been Neuengamme's chief killer by his own account. From early on after his arrest, his story had been consistent. He'd worked in the hospital and injected a stream of prisoners with phenol over a protracted period of time. More than a thousand had been killed in this fashion. It was direct. Bahr had done as he was commanded, but he'd done it nonetheless. A thousand prisoners, killing an almost daily occurrence. Mass murder in the guise of medical treatment. And that wasn't all. Willi Bahr admitted to obeying the order to gas nearly two hundred Russian prisoners using Zyklon B. He hadn't judged his actions at the time, made no complaint and voiced no opposition.

Later, Bahr's lawyer would deliver a speech in his defence. There was no doubt about guilt: Bahr had confessed. But Dr Kroell, his attorney, posed the argument: Bahr was 'intellectually inferior to a high degree' and this condition made him incapable of challenging any order, even one which could have been judged objectively as 'illegal'. 'The overwhelming majority of the German people had, through years of propaganda and terrorist methods,' Dr Kroell would say, 'succumbed to a psychosis so that their ideas of justice became more and more confused.' A collective incapacity that made opposition impossible. And Bahr feared disobedience would bring about his own destruction. How could he be culpable when so conditioned?

It was an argument that could not be allowed to succeed. Moral responsibility would be reduced to an IQ test or simply an assumption that everyone in the country had been duped. What would that say about our humanity? 'Crimes *against* humanity' related as much to the perpetrators as to the victims: these were crimes because they were carried out by human beings against human beings. Bahr was one agent who made that possible. Let him escape and who would be left to take the blame?

Willi Bahr may have been the lowest of the low but he was a crucial figure. He couldn't have known this, let alone cared about it. His capacity for any thought for his position was either non-existent or very well suppressed. But he was the man who linked Neuengamme and all those in power there to Auschwitz, to the phenomenon of extermination through gassing, and to the institutionally approved killing of anyone without due cause or sanction. Of all the figures I came across in the British trials, I thought Bahr was the one who should have been called to give his evidence before the tribunal of the Major War Criminals at Nuremberg. If one so lowly could have been trusted to use the gas Zyklon B in order to kill nearly two hundred Russian prisoners *and* spend his time in the camps disposing of sick inmates by injecting them with petrol, Bahr showed how the whole system was debased from top to bottom.

13.

On 2 May 1946, Judge Advocate Carl Stirling summed up the Neuengamme case for the benefit of the officers on the panel and the few members of the public and press still watching. He said,

> The case for the prosecution is that year in, year out, day in and day out there was a system at this camp based on over-work, under-nourishment, insufficient clothing, brutality, *Appel*, ill-using them in air raids, lack of sleep, inattention in the medical ward and all the other things you have heard; and the case for the prosecution is that

every one of the accused in the dock, starting with the commandant
Pauly down to that man Bahr, was each in his own way and in his
own sphere not merely being in the camp behaving decently and doing
what he could in his duty but that they all were actively supporting
and maintaining this abominable system and that it was such a system
that any man of ordinary intellect must have known that what was
going on would inevitably cause suffering and in many cases the death
of people for whom they had the responsibility of looking after.

It was hardly the most articulate of summaries. Any newspaper
reporter would have had to translate the clumsy sentences so that
their readers could follow the logic, *if* they'd been interested in the
case, that is.

Stirling qualified his reasoning immediately. He said that, in his
view, 'justice cannot be done if you convict a man merely because
he was on the staff of the Neuengamme camp'. It was a theme he'd
carried over from his Belsen trial summary: each accused had to be
shown to have committed some act of illegitimate violence. There
were few difficulties in this case. Stirling addressed all the evidence
against each of the accused and the defences they had presented. He
was fair, noting any points in the defendants' favour. From Max Pauly
down he reviewed their testimony and the proof there was against
them. When he came to Bahr it was as though he threw up his hands
in despair.

'There seems very little I can do as Judge Advocate on behalf of
Bahr,' he said.

Was there a hint of sympathy? Or resignation?

He said to the panel, 'I am sure the court will form a view as to
his intellectual capacity … You have to consider in the light of the
evidence whether Willi Bahr was really so stupid as is made out and
whether he really was objecting to carrying out the orders which
were undoubtedly given to him.' Did he have the intelligence to
think it was right to inject phenol and petrol into helpless prisoners
or gas the two hundred Russian POWs? 'I do not want to be hard
on Willi Bahr,' said Stirling, 'and I am perfectly prepared to put him
before you as a man of limited intelligence who was exploited by
his superiors; but I am not prepared to put before you … that at any

time he was insane in the sense that we require, that he did not know the nature and quality of his act or, if he did, that he did not know it was wrong.'

After more than a day of analysing the evidence, Stirling gradually brought proceedings to a close.

All the accused were found guilty. The defence lawyers made their pleas in mitigation. Dr Weissig, for Max Pauly, quoted Dostoevsky and noted the 'dumb cadaverous obedience, which was bred in the Third Reich and particularly in the SS'. It made no impact on the judging panel. Pauly, Thumann, Dr Trzebinski, Speck and Bahr were all sentenced to death. No one was acquitted this time.

The verdict attracted little attention. This was the extent of the *Times'* report:

> The trial of the staff of the Neugammer concentration camp closed
> in Hamburg this afternoon, when sentences of death by hanging were
> passed on Max Pauly, commandant of the camp, and on 10 others of
> the 14 defendants. Sentences of imprisonment for long terms were
> passed on the remaining three. The charge against the prisoners was
> that of ill-treating and causing the death of 40,000 allied nationals.
> Evidence was produced during the trial that experiments were carried
> out on children which led to their deaths.[18]

They couldn't spell the camp's name properly. The speck of detail concerning the children was misleading. It wasn't clear whether the trial was run by the British. Despite the weeks of proceedings, this was all the newspaper of the establishment had to say.

Throughout the proceedings no one reported on how the inmates of Neuengamme KZ came to leave the camp, make the treacherous journey to Lübeck and on to Neustadt, be unloaded from their cattle trucks onto ships in the bay, become pressed into the holds of those ships as barely living cargo, and then, when liberation was no more than a few hours away, were attacked by RAF fighter-bombers so that within a matter of minutes 7,000 of them had drowned, been burned, blown to bits or machine-gunned by the British aircraft, only for the survivors to be left to die in the water by their guards and shot at again by Germans troops if they managed to make the shore.

The prosecutors and defence lawyers were loath to mention the sordid details. As I flicked through the transcript and read the submissions and the arguments and the testimony delivered in that grand building in Hamburg, I could only find passing, reluctant reference to the disaster. The omission seemed to have troubled the Deputy Judge Advocate, but there had been little he could do to change the course of proceedings. When Phillip Jackson, the teenager who was the first to be interviewed by Noel Till in Neustadt, had appeared as a witness he'd been asked about the Dutch 'Torsperre' condemned to death, and had said they'd all been hanged, all 'except a matter of two or three', one of whom, he'd said, 'was on the *Cap Arcona* and was saved'. I thought immediately of Piet Ketelaar and his high-pitched voice recalling his escape, but perhaps Jackson had meant another Dutchman. Yet the mention of the ship had alerted Stirling. He'd interrupted the prosecution. He'd been confused. Why hadn't the court been told about the catastrophic number of deaths? He'd asked Jackson to tell them what had happened. Major Stewart explained that the disaster didn't form part of the charge so there was no need to address it in evidence.

Stirling was entitled to quiz the witness and, despite Stewart's explanation, he'd taken the opportunity to ask Jackson about those days after he left Neuengamme.

'We were taken by rail to Lübeck, there we remained about ten days in the trucks on the quayside while other prisoners were being loaded in the ship. Eventually we were loaded on the ship *Thielbek* on 2 May in the morning and we sailed from Lübeck in the afternoon.'

'For where?'

'For a place in Lübeck Bay which was actually in front of Neustadt.'

'Then what happened?'

'Then on 3 May at 3.30 p.m. we were sunk by the RAF.'

'By bombs?'

'Yes.'

'And you survived and your father was drowned, is that correct?'

'Yes.'

'Were you still prisoners or did you gather you had been released?'

'We were still prisoners on the ships.'

Major Stewart had been forced to intervene. Now that the Judge Advocate had shown an interest he couldn't ignore it any longer.

'Will you tell the court how you were evacuated from Neuengamme Camp?' Stewart had asked Jackson, re-examining him.

'We were evacuated by rail in cattle trucks, fifty in a truck, and I was with the revier [sick bay] with the sick.'

They were in there from 9 p.m. until midday the next day. They didn't receive any food on the journey. Then 2,000 prisoners were put on board the SS *Thielbek*.

'Will you describe to the court the conditions below deck where you were kept?'

'The conditions below deck were appalling. There were two floors, actually the bottom of the ship. The people were so packed that it was quite difficult to lie down ... There were quite a number of sick people ... and the stench was absolutely appalling. We were in very, very poor conditions.'

'Was there a white flag or a Red Cross sign or any indication on the ship to indicate to the Royal Air Force that the cargo of the ships were human beings and prisoners as opposed to military objectives?'

'No, there was absolutely no such flag. There was a German flag.'

That was the limit of his knowledge and Stirling had allowed the proceedings to move on, though it must have festered, for later, when Max Pauly had been giving evidence, Stirling had intervened once again. Someone had to be responsible for the single largest killing of the prisoners, 7,000 or more, aboard those ships.

Stirling asked Pauly, 'What was the idea at the back of moving all these people from the concentration camp at Neuengamme somewhere else? Why could they not have been left there so as to be taken over by the Allies?'

Pauly said the liberation of Buchenwald, the publication of the photographs, caused the *SS-Reichsführer* Himmler to order Neuengamme's evacuation.

'Where were they going to be put?'

Pauly said the SS commander in Hamburg had the idea to move them to Schleswig-Holstein. To an island.

'Were you going with them?'

'Yes.'

But he hadn't. He went to Bullenhuser Damm first, where the children had been killed. And soon after he'd been captured by the British Army. He knew nothing more about the inmates.

Stirling had heard enough. He'd been bemused that Stewart hadn't made anything of the matter. He'd asked him directly whether he thought the tragic deaths of the prisoners weren't connected with the charge that the accused had violated the laws of war. Wasn't the evacuation under terrible conditions, as various inmate witnesses had testified and no one had disputed, 'one of the most serious kinds of ill-treatment' presented to the court?

Stubbornly Stewart altered none of his thinking. The evacuation, the sinking of the *Cap Arcona* and other ships and the resulting huge loss of life, wasn't part of the case against the men in the dock. But, he'd said, key figures would be appearing later for the defence. General Bassewitz-Behr and *Gauleiter* Kaufmann, the men who'd come up with the idea of evacuation to the ships, were due to give evidence. They might satisfy Stirling's curiosity.

Indeed, Karl Kaufmann, then in custody awaiting his own trial, had been called by Dr Weissig as a witness for Pauly. Kaufmann had been *Gauleiter* of Hamburg, a Nazi party leader for the region, as well as *Reichsstadthalter* and chief commissioner for transport. It was the highest administrative position in the city. Although the camp hadn't come within his jurisdiction he'd said he'd visited three times, to view the brickworks and suchlike. When asked about the evacuation of Neuengamme he'd said, 'At the beginning and middle of March, Count Bassewitz-Behr who was the senior SS police officer came to me almost daily and told me that in his area there were a large number of prisoners of war and refugees owing to the advance of the Eastern and Western fronts.' He was told about gross overcrowding at Neuengamme. Kaufmann claimed that the Danish consul had asked him to help the Red Cross take the Scandinavians away. He'd asked Pauly to release them, which eventually happened when higher authority approved. He'd then tried to persuade Bassewitz-Behr to 'get the Swedish or Danish Red Cross to also assist the other prisoners in their release', and advised Bassewitz-Behr to move the prisoners overland to Denmark. But Bassewitz-Behr thought the risk of bombing was too great. Kaufmann had said he knew that Bassewitz-Behr had tried to get ships for the prisoners, for their transport to Sweden. It was only much later that he'd found out what had happened.[19]

When Bassewitz-Behr had come as a witness too, he'd admitted he had given the order for taking the prisoners onto the ships. And he'd admitted that a command had been received from Berlin that the inmates of concentration camps were not under any circumstances to be allowed to fall into enemy hands.

'Where were they to land these people?'

'They should remain in the bay at Neustadt.'

'Anchor in the bay and where would they land?'

'My idea was that in the case of an Armistice to ask Himmler to get permission to bring those people from the bay in Neustadt to Sweden.'

He'd said he didn't know that Pauly hadn't gone with the prisoners. He knew nothing: about the camp, about the ill-treatment, about the conditions, about the experiments, about the children.[20] Nothing more could be extracted from the defendants, the witnesses or from the prosecution. There was to be no explanation or scrutiny of any distinction.

At the very last moment of the trial, during his summing up, Carl Stirling had let one last reference enter the record. The prosecution's decision to ignore it as part of the indictment troubled him, but he had no power to alter the case against Pauly, the only man on trial here who would have had direct responsibility for putting the inmates on those ships.

Stirling had said, 'Why it was necessary to move these unfortunate people I do not know; but the prosecution are not making it part of their case and therefore I leave it as a matter of history as to how this camp ended.'

There it was: the plea to history, a plea directly to me, I felt, sitting in the air-conditioned reading room of the British National Archives. There was no easy resolution for the victims of the *Cap Arcona* and the other bombed ships. Those who'd died in the camps had been represented in this court. Those who'd died outside during the evacuation had not. Stirling's close of proceedings was exactly one year after the thousands of Neuengamme prisoners perished on the ships in Neustadt Bay. It was 3 May 1946. The anniversary went unmarked.

14.

Press interest in war crimes, in prosecuting the Nazis at all levels, was seeping away. That much was clear. Ten days after the Neuengamme proceedings the American-run Mauthausen KZ case concluded with all defendants convicted and fifty-eight death sentences handed down. That too only warranted a paragraph in *The Times*.[21] Two weeks later, another camp commandant, Martin Gottfried Weiss of Dachau, and fourteen other personnel were hanged in Landsberg prison.[22]

The superficial coverage led me to think all the concentration camp cases had become reduced to a few short paragraphs of mundane announcements or the occasional lurid anecdote. And it made me think that Judge Advocate Stirling's surrender of the *Cap Arcona* to history was already underway for the camps and the evils they sustained too. The grand and furious programme of retribution was losing its soul as he signed off yet another trial.

9

Nuremberg

1.

Perhaps by the time I visited Nuremberg, entering its outskirts from the direction of Munich, I was too full of tales of atrocity and fragile, possibly fruitless trials, evidence of a fury more vented than practised. Perhaps I'd reached that point on a pilgrimage when doubt, induced by the contemplation of finishing the journey, questioned its premise and wisdom. More likely it was the disappointment at what I could see, driving into the city from the south, along Route 73 and then towards Galgenhof, straight into the Luitpoldhain and its broad parkland.

As soon as I saw the open city field I recognised something from the car window. I parked at the roadside and walked towards the sturdy concrete structure that had caught my eye between the trees. Its rear was a wall of grey slab tarnished with eight decades of weather stains. Rounding the structure didn't improve the sight. Several plinths guarded both sides of a wide sloping terrace leading to a three-storey-high nine-arched altar. It was bleak, thickly concreted and cold. Turning around I could see a grassy expanse. This was the place, I knew, where thousands of German troops and SS and SA storm troopers gathered

in perfect positioning, flanking an avenue along which Hitler and
Himmler walked in 1934. This was where the might of the Nazis was
presented as a demonstration of power, resolve, intent. Here, on the
periphery of the city, the magnitude of their power was displayed to
Germany and to the world.

Standing in the remains of the Hall of Honour, where Hitler
presided over the commemoration of the dead, I could imagine how
overwhelming the display of massed support must have been. I didn't
think this was only 'dumb cadaverous obedience', as Max Pauly's
lawyer had called it. A deeper and more conscious commitment to
the message and to the means offered by the Nazis seemed to me
more likely.

And then I wondered how so many seemingly ordinary men and
women could have been infected by such an epidemic of inhumanity
that they would allow a world, even their own, to be destroyed in
their name and, for many, with their connivance, and, for some,
with their delight.

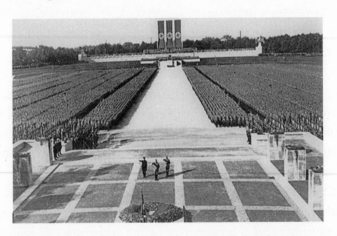

But I remembered Primo Levi cautioning against interpreting the
Nazi case as unique, either in history or as a possibility for the future.
He warned about the facility of any society to be overcome by loathing
for a distinct people or race or religion, telling a story over and over
again to the point when it became 'true' beyond contradiction. It isn't
a distant danger. The risk of public and politicians and press conspiring
in the creation of a myth of hatred that provokes violence and war
is ever-present. Levi wrote,

Many people – many nations – can find themselves holding, more or less wittingly, that 'every stranger is an enemy'. For the most part this conviction lies deep down like some latent infection; it betrays itself only in random, disconnected acts, and does not lie at the base of a system of reason. But when this does come about, when the unspoken dogma becomes the major premise in a syllogism, then, at the end of the chain, there is the *Lager*.[1]

Facing out from the ugly Luitpold Arena monument, no more than a concrete monstrosity now if it had ever been anything else, I thought about Levi and his thesis. I thought how in 2002 I like many others had marched against the impending invasion of Iraq by the US and Britain. I did so for a number of reasons. Many aspects had worried me. I understood the argument that Saddam Hussein was a tyrant responsible for terrible oppression and crimes against humanity and was capable of more. But I didn't believe the proposed attack was properly considered. I didn't believe it was legal, for what that judgement was worth, a judgement founded on the principles enshrined in this city of Nuremberg and the Allies' grand gesture of condemnation of aggressive war. I also worried that a hostile occupation of Iraq could lead to many innocents suffering. The seemingly insatiable need for 'intelligence' was unlikely to be discriminating when faced with Iraqis, civilian or otherwise, caught up in the business (and it is a business now) of incarceration, interrogation, punishment. Guantanamo Bay was already an iconic representation of the dangers, a pitiless place that could too easily be replicated on a grander scale.

So it proved. The year after the invasion, once British occupation of southern Iraq had become entrenched, I'd then become involved on the periphery of a legal action, offering occasional and informal advice about aspects of law that might be relevant.[2] The matter concerned a number of Iraqi civilians killed by British troops in Basra, on the streets, in homes or in an army base. Baha Mousa was the one who'd died in custody, in the headquarters of the 1st Battalion of the Queen's Lancashire Regiment. The details were sparse though. Mousa was working in a hotel as a receptionist, arrested by British soldiers looking for insurgents, taken into custody for questioning. Thirty-six hours later he was dead. Any death in custody is worthy of investigation. There's always the chance that some violence has been done, some cruelty unleashed sufficient to end a man's life without cause. And with that possibility comes the questions: what law applies? What standards of behaviour should be expected of the soldiers involved? If I'm honest, they were for me at that moment rational, academic, legal conundrums.

Then I'd been shown the post-mortem report and photographs of Baha Mousa's body. They showed a face distorted, almost unrecognisable, bloodied and swollen. A torso livid with huge swathes of bruising the size of footballs. Wrists with rings of cut flesh. A strangulation line across the throat. These were pictures of someone mauled over a protracted period of time, tortured, beaten and treated as ... what? A *Häftlinge*, a 'Muselmann', as they called them in the concentration camps, someone who had no future, no past, who was a thing to be dealt with, a thing without a name, only a number, 'the demolition of a man', as Levi wrote; a person subjected to 'useless violence ... occasionally having a purpose, yet always redundant, always disproportionate to the purpose itself'.

As I'd learned more about the death of Mousa, examined the details of his detention, the 'demolition' of this man provoked eerie echoes of another time. But I asked myself: was it absurd to suggest any kind of comparison between the suffering endured by Mousa and the men detained with him and those millions of inmates in the German concentration camps?

It would be tempting to say 'yes' and refute any meaningful link. No one could compare the whole system of the *Lager*, from labour to extermination camps, lightly; that would undermine the conviction that what was perpetrated by the Nazis represented a nadir for humanity. If it was the worst that humankind could do, then all other monstrous acts were, by definition, lesser wrongs. And wouldn't it diminish our understanding of the Nazi system to equate (rather than simply compare) it with the terrible actions of bad men (and women) whenever and wherever they may happen?

But it seemed to me that to deny *any* connection, to suggest that there were easily separable categories of brutality, would be equally absurd. Not because there was some identification of thought or ideology behind Mousa's murder as part of a mass exercise in torture or extermination. Nor because the circumstances and conditions of that British Army base in Basra resembled in any way the operation of a concentration camp. Nor because the whole culture of the British Army may have been infected with a violent hatred for everyone who appeared alien and different and dangerous. Nor that the British nation had become beset by obedience to a warped ideology. None of those characteristics of the Nazi and German experience could have been applied, or at least I didn't have the evidence to confirm them one way or another. The link was rather in parallel and very personal institutionalised relationships: the relationship between those men who kicked, punched and humiliated the man in their custody, who had his head encased in sandbags and his body assaulted to the point of collapse and death; the relationship between those perpetrators and the people whom they served and whose orders they followed, those officers and officials who shaped the culture of their units; the relationship between those who were sent to undertake the dirty task of fighting and the people who sent them. No matter what the era, institutional brutality always involves such individual and physical and hierarchical connections: the banality of evil enchaining once more those who decide a course of action and those common people, the functionaries and ordinary folk ready to act without asking questions or who turn away without demanding to know what's happening.

That much at least, I believed, was a crucial recognition underpinning all the investigations and trials I'd examined which involved the British after 1945. Guilt attached to those who'd committed personal acts of cruelty *and* those who served to enable systemic wrongs to occur. In that sense, relating what is done in *our* name now to what was done by the most heinous regime we can recall serves a purpose: it's a reminder, or perhaps a test, of the proximity of hatred or indifference, the proximity of the camps. They're always there, those places and institutions of malignancy, lying deep in the imagination to emerge into practice unless we're very, very watchful. Which, of course, too frequently, we're not.

Seven British soldiers were prosecuted in relation to the killing of Baha Mousa and ill-treatment of nine other Iraqi civilians held with him. There was a trial. Evidence was brought and witnesses examined. All were acquitted of having any responsibility for the death. Though the result might have been questionable, the process was sacred and it followed the form used in all the British trials after 1945.[3] But the matter didn't end there. After I'd finished writing the book on Baha Mousa I began to learn of similar stories. More allegations were brought to the High Court. They spoke of insidious treatment: sexual abuse, threats of execution, of being sent to Guantanamo. There were multiple allegations of forced nakedness; threats of rape against detainees or their family members; coercion into simulated sexual positions; sleep deprivation; persistent and prolonged use of hooding with sand or cement bags in suffocating temperatures; sound bombardment; mock execution; the playing of pornographic videos outside cell doors; and beatings. They were not the accumulation of isolated reports, arising against various units in army posts across southern Iraq. The allegations related to a small number of mass detention centres, camps designed to detain Iraqis suspected of being involved in insurgent action of some kind and to subject them to questioning. The British and Americans needed a place to hold people and carry out their interrogations.

Apart from localised army bases, such as Battle Group Main in Basra, where Baha Mousa was held and killed, there were Shaibah Logistics Base, Camp Abu Naji, Camp Bucca, Camp Breadbasket, Camp Akka. And a British outfit called the Joint Forward Interrogation Team (JFIT), which specialised in questioning techniques and were responsible for extracting intelligence, operated in little compounds within some of these camps. Gradually allegations about their methods emerged. Whether true or not, the allegations have been made before the courts in Britain and some have been passed to the Iraq Historic Allegations Team set up by the Ministry of Defence in 2010 to investigate. At the time of writing, more than a thousand cases have been lodged with them.[4]

Standing at the Luitpold Arena it occurred to me that the point of Nuremberg and all those trials under the terms of British justice was to show that the standards to be applied in the judgement of *anyone* suspected of war crimes, of international crimes, would be the same no matter who they were or where those crimes were committed. Justice was to be done for the victims, for all offended to the core by the infliction of an unnecessary and indiscriminate brutality. That applied to Britain as to anywhere else. Of course, I knew that since the judgment in 1946 nobody has been prosecuted for the crime of aggression. Despite the construction of an International Criminal Court in 1998 (a successor to the spirit of Nuremberg), that offence remains outside the ambit of international legal action, opposed by the major world powers; there will be no criminal action with regard to the 2003 Iraq War. Many people have, however, been brought before international tribunals since 1990 to answer charges of war crimes, genocide and crimes against humanity. All those proceedings in The Hague against those responsible for atrocities in the Former Yugoslavia, and in Rwanda, and in other areas of conflict, have their roots in the great trial conducted here in this German city. And those investigated, if not prosecuted, in Britain for crimes committed in Iraq are, whether we like it or not, inextricably linked with the British trials of 1945 onwards. They were linked, too, I thought, with the flaws and errors and political indifference and diminishing enthusiasm that eventually defined them. It made me angry. Not because the allegations were necessarily true. I have not seen enough evidence to decide one way or another. I was angry because after the death of Baha Mousa and all I knew about that murder, the national resolve to unpick the truth and prosecute those responsible was absent. I was angry too because for all the rhetoric of justice and intolerance of impunity for war crimes and atrocity, I thought history was once again more likely to be the judge than a court of law.[5]

★ ★ ★

I walked away from the Arena, returned to my car, and then drove the couple of miles to the Palace of Justice. Seventy years ago the *Daily Mail* had described what was left of the city: 'It is a jewel no longer. It is little but a heap of ruins, its roads mere alleys between mountains of rubble, its once-beautiful houses but shells and blind walls. Its people live here like rats in sewers.'[6] Areas remain pockmarked by that destruction, but the extraordinary rehabilitation, economically, politically and socially, of Germany over the intervening time has transformed this place. The Palace of Justice has been maintained and refurbished and looks unblemished by its history. Like the Luitpold Arena, it too is inhabited by myth, though I'd like to believe a myth of virtue for the most part.

It was late in the afternoon, but the Palace was still open. I toured the exhibition, detailed and honest as so many of these commemorations of justice are, and then wandered into the original courtroom. I sat on one of the benches looking up to the judges' high-backed leather chairs, everyone hushed as though in church. Those other trials across Germany I'd examined came to mind. I wondered whether they'd achieved anything between them all. Some men and women had been put to death or sentenced to imprisonment, but beyond those small retributive acts (small relative to the scale of crimes committed and the numbers of those who'd committed them or been associated with them or enabled them to happen by their silence), what had been accomplished? Who remembered them really?

And then I thought how Nuremberg, the court, the procedure, meant little without all those 'minor' war crimes trials. If Britain and the USA and France and the Soviet Union and all those occupied countries hadn't prosecuted the killers and torturers then the proceedings in this courtroom would have been diminished and more easily dismissed as tokenistic. The prosecutor Thomas Dodd had promised that the scenes of mass suffering shown in films and documents and heard from witnesses would be punished by the Allies. Of course all the defendants, the Major War Criminals, would be held to account for bringing about war and the conditions for persecution and slaughter, but that would have been undermined if the individuals who'd carried out the atrocities weren't brought to justice too. Those investigations and trials I'd scrutinised defined Nuremberg and gave it meaning, completed it as a web of retribution.

It also occurred to me that in contributing to this grand scheme, a myth of modern Britain's own virtue was founded. The justice delivered after the war fixed an image of self-purity in the British historical psyche, one to be trotted out whenever it was needed to define 'us' against the rest of 'them': Britain had fought the Good War and had defeated the evil one; it had seen the horrors committed by that enemy and had not lost its balance; it had joined with others to bring civilised retribution to those who'd deserved it. Whatever else Britain might have done or would do, whatever crimes might be committed, would be wiped cleaner by the memory of that time of controlled and righteous fury.

Like all myths there was truth here. And like all myths there were lies too. What worried me, though, was that the selected memories of that time had so ingrained themselves that 'we' could forgive ourselves anything. We could go to war, we could occupy, we could torture, we could treat people as numbers, we could excuse any violence with the memory of our justice and the myth of our goodness to comfort us. For we were the virtuous, the heroic, and could always say: we distinguished ourselves from 'them', those who ordered invasions, the extermination of peoples, the destruction of individuals, the killing of children, the use of men and women as tools and for experiments. We could say we put them on trial, we treated them fairly, and then we punished them. That had to make us the brighter star.

As the sun poured through the high windows of the Nuremberg courtroom I felt suddenly weary. I no longer cared about the men who had been prosecuted here, who they were or what they said or what became of them. They were insignificant. Those twenty-odd individuals lined up to be condemned for a nation's corruption didn't interest me. They were little different from any other debased politicians or public leaders; people like that have always been amongst us. Every society has them, though perhaps not conjoining to such extremes. There have been (and remain) men and women who've held positions of power in Britain and made decisions that have deliberately taken lives and meted out suffering in pursuit of some dubious policy or interest or notion of security. We will never be rid of such unscrupulous men and women. Goering, Hess, Speer, Rosenberg and the rest – who were they but mythic figures deemed necessary to subject to months of ritualistic confrontation so that no one could doubt they were in the wrong and everything they did was hateful and fraudulent? Their evil reflected the Allies' goodness. They could even serve to absorb the guilt of their enemy. By placing blame on the Germans for the Katyn Forest massacre perpetrated by the Soviets they were put in the same position as the Gadarene pigs, chosen by Jesus to take within them the demons of others. They were men who deserved nothing more.

In comparison, I thought, those individuals like Pauly and Thumann and Speck and Bahr and Grese and Klein and Frahm and Jauch and Trzebinski and all those brought before the British trials were the ones who needed to be examined and their characters dissected, their stories told, believed, understood, because they were closer and more familiar and more connected to me and to those I identified as 'us' than I cared to admit.

2.

The scheme of retribution ground on remorselessly throughout the spring and into the early summer of 1946. A bevy of cases pursued by the British were heard, though proceedings at Nuremberg dominated attention as each defendant had the opportunity to take the stand and justify his actions and position within the Nazi hierarchy. Some did so successfully. Hans Fritzsche, a rather lowly figure in the Nazi-controlled press division and Propaganda Ministry, was adamant that his work had nothing to do with the crimes charged. Under cross-examination by General Rudenko, the Soviet prosecutor, he admitted only 'that German propaganda spread the racial theory but I deny most emphatically that German propaganda had made preparations for, or had called for, the mass murder of Jews'.[7] He maintained ignorance of atrocities and said he was but a functionary conducting propaganda dictated by his superior, Josef Goebbels. The judges believed him. Hjalmar Schacht, economist and banker for the Reich, was equally convincing as to his innocence. So too Franz von Papen, one-time Chancellor of Germany before Hitler. Though he was a Nazi supporter in general, the evidence presented at the trial couldn't connect him sufficiently to the crime of aggression or any other charge. He'd served most of the war in Turkey as Germany's ambassador. He would be acquitted, although the Soviet judge would register his dissent against the generous judgment given by his three Allied colleagues on the tribunal.

The other defendants were to be found guilty. After months of defence statements and witnesses, and then a period of deliberation, the panel of judges led by its President, Lord Justice Lawrence, began to read out its judgment on 30 September 1946. Over two days,

Lawrence and his colleagues took turns to set out their summary of the tribunal's history, the charges, the evidence, their interpretation of the law. They relied on the Auschwitz commandant Höss and those credible accounts of extermination and atrocity to describe the crimes against humanity, though in truth those testimonies could never have been as impressive as the film of the liberated concentration camps shown to the court the previous November.

The judges then assessed the guilt of each defendant. That element of the judgment didn't last long. Goering was dealt with in a matter of minutes with the conclusion that 'there is nothing to be said in mitigation'. None of the others received any greater attention.

Finally at 2.50 p.m. on 1 October 1946 the sentences were pronounced. Goering, von Ribbentrop, Keitel, Kaltenbrunner, Rosenberg, Frank, Frick, Streicher, Sauckel, Jodl and Seyss-Inquart were sentenced to death. Hess was imprisoned for life, as were Raeder and Funk. The others received ten to twenty years. And so their names were entered into history as the worst of men.

The press indulged themselves. *The Times* registered the process as 'the greatest trial in history, whether for the amazing breadth of its canvas or as a fount of knowledge and guidance for the jurist and the historian'.[8] It made it sound a very academic enterprise and it's not difficult to see why when reading the transcripts for all those months of advocacy. The *Daily Mail* produced an editorial that was more ambivalent about the whole affair. 'What has been its purpose – what its value?' the paper asked. 'The purpose of this trial has been to establish beyond question the fourfold guilt of the Nazis, both as individuals and as a hierarchy. On all four counts the Nazis were double-dyed in guilt, and everyone knew it before even the trial began.' So why was it necessary to 'prosecute, to defend, to give judgment'? The answer the paper gave was 'that for the first time in history a case against a criminal government has been built up, step by step, on unassailable evidence and proved in a way which posterity will be unable to challenge'. And for 'the first time the heads of State have been arraigned before an international tribunal, and in that respect it is unique'. But the newspaper warned that 'Nuremberg has set a dangerous precedent. In the absence of safeguards some nations may mistake its meaning and imagine that it has become proper to arraign and execute the leaders of the losing side merely because they have lost.' It recommended that the procedure followed should be meticulously laid down to protect against such injustice. 'The Nuremberg Tribunal has modelled itself largely on British observances, which are famous for their openness and impartiality.'[9]

The Times was less parochial in its evaluation: 'The long proceedings have made it sufficiently clear to all that the judges have purged their minds of passion, and approached their task with no motive but the desire to do justice according to the law.'[10] It concluded with its own warning: 'Now an even greater responsibility rests upon the peoples and their Governments for giving the rule of law an ever wider and ever more positive jurisdiction until the human rights so cynically and brutally set at naught by the Nazi dogma and its exponents are granted and guaranteed universal observance.'

On 16 October 1946, those sentenced to death were hanged, except for Goering, who'd committed suicide the day before, having somehow obtained or kept hidden on his body a cyanide pill.

The quick delivery of punishment didn't mark the end of the Nuremberg proceedings. The Americans had always been intent on trying representatives of various facets of the Nazi state and its supporters and they still had in custody men whom they considered to be major figures in the commission of the most serious of crimes. The British weren't keen. Though they would support further trials, handing over many suspects they had in custody, they would have no formal role. Nor would the other powers. The US would undertake the prosecutions alone.

That had been predetermined: in January 1946 President Truman had already approved by executive order the continuation of proceedings once the International Military Tribunal had reached its judgment.[11] Justice Jackson was to be replaced by Col Telford Taylor as the Chief of Counsel. Under his direction and over the next two years twelve trials were held. Doctors, leaders of the *Einsatzgruppen* who'd massacred Jews and Soviets as the German army advanced into Russia, members of the Nazi judiciary, industrialists, government ministers, and SS officers including Oswald Pohl, whom the British War Crimes Investigation Team had apprehended, were all prosecuted and the majority found guilty. A relatively small number were executed following the trials; most received prison terms that would be commuted soon after proceedings ended. The vast majority were released in a few years.

3.

Eight days before the Nuremberg defendants were hanged, Max Pauly, Anton Thumann, Dr Trzebinski, Adolf Speck and Willi Bahr, to little acclaim or notice, were executed too.

By the time these penalties were delivered, the British commitment to war crimes trials was unravelling. Group Captain Somerhough and Lt Col Nightingale were overseeing a professional and largely dedicated war crimes investigation operation, but they were being undermined by government insouciance for their task, not that they had ever received unqualified logistical support. In September 1946, they again reformed 'in view of the imminent re-organisation of war crimes investigation in the British zone of Germany and an anticipated change in Government policy'. All investigations were now to be centralised at HQ BAOR, and they would be called the War Crimes Group (North West Europe), served by approximately 76 officers and other ranks making a total of 292, though 'economies have been effected wherever feasible'.[12] This supposedly made them more efficient.

The summer of 1946 also saw the Foreign Office recommending that cases involving the ill-treatment or killing of British troops by the Germans should take priority, with a view to winding up the whole programme sooner rather than later. The Cabinet confirmed the idea in November, and looked towards a discontinuance as soon as practicable.[13] In fact, the emphasis on crimes committed against British service personnel had already been adopted. Cases being pursued as at December 1946 reflected the preference: for No. 1 team nine of their fifteen investigations underway involved the murder of British soldiers or airmen. No. 2 team had eight out of ten, No. 3 eight out of thirteen, No. 4 nine out of eleven, No. 5 eight out of nine.[14] It didn't mean they would ignore more general concentration camp cases, but the appetite for wide-ranging examination of atrocities was diminishing. Over the next year or so, a number of camps were the subject of prosecution: Beendorf, Hamburg-Sasel, Gaggenau, Kiel-Hasse, Lahde-Weser, Hamburg-Neugraben and -Tiefstack, Schandelah, Hannover-Ahlem, satellite camps of Neuengamme where familiar conditions and killings had occurred. The British pursued each one to trial, prosecuting those few SS members whom they'd been able to find. Nevertheless, there had been over seventy-five of these sub-camps of varying size that had operated during the war. The investigators couldn't pursue them all, not once preference for crimes committed against British troops had been made policy.

And apart from the investigation into Ravensbrück KZ, where British interest was piqued by the ill-treatment and killing of women SOE agents in the camp, it was determined by the end of 1946 that '[w]ork on cases of concentration camps not in the British Zone ... will cease and accused will be handed over to nation territorially concerned'. It meant there would be no proceedings pursued against those involved in any of the extermination camps. There would be no repeat of the Bergen-Belsen trial, when defendants had to answer for the mass killings of Jews and many others at Auschwitz or elsewhere.

From that point on, the War Crimes Group had to cope with losing experienced officers and other ranks who were demobbed from time to time. Though diligent in chasing down cases, they were continually pressed to complete their work. As far as I could tell, this they did with as much professional order as possible in the circumstances. Over the course of the next three years, they prosecuted 937 persons on war crimes charges. Of those, 667 were convicted and 230 sentenced to death.[15] It seems a lot. But the Russians in their occupied zone of Germany tried 14,240 over the same period with only 142 acquittals.[16] Most probably the attachment to the standards of fair trial and proper proof was less apparent in the Soviet zone, though they adhered to the same format of trial and punishment.[17] Even so, there were thousands of camp guards and officers and functionaries who were in the British-controlled territory who had been kept in custody and who might have been subjected to prosecution. It had, however, become logistically impossible and politically undesirable to do so.

The inevitable decision was confirmed in May 1949.[18] In a statement to the House of Lords, Lord Henderson, Parliamentary Under-Secretary of State for Foreign Affairs, announced that as far as the prosecution of war crimes was concerned, 'No trials have started since September 1, 1948, and none will be started in the future, apart from that of Field-Marshal von Manstein. All those started before that date have now finished, and the sentences have been put into execution.'[19] Any cases that related to crimes against humanity, Lord Henderson said, were the preserve of the German authorities. They had been responsible since the Control Council Law No. 10 for prosecuting them and they would be solely responsible for continuing to do so. It was 'no part of His Majesty's Government's policy to interfere'.

The German courts continued to prosecute war crimes and crimes against humanity for many years, though in increasingly smaller numbers. Political sentiment focused instead on obtaining the release of those war criminals sentenced to imprisonment and ending the purging of the Nazis from West German society. There was to be a general and overarching rehabilitation that would bind the country to its new allies, forging, into the bargain, a barrier against the feared expansion of the Soviet Bloc.

Germans convicted of war crimes who escaped the death penalty were quickly released in the early years of the 1950s. All those long, often life, sentences of imprisonment handed down by courts who thought that they were imposing a reckoning on the Nazi criminals were reduced to a matter of a few years. The men and women who'd committed the worst of acts were let go. Denazification as a policy was abandoned and, as far as possible, overturned. For all that effort in the name of British justice, only the irreversibly executed death penalties stood intact. Even the Americans, once stalwart in their resolve to convict those responsible for the camps they'd liberated, became reticent. After the flurry of hangings that had marked the early Dachau trials in 1946, sentences became more lenient. Life terms were imposed when once death would have been the only result. These were now reduced on appeal to the point when all were released too.

As if such clemency wasn't enough, the US instituted a period of self-examination regarding its original conduct of trials at Dachau.

Various inquiries were ordered to examine claims that the rights of the accused had been seriously abused, with torture and threat and subterfuge used as means of acquiring false confessions. In February 1949, an Administration of Justice Review Board found that there had been mock trials where SS prisoners had been forced to don black hoods and stand before fake judges so they would confess.[20] All manner of techniques were uncovered that would have been condemned out of hand if perpetrated by the Gestapo. Though not entirely proven, the allegations were substantiated to such a degree that the American administration stopped all executions yet to be carried out. From that moment it was only a matter of a few years before those convicted were all released. War crimes trials had in any event ceased altogether for the Americans by 1949.

By the turn of the decade, the fury had subsided to such a point that West Germany could be welcomed back into the arms of its Western enemies. Though all was not yet forgiven, there was a political desire to forget. The investigators and lawyers moved on, back home, into other jobs, returning to their pre-war work or some other profession. Some I've managed to track.

Tony Somerhough became a public prosecutor in Kenya. He achieved a certain fame when he prosecuted Jomo Kenyatta as leader of the Mau Mau movement. He died at the age of fifty-three of a heart attack in October 1960 in Northern Rhodesia, as it was then called.

Fred Pelican returned to the UK when demobbed and started a building firm. He persisted with that for a few years and then later opened a carpet shop in north London, working through to retirement.

Carl Stirling remained one of the most prominent Judge Advocates until 1952. He died in 1983 aged eighty-two.

Noel Till returned to practise as a solicitor in Yorkshire. He died in 1993.

Leo Genn maintained his acting career until shortly before his death in 1978. He achieved a good deal of success in the 1950s and '60s, though in his later life the film roles became depressingly obscure.

Walter Freud left the War Crimes Team in September 1946. I'm not sure whether it is a mark of irony after his pursuit of Bruno Tesch, but he became a renowned industrial chemist. Boxes of his papers were deposited with the archives of the Imperial War Museum. There were no detailed accounts of his war crimes investigation work within them. He died also aged eighty-two, in 2004.

Lord Shawcross, senior British prosecutor at Nuremberg, was a public figure for many years and died in 2003 at the age of 101. He helped found Justice, which became a significant human rights and rule of law organisation, took on many major firm directorships and was a cross-bench peer in the House of Lords.

Thomas Backhouse, the Belsen trial prosecutor, returned to Britain and became a county court judge. He didn't live long, dying in 1955 at the age of fifty-one, but it was long enough to have seen some of those sentenced to imprisonment under his prosecution released.

Stephen Stewart became as English as it was possible for an Austrian to be. He prosecuted many trials, including the Ravensbrück KZ case. On return to Britain, he was called to the Bar in 1948 and ended up specialising in matters of intellectual property. He was eighty when he died in 1995.

Gerald Draper became a legal academic of note. He specialised in the laws of war. Though many would say he'd been afflicted by what he'd learned of the Holocaust and the inhumanity practised by the Nazis he'd encountered (he'd interviewed Commandant Höss after his arrest), his faith in the law to give some response never seemed to dim.

Of the others, Robert Jackson died in 1954; David Maxwell Fyfe became Lord Chancellor in Churchill's government of 1954 and died in 1967. Telford Taylor continued as a prominent lawyer and writer and legal academic. He died in 1998 aged ninety.

But whoever was involved, they all ended up the same, victim, prosecutor, perpetrator, judge, except perhaps in the judgement one might make of their lives.

4.

What remains to be said? A terrifying amount. There always is when atrocity is the subject. But I began to think I had no sense of its limits. So many stories and interconnecting lines of enquiry. If I took twenty

years I might chart much of what happened in some form of pack-
aged chronology, describe the men and women involved, what they
said, the words they used, the phrases and sentences and pages of
their speech, record their actions, a hanging maybe, an interrogation,
and I could move from archive to library to records office to private
collection, extracting more words and detritus of someone's flawed
memory, cross-reference them with each other, piecing together a
puzzle that had no solution, and I could visit every concentration
camp and court building still standing, every relic of those places
where the events I described took place, all in trust that by the accumulation of this evidence I would be serving the interests of some
complete truth which relayed every nuance and vital fact about a
time and location when and where a fleeting fury erupted, burned
and quickly exhausted itself. I might do all this and even then I would
not capture the totality of this story. But I couldn't give up.

On my return from Nuremberg, I continued to search through the
records of trials and investigations. I was mopping up the cases I'd
been examining, not quite sure what I was looking for any longer.
Some fell into that category of 'trivial' that I couldn't help but think
were used to make up the numbers in the (unsuccessful) pursuit of
500 war crimes prosecutions by April 1946 demanded by the British
government from the War Crimes Teams.[21] They consisted of minor
infractions of the laws of war (the alleged withholding of food pack-
ages, the failure to comply with orders not to scupper one's ship,
dubious interrogation practices). Most, though, involved the isolated
killings of British forces personnel, the murders which had incensed
the investigators like Leo Genn and made up the core of the War
Crimes Teams' work. Reading their details worried me on occasion.[22]
I wasn't always convinced that justice had been done.

Then I came to the Bullenhuser Damm transcript. I think I had
been avoiding it. Though it appeared in the lists and records as just
another war crimes case, I already supposed it epitomised the deep
descent into inhumanity that had gripped the German nation. All
those involved had known that the war was ending, that they were
days away from surrender, capture, perhaps punishment, and yet the
perpetrators of this one atrocity hadn't paused for a moment before
killing those twenty Jewish children.

I scrutinised every page of the trial and the reports made in its wake. At the front of the file was a final review by the prosecuting officer, Captain Cleaver from JAG. He reported after the proceedings had concluded in the summer of 1946. Various matters troubled him. He said that the trial was covered by the controlled German press only, failing to attract any coverage from the British correspondents. Everyone back in Britain was waiting on the Nuremberg Tribunal, desire for yet more accounts of terrible happenings almost expunged, no doubt. Even so, I couldn't understand the apathy. 'A small number of German spectators attended from time to time,' Cleaver wrote. No one was interested. Even the British authorities in Hamburg seemed to have become indifferent. Cleaver also said HQ Hamburg District did nothing to help the trial preparations unless 'requested, entreated or threatened'. He couldn't get easy access to Fuhlsbüttel, where two of the accused were held. He wasn't given an interpreter and 'the prison staff were even more reluctant to let me out of the gaol than they had been to let me in.' He'd been confused with a witness under sentence of death. There was no officer detailed to assist the defence and the defence counsel only learned 'by accident where the trial was to take place'.[23]

The transcript revealed a by now familiar story of British criminal proceedings. It had all been over relatively quickly. Of those involved in the killings, Dreimann, Dr Trzebinski and Speck had already been sentenced to death in the main Neuengamme camp trial. Max Pauly was called from his death row cell by the prosecution. He was cooperating. Up to a point. He maintained that the execution of the children, whose treatment in the hospital he'd known about, was ordered by SS General Pohl in Berlin at the request of Professor Heissmeyer. Pauly said he'd left all the arrangements to Dr Trzebinski and had nothing to do with the executions.

The doctor also came to give evidence. He told the court about Heissmeyer and the orders to conduct the experiments on the children, experiments that had been sanctioned by Himmler. Trzebinski knew the children were Jewish. When they got to Bullenhuser Damm he injected them with morphine to put them to sleep. Then Frahm hanged them one by one. The prisoner male nurses and doctors who had looked after the children at Neuengamme were also hanged, but without the benefit of morphine.

When the defence had their turn to present evidence, it all seemed hopeless. Not one disputed his involvement though they all shifted blame to someone else. 'Orders are orders' was the reply Dr Trzebinski had supposedly given to Jauch when asked at the time whether the hangings were necessary. That had been the limit of opposition to the killings.

The trappings of execution had followed a familiar pattern even for these children. They were made to undress and told they were to have a bath for onward journey to Theresienstadt, the main concentration camp in the then Czechoslovakia. They looked pleased at this, said Jauch. Then they were injected by Dr Trzebinski. He said he went outside before any hanging took place. But he knew they were to be killed.

The death sentence was pronounced for Frahm and Jauch. They were executed together on 11 October 1946 at 11.26 a.m.

Before the executions were carried out Lord Russell, Deputy Judge Advocate General, had to give his interpretation of the proceedings, to recommend whether or not the sentences should be confirmed. His opinion was brief. 'None of the petitions discloses any adequate grounds for interfering with the sentences awarded.'[24] It didn't matter to Russell that Jauch had said he'd tried to object. He was in charge of Bullenhuser Damm at the time. That was enough, coupled with his presence during the executions. Was Jauch the victim of blind obedience? His counsel said he did nothing deserving of condemnation before that night. He wasn't suspected or named in connection with any other war crime at any camp. That was hardly the point. He bore responsibility. One atrocious act was sufficient.

Sitting with the file of the trial before me, the testimony and proceedings written by hand, I realised I'd gone too far. Though I knew them well enough, having read Walter Freud's investigation report, I couldn't take the details any more. I couldn't bring myself to unpick the minutiae. The more I thought about those children in that cellar and those inmates who had been looking after them strung up so callously because of orders, the more I felt defeated. Even if the investigation and trial were necessary, a moral imperative, they signified failure. Though British justice may have been flawed and further undermined by political indifference, the best it could do was acknowledge the manifold nature of corruption inherent in humanity.

The Bullenhuser Damm case was the last one I examined. The search I'd begun years before should end there, I thought, the obsession triggered by my ignorance of Neuengamme and the fate of its inmates and the programme of justice effected by the British exhausted. What else could I possibly want to know?

Epilogue

There is one place I haven't visited. I know I should but I can't steel myself to do so now. It's an act of cowardice, I suppose. Though I've mentioned Auschwitz more times than I can remember in this book, I will not go there. It may be synonymous with Nazi evildoing but I'm frightened that it's beyond my capacity to assimilate. I've become saturated. There are so many more stories and many more cruelties and killings to recount, stories that remain to be uncovered amongst the hundreds of case files in the archives of the British and other prosecuting nations, stories that were never subjected to formal investigation let alone trial. But they are too much for me to contain at the moment, if at all. There comes a point when the reality of humanity's aptitude for cruelty is simply crushing. Then the desire to look away is a matter of self-preservation. Forgetting supplants fury because a perpetual state of anger is untenable.

Except …

As I was writing this book I took a holiday with my family in Catalonia. One day we visited Tarragona Cathedral. I thought it would be a cool haven from the heat of the city. In one of the rooms attached to the cloisters was a museum. I went through the glass doors, attracted by the visible splendour inside. Protected by glass cases were various triptychs, beautifully colourful paintings in gold leaf and oils depicting the lives of the saints honoured within the various chapels of the cathedral: St Tecla, St Michael, St Fructuosus, many others.

From a distance the paintings sparkled. My eyes wandered over the depicted scenes, two or three to each panel. It was an idle gaze in that lazy way of noticing little but the colours and the cracks in the gold leaf and wood beneath, a cursory examination that expects only mild pleasure, nothing engaging. But then even in that unimaginative state one scene began to register: a saint hanging from a rope attached to a staff. Two men with giant scissors, like sheep shearers, standing each side of him. They were cutting the skin from his hands and arms, folding it back still in bodily shape. Two others were at the man's feet. They were doing the same to his legs. The saint's face was raised but without great agony. It was possessed by something beyond anguish.

By this stage I was transfixed. I looked at the other panel: a headless corpse, still kneeling, the executioner holding the head by its hair. The face of the severed head had the same expression as the man being flayed. Was one or the other St Bartholomew? I didn't care. I felt sick. I turned away, though it took an effort, as though I was compelled to scrutinise the details.

I glanced across at another painting. A woman tied spreadeagled to an X-shaped cross, naked and covered with splashes of red, a man tearing at her body with a pair of long pincers.

And another: a man on all fours, head up, a soldier with a long curved sword held high, ready to swing at his neck.

I thought, these pictures weren't displaying the lives of the saints: they were glorifying their excruciating deaths. And deaths which were celebrated, admired, beautified. 'You will see that by God's power I am stronger in being tortured than you are in torturing me,' said St Vincent, according to *The Golden Legend*.

I hustled my daughters away and outside, telling them they shouldn't look, that there were pictures they shouldn't see.

In the cloister garden as I watched my children playing amidst the jackfruit trees and fountains and close-cropped grass, I thought those paintings made little sense.

Now, at the end of this book, as I've decided to look no further, I'm tempted to believe the complete opposite. If the term that's been present throughout, those words 'crimes against humanity', is to have any meaning, how can I disregard what that humanity is? Looking at those terrible pictures, remembering the files and files I'd read of other atrocities, remembering the camps I'd visited where the physical residue of countless cruelties is ever present, it would be naïve, perhaps negligent, to think it didn't include the propensity to inflict violence and harm on other people. To do so would leave the term superficial and incomplete. It would be hopelessly romantic.

But I should have known that. Reading Susan Sontag's *Regarding the Pain of Others* I found this passage:

> Someone who is perennially surprised that depravity exists, who continues to feel disillusioned (even incredulous) when confronted with evidence of what humans are capable of inflicting in the way of gruesome, hands-on cruelties upon other humans, has not reached moral or psychological adulthood. No one after a certain age has the right to this kind of innocence, of superficiality, to this degree of ignorance, or amnesia.[1]

She's right.

But she tempers this, recognising that 'too much remembering' can be embittering and thus destructive. 'To make peace is to forget,' she wrote. 'To reconcile, it is necessary that memory be faulty and limited. If the goal is having some space in which to live one's own life, then it is desirable that the account of specific injustices dissolve into a more general understanding that human beings everywhere do terrible things to one another.'

Now, thinking about all I have found and all I have chosen to write, I can see the fury set loose in retribution against those caught and put on trial after the war suffered from this contradiction. It began as a romantic gesture. And like any romance and like any gesture, the gloss of virtue soon fell away to reveal a hard, pragmatic under-coat. The enormity of the task meant the participants didn't have the resolve to sustain it. It was beyond them as it would be beyond anyone. Perhaps, though, anger as a spur to justice is romantic too. For the most part it's temporary. Resentment might remain but unrelenting fury is hopeless and rare and often refuels hatreds.

I wonder then, for the last time, what they achieved, Nuremberg and all those thousands of investigations and thousands of trials and thousands of hangings and thousands of prison sentences ultimately cut short, as fury passed and was replaced not by forgiveness nor by forgetting but a strange shrug of self-preservational indifference. Did they provide any justice to the victims? I think about the 7,000 people who were killed in Neustadt Bay: no one bore responsibility for that catastrophe. No one was held accountable. How many more deaths and tortures were similarly ignored, and how many perpetrators escaped, both having to be disregarded because there were simply too many to address? For all Nuremberg's value in confronting the overarching systems of Nazi inhumanity, the victims were only numbers. That's what law and trial invariably promises: an impersonal and imperfect reaction to human cruelty and human suffering.

Perhaps, though, I should expect no more. Perhaps I should value the small but significant resistance to maleficence marked by the retribution. It may have been symbolic, shambolic, illusory, as are all schemes of justice, and for the greater part wholly obscured, but it was essential for all that. What else could they have done? That much is worth remembering when so much has been forgotten.

Sources and Bibliography

The material available charting the history of the concentration camps, the atrocities committed by the Nazi regime, the perpetration of the Holocaust, the proceedings at Nuremberg, and the political machinations accompanying all of these matters, is huge. Rather than try to list these I've outlined those sources I found the most revealing, before listing the works cited in this book.

Of first importance are the literature and artefacts and memorials I found at the various sites I visited across Europe. Noteworthy amongst these were Bergen-Belsen, Flossenbürg, Neuengamme, Dachau, Buchenwald and Mittelbau-Dora, but I should also mention Colditz, Fossoli in Italy (where Primo Levi was first incarcerated before being transferred to Auschwitz), Plötzensee in Berlin and the Palace of Justice at Nuremberg. For the most part, the displays and exhibitions provided significant insights and directions that were invaluable in helping me understand the enormity of both the wrongs done and the Allied response. At most of these places there were people ready to open doors, show items and buildings of interest and treat every visitor with respect. They could each point to remarkable collections and records which even after seventy years have yet to reveal their full histories.

Occasionally, as I've mentioned in the book, local interest in preserving the memories of atrocities I found to be sometimes dulled or even suppressed. Finding information beyond graves or commemorative stones recording the numbers or names of the dead was sometimes difficult. I do wonder whether as generations pass, the German people and authorities will remain conscious enough of their country's history to reinforce their abhorrence for those brutal times. If the last ten years are a good indication, when many memorials and museums, particularly at concentration camps, have been opened, there is still an apparent appetite for reflection. That can only be for the good. But the sense of responsibility to preserve the records and memories are bound to be strained. In the meantime, the sources of information are probably more fecund now than ever before despite the passing of the victims and perpetrators and avengers.

The second source to which I came to feel inextricably attached were the public collections at the National Archives and the Imperial War Museum. At both institutions the genial but professional assistance was uniform. Research can be a self-perpetuating enterprise and on more than one occasion the sense of discovery as I opened file after file was extraordinary. No one should rely on published books or articles for their inspiration or understanding of any subject if they can help it. The physical archive is a wonderful invention.

Though I prefer the public records, if only for their delivery of revelations that without exception I thought (often wrongly) were unique, I value highly the secondary source: those memoirs and histories and academic analyses, some of which appear in the bibliography. But there were few works that could tell me what I wanted to know. The story of the British military trials is an obscure one. Why no one has found it interesting enough to tell in any detail I do not understand. Perhaps lawyers and detectives make poor analysts and historians; they're too steeped in taking a position, a brief, to see things from a variety of perspectives. Perhaps the experience of investigating and prosecuting atrocity simply saps the will to revisit the detail of death and suffering and the 'evil' (as many would describe it) of those crimes. Nonetheless, there are some accounts which help understand what happened during those few years after the war's end and which I've mentioned in the bibliography below.

Angier, Carole, *The Double Bond: Primo Levi: A Biography* (London: Penguin, 2013)
Arendt, Hannah, *Eichmann in Jerusalem: A Report on the Banality of Evil* (London: Penguin, 1992)
Arendt, Hannah, *The Origins of Totalitarianism* (New York: Schocken Books, 2004)

Barnard, Clifford, *Two Weeks in May 1945* (London: Quaker Home Service, 1999)

Baron-Cohen, Simon, *Zero Degrees of Empathy: A New Theory of Human Cruelty and Kindness* (London: Penguin, 2012)

Bauman, Zygmunt, *Modernity and the Holocaust* (Cambridge: Polity, 1989)

Beimler, Hans, *Four Weeks in the Hands of Hitler's Hell-Hounds: The Nazi Murder Camp of Dachau* (London: Modern Press, 1933)

Ben-Naftali, Orna and Tuval, Yogev, 'Punishing International Crimes Committed by the Persecuted: The *Kapo* Trials in Israel (1950s–1960s)' (2006), *Journal of International Criminal Justice*, Vol. 4, pp. 128–78

Bernadotte, Folke, *The Curtain Falls* (New York: A.A. Knopf, 1945)

Bloxham, David, *Genocide on Trial: War Crimes Trials and the Formation of Holocaust History and Memory* (Oxford: Oxford University Press, 2001)

Bower, Tom, *Blind Eye to Murder: Britain, America and the Purging of Nazi Germany – A Pledge Betrayed* (London: Andre Deutsch, 1981)

Churchill, Winston, *History of the Second World War, Vol. VI* (London: Penguin Classics, 2005)

Collis, W.R.F. and MacClancy, P.C., 'Some Paediatric Problems Presented at Belsen Camp' (1946), *British Medical Journal*, No. 4442, pp. 273–5

Cox, Graham, 'Seeking Justice for the Holocaust: Herbert C. Pell vs the US State Department' (2014), *Criminal Law Forum*, Vol. 25, pp. 77–110

Earl, Hilary, *The Nuremberg SS-Einsatzgruppen Trial 1945–1958: Atrocity, Law, and History* (Cambridge: Cambridge University Press, 2009)

Frankl, Viktor, *The Doctor and the Soul: From Psychotherapy to Logotherapy* (New York: Vintage Books, 1973)

Frankl, Viktor, *Man's Search for Meaning* (London: Rider, 2004)

Friedländer, Saul, *The Years of Extermination: Nazi Germany and the Jews 1939–1945* (London: Phoenix, 2008)

Friedman, Jonathan, 'The Sachsenhausen Trials', in Patricia Herber and Jürgen Matthäus, *Atrocities on Trial: Historical Perspectives on the Politics of Prosecuting War Crimes* (Lincoln: University of Nebraska Press, 2008) pp. 159–84

Gellately, Robert, *The Nuremberg Interviews: Conversations with the Defendants and Witnesses Conducted by Leon Goldensohn* (London: Pimlico, 2007)

Gilbert, G.M., *Nuremberg Diary* (New York: Da Capo Press, 1995)

Gilbert, Martin, *Auschwitz and the Allies* (London: Mandarin, 1991)

Goldhagen, Daniel Jonah, *Hitler's Willing Executioners: Ordinary Germans and the Holocaust* (London: Abacus, 1996)

Green, Joshua M., *Justice at Dachau: The Trials of an American Prosecutor* (New York: Broadway Books, 2003)

Hackett, David A. (ed. and tr.), *The Buchenwald Report* (Boulder: Westview Press, 1995)

Halliday, Hugh A., 'Relief Amid Chaos: The Story of Canadian POWs Driving Red Cross' (2002), *Canadian Military History*, Vol. 11: 2, Article 7, available at http://scholars.wlu.ca/cmh/vol11/iss2/7

Harding, Thomas, *Hanns and Rudolf: The German Jew and the Hunt for the Kommandant of Auschwitz* (London: Windmill Books, 2014)

Hardman, Leslie and Goodman, Cecily, *The Survivors: The Story of the Belsen Remnant* (London: Vallentine Mitchell, 1958)

Helm, Sarah, *A Life in Secrets: Vera Atkins and the Lost Agents of SOE* (London: Abacus, 2006)

Herber, Patricia and Matthäus, Jürgen, *Atrocities on Trial: Historical Perspectives on the Politics of Prosecuting War Crimes* (Lincoln: University of Nebraska Press, 2008)

HMSO, *Law Reports of Trials of War Criminals: Selected and Prepared by the United Nations War Crimes Commission* (London: HMSO, 1949)

Hughes, Ted (tr.), *Aeschylus: The Oresteia* (London: Faber and Faber, 1999)

Isherwood, Christopher, 'Berlin Diary', in *Goodbye to Berlin* (London: Minerva, 1989)

Fermor, Patrick Leigh, *A Time of Gifts* (London: John Murray, 2004)

Jackson, Sophie, *British Interrogation Techniques in the Second World War* (Stroud: The History Press, 2012)

Jardim, Tomaz, *The Mauthausen Trial: American Military Justice in Germany* (Cambridge: Harvard University Press, 2012)

Jones, Priscilla Dale, 'Nazi Atrocities against Allied Airmen: Stalag Luft III and the End of British War Crimes Trials' (1998), *Historical Journal*, Vol. 41:2, pp. 543–65

Kemp, Anthony, *The Secret Hunters* (London: Michael O'Mara Books, 1986)

Kershaw, Ian, *The End: Germany 1944–45* (London: Penguin Books, 2012)

Kogon, Eugen, *The Theory and Practice of Hell: The German Concentration Camps and the System Behind Them* (London: Secker & Warburg, 1950)

Kramer, Rita, *Flames in the Field: The Story of Four SOE Agents in Occupied France* (London: Penguin Books, 1996)

Lange, Wilhelm, 'Cap Arcona: Summary of the Cap Arcona Disaster in the Bay of Neustadt on 3 May 1945 – On Behalf of the town of Neustadt' (1996)

Lawrence, Geoffrey (Lord Oaksey), 'The Nuremberg Trial' (1947), *International Affairs*, Vol. 23:2, pp. 151–9

Lemkin, Raphael, *Axis Rule in Occupied Europe: Laws of Occupation; Analysis of Government; Proposals for Redress* (Washington DC: Carnegie Endowment for International Peace, 1944)

Levi, Primo, *If This is a Man* (London: Abacus, 1979)

Levi, Primo, *The Drowned and the Saved* (London: Abacus, 1988)

Lewis, J.T., 'Medical Problems at Belsen Concentration Camp (1945)', reprinted in *Ulster Medical Journal*, Vol. 54:2, pp. 122–6 (October 1985)

Longerich, Peter, *Heinrich Himmler* (Oxford: Oxford University Press, 2012)

Lord Russell of Liverpool, *The Scourge of the Swastika: A Short History of Nazi War Crimes* (New York: Philosophical Library, 1954)

Marcuse, Harold, *Legacies of Dachau: The Uses and Abuses of a Concentration Camp, 1933–2001* (Cambridge: Cambridge University Press, 2001)

Margolian, Howard, *Conduct Unbecoming: The Story of the Murder of Canadian Prisoners of War in Normandy* (Toronto: University of Toronto Press, 1998)

Megargee, Geoffrey P. (ed.), *Encyclopedia of Camps and Ghettos 1933–1945*, Vol. 1, Parts A & B (Bloomington: United States Holocaust Memorial Museum, 2009)

Meyer, M. and McCoubrey, H. (eds), *Reflections on Law and Armed Conflicts: The Selected Works on the Laws of War by the Late Professor Colonel G.I.A.D. Draper OBE* (The Hague: Kluwer, 1998)

Milgram, Stanley, *Obedience to Authority: An Experimental View* (London: Tavistock Publications, 1974)

Mollison, P.L., 'Observations on Cases of Starvation at Belsen' (1946), *British Medical Journal*, No. 4435, pp. 4–8

Moorehead, Alan, 'Belsen', in Cyril Connolly (ed.), *The Golden Horizon* (London: Weidenfield & Nicolson, 1953), pp. 103–12

Mullins, Claud, *The Leipzig Trials: An Account of the War Criminals' Trials and a Study of German Mentality* (London: H.F. & G. Witherby, 1921)

Niremberski, M., 'Psychological Investigation of a Group of Internees at Belsen Camp' (1946), *Journal of Mental Science*, Vol. 92, pp. 60–74

Padfield, Peter, *Himmler: Reichsführer SS* (London: Papermac, 1991)

Pelican, Fred, *From Dachau to Dunkirk* (London: Vallentine Mitchell, 1993)

Schawe, Karin (ed.), Georg Felix Harsch (tr.), *The Neuengamme Concentration Camp Memorial – A Guide to the Site's History and the Memorial* (Hamburg: Neuengamme Concentration Camp Memorial, 2010)

Sebag-Montefiore, Hugh, *Dunkirk: Fight to the Last Man* (London: Penguin Books, 2007)

Sereny, Gitta, *Into That Darkness: An Examination of Conscience* (London: Picador, 1974)

Sontag, Susan, *Regarding the Pain of Others* (London: Penguin Books, 2003)

Staub, Ervin, *The Roots of Evil: The Origins of Genocide and Other Group Violence* (Cambridge: Cambridge University Press, 1989)

Taylor, Telford, *The Anatomy of the Nuremberg Trials* (London: Bloomsbury, 1993)

Todorov, Tzvetan, *Facing the Extreme: Moral Life in the Concentration Camps* (London: Phoenix, 1999)

Tusa, Ann and Tusa, John, *The Nuremberg Trial* (London: Macmillan, 1983)

Vaughan, Hal, *Doctor to the Resistance: The Heroic True Story of an American Surgeon and his Family in Occupied Paris* (Washington DC: Brassey's Inc., 2004)

Wachsmann, Nikolaus, *KZ: A History of the Nazi Concentration Camps* (London: Little, Brown, 2015)

Waller, James, *Becoming Evil: How Ordinary People Commit Genocide and Mass Killing*, 2nd edn (Oxford: Oxford University Press, 2007)

Wiesel, Elie, *Night* (London: Penguin, 2006)

Winstone, Martin, *The Holocaust Sites of Europe: An Historical Guide* (London: I.B. Tauris, 2010)

Wyman, David, *The Abandonment of the Jews: America and the Holocaust 1941–1945* (New York: Pantheon Books, 1984)

Endnotes

Part 1 - Neuengamme

1 Karin Schawe (ed.), Georg Felix Harsch (tr.), *The Neuengamme Concentration Camp Memorial – A Guide to the Site's History and the Memorial* (Hamburg: Neuengamme Concentration Camp Memorial, 2010), p. 44.

2 Statement on Atrocities signed by President Roosevelt, Prime Minister Churchill and Premier Stalin as part of the Joint Four-Nation Declaration (the 'Moscow Declaration') issued at the Moscow Conference, October 1943.

3 Ted Hughes's translation of Aeschylus' *The Oresteia* (London: Faber and Faber, 1999), p. 169.

4 The Rt. Hon. Clement R. Attlee, introducing an address by Geoffrey Lawrence (Lord Oaksey), together published as 'The Nuremberg Trial', *International Affairs*, Vol. 23:2 (1947), pp. 151–159.

Part 2 - Buchenwald

1 *The Times*, 9 April 1945.

2 The Buchenwald Report was written in 1945 largely by one of its surviving inmates, Eugen Kogon. It refers to the zoo as another excuse for causing suffering to the inmates. If any animal or bird was injured or fell ill, the inmates would be called to account. David A. Hackett (tr. and ed.), *The Buchenwald Report* (Boulder: Westview Press, 1995), pp. 130–131.

3 *The Times*, 23 April 1945.

4   *The Times*, 1 May 1945. Sixty years on, this reflection still holds good. Photographs and film of abuse of civilians in Iraq by British soldiers in Basra and Americans in Abu Ghraib prison removed doubt that people had been cruelly mistreated. The pictures showing US soldiers, a young elfin-like woman amongst them (I'm not sure why I mention this though it seems to accentuate the callousness somehow and echoes, as I found, some of the prurient interest in Irma Grese, an SS guard at Auschwitz and Bergen-Belsen, during her trial in 1945), piling up naked Iraqi prisoners, pulling them on dog leads and laughing at their nudity, provoked outrage. The same occurred with the British version at Camp Breadbasket the year before: pictures of detainees strapped to forklift trucks or forced to simulate anal sex. Even with a world now inundated with horrific images, those photographs conveyed a truth that no end of case reports could achieve. The *Guardian*'s online report on the scandal was available at the time of writing at http://www.theguardian.com/Iraq/breadbasket/0,15804,1419469,00.html.

5   Susan Sontag's *Regarding the Pain of Others* (London: Penguin Books, 2003) was an important book for me when thinking of the images of the camps and the Holocaust. This quote comes from p. 102.

6   Christopher Isherwood, 'Berlin Diary' in *Goodbye to Berlin* (London: Minerva, 1989), p. 245.

7   Patrick Leigh Fermor, *A Time of Gifts* (London: John Murray, 2004), pp. 31–32.

8   Various incidents were reported over the years but it's worth looking particularly at the *Daily Mail* coverage: for instance, on 12 December 1925, 26 April 1927 and 16 September 1929.

9   *The Times*, 19 April 1930.

10   *The Times*, 18 September 1930.

11   *The Times*, 18 June 1901.

12   *The Times*, 9 March 1901.

13   Coincidentally, on the same day that the concentration camps of Germany were first described in the British press, one of the men who in 1945 would become central to the prosecution of those responsible for their operation made his debut in the newspapers. On 21 March 1933 the *Manchester Guardian* reported a story featuring a Major Henry Shapcott. He was the prosecutor at a sensational court martial in London. Some twelve years later, Shapcott would be a senior figure in the British Army's investigation and trials of Nazis, but on that day, he was concerned with Lieutenant Norman Baillie-Stewart, an officer

in the Seaforth Highlanders accused of breaching the Official Secrets Act. Baillie-Stewart had been passing military information to the Germans since 1931, well before the Nazis came to power. He had been in the thrall of Germany for some time and had agreed to become a spy in return for a modest amount of cash. After a short trial Baillie-Stewart was found guilty and sentenced to five years in prison. In one of those twists that make fact seem absurdly fanciful, Baillie-Stewart would leave the UK after his release from prison shortly before World War II broke out. He would travel to Germany and become the English voice for German radio in the lead-up to the conflict, paving the way for Lord Haw-Haw to take his place. Baillie-Stewart was arrested in Vienna in 1945 and put on trial once more: this time for aiding the enemy. It was one of those that added to the mix of cases the British would pursue after the war.

14   In the same edition, the paper also reported a raid upon Albert Einstein's house near Potsdam after 'local political and emergency police' searched his villa following a tip-off that arms and ammunition were hidden there. Einstein wasn't in the country. He was on his way home from the USA at the time and had already made public his refusal to return to Germany 'owing to the persecution of the Jews': *Manchester Guardian*, 21 March 1933.

15   *Manchester Guardian*, 27 May 1933.

16   Hansard, House of Commons Debate, Vol. 287 cols 367–485 (14 March 1934) at 456 onwards.

17   Hansard, HC, House of Commons Debate, Vol. 276 cols 2750–824 (13 April 1933).

18   *Manchester Guardian*, 23 June 1933.

19   *The Times*, 26 August 1933.

20   *The Times*, 6 September 1933.

21   *Manchester Guardian*, 1 January 1934.

22   Letter to the Editor, *Manchester Guardian*, 4 January 1934.

23   *Manchester Guardian*, 16 January 1934.

24   *Manchester Guardian*, 22 January 1934. The *Illustrated London News* provided the first pictures of Dachau soon after, although towards the back of the magazine, after the rare chinchillas and reports on the 'kinema'. Twenty-four pages into the 10 February 1934 edition, photographs of inmates and guards were shown. They bore no resemblance to those that would appear eleven years later.

25   *Manchester Guardian*, 7 May 1935.

26   *Manchester Guardian*, 20 April 1935.

27   *Manchester Guardian*, 20 September 1935.

28   *The Times*, 8 November 1935.

29   *The Times*, 15 November 1938.

30   *The Times*, 19 November 1938.

31   Hans Beimler, *Four Weeks in the Hands of Hitler's Hell-Hounds: The Nazi Murder Camp of Dachau* (London: Modern Press, 1933).

32   Letter to the Editor, *Manchester Guardian*, 10 July 1935.

33   Letters to the Editor, *Manchester Guardian*, 13 July 1935.

34   The *Manchester Guardian* printed an interesting article on 'The Prince and Germany' on 12 June 1935.

35   Letter to the Editor, *Manchester Guardian*, 27 July 1935.

36   Hansard, HC, Vol. 337 cols 79–189 (14 June 1938).

37   Hansard, HC, Vol. 341 cols 1987–2107 (24 November 1938) at 2052.

38   *The Times*, 31 October 1939.

39   *The Times*, 12 December 1939.

40   *The Times*, 12 November 1940.

41   *The Times*, 14 February 1940.

42   *The Times*, 27 October 1941.

43   *The Times*, 14 January 1942.

44   Lord Maugham made the statement during a House of Lords debate. See Hansard, House of Lords Debate, Vol. 124 cols 555–94 (7 October 1942).

45   *The Times*, 7 October 1942.

46   I found these particular entries in a volume of periodic summaries produced by the Government Code and Cypher School working out of Bletchley Park (National Archives, HW16/6). It contained detailed information intercepted from German police communications and deciphered. There are a hundred or so of these volumes. This one shows clearly that the British government had access to information from as early as 1941 mentioning gas chambers and mass executions.

47   *New York Times*, 18 December 1942, and *The Times*, 18 December 1942.

48   *The Times*, 16 October 1942.

49   Lord Maugham talked at length to the House of Lords about the failure of the Leipzig Trials. The experience seemed to have marked the government's attitude towards post-war justice. See note 44 above.

50   Claud Mullins, *The Leipzig Trials: An Account of the War Criminals' Trials and a Study of German Mentality* (London: H.F. & G. Witherby, 1921).

51 Statement on Atrocities signed by President Roosevelt, Prime Minister Churchill and Premier Stalin as part of the Joint Four-Nation Declaration (the 'Moscow Declaration') issued at the Moscow Conference, October 1943.

52 The tortuous history of accepting 'crimes against humanity' as a legitimate offence in international criminal law is told in Graham Cox's 'Seeking Justice for the Holocaust: Herbert C. Pell vs the US State Department' (2014), *Criminal Law Forum*, Vol. 25, pp. 77–110.

53 The official account of this development is told in *The History of the United Nations War Crimes Commission and the Development of the Laws of War* (London: HMSO, 1948), which is now available online at http://www.unwcc.org/documents/.

54 National Archives, WO 311/6 'War criminals: proposals to bring suspects to trial during war time'.

55 A full account of this initiative is described from a Canadian perspective in Howard Margolian, *Conduct Unbecoming: The Story of the Murder of Canadian Prisoners of War in Normandy* (Toronto: University of Toronto Press, 1998).

56 National Archives, FO 371/50968 'German war criminals: crimes against Jews: atrocities in occupied territories'.

57 National Archives, TS 26/856 'Shooting of Allied Prisoners of War by 12 SS Panzer Division (Hitler Jugend) in Normandy, 7th–21st June 1944'.

58 The series of reports on these inquiries can be found at National Archives, FO 371/50968 onwards.

59 National Archives, FO 371/50970, correspondence on proposed republication in the United Kingdom of the 21st Army Group Report on German Atrocities in Belgium January 1945.

60 Ibid.

61 FO 371/50970, note 59 above, letter from FO to Sir Cyril Radcliffe Minister of Information, 15 February 1945.

62 The report is reprinted in Anthony Kemp, *The Secret Hunters* (London: Michael O'Mara Books, 1986). Papers relating to Galitzine's investigations at Natzweiler are also available at the Imperial War Museum, 'Private Papers of Captain Y. Galitzine' (Document No. 16000).

63 According to Anthony Kemp (note 62 above), Galitzine never lost his belief that the British had failed in their duty towards pursuing war criminals. But his initial investigations would be vital in one of the more successful war crimes investigation operations: the pursuit of

those responsible for the murder of British SAS and SOE operatives. That was a priority before the war concluded *and* once the initial burst of enthusiasm for punishing the Nazis had begun to dissipate. Some of this story is told in Rita Kramer, *Flames in the Field: The Story of Four SOE Agents in Occupied France* (London: Penguin Books, 1996), and Sarah Helm, *A Life in Secrets: Vera Atkins and the Lost Agents of SOE* (London: Abacus, 2006).

64 National Archives, WO 208/4296 'Papers recovered from Lt Col A.P. Scotland: German concentration camps; POW interrogation reports'.

65 *The Times*, 12 August 1944.

66 FO 371/50970, note 59 above.

67 Statement by the President released to the press on 24 March 1944, which I found in Robert H. Jackson, *Report of Robert H. Jackson, United States Representative to the International Conference on Military Trials* (Washington: Department of State, 1949), pp. 12–13.

68 Winston Churchill, *History of the Second World War, Vol. VI* (London: Penguin Classics, 2005), Appendix C.

69 David Wyman, *The Abandonment of the Jews: America and the Holocaust 1941–1945* (New York: Pantheon Books, 1984).

70 Martin Gilbert, *Auschwitz and the Allies* (London: Mandarin, 1991), p. 341.

71 Elie Wiesel, *Night* (London: Penguin, 2006), preface to new translation, p. x.

72 Memorandum to President Roosevelt from the Secretaries of State and War and the Attorney General, 22 January 1945, in *Report of Robert H. Jackson, United States Representative to the International Conference on Military Trials, London 1945* (Washington: US Department of State, 1949), pp. 3–17.

73 The Malmedy massacre above all received the kind of publicity and public outrage in the US as had in Britain the killing of the fifty British and Allied officers who'd escaped from Stalag Luft III earlier in 1944. During the last grand offensive launched by the Germans against the Allies in the west, men of the 1st SS Panzer Division, 'Leibstandarte Adolf Hitler', captured over one hundred US troops at the village of Malmedy in the Ardennes, disarmed them and shot them. It was by no means a unique event. But this time, news reports of the discovery in the snow of more than eighty soldiers, with clear evidence of their having been shot at close range ('Slaughtered in Cold Blood' was the headline), couldn't be wrapped up in the general condemnation of Nazi crimes. The killing of the

GIs was made very personal and wouldn't diminish over time. I found newspaper reports from the 1970s that charted the story of the SS officer in command of the unit, Joachim Peiper, who was convicted for the massacre in a US-led trial in 1946 and sentenced to death. The penalty was commuted to life imprisonment in 1951 and reduced further so that he was released in 1957. Peiper was eventually killed in his house in Traves, France, where he'd settled with his family and was purportedly writing his memoirs, on Bastille Day, 1976. A tract denouncing him as a war criminal had been circulated in the area and Peiper, receiving a death threat in the post, had sent his wife and daughters back to Germany. A couple of days later his house was attacked by armed men and firebombed. He died in the blaze. See *The Times*, 15 July 1976.

74 The most recent book to chart the development of the Nazi concentration camp system is Nikolaus Wachsmann, *KZ: A History of the Nazi Concentration Camps* (London: Little, Brown, 2015).

75 One element of the order was highlighted by the prosecution at the Nuremberg Tribunal to indicate the draconian nature of punishment employed in the concentration camps. The order stated that those to be hanged would include: 'Anyone who, for the purpose of agitating, does the following in the camp, at work in the quarters, in the kitchens and workshops, toilets and places of rest: holds political or inciting speeches and meetings, forms cliques, loiters around with others; who, for the purpose of supplying the propaganda of the opposition with atrocity stories, collects true or false information about the concentration camp and its institution, receives such information, buries it, talks about it to others, smuggles it out of the camp into the hands of foreign visitors or others by means of clandestine or other methods, passes it on in writing or orally to released prisoners or prisoners who are placed above them, conceals it in clothing or other articles, throws stones and other objects over the camp wall containing such information, or produces secret documents; who, for the purpose of agitating, climbs on barracks roofs and trees, seeks contact with the outside by giving light or other signals, or induces others to escape or commit a crime, gives them advice to that effect or supports such undertakings in any way whatsoever.' Presentation of the case concerning concentration camps by Thomas Dodd US prosecutor 13 December 1945 which I found at http://avalon.law.yale.edu/imt/12-13-45.asp#camps.

Part 3 – Lüneburg Heath

1   Ian Kershaw's *The End: Germany 1944–45* (London: Penguin Books, 2012) conveys the scale of chaos that existed then and the desperately dangerous conflict that was still underway deep into 1945.

2   The Office of the Prosecutor, ICC, 'Communication concerning the situation in Iraq', 9 February 2006, available on the International Criminal Court's website at http://www.icc-cpi.int/NR/rdonlyres/04D143C8-19FB-466C-AB77-4CDB2FDEBEF7/143682/OTP_letter_to_senders_re_Iraq_9_February_2006.pdf.

3   *The Times*, 14 April 1945.

4   Gerard Mansell, 'From Belsen to Lübeck', *Illustrated London News*, 25 May 1985.

5   *The Times*, 19 April 1945.

6   Ibid.

7   *Daily Mail*, 19 April 1945.

8   P.L. Mollison, 'Observations on Cases of Starvation at Belsen' (1946), *British Medical Journal*, No. 4435, pp. 4–8.

9   J.T. Lewis, 'Medical Problems at Belsen Concentration Camp (1945)', reprinted in the *Ulster Medical Journal*, Vol. 54:2, pp. 122–6 (October 1985).

10   W.R.F. Collis and P.C. MacClancy, 'Some Paediatric Problems Presented at Belsen Camp' (1946), *British Medical Journal*, No. 4442, pp. 273–5.

11   M. Niremberski, 'Psychological Investigation of a Group of Internees at Belsen Camp' (1946), *Journal of Mental Science*, Vol. 92, pp. 60–74. The observations are confirmed by the remarkable Viktor Frankl who was an inmate of Buchenwald, a psychologist capable of reflecting on his experiences during and after his captivity. His book, *The Doctor and the Soul: From Psychotherapy to Logotherapy* (New York: Vintage Books, 1973), is a remarkable account of his time in the concentration camps.

12   National Archives, WO 309/1697 'No. 1 War Crimes Investigation Team depositions: 1–175', deposition of Hughes, 22 June 1945, sworn before Lt Col Genn.

13   *Daily Mail*, 21 April 1945. Edwin Tetlow's description of the 'final horror' is remarkable for his personal involvement in the story. After describing the terrible scenes, he signs off with, 'All this I saw, and I do not want to see anything like it again.'

14 Leslie Hardman and Cecily Goodman, *The Survivors: The Story of the Belsen Remnant* (London: Valentine Mitchell, 1958), p. 16.

15 See note 13 above.

16 Alan Moorehead, 'Belsen', in Cyril Connolly (ed.), *The Golden Horizon* (London: Weidenfield & Nicolson, 1953), pp. 103–12.

17 Thomas Harding, *Hanns and Rudolf: The German Jew and the Hunt for the Kommandant of Auschwitz* (London: Windmill Books, 2014).

18 Ibid., p. 179.

19 *Manchester Guardian*, 28 June 1945.

20 WO 309/1418 'War crime investigation teams: formation of unit'.

21 Ibid.

22 Ibid.

23 The accounts of the two massacres are told in Hugh Sebag-Montefiore, *Dunkirk: Fight to the Last Man* (London: Penguin Books, 2007). Despite much effort by the British war crimes investigators no one has ever been brought to justice for these crimes. Identifying those responsible was difficult, finding them more difficult still, and constructing a case that would satisfy the legal standards of a criminal trial the most difficult of all.

24 Winston Churchill, *History of the Second World War, Vol. VI* (London: Penguin Classics, 2005), Appendix C.

25 'Aide-memoire from the United Kingdom April 23 1945', in *Report of Robert H. Jackson, United States Representative to the International Conference on Military Trials, London 1945* (Washington: US Department of State, 1949), pp. 18–20.

26 A good account of Jackson's appointment is told in Ann Tusa and John Tusa, *The Nuremberg Trial* (London: Macmillan, 1983).

27 'American Draft of Definitive Proposal, Presented to Foreign Ministers at San Francisco, April 1945', in *Report of Robert H. Jackson, United States Representative to the International Conference on Military Trials, London 1945* (Washington: US Department of State, 1949), pp. 22–7.

28 These complaints were repeated in copies of a draft report by the senior investigating officers at Bergen-Belsen amongst the 'Private Papers of Lieutenant Colonel S.G. Champion' held at the Imperial War Museum (Document No. 2323).

29 Major Smallwood gave his evidence on Wednesday, 26 September 1945. The transcript of the Bergen-Belsen and Auschwitz concentration camp trial can be found in several volumes at the National Archive, WO 235/12 onwards. A full version of the transcript is also

available online now at http://www.bergenbelsen.co.uk/pages/TrialTranscript/Trial_Contents.html.

30 National Archives, WO 309/1697 'No 1 War Crimes Investigation Team depositions: 1–175', Exhibit 24.

31 Walter Freud's private papers can be found at the Imperial War Museum (Document No. 13326). These alerted me to Fred Warner's papers also stored there, which included a full version of his memoirs (Document No. 7965).

32 National Archives, WO 311/856 'Setting up of a Supreme Headquarters Allied Expeditionary Force (SHAEF) court of inquiry to record evidence of atrocities'.

33 National Archives, TS 26/854 'Shooting of Allied Prisoners of War at Tilburg, Holland, 9 July 1944: Report of SHAEF Court of Inquiry'.

34 National Archives, TS 26/858 'Shooting of Allied Prisoners of War: In the vicinity of Le Paradis, Lestrem, Pas-de-Calais, 27 May 1940: Report of SHAEF Court of Inquiry'.

35 Leo Genn's papers concerning his military service are listed in the catalogue of the National Archives as held at the Imperial War Museum's Department of Documents. When I enquired after them I was told that they were in the process of being curated at their Duxford repository and wouldn't be available for the public for some time. Stephen Walton, the Senior Curator, very kindly sent me photocopies of documents that he thought would be of interest to me. Amongst these I found material which shed considerable light on the attitudes and experiences of the investigators at Bergen-Belsen.

36 See note 28 above.

37 Raphael Lemkin, *Axis Rule in Occupied Europe: Laws of Occupation; Analysis of Government; Proposals for Redress* (Washington DC: Carnegie Endowment for International Peace, 1944).

38 Ibid.

39 National Archives, WO 309/1418 'War crime investigation teams: formation of unit'.

40 See note 28 above.

41 A draft of this announcement was within Lt Col Champion's papers referred to in note 28 above.

42 *The Times*, 12 May 1945.

43 *The Times*, 24 May 1945.

44 *The Times*, 24 May 1945.

45 *Manchester Guardian*, 25 May 1945.

46 Though in 2005 someone wanted to fix the deck of proof and placed forged documents in the files at the National Archives in Kew that suggested the British wanted to kill 'HH' in case he gave evidence of an embarrassing collusion with the British. No one was ever charged for this offence. The story was reported by the *Guardian* as '29 fakes behind a rewriting of history', 5 May 2008. The National Archives have now introduced spy cameras in the reading rooms to prevent something similar happening again.

47 One account by a 'British officer who was formerly in the Salford City Police' was printed in the *Manchester Guardian*, 29 May 1945, telling the story of how Himmler revealed his identity when in British custody. This could only have been Capt. Selvester. Others have emerged over the years. Corporal Harry Jones purportedly wrote about what he'd seen as part of the unit that had Himmler in custody (*Daily Mail*, 2 August 2010). Biographers of Himmler have also compiled accounts of his last moments: see Peter Padfield, *Himmler: Reichsführer SS* (London: Papermac, 1991), and more recently, Peter Longerich, *Heinrich Himmler* (Oxford: Oxford University Press, 2012).

48 Selvester retold his story to the *Herald*, which reported it on 4 July 1998.

49 The film clip is now available online at http://www.britishpathe.com/video/death-of-himmler.

50 *Manchester Guardian*, 25 May 1945.

51 *Collier's*, 22 September 1945. When I read the article it cast into doubt some accounts of the showing of the same film, expanded to cover many other camps, which would be shown at Nuremberg. The impression given then was that that was the first time the film had been seen by the defendants. This account by journalist George Tucker suggests otherwise.

52 National Archives, WO 311/838 'Opening of prison for high ranking civilian prisoners at Mondorf-les-Bains, Luxembourg, codename "Ashcan"'.

53 National Archives, WO 208/3154 'Special detention centre "Ashcan": interrogation reports'.

54 *The Times*, 29 May 1945.

55 *The Times*, 1 June 1945.

56 'Report to the President by Mr Justice Jackson, June 6, 1945', in *Report of Robert H. Jackson, United States Representative to the International*

Conference on Military Trials, London 1945 (Washington: US Department
of State, 1949), pp. 42–54.

57   National Archives, WO 311/61 'War Crimes Investigation Unit
     (WCIU), London District Cage (LDC): general correspondence on
     war crimes'.

58   No mention was made about the still highly secret material gathered
     from breaking the German Enigma machine code system. No one
     was going to admit to that in public or even to the Soviets.

59   The massacre of the fifty was first announced to the House of
     Commons on 19 May 1944 by the Foreign Minister, Anthony Eden.
     It left a deep impression on the British public, perhaps because there
     were so many thousands of British POWs in German hands that
     families were from then on fearful for their safety. More than a year
     later, it hadn't been forgotten and it remained a priority for investiga-
     tion and prosecution. See Priscilla Dale Jones, 'Nazi Atrocities against
     Allied Airmen: Stalag Luft III and the End of British War Crimes
     Trials' (1998), *The Historical Journal*, Vol. 41:2, pp. 543–565.

60   The statement was read out in its entirety during the Bergen-Belsen
     trial on 2 October 1945.

61   The name Mengele would become synonymous with a particular
     form of Nazi atrocity, a product of an ideology that denied respect
     as 'human' to all but a select band, and one that the American pros-
     ecutors would take up in years to come. The British investigators in
     May 1945 didn't yet understand the implications of the Dr Mengele
     story (he was largely an unknown figure then), but he would come
     to represent a twisted mentality within the Nazi movement that
     defined an extraordinary disassociation from humanity. Whole
     swathes of peoples may have been the specific target of their callous
     violence, Jews and Roma and gays and Slavs and the disabled, but
     any person could find themselves persecuted and unrecognised as
     human and subjected to treatment that denied any value they may
     have as a life. Such thinking would allow people to be used (and once
     used and no longer serving a function they would be disposed of like
     any utensil) for whatever purpose the Germans desired: labourers,
     killers, playthings, objects of display. Mengele was one of a cohort
     of medical practitioners who extended the list to guinea pigs. But the
     story told about Mengele and the Nazi doctors could only be passed
     back to London. It served little purpose for the immediate gathering
     of evidence against those in custody in Bergen-Belsen, though similar

stories of experimentation were being uncovered in the other camps investigated by the British at Neuengamme, Ravensbrück and Natzweiler.

62   The question was asked for good reason. It was believed that certain SAS and SOE agents were imprisoned in Natzweiler. Investigators wanted to know if Kramer had any idea about their fate, it not being clear at that point what had happened to a number of agents. It was an issue that would assume significance later, although for now the focus was on Belsen and Auschwitz.

63   Affidavit of Renée Erman, 26 May 1945, contained within the Bergen-Belsen trial documents and available online at http://www.bergen belsen.co.uk/pages/TrialTranscript/Trial_Contents.html.

64   Dr Charles Bendel would give his evidence at the Bergen-Belsen trial on 1 October 1945.

65   National Archives, WO 309/1697 'No 1 War Crimes Investigation Team depositions: 1–175'.

66   Klein's statement was read out at the Bergen-Belsen trial on 5 October 1945.

67   The song and invitation cards are amongst Leo Genn's military papers deposited with the Imperial War Museum: see note 35 above.

68   The assumption of fanaticism as characteristic of all SS members would later affect the Bergen-Belsen trial. Though it might be true, little evidence of that fanaticism came to light then. The SS personnel accused portrayed themselves as anything but fanatics. They were worker bees, they would claim, drones, automatons carrying out the commands of absent others.

69   *The Times*, 17 June 1945.

70   Lt Col Champion gave evidence to this effect at the Bergen-Belsen trial on 28 September 1945 when he was brought to explain how investigations had been carried out at the camp.

71   National Archives, WO 309/372 'War Crimes Investigation Unit: formation of units and organisation'.

Part 4 – Neustadt

1   *Der Spiegel*, 22 June 2007.

2   *Guardian*, 23 March 2015.

3   Wilhelm Lange, 'Cap Arcona: Summary of the Cap Arcona Disaster in the Bay of Neustadt on 3 May 1945 – On Behalf of the town of Neustadt' (1996).

4   This wasn't entirely accurate. 30 Assault Unit, a British intelligence gathering team, had operatives at Neustadt on the day of the sinking. Two SS guards were captured by them. The History of the unit stated that these guards were 'summarily executed': National Archives, ADM 223/214 'Appendix 1 (Part 5): History of 30 Commando (later called 30 Assault Unit)'.

5   National Archives, WO 309/1592 'Neustadt Bay, Germany: death of allied nationals on board ship and investigations into conditions at Neuengamme Concentration Camp, Germany', Report by Col. J. Christopher to Comd 8 Corps, 14 May 1945.

6   The story of Brigadier Mills-Roberts' treatment of Field Marshal Milch has passed into general British commando lore. I'm unsure of its truth.

7   Lt Charlton's statement was part of the evidence presented at the Neuengamme Concentration Camp trial held in 1946: National Archives, WO 235/167 'Exhibits 1–40 Place of Trial: Hamburg'.

8   National Archives, WO 309/480 'Bergen-Belsen Concentration Camp: First Trial: Administrative arrangements and general correspondence', Memo to 21 Army Group received 27 April 1945.

9   National Archives, WO 309/517 'Sandbostel Concentration Camp, Germany: killing and ill-treatment of allied nationals', Analysis of Inquiry into Sandbostel Camp by Captain Stewart, July 1945.

10   Clifford Barnard, *Two Weeks in May* 1945 (London: Quaker Home Service, 1999). Barnard was a member of the Friends Ambulance Unit which was sent to Sandbostel on its liberation. In his book, he describes his experiences and the correspondence he had with local Germans about the camp in the late 1990s.

11   National Archives, WO 309/517, note 9 above.

12   National Archives, WO 309/517, Report on Search for Missing of Sandbostel Camp, 18 July 1946.

13   National Archives, WO 309/1418 'War crime investigation teams: formation of unit', Report on organisation of War Crimes Investigation teams, 3 June 1945.

14   *The Times*, 20 January 1993.

15   There are a number of files held by the National Archives that contain information about the Neustadt Bay disaster. WO 309/637, WO

309/851, WO 309/1592 and WO 309/1788. Major Till's investigation papers are mostly within WO 309/1592.

16   Missing from the statement, however, were comments Phillip Jackson had made in letters apparently written by him on 8 and 10 May 1945. I don't know precisely to whom these letters were addressed nor have I seen copies. They're referred to in a book by Hal Vaughan called *Doctor to the Resistance* which tells the story of Phillip's father, Dr Sumner Jackson. Vaughan quotes from letters he says are held by the Jackson family. They seem to retell the same account as relayed to the War Crimes Investigation Team. A couple of inconsistencies appear nonetheless. According to Vaughan, Phillip had written that prisoners who'd made it into the water from the *Thielbek* 'were hit by cannon fire from the Typhoons'. He also wrote that after being taken to shore, he and the other rescued survivors, about 200 in all, were put against a wall. 'The SS set up machine guns to get rid of us. Then a British tank arrived. That was our liberation.' Jackson's tale was less dramatic in his formal statement given a couple of weeks later (perhaps the result of its composition by his interviewer), but it was odd that no mention was made of the Typhoons strafing the prisoners in the water in his official statement. If he meant that the aeroplanes returned to attack the men, whether inmates or guards who'd jumped overboard, that would be a serious charge: it could be interpreted as a war crime, something that wasn't acceptable under the Geneva Convention. Maybe all he saw was the ongoing attack by the planes against the many targets in the bay that afternoon. People in the water would have been caught in the crossfire. Whatever it might have implied, this part of his account didn't find its way into the statement. It only appeared in those reported letters. Hal Vaughan, *Doctor to the Resistance: The Heroic True Story of an American Surgeon and his Family in Occupied Paris* (Washington DC: Brassey's Inc., 2004), pp. 152–3.

17   Voth was the spelling in Till's transcript, but it's possible this was Ewald Foth. He matches Dora's description. Foth was handed over to the Polish authorities and tried in 1946. He was sentenced to death and hanged in Gdańsk in 1947 for his crimes committed at Stutthof KZ. See Geoffrey P. Megargee (ed.), *Encyclopedia of Camps and Ghettos 1933–1945*, Vol. 1, Part B (Bloomington: United States Holocaust Memorial Museum, 2009), p. 1467.

18   David A. Hackett (ed. and tr.), *The Buchenwald Report* (Boulder: Westview Press, 1995), p. 159.

19   Eugen Kogon, *The Theory and Practice of Hell: The German Concentration Camps and the System Behind Them* (London: Secker & Warburg, 1950), p. 62.

20   Ibid., pp. 276–7.

21   Viktor Frankl, *Man's Search for Meaning* (London: Rider, 2004), p. 93.

22   Primo Levi, *The Drowned and the Saved* (London: Abacus, 1989), pp. 28–9.

23   It wasn't just the Allied forces' prosecutors who saw the *Kapos* as potential accused. The Israeli state conducted forty largely unpublicised prosecutions of *Kapos* during the 1950s and '60s under its Nazi and Nazi Collaborators Law 1950, which was also used to prosecute Adolf Eichmann. For one of the few analyses of these trials see Orna Ben-Naftali and Yogev Tuval, 'Punishing International Crimes Committed by the Persecuted: the *Kapo* Trials in Israel (1950s–1960s) (2006), *Journal of International Criminal Justice*, Vol. 4, pp. 128–78.

24   I found details of the Dora Love Prize, and an account of her life, at the following web page of the University of Essex: http://www.essex. ac.uk/history/holocaust_memorial_week/dora_love_prize/dora_love.html.

25   What Till didn't know was how de Blonay came to be there. It was an extraordinary tale in itself. Even amidst the chaos and desperate fighting at the end of the war, the Swiss-based organisation was able to gain passage across the battle zones. In March 1945, it had arranged for a fifty-car train laden with trucks and supplies to leave Switzerland and steam to a POW camp near Munich, Stalag VII-A. The consignment was unloaded by Allied prisoners, many of them Canadian. Two days later, de Blonay turned up at the camp asking for volunteer drivers from amongst the prisoners. More than fifty Canadians and Americans gave their word to the German authorities not to escape and then drove the convoy all the way to Lübeck. The Allied POW drivers may have moved on from Holstein, sent back across Germany in a remarkable feat during the final days of the war, but de Blonay was still in Lübeck on 2 May. Hugh A. Halliday, 'Relief Amid Chaos: The Story of Canadian POWs Driving Red Cross' (2002), *Canadian Military History*, Vol. 11:2, Article 7, available at http://scholars.wlu.ca/cmh/vol11/iss2/7.

26   Imperial War Museum, Piet Ketelaar Interview (1987) (Catalogue No. 9725).

27   Imperial War Museum, Private Papers of Lt Col S.G. Champion (Documents No. 2323).

28 One of those whom Till was investigating was Keith Meyer, who was known to have been captured by the Germans but whose destination couldn't be located. As it happened, Champion sent his draft interim report on Belsen to Till for his comments and in that Champion mentioned that they had found only one British national who was killed at Belsen. That was Keith Meyer. Till wrote to Champion that they had been presuming Meyer was at Sachsenhausen. 'It's rather upset our story his turning up at Belsen!' Till wrote.

29 Royal Warrant, 18 June 1945, Regulations for the Trial of War Criminals.

30 Imperial War Museum, Champion Papers (note 27 above).

31 Count Folke Bernadotte was something of a controversial figure during the latter stages of the war. He spent many weeks at the beginning of 1945 attempting to negotiate with Heinrich Himmler for the release of prisoners from concentration camps. With a degree of self-publicity, he wrote about his efforts immediately after the end of the war in a hastily composed autobiography: Folke Bernadotte, *The Curtain Falls* (New York: A.A. Knopf, 1945).

32 'Planning Memorandum distributed to Delegations at the beginning of the London Conference June 1945', in *Report of Robert H. Jackson, United States Representative to the International Conference on Military Trials* (Washington: Department of State, 1949), pp. 64–8.

33 Raphael Lemkin, *Axis Rule in Occupied Europe: Laws of Occupation; Analysis of Government; Proposals for Redress* (Washington DC: Carnegie Endowment for International Peace, 1944).

34 Telford Taylor, *The Anatomy of the Nuremberg Trials* (London: Bloomsbury, 1993), p. 62. Taylor was one of the senior lawyers on Jackson's US team. He would become chief prosecutor for those trials at Nuremberg which took place after 1946 and the conclusion of the main tribunal hearing.

35 Berlin Potsdam Conference, Protocol of Proceedings, 1 August 1945, Part VI, 'War Criminals'.

36 *The Times* published the text of the Leaders' Statement from the Potsdam Conference in Berlin on 3 August 1945. Truman, Churchill and Stalin all endorsed the form of trial constructed by the Americans in London.

37 'Agreement and Charter of the International Military Tribunal, 8 August 1945', in *Report of Robert H. Jackson, United States Representative to the International Conference on Military Trials* (Washington: Department of State, 1949), pp. 420–28.

38   Protocol to Agreement and Charter, 6 October 1945.

39   I did, however, happen across a note from Nuremberg US prosecutor
      Col Amen suggesting that Kramer 'will testify that the principal
      officers in charge of concentration camps, Glücks and Pohl, did
      nothing to alleviate conditions at Belsen' and should be brought to
      the tribunal to give that evidence. No mention was made of Kramer's
      role at Auschwitz and he wasn't brought as a witness. See 'Potential
      witnesses for trial', Amen memo 2 November 1945, 'Witnesses compe-
      tent to testify at trial', and Amen memo 17 November 1945, both
      available in the online archive of Nuremberg Tribunal papers collected
      by another member of the US prosecution team, General William
      Donovan   (http://library2.lawschool.cornell.edu/donovan/show.
      asp).

40   The Times, 9 August 1945.

41   Telford Taylor, The Anatomy of the Nuremberg Trials (London:
      Bloomsbury, 1993), p. 80.

42   The matter was revisited after the tribunal began. The Poles wanted
      to submit evidence, unsurprising given the years of occupation.
      But there was resistance from the British. They thought it would
      be unmanageable. National Archives, FO 371/51001 'German war
      criminals: crimes against Jews: atrocities in occupied territories:
      Nuremberg war crimes: Belsen trials: minutes of Nuremberg trials.
      Code 73 File 16 (papers 9708–9804)', Memo FO to Warsaw Embassy
      11 December 1945.

43   Manchester Guardian, 30 August 1945.

Part 5 - Lüneburg

1   National Archives, WO 309/480 'Bergen-Belsen Concentration Camp:
      First Trial; Administrative arrangements and general correspondence'.

2   Imperial War Museum, Private Papers of Major T.C.M. Winwood
      (Documents No. 11522).

3   Illustrated London News, 29 September 1945.

4   Hannah Arendt, The Origins of Totalitarianism (New York: Schocken
      Books, 2004), p. 568.

5   Daily Mail, 18 September 1945.

6   Manchester Guardian, 22 September 1945; Jackson accepted that other
      defendants could be added to the list of accused later. The main news

he wanted to communicate, though, was that the Gestapo and the SS were to be tried as 'organisations'. If convicted, it would mean 'all members would be guilty to the extent of their active participation,' Jackson said.

7   *Daily Mail*, 25 September 1945.

8   *The Times*, 18 September 1945.

9   National Archives, WO 309/484 'Administrative arrangements and general correspondence', Memo, 14 November 1945, HQ 30 Corps District 336/1/A(PS).

10 *The Times*, 17 October 1945.

11 *Manchester Guardian*, 1 October 1945.

12 Decision on Prosecution Motion for the Admission of Transcripts in Lieu of Viva Voce Testimony Pursuant to 92 bis (D) 30 June 2003 Trial Chamber III (Judges May [Presiding], Robinson & Kwon).

13 *Manchester Guardian*, 5 October 1945.

14 I accessed the archive of the board at http://www.jta.org/1945/10/11/archive/board-of-deputies-protests-against-anti-jewish-slur-by-british-officer-defending-nazis#ixzz3JhF6FJFk.

15 *The Times*, 10 October 1945.

16 Though as far as the British were concerned he was going to hang whatever happened. The War Office noted a request from the French government in October 1945 to hand Kramer over to them in the event of him not being condemned to death. He was required 'for trial by Military Court at Strasbourg for the crimes committed at Struthof'. The note commented: 'We imagine that, in the unlikely event of Kramer not being condemned to death, the Polish Government might also ask for him for trial on account of his crimes at Auschwitz.' National Archives, WO 309/484, War Office note to BAOR, 21 October 1945.

17 *Manchester Guardian*, 4 October 1945.

18 G.M. Gilbert, *Nuremberg Diary* (New York: Da Capo Press, 1995).

19 *Daily Mail*, 17 October 1945.

Part 6 – Dachau

1   US Joint Chiefs of Staff Directive on the Identification and Apprehension of Persons Suspected of War Crimes or Other Offenses and Trial of Certain Offenders, 1023/10, 8 July 1945.

2   Documents of the International Military Tribunal at Nuremberg,
       'Nazi Conspiracy and Aggression Volume IV', Document No. 2222-PS,
       Report of Investigation of Alleged War Crime committed in 31 concen-
       tration camps all in the vicinity of Nordhausen, Germany.

3   For reports on some of the major cases tried, see *Law Reports of Trials
       of War Criminals: Selected and Prepared by the United Nations War Crimes
       Commission* (London: HMSO, 1949). There are also two excellent
       narrative-based accounts I came across: Joshua M. Green, *Justice at
       Dachau: The Trials of an American Prosecutor* (New York: Broadway
       Books, 2003), and Tomaz Jardim, *The Mauthausen Trial: American
       Military Justice in Germany* (Cambridge: Harvard University Press, 2012).

4   *Manchester Guardian*, 23 September 1945, which reported 40,000 were
       killed at the institution.

5   Case No. 4, The Hadamar Trial of Alfons Klein and six others,
       8–15 October 1945, *Law Reports of Trials of War Criminals: Selected
       and Prepared by the United Nations War Crimes Commission, Vol. I*
       (London: HMSO, 1949).

6   *The Times*, 17 November 1945.

7   Case No. 60, The Dachau Concentration Camp Trial of Martin
       Gottfried Weiss and Thirty-Nine Others, 15 November–13 December
       1945, *Law Reports of Trials of War Criminals: Selected and Prepared by
       the United Nations War Crimes Commission, Vol. XI* (London: HMSO,
       1949).

8   Donovan Research Collection, Vol. XIX s 61.01 (http://library2.
       lawschool.cornell.edu/donovan/show.asp). Such was the desire to
       present a prosecution untainted by accusations of crimes committed
       by the Allied nations that all mention of the Soviet invasion of Poland
       (which followed a secret pact between Hitler and Stalin) was also
       suppressed.

9   Although for three days the court had been preoccupied with prelim-
       inary legal points (whether Martin Bormann could remain one of
       the accused in absentia (accepted), whether the proceedings should
       be postponed because the accused Gustav Krupp was ill (rejected),
       whether his son Alfred could be added to the accused (rejected)). On
       Tuesday 20 November the real event began.

10   *Daily Mail*, 21 November 1945.

11   *The Times*, 21 November 1945.

12   *Manchester Guardian*, 30 November 1945.

13   *Daily Mail*, 30 November 1945.

14   Gilbert's engagement wasn't part of any general attempt to under-
      stand the 'Nazi mind'. Gilbert described his duties as 'to keep the
      [Nuremberg] prison commandant, Colonel B.C. Andrus, aware of
      the state of [the defendants'] morale, and to help in any way possible
      to assure their standing trial with orderly discipline'. He would also
      take part in assessments of the mental health of any prisoner.
      G.M. Gilbert, *Nuremberg Diary* (New York: Da Capo Press, 1995), p. 3.
      Psychological profiling had already been used by the Allies during
      the war in their attempts to understand their enemy leaders and find
      their weaknesses. The US Office of Strategic Studies commissioned
      a psychological profile of Hitler in 1943, which of course identified
      aspects of his upbringing as contributing reasons for his perpetrating
      atrocities. You can find the report entitled 'Analysis of the Personality
      of Adolph Hitler' by Dr Henry A. Murray in the Donovan Nuremberg
      Trials Collection at Cornell University Law Library, available online
      at http://ebooks.library.cornell.edu/n/nur/analysis.php.

15   *Daily Mail*, 1 December 1945.

16   Documents of the International Military Tribunal at Nuremberg,
      Nazi Conspiracy and Aggression, Volume 3, Document No. 1061-PS.

17   Stroop was prosecuted by the Americans at Dachau for the murder
      of nine American POW flying crew in 1947. He was then extradited
      to Poland, where he was tried and convicted and sentenced to death
      for the Warsaw Ghetto atrocity.

18   G.M. Gilbert, *Nuremberg Diary* (New York: Da Capo Press, 1995), p. 98.

19   Primo Levi, *The Drowned and the Saved* (London: Abacus, 1988), p. 97.

20   Stanley Milgram, *Obedience to Authority: An Experimental View* (London:
      Tavistock Publications, 1974).

21   Jeremiah 17:9 (English Standard Version). I'm no scholar of the Bible.
      I came across the reference in the council chamber of the medieval
      castello of Gradara in Italy.

22   Hannah Arendt, *Eichmann in Jerusalem: A Report on the Banality of Evil*
      (London: Penguin, 1992).

23   I can't leave this subject without mentioning a number of works that
      have been instrumental in shaping consideration of the human capacity
      for atrocity. Foremost amongst these, at least as regards the minds of
      those who exercised authority in the concentration camps, is Gitta
      Sereny's somewhat forgotten masterpiece, *Into That Darkness: An
      Examination of Conscience* (London: Picador, 1974). An account of her
      interviews with the ex-commandant of the extermination camps at

Sobibór and Treblinka, this book searches deeply within the psyche of
both the Nazi officer and his wife. It is an extraordinary read. Others
that I haven't already mentioned include: Simon Baron-Cohen, *Zero
Degrees of Empathy: A New Theory of Human Cruelty and Kindness* (London:
Penguin, 2012); Ervin Staub, *The Roots of Evil: The Origins of Genocide
and Other Group Violence* (Cambridge: Cambridge University Press, 1989);
Tzvetan Todorov, *Facing the Extreme: Moral Life in the Concentration
Camps* (London: Phoenix, 1999); and James Waller, *Becoming Evil: How
Ordinary People Commit Genocide and Mass Killing*, 2nd edn (Oxford: Oxford
University Press, 2007). There are many others.

Part 7 - Hamburg

1   Imperial War Museum, Private Papers of Lt Col Leo Genn.
2   Hansard, HC, Vol. 416 cols 1909–10 (3 December 1945).
3   The Foreign Office collected stories about the Bergen-Belsen trial
    from the world's press to assess public reaction to the proceedings.
4   National Archives, WO 32/12197 'War Criminals: general: war crimes
    policy'.
5   National Archives, WO 311/682 'Establishment of Special Search Units
    to aid investigation of war crimes', Message to War Office AG3(W),
    16 December 1945, from Major General Chilton.
6   WO 311/682, Message War Office to BAOR, 30 December 1945.
7   A story in its own right and told by Sarah Helm, *A Life in Secrets: Vera
    Atkins and the Lost Agents of SOE* (London: Abacus, 2006).
8   The comment was included in an interview with Vera Atkins recorded
    on tape by the Imperial War Museum in 1986: Imperial War Museum,
    Recording – Vera Atkins (Catalogue No. 31590).
9   National Archives, WO 311/694 'SAS war crimes investigation: policy'.
10 Marked in the margin of this letter was a note that JAG denied Harris's
    claim, instead asserting that Barkworth's evidence was more than
    enough: WO 311/694 (note 9 above).
11 Letter, 6 October 1945, Harris to Col G.R. Bradshaw DDPS(c), War
    Office. WO 311/694 (note 9 above).
12 National Archives, WO 311/682 'Establishment of Special Search Units
    to aid investigation of war crimes'.
13 National Archives, WO 309/2204 'War crimes: statistics; prisoners held
    in custody by War Crimes Group (North West Europe); cases held by
    Field Investigation Section; allocation of cases; progress reports'.

14 Imperial War Museum, taped interview with Ian Neilson in 1998 (Catalogue No. 18537).

15 WO 309/2204, note 13 above.

16 National Archives, WO 309/1672 'War Crimes Group (NWE): formation, organisation and standing instructions'.

17 National Archives, WO 309/1826 'War Crimes Investigation Unit: administrative records'.

18 Ibid.

19 Ibid.

20 Ibid.

21 National Archives, WO 309/1673 'War Crimes Investigation Unit, BAOR and War Crimes Group NWE: war establishment'.

22 Ibid.

23 National Archives, WO 311/15 'Deputy Judge Advocate General (DJAG) British Army of the Rhine (BAOR) personnel: interrogating teams and interpreters'.

24 WO 309/1673 (note 21 above).

25 National Archives, WO 309/64 'Neuengamme Concentration Camp, Germany: killing and ill-treatment of allied nationals'.

26 National Archives, WO 309/1602 'Supplying poison gas (Zyklon B) for use in extermination of allied nationals in concentration camps'.

27 There were, perhaps surprisingly, many letters written to the British forces by German citizens. I came across one dated 24 August 1945 from an Eric Anders, who'd been a political prisoner in Neuengamme. He sent a well-crafted condemnation of *SS-Oberscharführer* Reese: (National Archive, WO 309/64 (note 25 above)). It contributed to the general file of information against Reese, who was eventually brought to trial in 1946.

28 Further Deposition by Ada Bimko, 28 May 1945.

29 International Military Tribunal at Nuremberg, Trial proceedings, 17 April 1945, p. 554.

30 M. Meyer and H. McCoubrey (eds), *Reflections on Law and Armed Conflicts: The Selected Works on the Laws of War by the Late Professor Colonel G.I.A.D. Draper OBE* (The Hague: Kluwer, 1998); Biographical note by Brevet Major The Count de Salis.

31 Imperial War Museum, 'Private Papers of Major A.W. Freud' (Document No. 13326).

32 Pelican was another of those who recorded his experiences for the Imperial War Museum (Catalogue No. 9222). You can still access his

tapes. But he also published a memoir as part of a series of Holocaust Testimonies. This was in 1993. He was seventy-five years old. Fred Pelican, *From Dachau to Dunkirk* (London: Vallentine Mitchell, 1993).

33   Ibid., p. 113.

34   WO 309/1602 (note 26 above).

35   National Archives, WO 235/641 'Defendant: Bruno Tesch DJAG No. 168'.

36   I've tracked down the history of only one other of these named SS men trained to use Zyklon B. Adolf Theuer was only nineteen at the beginning of the war but worked at Auschwitz. His job was to insert the tin of Zyklon B into the gas chamber pipe. After the camp's evacuation, he served at Ohrdruf KZ. He was captured, tried, sentenced to death and executed in Czechoslovakia in 1947.

37   National Archives, WO 208/4294 'Papers recovered from Lt Col A P Scotland: notes on operation of War Crimes Interrogation Unit, work and organisation of Prisoners of War Interrogation Section (Home) and miscellaneous subjects'.

38   See, for instance, Sophie Jackson, *British Interrogation Techniques in the Second World War* (Stroud: The History Press, 2012). Scotland always denied claims of abuse.

39   The same sentiments governed high-level policy discussions about the prosecution of industrialists who were complicit in the maintenance and supply of the Nazi regime, enabling it to function efficiently, who were complicit also in subjecting millions of workers to inhuman conditions, and who benefited fantastically from that arrangement. IG Farben, chemical giants and the manufacturers of Zyklon B, would be the subject of a later trial run by the Americans a year after the Nuremberg Tribunal was over, as would owners and directors of the arms manufacturing corporation Krupps and the mining and industrial conglomerate Flick KG.

40   National Archives, WO 309/388 'Killing of allied children and ill-treatment of allied nationals'.

41   Kurt Heissmeyer avoided capture, returned to Magdeburg and continued to practise as a TB specialist despite being named as a culprit of this atrocity in Lord Russell's notorious bestselling book on Nazi war crimes in 1954 (Lord Russell of Liverpool, *The Scourge of the Swastika: A Short History of Nazi War Crimes* (New York: Philosophical Library, 1954), pp. 189–190). He was eventually identified and put on trial in East Germany in the 1960s and sentenced to life imprisonment. He died in 1967.

42 National Archives, WO 309/585 'Velpke, Germany: killing of children of allied nationals by neglect'.

43 Ibid., letter, 2 February 1946, Director of Personal Services War Office to HQ BAOR.

44 WO 309/585 (note 42 above).

45 International Military Tribunal at Nuremberg, trial proceedings, 3 January 1946.

46 Col Amen Memorandum on Potential Witnesses for Trial, 17 November 1945, General Donovan Archive papers (http://library2. lawschool.cornell.edu/donovan/show.asp).

47 Telford Taylor, *The Anatomy of the Nuremberg Trials* (London: Bloomsbury, 1993), p. 248.

48 G.M. Gilbert, *Nuremberg Diary* (New York: Da Capo Press, 1995), p. 101.

49 *The Times*, 4 January 1946.

50 Ibid.

51 *The Times*, 21 January 1946; Wilson Harris MP wrote on 'An Atmosphere of Scrupulous Justice'.

Part 8 - Hamburg Revisited

1 *John Bull*, 22 October 1949.

2 National Archives, WO 235/641 'Defendant: Bruno Tesch DJAG No. 168'.

3 National Archives, HO 334/161/17843 'Naturalisation Certificate: Karl Stephan Strauss. From Germany. Resident in B.A.O.R. Certificate AZ17843 issued 25 March 1946. Alias: Stephen Malcolm Stewart'.

4 The Neuengamme trial proceedings are recorded in several thick lever arch files. See National Archives, WO 235/163-169 'Neuengamme concentration camp case'.

5 Christopher Sidgwick was an occasional writer for the *Manchester Guardian* even whilst serving with the British Army in Germany after the end of the war. The paper published one article by Sidgwick on Neuengamme KZ and the trial: *Manchester Guardian*, 13 May 1946.

6 *Manchester Guardian*, Letters to the Editor, 7 April 1936.

7 *Daily Mail*, 16 February 1946.

8 International Military Tribunal at Nuremberg, trial proceedings, 14 March 1946.

9   Telford Taylor, *The Anatomy of the Nuremberg Trials* (London: Bloomsbury, 1993), p. 330.

10   *Daily Mail*, 15 March 1946.

11   *The Times*, 14 March 1946.

12   *The Times*, 15 March 1946.

13   Telford Taylor, *The Anatomy of the Nuremberg Trials* (London: Bloomsbury, 1993), p. 335.

14   The letters were made public in 2009. See *Guardian*, 20 March 2009.

15   *Daily Mail*, 22 March 1946.

16   *The Times*, 22 March 1946.

17   News of the trial and conviction was covered extensively by the BBC. See http://www.bbc.co.uk/news/uk-24870699.

18   *The Times*, 4 May 1946.

19   Kauffmann would be tried and convicted, sentenced to a prison term but released early in 1953. He died in 1969.

20   Bassewitz-Behr would be controversially acquitted by a British court of responsibility for killing and ill-treatment at Fuhlsbüttel prison, but then immediately extradited to the Soviets for crimes committed in Russia, the killing of Jews, forced labour. The Russians convicted him and he died in Siberia whilst serving his sentence of hard labour.

21   *The Times*, 12 May 1946.

22   *The Times*, 29 May 1946.

Part 9 - Nuremberg

1   Primo Levi, *If This is a Man* (London: Abacus, 1979), p. 15.

2   Anyone, if interested, can read the judgment of the courts that examined the case on the internet. The official title of the case was *R. (Al-Skeini) v. The Secretary of State for Defence*.

3   But no such legal procedure or court has examined the choice to go to war in the first place and the inquiry established to look into that question (the Chilcot Inquiry) quickly became an exercise in futility. The Chilcot Inquiry was established by the government of Gordon Brown in 2009. One of its members was the historian Sir Martin Gilbert, who had written extensively on the Holocaust and in particular the Allies' knowledge and lack of response to its execution; see Martin Gilbert, *Auschwitz and the Allies* (London: Mandarin, 1991). He died in February 2015 before the report was published.

4   Iraq Historic Allegations Team, Quarterly Update – October to December 2014, https://www.gov.uk/government/uploads/system/uploads/attachment_data/file/411437/20150216-Qupdate_Oct_Dec2015.pdf.

5   Though there was a public inquiry that condemned British practices of interrogation and named many soldiers who were believed to be responsible for Baha Mousa and the other detainees' injuries and those who'd failed to prevent such abuses, no one has been brought to justice for the death. At the time of writing, the spring of 2015, some twelve years after Baha Mousa was killed, the IHAT can only promise that they are pursuing new lines of enquiry.

6   *Daily Mail*, 16 February 1946.

7   International Military Tribunal at Nuremberg, trial proceedings, 28 June 1946.

8   *The Times*, 29 September 1946.

9   *Daily Mail*, 1 October 1946.

10 *The Times*, 2 October 1946.

11 Executive Order No. 9679, 16 January 1946. The Americans prosecuted a further twelve cases after the main trial of Goering et al. They were led by Telford Taylor. A full report of these proceedings can be found in 'Trials of War Criminals Before the Nuremberg Military Tribunals Under Control Council Law No. 10', available online at http://www.loc.gov/rr/frd/Military_Law/NTs_war-criminals.html.

12 National Archives, WO 309/1672 'War Crimes Group (NWE): formation, organisation and standing instructions'.

13 National Archives, FO 371/57587 'Proposed trial before a United States Zonal Court of Alfred Krupp and other German industrialists'.

14 National Archives, WO 309/1826 'War Crimes Investigation Unit: administrative records'.

15 Hansard, HC, Vol. 468 col. 193W (28 October 1949), reply of Mr Shinwell.

16 Hansard, HL, Vol. 179 cols 1039–40WA (16 December 1952), Parliamentary answer by Parliamentary Under-secretary of State for Foreign Affairs.

17 We're largely in the dark about the Soviet prosecutions. There are few sources available to judge though some snippets of information have found their way into Western academic analysis. See, for instance, Jonathan Friedman, 'The Sachsenhausen Trials', in Patricia Herber and Jürgen Matthäus, *Atrocities on Trial: Historical Perspectives on the Politics of Prosecuting War Crimes* (Lincoln: University of Nebraska Press, 2008), pp. 159–84.

18   The War Crimes Group ceased to function officially on 15 September
      1948. Its cases were handed over to Legal Division. No general warning
      was issued amongst the forces on mainland Europe. The Allied
      Commission for Austria complained, 'Although we have always fore-
      seen the possibility of War Crimes Group closing, it was not antici-
      pated that we should get no warning.' National Archives, FO 1020/776
      War crimes: policy: Brief for AAG, 26 August 1948.

19   Hansard, HL, Vol. 162 cols 376–418 (5 May 1949).

20   A report of the investigation into the Malmedy massacre trial prep-
      arations was particularly damning. Report of Subcommittee of the
      Committee of Armed Services United States Senate 81st Congress,
      available in its entirety at http://www.loc.gov/rr/frd/Military_Law/
      pdf/Malmedy_report.pdf.

21   One struck me in particular for its echoes in those allegations made
      against British forces in Iraq during its occupation after 2003. The
      Dulag Luft trial made little sense to me when placed in the same
      category as those trials I'd followed from 1945 and 1946. According
      to Sir Frank Soskice QC, a member of the British War Crimes
      Executive and Solicitor General in Attlee's government, it repre-
      sented 'one aspect of the skein of events which formed the context
      of Nazi war brutality'. But I wasn't convinced. Dulag Luft had been
      the German Air Force's intelligence centre. It was a prison through
      which nearly 40,000 Allied aircrew had passed during the war, taken
      for short periods of time in order to extract information. The SS
      weren't involved, nor the Gestapo directly. Luftwaffe serving
      personnel controlled operations at the prison and directed the
      methods of interrogation that were alleged by the British prosecution
      to be 'war crimes'.
          Dulag Luft camp was a wooden building consisting of about
      two hundred identical separate cells. They were built to be sound-
      proof. Each was small, about 3 metres by 2 metres, and had a tiny
      window to the outside. The windows couldn't be opened. Under
      the window was a tubular heater controlled from the corridor. The
      cells housed Allied airmen who had been shot down over occupied
      Europe. They were brought here as a matter of course to be inter-
      rogated. First given a questionnaire to complete, the men were then
      seen separately, either in their cells or the office of the interrogating
      officer. The interrogations were short for gunners, who wouldn't be
      expected to know much, and longer (perhaps three or four days) for

a pilot so as to extract information about general air force operations. Servicemen might stay in solitary confinement for several weeks waiting to be interrogated before being transferred to one of the various POW camps about Germany. The official interpretation was less damning, as I discovered whilst reading some of the records of the London-based British War Crimes Executive, which collated evidence for the Nuremberg Tribunal. Group Captain Felkin had reported on Dulag Luft in the middle of 1945. He'd said, 'Interrogation of many German interrogators and of some of the leading figures in German Air Force Intelligence indicates that the handling of our air crew for interrogation purposes was not out of the ordinary … To our knowledge, all cases of gross mistreatment and murder of prisoners of war may be allayed to the Gestapo or SS.'

Though interrogation of POWs wasn't sanctioned by the Geneva Convention, everyone knew that both sides asked questions. Indeed, Dulag Luft had been taken over by the US Air Force in 1945 and was also used as an interrogation centre, this time for SS and other Nazis. Neither side stopped with polite questioning. Whether the process slipped into torture or ill-treatment was always a matter of degree and judgement.

The prosecution was headed by Major Gerald Draper, who claimed in his opening speech that the heating of the cells had been turned up to excessive temperatures to soften up the airmen before interrogation. He said threats were made of transfer to the Gestapo if questions weren't answered satisfactorily, medical attention had been refused for those in need, solitary confinement had been prolonged and in some cases ('very few', the prosecution accepted) blows were struck.

One of the first prosecution witnesses, WO Robert Lang, said he'd been shot down north of Amsterdam in April 1943. After his capture he'd been transferred to Oberursel, where the Dulag Luft camp was located. Lang had been put in one of the cells. A German officer came to see him and asked him to complete a form. He filled out the standard information and crossed out everything else. The officer had raved at him, Lang said, before leaving him alone. Then Lang heard the noise of a switch being pulled outside. The radiator began to vibrate and the room had become hotter and hotter. 'The heat became so intense that I had to strip to my underpants and lie on the floor.'

Major Draper asked about his condition at the time. He was still bruised from his crash a couple of weeks previously, he said. And then there was his finger. He'd broken it on landing and it had been set in the hospital in Amsterdam. But it still hurt at Dulag Luft, he said. He'd asked for medical attention. None ever came, though admittedly his finger healed soon after, he said.

The heat treatment had continued for a few days. The radiator had been turned on and he'd been left to stew. He'd only gained some relief when he'd banged on the door and persuaded the German guard to take him to the lavatories. He'd been very weak, he said. They'd kept asking him questions. He'd refused to answer and the heat had been turned on again. Eventually, the German officer had asked him to confirm the number of his squadron and he'd done so. That was all, he rushed to say. Lang had told the interrogator what he'd wanted to know. Just that and nothing more, he said. After that and later the same day he'd been taken from his cell to a transit camp.

The defendants were the high-ranking officers of the camp. *Oberleutnant* Erich Killinger, the commandant of Dulag Luft, was presented as the senior officer in charge of the installation and, under the terms of the royal warrant, responsible for any war crime committed by his unit. But Killinger was patently no Nazi. He'd refused to join the Nazi party. As the trial continued and the defence offered its evidence, it was accepted that Killinger had known little if anything of the heat treatment. When he'd finally learned about it he'd issued orders forbidding the practice and it hadn't been used again. What was more, during his time as commandant, with so many thousands of prisoners passing through his hands, he'd managed to attract the commendation of several British POWs. The same could be said for the other defendants. A long list of affidavits from British officers reflected the high regard in which they were all held. It seemed bizarre that the main defence witnesses were British serving personnel. And high-ranking at that.

Air Vice-Marshal Ivelaw-Chapman, Air Commodore in 1944 and in command of Base 13, Bomber Command, had been shot down in his Lancaster on 6 May 1944. Kept by the Gestapo for three days, he'd then been released to the Luftwaffe and sent to the hospital at Dulag Luft. From that moment, he said, he was treated properly. He told the court he was even allowed outdoor exercise. 'I had the right to walk round the wire surrounding the grounds' and 'I was allowed to go up in the

Taunus hills for exercise and managed to get winter-skiing.' One of
the accused, Eberhardt, had taken him. The extraordinary story, deeply
contrasting with commonly held suspicions about the German military
character, punctured any notion that the court was dealing with a
committed Nazi. Ivelaw-Chapman had little but good to say of the
German officers and medics he'd encountered.

He wasn't alone. Affidavits from other British officers were
provided. Of Eberhardt, Group Captain Harry Day MC said his
behaviour 'was always most considerate'. Flight Lieutenant Hardy
said 'his behaviour towards me was always correct'. And then there
was Douglas Bader, the fêted flier, who was a prisoner at Dulag Luft
for a month during 1941. Eberhardt questioned him 'pleasantly and
quietly and in every way correctly'. All the prisoners had been treated
fairly, Bader said. By common account, the accused were honourable
military personnel.

It counted for little. Major Draper's closing speech scorned the
attempt to present the accused in such a way. If they hadn't known
about the heating and the threats of transfer to the Gestapo, then
they should have done. There can be no excuse, he said, for presiding
over an abusive operation, one that contravenes the rules of war.
Even if the accused didn't participate directly, should we believe them
when they say they didn't approve of the methods? He said the
complaints brought by the British servicemen were serious and
shouldn't be taken lightly. They indicated a brutal and calculated
process.

Three of the accused, Killinger and Eberhardt included, were
found guilty of the charges. Eberhardt was sentenced to three years'
imprisonment, Killinger to five. The *New York Times* reported the case
as: 'Allies Jail 3 Torturers'. That was how the case was presented:
heinous torture of Allied aircrew.

Reading Draper's closing speech seventy years later, I wondered
whether the prosecution of Erich Killinger and the others of Dulag
Luft had any place in that scheme of justice devised in righteous fury
before the end of the war. If the matter was too petty to place in
the same bracket as 'war crime' as employed at Bergen-Belsen, then
perhaps not. But if we think of these post-World War II trials as
setting a precedent, then maybe Draper was right: there was no room
for being lenient or, worse, condoning the methods used – that would

legitimate them. Even if the British had been just as free with coercive interrogation techniques, that wouldn't make the German Luftwaffe officers any less culpable. If you started forgiving such techniques, where would you stop?

A direct test for the British during their occupation of Germany came a few years later. During 1947 a number of deaths of Nazi suspects still held in British custody were investigated. The internment camp at Bad Nenndorf appeared to have operated a regime that was brutal in the extreme. Capt. John Stuart Smith of the Royal Army Medical Corps as doctor at the prison was one of those prosecuted for neglect. Several suspected war criminals had been kept in cells with no heating during a bitterly cold winter, were left untreated when they developed frostbite, were allowed to deteriorate and only sent to the local hospital when it was too late to save them. Dr Smith was found not guilty of manslaughter but guilty of neglect and dismissed from the services. Others were similarly prosecuted. That at least would suggest an institutional intolerance for coercive techniques.

22   The 'Essen-West' case, for instance, involved seven Germans, a mix of soldiers and civilians, who were charged with a war crime being 'concerned in the killing of three unidentified British airmen POWs'. The year previously, during a massive RAF bombing raid over Essen, in the industrial centre of the Ruhr, several aircraft had been shot down. Some crews parachuted to safety. Three flyers (their identity would never be known) had been picked up by the police and were to be taken to the local military barracks. Feelings amongst the German civilians against the bombers were intense. They hated these 'terror fliers', as the RAF and USAF were called. The bombing would kill indiscriminately, hitting civilian targets during the night or day without warning. That was the nature of the relentless bombing campaign fought by the Allies. When some of the flying crew escaped from their planes and parachuted into the middle of the places where they had been bombing, civilians would sometimes attack and kill them. Hitler had issued orders to German forces that they shouldn't interfere if civilians decided to exact mob revenge.

That night in December 1944, citizens of Essen-West heard of the capture of the three RAF crew. A hundred or so intercepted them being marched to the local barracks. Shouts were heard: 'Kill them.' They attacked the crew with hammers, threw bricks at them, hit them with sticks. When they reached the Wickenburg bridge the RAF men were thrown into the valley below. Shots were fired to finish them off. Some citizens went down to see they were dead, stripped them and pushed their bodies into the stream. Throughout, the soldiers guarding the RAF men kept to their instructions not to interfere. They were commanded by *Hauptmann* Erich Heyer.

When the British occupied Essen-West they were told of the killings. Why some of the German civilians came forward with the story is unclear. But Heyer, who was arrested along with various other named soldiers and civilians, called them 'denouncers'. Perhaps scores were being settled. Perhaps consciences were too troubled to keep silent. Whatever the motivation, the story was undoubtedly true as during the investigations then launched, the British confirmed the basic details as told to them. Even those arrested did not dispute how the RAF men had died.

Various affidavits were collected that implicated the six men eventually placed under arrest. All denied delivering the fatal blows or firing the shots. But they'd been named as involved in one way or another. When the case came to be heard at the end of 1945, proceedings lasted several days. Heyer admitted to giving his men the order sent down to him by Battalion to the effect that if the civilians attacked the British crew, the soldiers shouldn't prevent them. He admitted it wasn't an order he agreed with but 'an order was an order'.

Heyer didn't accompany the guard on the march to the barracks, deciding, he said, to go to dinner instead. No one suggested he took part in the attacks or the killing. The evidence against him was that he'd incited the crowd and had been overheard giving orders to a couple of the soldiers in the guard company that the flyers should be shot, though that was never firmly established. Under examination by his British Army attorney he claimed that he became 'ashamed of my fellow German-countrymen' when he'd heard what had happened. He denied giving any reason for the guard or the civilians to harm the flyers.

By the end of the trial, Heyer and one other (Johann Braschoss, against whom testimony had been given that he'd been involved in the attacks on the bridge) were sentenced to death. Karl Kaufer, another civilian present that night, was given life imprisonment even though there was little to separate him from the rest of the crowd other than an eyewitness's account that suggested he'd tried to take a rifle from one of the German guards, supposedly to shoot the RAF men.

I couldn't tell from reading the files whether the trial conducted was fair. Since the information had come to light, it seemed right that the prosecution was brought. And reading through the transcript of proceedings, the questioning and representation appeared competent and reasonable. But later in the file I saw that an appeal against Kaufer's sentence had been lodged in 1949 by his wife with the intervention of the Bishop of Cologne's office. It was considered by Lord Russell of Liverpool, Deputy Judge Advocate General, one of the London government lawyers at the heart of war crimes prosecutions. He read the case papers (you can see some of his markings on the transcripts where he'd come across some detail he thought important) and concluded that Karl Kaufer hadn't deserved to be convicted, let alone sentenced to life imprisonment. Lord Russell wrote that the case against Kaufer was based on 'flimsy material', hearsay and unreliable witness testimony. He should never have been convicted, he concluded.

Kaufer was released. There was nothing Lord Russell could do for Heyer or Braschoss, of course, and he didn't look at their convictions. A review had confirmed the sentence shortly after it had been pronounced, as was the procedure, and nothing untoward had been noticed then. But in 1945 the desire to forgive, to give the benefit of the doubt, to be wary, was limited. The virtue of mercy would only come later. Until then retribution was allowed to run its course where it might.

23   National Archives, WO 309/388 'Killing of allied children and ill-treatment of allied nationals'.

24   National Archives, WO 235/189 'Bullenhuser Damm Trial: Neuengamme Case No. 3'.

Epilogue

1   Susan Sontag, *Regarding the Pain of Others* (London: Penguin, 2004), p. 102.

Acknowledgements

This book wouldn't have been written were it not for Patrick Bradley. His encouragement and enthusiasm have been inexhaustible. But it's his friendship that I value above all else: I can't thank him enough for that.

I would also like to thank Dan Franklin at Jonathan Cape, Andrew Gordon at David Higham and Maureen Freely at Warwick, who have been instrumental in bringing this book to life.

As always, however, the ones who have made it all worthwhile are Kathy, Antonia and Claudia.

Picture Credits

Index

Abas, Reina, 129
Abraham, General, 190, 191
Abu Ghraib, 440
Afghanistan, 384–6
Alexander, Captain Hanns, 84–6, 98, 130, 317, 372
Allied armed forces, atrocities against: during Battle of Normandy, 45–6; British attitude, 89; British investigations, 96–7, 185, 311–13, 419–20, 455; Dulag Luft, 466–70; 'Essen-West' case, 470–72; Great Escape massacre (1944), 89, 123, 365, 450; Malmedy, 444–5, 466; SAS victims, 312–13; SOE victims, 55, 311–12, 420
Almaleh, Dora, 233–5
Amen, Colonel John, 341–2
Amper, Frau, 93
Anders, Eric, 461
Andrus, Colonel B.C., 112, 459
Ansell, Lieutenant, 178
Arendt, Hannah, 212, 303
Arnoldsson, Dr Hans, 143, 190
Ashcan (Palace Hotel, Mondorf), 111–16
Athen, SS, 153, 154, 177, 178, 180–82, 189; *see also* Neustadt Bay bombing
Atkins, Vera, 311–12
Attlee, Clement, 15
Audrieu massacre (1944), 45
Aurdzieg (*Kapo*), 218
Auschwitz and Auschwitz II-Birkenau: Allied knowledge of conditions, 49, 50; author's inability to visit, 429; gas chambers, 322–3; history and conditions, 61, 62, 63, 100, 125 126–7, 128–30; Höss on trial, 372–80; selection process, 225–7, 237–9, 254, 255; war crime trial *see* Bergen-Belsen trial
Austin, Sergeant Major Edwin, 108, 110

Backhouse, Colonel Thomas (Tommie), 210; background, 212; Bergen-Belsen trial opening speech, 212, 213, 214–20, 225; Bergen-Belsen trial defendant cross-examination, 244–6, 248, 254, 255, 256; Bergen-Belsen trial evidence presentation, 233, 234–5; Bergen-Belsen trial witness examination, 224–6; later life, 423
Bad Nenndorf, 470
Bader, Douglas, 469
Bahr, *SS-Rottenführer* Willi: arrest and interrogation, 330–33; death, 419; named in investigations, 158, 164; sentence, 399; trial, 337, 357, 358, 395–7, 398–9
Baillie-Stewart, Norman, 440–41
Banda, Hastings, 297–9
Barkworth, Major Eric 'Bill', 312–13
Barnard, Clifford, 452
Barnes, Sir Thomas, 121
Barsch (alleged war criminal), 217
Bartlett, Vernon, 310
Bassewitz-Behr, *Gruppenführer*, 190, 191, 367, 402–403, 464
Becklingen War Cemetery, 67–8
Bedford College, 33
Beendorf, 420
Beimler, Hans, 33
Beining, August, 158
Bell, Major, 92, 99, 129
Belsen *see* Bergen-Belsen
Belzec, 62
Bendel, Dr Charles, 128–9
Berg, Margarete, 129
Bergen-Belsen, 69; history and conditions, 63, 74–81, 127–8; liberation, 68, 73–87, 76, 86; 286; Olivier and Thorndike visit, 131; site, 12; overview, 69–88; tour round, 69–73; war crime investigations, 87, 88, 92–101, 123–34, 184, 232

Bergen-Belsen trial: criticisms, 309–10; defence case, 235–48, 252–6; defendant overview, 216–18; defendants' right to defence, 220–24; evidence presentation, 233–5; executions, 294; investigation's inadequacy, 232; Judge Advocate's summary, 256–7, 259–62; overview, 205–48, 252–62; premise of prosecution case, 212–15; prosecution team, 210; venue, 208, 209–10; verdicts and sentences, 257–9; witnesses and cross-examinations, 224–32, 322–3
Berlin, Plötzensee prison, 12
Bernadotte, Count Folke, 177, 190, 455
Berney-Ficklin, Major General, 239
Bertram, Captain, 177, 178, 189–90
Bethnal Green tube disaster (1943), 354–5
Bidault, Georges, 91
Biddle, Francis, 52, 279
Bimko, Ada, 224, 322–3
Birkenau *see* Auschwitz and Auschwitz II-Birkenau
Blaskowitz, *Generaloberst*, 115
Bletchley Park, 37
Blonay, Paul de, 177–8, 454
Boer War (1899–1902), 27–8
Boetticher, Friedrich von, 113
Bormann, Johanna, 216–17, 225, 227–9, 228, 294
Bormann, Martin, 111, 280, 343, 458
Bothe (alleged war criminal), 218
Bradley, General Omar, 23
Braschoss, Johann, 471, 472
Breendonk Fort, 46, 285
Brems, *Blockführer*, 382
Bridgeman, Major General the Viscount, 122
British Legion, 34–5
British War Crimes Executive (BWCE), 121–2, 200, 310
Brown, Captain, 234
Brownjohn, Major General, 319

Buchenwald, 22; Allied knowledge of conditions, 36, 49; history and conditions, 61, 167–8; liberation, 23–5, 285–6; in Nuremberg film, 285–6, 287; overview, 17–25; satellites, 19–20; site, 13, 21; tour round, 21–3; zoo and falconry, 22–3, 439
Bullenhuser Damm atrocity: building and exhibition, 308–309, 334; events, 334–7; Neuengamme trial mentions, 354, 358–9, 366, 371, 381, 393–4; site as shrine, 13; trial, 337, 347, 424–7
Bulowski, Władysław, 50
Burgraf (Kapo), 218
Bürkner, Leopold, 113
BWCE see British War Crimes Executive

Cadogan, Sir Alexander, 47, 89–90
Camp Breadbasket, Iraq, 440
Cap Arcona, SS, 10–11, 137–46, 153–5, 177, 178, 179–83, 188–90, 400; see also Neustadt Bay bombing
Cap Arcona museum, 142–4
Cartmell, Major, 319
Central Registry of War Criminals and Security Suspects see CROWCASS
Chamberlain, Sir Austen, 29
Champion, Lieutenant Colonel Savile, 98–9, 101, 133, 184–5, 187, 233, 316
Charlton, Lieutenant, 146–7, 360–61
Chełmno, 62
Chilcot Inquiry, 464
Chilton, Major General, 311
Christopher, Colonel Jack, 144–6, 177
Churchill, Rhona, 280
Churchill, Winston: attitude to war crimes, 36, 41–2, 51, 89; description of Nazis, 387; and war crime trials, 455
Clark, Ronald, 351
Clauberg, SS Dr, 128
Cleaver, Captain, 425
Colditz, 12
Collis, W., 79
concentration camps: Allied knowledge of conditions, 25–39, 47–53, 442; economic aspect and forced labour, 55–6, 60–61, 62–4, 265–72; film of conditions shown at Nuremberg, 284–9; German public knowledge of, 64; opening of first German, 28, 58–60; origins, 27–8; overview of victims and sites, 12–13; psychological impact, 80–81; punishments in, 445; scale and breadth of

system, 57–64; staff mentality, 246–8; treatment of staff in immediate wake of liberation, 84–7; visiting nowadays as moral issue, 275–6; see also individual camps by name
Cranfield, Major, 211, 223, 224–5, 226, 229, 254–5, 259
Crosfield, Colonel, 34
CROWCASS (Central Registry of War Criminals and Security Suspects), 122, 313–14

Dachau: Allied knowledge of conditions, 29, 30–31, 33, 34, 35, 49, 441; history and conditions, 28, 59–60, 116, 124–5; site, 12–13; tour round, 275–6, 286
Dachau trial, 272–5, 277–8, 294–5, 404, 421–2
Darré, Richard, 113
Day, Group Captain Harry, 469
death statistics, 72–3
Degesch (company), 328
Deutschland, SS, 177, 178; see also Neustadt Bay bombing
Dewar-Duncan, Father, 148–9
Diner, Cescha, 162
Dodd, Thomas, 291–2, 294, 395, 414
Doenitz, Admiral Karl, 103, 114, 199, 252, 288
Dolin, Dora, 162
Dolin, Lea, 162
Donnedieu de Vabres, Judge Henri, 279
Donovan, General, 278–9
Dörr (alleged war criminal), 218
Draper, Major Gerald: colleagues' comic verse about, 131; and Dulag Luft, 467–9; later life, 423; and Tesch & Stabenow, 323, 327, 332, 333; and Warner, 94
Dreimann, SS-Oberscharführer Willy, 153, 187, 336, 337, 381, 393
Drosihn, Dr Joachim, 328, 329, 332, 352
Dujeu, Raymond, 226
Dunkirk evacuation (1940), 89, 97
Durham Miners' Association, 33

Eberhardt (Dulag Luft staff member), 469
Eden, Anthony, 51, 89, 91, 450
Edward VIII, 34
Egersdörfer, Karl, 218, 234–5, 258
Ehlert, Herta, 217
Eichmann, Adolf, 303, 373, 376, 454
Eicke, Theodor, 59, 60
Einstein, Albert, 441
Eisenhower, General Dwight D., 23, 45, 285
Elwyn Jones, F., 340
Enigma, 450
Epp, Franz Ritter von, 111

Erman, Renée, 128
'Essen-West' case, 470–72
euthanasia programme, 273–5, 285
Everaert, Joanneas, 358–9
evil, existence and meaning of, 168, 295–304

Farge, 13
Faure, Edgar, 340
Felkin, Captain, 467
Fetherston-Godley, Major Francis, 34–5
Fiest (alleged war criminal), 218
First World War (1914–18), 39–41
Flensburg, 103
Flick KG, 462
Florence, Professor Gabriel, 336, 371
Flossenbürg, 13, 55–8, 56, 61
Flrazich, SS-Rottenführer, 217, 226
Forbes, Captain Alexander, 129
Ford, John, 284
Forster, Albert, 103
Förster, Ida (alleged war criminal), 217
Förster, Ilse (alleged war criminal), 217
Foth, Edward see Voth, Oberscharführer
Fox, Captain Alfred, 85, 92, 128, 130
Frahm, Blockführer Johann, 336, 337, 393, 425–6
France, Allied invasion of (1944), 45
Frank, Anne, 71, 183
Frank, Hans, 112, 114, 199, 417, 418
Frank, Hela, 93
Frank, Margot, 71
Frankl, Viktor, 68, 446
Franks, Colonel, 312
Freud, Captain (Anton) Walter, 94, 317, 323–33, 335–7, 422–3
Freyend, Ernst John von, 113
Frick, Wilhelm: in captivity, 114; death, 148; and the Jews, 26–7; named as war criminal, 103; and 'protective' custody, 58; sentence, 417; trial, 199, 252
Fritzsche, Hans, 416
Fuhlsbüttel prison, 13, 367, 370, 382–3, 464
Funk, Walther, 103, 114, 288, 417

Gaggenau, 420
Galitzine, Captain Prince Yurka, 48, 313–14, 443
gas chambers: gasses used and their suppliers, 307–308, 321–3, 326–33, 347, 352; gassing process, 375–6; selection process, 129–30, 225–7, 237–9, 254, 255, 375
Genn, Lt Col Leo, 95; background, 94–7; at Bergen-Belsen trial, 210, 212–13; demobbed, 130–31, 309; later life, 422; war crime investigations, 94–101, 130–32, 184

genocide: etymology, 100; use of concept in war crime trials, 191–2

German army units: 1st SS Panzer Division 'Leibstandarte Adolf Hitler', 444–5; 12th SS Panzer Division 'Hitler Youth', 45, 46

Gerthoffer, Charles, 280

Gestapo: at Breendonk Fort, 46; collective guilt concept, 457; notoriety abroad, 31, 32, 35, 36

Giannini, Major, 112

Gilbert, Gustave, 252, 288, 294–6, 342, 459

Gilbert, Martin, 51–2, 464

Glasgow, 33

Glücks, Richard, 125, 240–42, 374, 456

Goebbels, Josef, 26, 39, 60, 61, 102

Goering, Hermann: arrest, 102–103; and British Legion visit, 34; in captivity, 112, 114; death, 418; hagiographic photographs, 26; named as war criminal, 39; and Ohlendorf, 342; sentence, 417; trial, 199, 252, 280, 281, 288, 295–6, 362–6

Graf, Hans, 160

Grancey, General de, 358

Great Escape massacre (1944), 89, 123, 365, 450

Greiser, Arthur, 103

Grese, Irma, 210; character, 297; death, 294; and Kramer, 217; as press's favourite, 217, 219, 254, 440; trial, 211, 217, 219–20, 223, 225, 254–5, 440; verdict and sentence, 257, 259

Griffith-Jones, Lieutenant Colonel Mervyn, 346

Groß-Rosen, 61, 321

Gross (Kapo), 167

Grothmann, SS Colonel Werner, 106–107

Guantanamo Bay, 409

Gura, Ladislaw, 217

Guterman, Estera, 224

Hadamar asylum, 273–5, 285

Hahnel (alleged war criminal), 218

Hamburg: Curiohaus, 347; Messberghof, 307–308; see also Bullenhuser Damm

Hamburg-Neugraben, 420

Hamburg-Sasel, 420

Hannover Ahlem, 420

Harding, Thomas, 84–6

Hardman, Leslie, 82

Harris, Lieutenant Colonel A.J.M., 312–13

Harris, Lieutenant Colonel Whitney, 340–41

Haschke (alleged war criminal), 217

Heinrich (Kapo), 162–3

Heissmeyer, Professor: and Bullenhuser Damm, 425;

disappearance, 336; mentioned at Neuengamme trial, 359; named in investigations, 157, 158, 164, 335

Hempel (alleged war criminal), 217

Henderson, Lord, 421

Hess, Rudolf: and blind obedience, 237; and British Legion visit to Dachau, 34; in captivity, 114; named as war criminal, 39; sentence, 417; trial, 199, 252, 280, 281, 290, 396

Hessling, Kreisleiter, 338

Heydrich, Reinhard, 60, 62

Heyer, Hauptmann Erich, 471, 472

Hill, Major, 157

Himmler, Heinrich: atrocity reports received by, 37; and Bergen-Belsen, 75; Bernadotte negotiations, 455; and Buchenwald, 23; capture and death, 104–11, 104; and concentration camps, 60, 61, 62; and Dachau, 28, 59; and Final Solution, 373–4, 376; forged collusion with British, 449; life, 105–106; named as war criminal, 39; and Natzweiler-Struthof, 245; and Neuengamme, 401; and Neustadt Bay refugees, 177, 190; and Night of Long Knives, 60; and SS, 60, 106

Hitler, Adolf: Allied attitude to treatment of Jews, 32; and blind obedience, 237; and British Legion visit to Dachau, 34; British pre-war attitude, 27; and concentration camps, 58, 62; death, 90, 102; and downed enemy pilots, 470; Edward VIII's attitude, 34; Goering on his knowledge of the Holocaust, 365; hagiographic photographs, 26; and Munich putsch, 26; named as war criminal, 37, 39; and Night of Long Knives, 60, 105; psychological profile, 459

Hobhouse, Emily, 28

Holocaust see Jews

Horsell Heath, 67

Höss, Rudolf, 125, 227, 237–8, 370, 372–80, 417

Hössler, Lagerführer Franz, 216, 266, 294

Hughes, Glyn, 81

IG Farben, 462

Imperial War Museum oral histories, 179

industrialists, prosecution of, 462

Inspectorate of Concentration Camps, 60

International Military Tribunal see Nuremberg trial

International Red Cross, 177, 454

Iraq: allegations against British and US forces, 70–71, 73, 230, 440; Chilcot Inquiry, 464; Mousa case, 72, 73, 409–13, 465; other atrocities, 412; parallels between occupation of and Nazi concentration camps, 407–13; protests against war, 409

Iraq Historic Allegations Team, 412, 465

Isherwood, Christopher, 25

Israel, 454

Italy, Allied invasion of (1943–44), 45

Ivelaw-Chapman, Air Vice-Marshal, 468–9

Jackson, Phillip, 151–5, 400–401

Jackson, Justice Robert: appointed by Truman, 91; death, 423; and German collective guilt, 289; Goering questioned by, 364; guilt of SS and Gestapo, 131–2; and Nuremberg control, 198; Nuremberg performance, 121, 281–3; Nuremberg plans and preparations, 111, 116–20, 191–5, 249; Nuremberg start date announced by, 219

Jackson, Dr Sumner, 151–5, 177, 453

JAG see Judge Advocate General

Jäger, SS-Rottenführer, 156, 157–8, 164

Janner, Barnett, 29

Jauch, Oberscharführer, 336, 337, 393, 426

Jehovah's Witnesses, 59–60

Jews: Allied knowledge of Nazi treatment, 25–39, 47–53, 442; Bergen-Belsen trial's attitude to, 206–207, 218–19, 224–5, 237, 239, 242, 243–4, 261; ghettoes, 61, 292–3; Goering on, 362–3, 365; Kristallnacht, 61; Nuremberg indictment names, 251; overview of concentration camp treatment, 57–63; post-war care of orphans, 172; selection process at Auschwitz, 129–30, 225–7, 237–9, 254, 255, 375

Jodl, General Alfred, 103, 114, 199, 252, 417, 418

Jonas, Anni, 224

Jonas, Elvira, 224

Jones, Corporal Harry, 449

Judge Advocate General (JAG), 87, 101, 131, 332, 333, 338, 425

Kaczyński, Jarosław, 141

Kaen, Relli, 162

Kaltenbrunner, Ernst: brain haemorrhage, 280; in captivity, 114; death, 418; sentence, 417; trial, 199, 252, 340–41, 342, 372–3, 376–7

Kapos: guilt, 156–7, 161–73, 454; trials, 217–18, 255–6, 257
Katyn massacre (1940), 279, 415
Kaufer, Karl, 471–2
Kauffmann, Dr (attorney), 372–7
Kaufmann, Dr Charles, 155–7, 191
Kaufmann, *Gauleiter* Karl, 402–3, 464
Kaunas, 50
Keitel, Field Marshal Wilhelm: in captivity, 103, 114; death, 418; sentence, 417; trial, 199, 252, 280
Keith, Brigadier, 100
Kellog, Lieutenant, 284
Kemp, Anthony, 443
Kenya, 422
Kenyatta, Jomo, 422
Kershaw, Ian, 446
Kesselring, Albert, 112
Ketelaar, Jan, 179–80
Ketelaar, Piet, 179–83, 400
Kick, Wilhelm, 49–50
Kiel-Hasse, 420
Killinger, *Oberleutnant* Erich, 468, 469
Kirsch, Viktor, 294
Kitt, Dr, 358
Klein, Alfons, 274–5
Klein, Charlotte, 218
Klein, Dr Fritz, 86; arrested, 81; captivity and interrogation, 84–7, 130; death, 294; in Nuremberg film, 286; trial, 209, 216, 225, 236, 239, 254; verdict and sentence, 257, 258–9
Klippel, Josef, 217, 258
Koch, Erich, 103
Koebbels (*Kapo*), 156
Koenig, Dr, 381, 389–90
Kogon, Eugen, 167–8, 439
Koper (*Kapo*), 218
Koppel, Ruchla, 224
Kowalski, Dr Tadeusz, 157–8, 334–5
Kraft, *Lagerführer* Georg, 216, 236, 258
Kramer, Josef: and Bergen-Belsen's liberation, 77; in captivity, 81–2; death, 294; Galitzine's report, 48; and Grese, 217; interrogation, 124–8; and Nuremberg, 456; in Nuremberg film, 286; and Pauly, 370; trial, 208, 210, 216, 219, 225, 226–7, 236–48; verdict and sentence, 257, 259; as war criminal, 196
Kramer, Rosina, 240, 248
Kraus, Erwin, 112
Krause, *Obersturmführer*, 160
Krejči, Václav, 217
Kristallnacht (1938), 61
Kroell, Dr, 396
Krupp, Alfred, 458
Krupp, Gustav, 458
Krupps (company), 462
Kuchin, Captain, 280

Kulessa (alleged war criminal), 218
Kümmel, Walter, 129

Lahde-Weser, 420
Lang, WO Robert, 467–8
Lange, Wilhelm, 142–4
Lawrence, Lord Justice Geoffrey, 15, 24, 279, 280–81, 284, 416–17
Leigh Fermor, Patrick, 26
Leipzig Trials, 39–41
Lemkin, Raphael, 100
Levi, Primo, 168–9, 173, 300, 408–409, 410
Lewis, Dr Joseph, 79
Ley, Robert, 111, 115, 199, 237, 280
Lion, Leon, 95
Lisiewitz, Hilde, 217, 233–4
Litwinska, Sophia, 224
Lloyd George, David, 28
Lohbauer, Hilde, 217
London Conference (1945), 192–4
Longueil shooting (1944), 46
Lothe, Ilse, 217, 255–6, 257
Louts (*Kapo*), 156
Love, Dora (née Rabinowitz), 159–61, 172–5, 176
Lübeck Bay *see* Neustadt Bay bombing
Lublin *see* Majdanek
Lüdke, Albin, 356–8, 393
Luetkemeyer, *Lagerführer*, 357
Luftwaffe, 466–70
Lüneburg, 205–207, 208
Lüneburg Heath, 67–8, 109–10

MacClancy, P., 79
Macdonald, Colonel Bruce, 96–7
Macher, Major Heinz, 106–7
Mai, Mathis, 156
Majdanek (Lublin), 50, 62, 388
Malawi, 297–9
Malmedy massacre (1944), 444–5, 466
Mander, Geoffrey, 35
Mansell, Gerard, 76, 81–2
Manstein, General Fritz Erich von, 342, 421
Mathers, Lord, 309–10
Mathes (alleged war criminal), 217
Maugham, Lord, 37, 38, 442
Mauthausen, 49–50, 61, 125, 286, 404
Maxwell Fyfe, Sir David, 120–21, 279, 340, 364, 365–6, 423
medical experimentation: at Auschwitz, 127, 128–9, 450–51; at Dachau, 277; at Natzweiler-Struthof, 125–6; at Neuengamme, 158–9, 334–7, 358–9
Mengele, Dr Josef, 127, 129, 225, 255, 450–51
mentally ill, and euthanasia, 273–5, 285
Menthon, François de, 340
Meyer, August, 389, 391

Meyer, Keith, 455
Michalik, Stanisława, 129
Milch, Field Marshal Erhard, 145
Milgram, Stanley, 300–301
Milice, 156
Mills-Roberts, Brigadier, 145
Milošević, Slobodan, 230–2
Mittelbau-Dora, 13, 265–72, 267
Moller, Helmut, 175–6
Mollison, Captain, 77–9
Molotov, Vyacheslav, 91
Monckton, Sir Walter, 121
Mondorf *see* Ashcan
Montefiore, Leonard, 32
Montgomery, Field Marshal Bernard, 133
Moorehead, Alan, 82–4, 86
Moscow Conference (1943), 41–2
Möser, *SS-Obersturmführer* Hans, 272
Mounier, Pierre, 280
Mount Temple, Lord, 33
Mousa, Baha, 72, 73, 409–13, 465
Mullins, Claud, 40–41
Munich *putsch* (1923), 26
Munro, Major, 227–9
Murphy, Colonel Michael, 108

Nagel, Jakob, 112
National Archives, Kew, 347–8
Natzweiler-Struthof, 47–8, 49, 61, 125–6, 245, 451
Nazis, pre-liberation Allied knowledge of atrocities, 26–39, 47–53, 442
Neilson, Lieutenant Colonel Ian, 315–16
Neuengamme, 4; blockhouses, 3–4; commandant's house, 5–6, 6; exhibitions, 5; history and conditions, 8, 61, 152–3, 155–9, 331, 334–7, 359–61; House of Commemoration, 7–8, 8; liberation, 146–7; National Archives photographs, 348–9, 349; punishment cells, 4–5; satellite camps, 420; tour round, 3–11; war crime investigations, 149–51, 158–72, 173–8, 184–91, 320–1, 334–7; *see also* Bullenhuser Damm atrocity; Neustadt Bay bombing
Neuengamme trial, 9; case against Bahr, 395–7; defendants, 337, 350, 351; judge and lawyers, 351–3; Judge Advocate's summary, 397–9; Neustadt Bay mentioned, 399–403; overview, 8–10, 349–61, 366–72, 380–403; Pauly on the stand, 366–72; press coverage, 359; prosecution case, 353–9; Speck on the stand, 391–4; Thumann on the stand, 380–91; venue, 12, 347; verdicts and sentences, 399, 419

Neustadt Bay bombing: British
    liberation of Neustadt, 144–6;
    events, 10–11, 143–4, 145–6;
    memorials and museums,
    139–40, 140, 141, 142–4;
    Neuengamme trial mentions,
    399–403; public reaction,
    200–201; Till's inquiry, 153–5,
    170–71, 174–83, 187–91, 200–202;
    tour round Neustadt, 137–44
Nice, Geoffrey, 231
Night of the Long Knives (1934),
    60, 105
Nightingale, Lieutenant Colonel
    Alan, 316–19, 419
Nikitchenko, General, 279
Niremberski, Captain M., 80–81
Nordhausen, 285
Normandy, Battle of (1944), 45–6
Nuremberg, 407–408, 408, 413–14
Nuremberg Charter, 194–7
Nuremberg Laws, 32
Nuremberg trial: atmosphere,
    343–4; defendants list, 198–9;
    discussions and plans, 191–200,
    249–52; events, 279–96, 340–44,
    362–6; film shown, 284–9;
    Goering on the stand, 362–6;
    Höss on the stand, 372–80;
    indictment, 197–8, 250–52,
    279–80; Jackson's opening
    speech, 281–3; judges, 279;
    judges' summary, verdicts and
    sentences, 416–18; pleas, 280–81;
    prosecution case, 283–94,
    340–43; Rosenberg on the stand,
    391, 394–5; significance assessed,
    414–16, 417–18; start date
    announced, 219; symbolism
    of venue choice, 194; venue, 13,
    279, 407, 413–14

Ocampo, Luis Moreno, 73
Ochshorn, Izaak, 320–21
Ohlendorf, SS Major General Otto,
    341–3, 341
Ohrdruf, 19–20, 20, 23
Olivier, Laurence, 131
Opitz (alleged war criminal), 218
Ostrowoski (alleged war criminal),
    218
Otto, Blockführer Walter, 218, 258
Ozol, Lieutenant Colonel, 280

Panton, Selkirk, 104
Papen, Franz von, 102, 199, 416
Le Paradis massacre (1940), 89, 97
Patton, General George S., 23
Pauly, SS-Obersturmbannführer Max:
    and Bullenhuser Damm, 335,
    425; death, 419; guilt, 377,
    378–9; named in investigations,
    152, 164, 320–21; Neuengamme
    home, 5–6, 6; and Neustadt
    Bay bombing, 190, 191; and
    Nuremberg Charter, 196–7;

sentence, 399; trial, 337, 356,
    357, 366–72, 367, 380–81, 389,
    398, 401–403
Peiper, Joachim, 445
Pelican, Staff Sergeant Fred,
    323–33, 422
Pell, Herbert, 43
petrol/phenol injections, 84, 157–8,
    164, 331, 357, 396
Philip, Prince, Duke of Edinburgh,
    112
Philipp, Prince of Hesse, 112
Phillips, Captain, 211–12, 214, 235
Pichen (alleged war criminal), 217
Pohl, General Oswald, 62, 319, 367,
    418–19, 425, 456
Poland: Allied knowledge of condi-
    tions, 36, 38; concentration
    camps built in, 61; Katyn
    massacre, 279, 415; and
    Nuremberg, 199; ongoing quest
    for reparations from Germany,
    141; war criminals list, 103–104
Polanski, Blockführer, 218
Pollard, Major, 124
Potsdam Conference (1945), 193
psychological profiling, 459

Quenouille, Dr René, 335, 336, 371

Rabinowitz, Dora see Love, Dora
Radcliffe, Sir Cyril, 47
Raeder, Erich, 114, 199, 417
RAF: 'Essen-West' case, 470–72;
    and Neustadt Bay bombing,
    10–11, 137–46, 153–5, 176–83,
    187–91, 399–403
Rantzau, Captain, 317, 318
Rathbone, Eleanor, 33–4
Ravensbrück, 61, 129, 420
Red Cross see International Red
    Cross
Reese, SS-Oberscharführer, 461
Reinecke, General, 115
Rheinke, SS-Sturmmann, 156
Ribbentrop, Joachim von: in
    captivity, 112; death, 418; hunt
    for, 111; named as war crim-
    inal, 39; self-defence, 115;
    sentence, 417; trial, 114, 199,
    252, 280
Rice, Major, 107
Roberts, Major General George,
    178
Robichaud, Lieutenant, 98
Roosevelt, Franklin D., 36, 37, 39,
    41–3, 51, 91
Rosenberg, Alfred: arrested, 102; on
    blind obedience defence, 236–7;
    death, 418; named as war crim-
    inal, 39; sentence, 417; trial,
    199, 280, 323, 391, 394–5
Rosenman, Samuel, 90
Roth (Kapo), 218
Rothschild, James de, 35
Rozenwayg, Hanka, 224

Rudenko, General, 340, 416
Rudolph, Arthur, 270–71
Ruoff, Heinrich, 274–5
Russell, Lord, of Liverpool,
    426, 472
Russia, German invasion of (1941),
    61–2, 342–3
Rygiol, Henryk, 50

SA: definition, 27; eradication, 60,
    105; notoriety abroad, 27, 31;
    role in the early camps, 30
Sachsenburg, 32
Sachsenhausen-Oranienburg, 49,
    61, 125
Saddam Hussein, 409
Sandbostel, 148–51
SAS, 312–13, 314, 317, 443–4, 451
Sauckel, Fritz, 114, 417, 418
Sauer (alleged war criminal), 218
Schacht, Hjalmar, 416
Schandelah, 420
Schaulen, 160
Schilling, Klaus, 294
Schlomowicz, Ignatz, 218, 256, 257
Schmedidzt (alleged war criminal),
    218
Schon, Fritz, 153
Schonfeld, Nelly, 161–2
Schreirer, Heinrich, 217
Schumann, SS Dr, 128
Scotland, Lieutenant Colonel A.P.,
    49, 332–3
Sears, Colonel Hayden, 20
Sehm, Emil, 321–3, 326, 327
Selvester, Captain Thomas, 107–8,
    449
Sereny, Gitta, 459–60
Seyss-Inquart, Arthur, 114, 417, 418
SHAEF Court of Inquiry, 96–7, 98
Shapcott, Brigadier, 419
Shapcott, Major Henry, 440–41
Shawcross, Sir Hartley, 290–1, 310,
    423
Sidgwick, Christopher, 359–61
Simon, Viscount, 37
Sington, Captain Derrick, 75; truck
    used by, 76
Smallwood, Major, 92–3, 96, 99, 226
Smith, E.P., 309
Smith, Rennie, 31
Sobibór, 62, 459–60
Special Operations Executive (SOE),
    55, 311–12, 420, 443–4, 451
Sokoliska, Cila, 159, 161–2
Somerhough, Group Captain Tony,
    311–12, 313–14, 316–17,
    318–19, 419, 422
Sontag, Susan, 24, 431
Soskice, Sir Frank, 466
Soviet Union see Russia
Speck, Adolf, 392; death, 419;
    named in investigations, 336;
    sentence, 399; trial, 337, 356–7,
    381, 391–4
Speer, Albert, 62, 102, 252

SS: collective guilt concept, 457;
    Death's Head Battalions, 60;
    definition, 27; and fanaticism,
    131–2; Himmler's development,
    60, 106; membership as guilt
    by association, 131–2; notoriety
    abroad, 27, 31, 32; power over
    concentration camps, 60, 61
SS-Business Administration Main
    Office (WVHA), 62
Stalag Luft III escapees see Great
    Escape massacre
Stalin, Joseph, 41–2, 455
Stanhope, Lord, 24
Stärfl (alleged war criminal), 218
Starostka, Stanisława, 217
Stein, Ilona, 224
Stetler, Russell, 222
Stettinius, Edward, 52
Stevens, Lieutenant Colonel
    George, 284
Stewart, Major Stephen Malcolm, 9;
    background, 352–3; and
    Bergen-Belsen trial, 210, 213;
    and Kramer's interrogation,
    124, 127; later life, 423; and
    Neuengamme trial, 9, 352,
    353–6, 367–71, 390–91, 393–4,
    400–402; and Sandbostel, 149;
    and Velpke baby home, 337
Stimson, Henry, 52–3
Stirling, Judge Advocate Carl:
    appearance, 351; and Bergen-
    Belsen trial, 211, 233, 243,
    256–7, 259–60; later life, 422;
    and Neuengamme trial, 351–2,
    357, 358, 371, 397, 400–403;
    and Zyklon B trial, 352
Strasser, Gregor, 105
Streicher, Julius, 111, 112, 114, 199,
    417, 418
Strippel, SS-Obersturmführer Arnold,
    336
Stroop, SS-Brigadeführer Jürgen,
    292–4, 459
Stuart Smith, Captain John, 470
Stuckart, Wilhelm, 113
Der Stürmer (magazine), 111
Stutthof, 145, 146, 159–66, 170–74,
    366, 369
Sunschein, Lidia, 224
Synger, Paula, 224
Szafran, Dora, 224–9

Taliban, 384–6
Tarragona Cathedral, 429–30
Taylor, Lieutenant Colonel, 81
Taylor, Lieutenant Jack, 286
Taylor, Colonel Telford: later life,
    423; and Nuremberg, 198, 291,
    341, 361; and other trials,
    418–19, 455
Tesch, Dr Bruno, 322, 326–33, 352
Tesch & Stabenow, 307–308, 321–3,
    326–33, 352
Tetlow, Edwin, 82, 219

Theuer, Adolf, 462
Thielbek, SS, 10–11, 153–5, 177, 178,
    188, 400, 401; see also Neustadt
    Bay bombing
Thorndike, Sybil, 131
Thumann, SS-Obersturmführer
    Anton, 384; appearance, 383;
    arrested, 187; death, 419; moral
    choice, 383–7; named in inves-
    tigations, 152–3, 164, 320–21;
    sentence, 399; trial, 356, 366,
    370, 380–91, 394
Thumann, Frau, 389–91
Tiefstack, 420
Tilburg shooting (1944), 96–7
Till, Major Noel, 149–51, 158–72,
    173–8, 184–91, 201–2, 422
Till, Patrick, 150–51, 165–6, 172,
    178, 201–202
Tilling, Lieutenant Colonel
    Humphrey, 309
Totzauer, Karl, 356
Treblinka, 62, 459–60
Truman, Harry S., 91, 117, 418, 455
Trzebinski, Dr Alfred: and
    Bullenhuser Damm, 335–7,
    366–7, 393, 425–6; death, 419;
    and Neuengamme, 157, 358;
    sentence, 399; trial, 337
Tsipras, Alexis, 141

United Nations Organisation, 121
UN War Crimes Commission
    (UNWCC), 37–44, 54,
    116–17, 121
Ustica, 45

V2 rockets, 266
Vaughan, Hal, 453
Velpke baby home, 337–40
Volkenrath, Elisabeth, 217
Voorhees, Colonel John, 96–7
Voth, Oberscharführer (possibly
    Edward Foth), 160–61, 453

Wäckerle, Hilmar, 59
Wahlmann, Dr Adolf, 274
Walter, Frieda, 218
Wannsee Conference (1942),
    62, 113
war crime trials: for atrocities
    against Allied armed forces,
    45–6, 443–4; British trial proce-
    dures, 186–7, 196–7; cross-
    examinations, 224–32;
    defendants' right to defence,
    220–24; discussions and plans,
    36–44, 52–5, 89–92, 115–23,
    191–200; documentary
    evidence, 122–3; Dulag Luft,
    466–7; 'Essen-West' case,
    470–72; for First World War,
    39–41; and justice, 431–2; later
    trials, 418–22, 424–7; Major
    War Criminals procedure,
    191–2; as memorialisation,

276–7; press interest wanes,
    399, 403; prisoner release, 421–2;
    reasons for delays, 45–52; see also
    Bergen-Belsen trial; Bullenhuser
    Damm: trial; Dachau trial;
    Neuengamme trial; Nuremberg
    trial; Zyklon B: trial
war crimes: blind obedience
    defence, 236–7, 260–62, 297,
    343, 381; British accelerated
    programme to pursue, 309–40;
    crimes against humanity
    defined, 43–4, 195; definition,
    43–4; genocide concept, 191–2;
    German collective guilt, 140–41,
    288–9; guilt by association, 117,
    131–2; guilt of military, 199;
    inquiries into Allied atrocities
    during investigations, 421–2,
    466, 470; investigation process,
    184–7; investigations, 87–9,
    92–101, 114–16, 123–34,
    149–78, 184–91, 232, 311–13,
    320–1, 334–7, 419–20, 455; Kapo
    guilt, 161–73; man's inhu-
    manity to man, 429–31;
    mentality of the guilty, 246–8,
    295–304, 362; moral choice
    issue, 383–7; doubtful parallels
    between Nazi concentration
    camps and Iraq War, 409–13,
    466–70; pursuit, imprisonment
    and interrogation of senior
    Nazis, 102–16; selection process
    for interviewees, 183
War Crimes Group (North West
    Europe), 419–20
War Crimes Investigation Teams:
    appointment of Group Captain
    Tony Somerhough as head,
    311; criticisms by Galitzine,
    313–314; comparison with
    American teams, 148, 316;
    formation, 87–88;
War Crimes Investigation Unit,
    317–19, 320–40, 367, 372
Warner, Fred, 94
Warsaw Ghetto, 292–3
Weber, SS Dr, 128
Wedgwood, Colonel Josiah, 35
Weideinger, George, 29
Wein, Major P.S., 353, 387–8
Weinbacher, Karl, 328, 329, 332,
    357
Weingartner, Blockführer Peter, 216,
    236, 253, 253, 257, 259
Weiss, Martin Gottfried, 404
Weissig, Dr, 399, 402
Welles, Sumner, 37
Wells, Captain, 108
Werner (Kapo), 156–7
Westertimke, 107
Wiehagen, Heinrich, 336, 381
Wiesel, Elie, 52
Wilhelm II, Kaiser, 41
Willig, Karl, 274–5

Winwood, Major Thomas: Bergen-
Belsen trial defence cases put
by, 236–44, 248, 253; Bergen-
Belsen trial mitigation
speeches, 257–8; Bergen-Belsen
trial role, 208–9, 222, 223;
Bergen-Belsen trial witness
cross-examination, 226–7

Wirths, SS Dr, 128
World War One *see* First
World War
Wormhoudt massacre (1940),
89
Wright, Lord, 116–17
WVHA *see* SS-Business
Administration Main Office

Zaun, Alfred, 328, 329–30
Zelensky, Stefanie, 339
Ziereis, Franz, 49–50
Zimbardo, Philip, 300–301,
361
Zoddel, Erich, 218, *218*
Zyklon B, 307–308, 321–3, 326–33;
trial, 347, 352